PSYCHOLOGY
OF
MODERN
LIFE

High School Behavioral Science Series

Simple Experiments in Psychology:
A Laboratory Manual
W. W. Ray, Ph.D.

Developments in High School Psychology
H. Fisher, Ed.D.

Student's Guide to Conducting Social Science Research
B. B. Bunker, Ph.D.

Psychology of Modern Life
J.O. Whittaker, Ph.D.

PSYCHOLOGY
OF
MODERN
LIFE

James O. Whittaker, Ph.D.

Professor of Psychology and Social Science
The Pennsylvania State University

HUMAN SCIENCES PRESS

A Division of Behavioral Publications, Inc.
72 Fifth Avenue
NEW YORK

To My Mother and Father

Library of Congress Catalog Number 74-12622

ISBN: 0-87705-234-4

Printed in the United States of America
789 98765432

Library of Congress Cataloging in Publication Data

Whittaker, James Oliver, 1927-
  Psychology of modern life.

  Includes bibliographies.
  Includes index.
  SUMMARY: A study of human behavior for the high school student which includes chapters on such topics as learning, emotions, personality, mental health, marriage and family, and social problems.
    1. Psychology. [1. Psychology] 1. Title.

Contents

groups. . .Drugs and adolescent groups. . .What about soft drugs?. . .Crime and delinquency in adolescent groups. . .Conformity and non-conformity. . .What does this mean to you?. . .Chapter summary. . .Important terms from this chapter

Do we learn through association?. . .Cats in a puzzle box. . .Simple learning and classical conditioning. . .How fears are conditioned. . .Some principles of conditioning. . .What is operant conditioning?. . .Some conclusions about learning. . .How some children learn to be "spoiled brats". . .How animal trainers use operant conditioning. . .Conditioning human behavior. . .How are superstitions learned?. . .Punishment. . .Chapter summary. . .Important terms from this chapter

What affects learning?. . .*You* are the most important factor in learning. . .What is the I.Q.?. . .Are there different kinds of intelligence?. . .What does this mean to you?. . .How important is motivation?. . .Praise and sarcasm in the classroom. . .Emotions and learning. . .Learning and the material to be learned. . .How to study. . .Be an active learner. . .How to pick a book apart. . .Pay attention!. . .Should you distribute your learning?. . .How to take a test. . .Some other tips for good students. . .What happens when we forget?. . .What is overlearning?. . .Mnemonic devices. . .Theories of forgetting. . .Chapter summary. . .Important terms from this chapter

What are motives?. . .Where do motives come from?. . .The puzzle of curiosity. . .How strong are the various motives?. . .Some examples of human motives. . .Aggression. . .The need to be with others. . .The need to acquire. . .Money, money, money. . .What are personal motives?. . .Success, failure, and the level of aspiration. . .What causes frustration?. . .How do we react to frustration?. . .What is conflict?. . .Approach-approach conflicts. . .Avoidance-avoidance conflicts. . .Approach-avoidance conflicts. . .Chapter summary. . .Important terms from this chapter

The nature of emotions. . .How does the body react in emotion?. . .How the polygraph detects truth and lies. . .How do emotions develop?. . .How emotions help us. . .How emotions hurt us. . .The psychosomatic reactions. . .What are ulcers?. . .What causes high blood pressure?. . .Emotional problems of adolescence. . .How to deal with hostility. . .Dealing with sexual feelings. . .Feelings of inferiority. . .Other emotional problems of adolescence. . .Some final tips. . .Chapter summary. . .Important terms from this chapter

Preface

Psychology can no longer be considered an optional inclusion in the complete high school curricula. Psychology is in the news, and one can hardly hope to understand the day-to-day events of human affairs without some knowledge of environment and motivations, and without a degree of self-awareness. The ever-increasing interest in modern scientific psychology has made manifest the need for new teaching-learning materials.

High school programs of enrichment and acceleration have produced a "readiness" among pre-college students for a proper introduction to psychology. In response to this evident need, *Psychology of Modern Life,* has been written precisely for you at this important point in your formal education. Foundational knowledge is presented in an engaging manner. An expanded view of learning is explained along with personal helps on the skill of studying. The author details important data on the subject of personality development and personal relationships which lay a basis for understanding both normal and deviant behavior. The area of mental health and mental illness is realistically treated as a matter of adjustment within a changing society.

The text is not written from a guidance point of view, but rather from the position of the scientific student of psychology. The author has presented the subject of behavior in a way that will enhance self-understanding as well as increase understanding of others.

The vocabulary of behavior is tossed around rather glibly in the market place. A real need for accurate usage exists, making imperative not only accurate knowledge of terms, but also the ability to use them properly. The author gives at the end of each chapter a listing of technical terms and a precise rendering of the specific meanings in the body of the text.

No text can be a final word on any subject. It can only hope to stimulate further inquiry. May many satisfactions be achieved as you begin the grand adventure of studying the science of human behavior.

John Goodyear
Psychology Teacher
Cedar Cliff High School
Camp Hill, Pa.

Foreword

This book was written specifically for the high school student who wants to know more about his or her own behavior and the behavior of other people as well. In every chapter, wherever I could possibly do so, an effort was made to relate the material under discussion to the life and problems of the American teenager. In addition, throughout the book I have tried to emphasize the interdisciplinary approach. This approach stresses the fact that other disciplines such as history, economics, political science, religion, and sociology are as important as psychology in developing a comprehensive understanding of human behavior.

Personal problems, individuality and mental health have been given priority within the framework of a scientific approach. In other words, I have rejected the approach that treats these topics to the exclusion of all others in psychology. It seems to me that if high school psychology courses are to have any value at all, they should not be limited solely to the discussion of problems of adjustment in the white, middle-class adolescent. Some attempt certainly should be made to help the student understand not only his or her own behavior, but the behavior of members of minority groups, older people, and people living in other cultures as well.

The book is intended to be used in a one-semester course, although it can easily be supplemented with other readily available materials. At the end of each chapter we cite additional readings that can be used to expand the discussion. In addition, a laboratory manual, "Simple Experiments in Psychology" by Wilbert S. Ray (Behavioral Publications, New York), has recently been published. This manual sets forth nine interesting experiments that can be conducted with a minimum of equipment. It was developed specifically for the high school course.

A number of people contributed to the development of this book. My wife Sandra, a psychologist and former high school teacher, contributed two chapters of the text, as well as critical comments on the entire work. My teenage daughter read many different parts of the book and had much to do with the language and style of presentation. A number of high school teachers provided comments about their own teaching of the course, problems with currently available materials, and objectives they felt to be important. I appreciate their help and look forward to letters from teachers who use the final product.

James O. Whittaker
The Pennsylvania State University

About the Author

Dr. James O. Whittaker is Professor of Psychology and Social Science at The Pennsylvania State University. Since receiving his Ph.D. in social psychology at the University of Oklahoma under Muzafer Sherif in 1958, he has published more than thirty-five articles in professional journals. His research interests in cross-cultural psychology have taken him to Brazil, Peru, Lebanon, Hong Kong, and Viet Nam. In 1972 he was Visiting Professor at the University of Buenos Aires Medical School in Argentina under the auspices of the U.N. World Health Organization. More recently he was Visiting Professor at the University of Auckland in New Zealand where this book was completed. In 1974 he was one of the first western psychologists to visit the People's Republic of China as a member of a scientific delegation.

Dr. Whittaker is the author of *Introduction to Psychology*, a college text that has been used by more than a quarter of a million students in the U.S., South America, and Far East. He has also edited the book, *Recent Discoveries in Psychology*, which was published in 1972. Currently at work on a text in social psychology, Dr. Whittaker is a dedicated teacher and scholar. His interest in high school psychology stems from his concern that students going on to college be better prepared to meet the challenge, and also that those entering the world of work have a grasp of behavioral principles that will help them to become happier and more productive human beings.

Part I.

THE STUDY OF
HUMAN BEHAVIOR

Psychology: More than Common Sense

chapter 1

3

Most of the problems faced by human beings today are man-made. No divine power decreed that three-fourths of the human race should live in poverty, afflicted by disease, malnourished, and uneducated. No supernatural being created prejudice, war, or environmental pollution. Furthermore, problems such as these do not exist because of a lack of technology or failure to understand the physical world. We have—now—the machinery, tools, and scientific knowledge to solve almost all such problems. There are, of course, some diseases for which we lack cures, and we still lack the machinery to tackle other problems, such as removing the salt from sea water on a large scale. But by and large, man himself is the biggest obstacle to the solution of most of his difficulties.

Sciences which study man's behavior, such as psychology, are relatively new, and they have developed mainly in the world's richest countries. Perhaps this is not surprising since, for the most part, man turned his attention first to the physical environment. As long as most of his energies had to be devoted to growing or gathering food, fending off wild beasts, and so on, little energy or motivation remained to cause him to be seriously concerned with his own behavior.

It has only been for the last 80 years or so that some countries in the world have developed to the point where they could afford the relative luxury of supporting scientists studying man himself. In the less developed countries even today, the need is for engineers and public health specialists more than psychologists. These countries are faced with the fundamental problems of building roads, feeding people, and improving health standards. But gradually there has been a developing realization that knowledge of the physical environment is not enough. The expert in agriculture may know that crops could be increased if farmers changed their centuries-old methods, but the farmers themselves must be persuaded to change their behavior. The public health specialist may know that infant deaths could be reduced if mothers bathed their babies more often, but the mothers themselves must be convinced.

Psychology tries to explain behavior on something more than a common sense basis. It applies scientific method—the same method used by the chemist or physicist—to the study of man's behavior. In this chapter we will see that the old methods of the past, common sense in particular, have not

---

SOME COMMON MISCONCEPTIONS ABOUT BEHAVIOR*

Take the test given below and see how well you can do. Watch out—you may be fooled on some of these. Decide whether each statement is true or false.

1. A basic cause of war is that man is instinctively aggressive.
2. Preachers' children are apt to turn out badly.
3. The exceptionally intelligent child is apt to be as strong physically and as well-adjusted socially as the average child.
4. A person who learns rapidly remembers longer than a person who learns slowly.
5. The shape of the hands is practically worthless as an indicator of artistic temperament.
6. Women can drive a car just as well as men.
7. Too much study is never the cause of feeblemindedness.
8. The marriage of cousins leads to the deterioration of the family line.
9. A person who looks you straight in the eye may be just as dishonest as the person who cannot.
10. American Indians have no better hearing than white people.
11. Some animals lower than man are able to reason.
12. After learning something, you forget more of it in the first few hours than in the next several days.
13. Famous men tend to be born of poor but hard-working parents.
14. Boys who do poorly in academic work are apt to be superior in mechanical ability.
15. A person's I.Q. depends upon the test by which it is measured.
16. A genius has a special kind of intelligence not possessed by other people.
17. Peptic ulcers tend to occur in people who are basically unaggressive.
18. Child prodigies tend to maintain their superiority in later life.
19. Public opinion polls are frequently accurate within 1 or 2 per cent.
20. To see a dim object at night, it is best to look slightly to one side of it.

*Answers are given at the end of this chapter.

---

helped us solve human problems. We will look at how man himself has become the object of scientific study, at where psychologists work, and at how they go about finding answers to complicated problems.

WHAT IS PSYCHOLOGY?

Psychology is one of several sciences concerned with man's behavior. Its main goals are to predict what man will do under certain circumstances, and to control or regulate his behavior. These goals are often surprising to beginning students, who sometimes feel that it is impossible to predict behavior, and furthermore, that the idea of "controlling" behavior is offensive.

Is Behavior Predictable?

Every day each of us predicts what other people will do, and much of the time our predictions are correct. If it were not possible to make reasonably accurate predictions about the behavior of others, we could not live together at all. Think of what it would be like to drive a car if we could not predict what the other drivers would do. In some cases, of course, our predictions are inaccurate and accidents occur. But for the most part we are able

---

FIVE THINGS THAT WORRY TENTH GRADE STUDENTS

One of the jobs of the psychologist is to discover things that worry various age groups. Here are some of the worries expressed by 580 tenth graders. No matter what your age, do the same things worry you?

1. Girls thought they weighed too much. Boys didn't worry as much about weight but thought they were too thin in the arms and chest.

2. Boys who thought they were too short, and girls who thought they were too tall worried about height.

3. Both boys and girls who thought they were slow in maturing worried about their rate of development.

4. Pimples and blackheads caused more worry among the students than anything else.

5. Two-thirds of the students wished they could change themselves physically in some way.

to drive without bashing other fenders or having our own bashed, largely because behavior is predictable.

If it were possible for each of us to always predict the behavior of others, there would be little need for psychologists. The predictions about behavior made by psychologists, however, are based on observing large numbers of people under carefully controlled conditions. Thus they tend to be more accurate than those made by single individuals based on their own personal experience.

Should We Control Behavior?

Whether we like it or not, our behavior is controlled in many ways every day. For example, those who prepare television commercials seek to make us do certain things or buy certain products. Predicting and controlling behavior thus serves as the basis for a multibillion dollar industry.

On the face of it most of us do not like the idea of someone controlling our behavior. But if you ask if the control of behavior is good or bad, it is like asking if gravity is good or bad. Gravity is bad if you drop a piece of china and smash it. But it is good if you want to continue clinging to our spinning planet. In the same way, the control of behavior may be seen as bad or good. Controlling behavior is bad if someone makes us buy something we do not need or do something that is not good for us. But all of us would agree that it would be desirable to control behavior in such a way as to eliminate crime and mental illness. When the psychologist speaks about "controlling" or "regulating" man's behavior, then, it is problems such as these that concern him. He wants to learn enough about the causes of such problems so that they may be eliminated.

Fat People and Thin People

The attempt to understand human behavior did not originate with psychology. As long ago as the time of the ancient Greeks, philosophers were writing about the behavior of man.

Among the theories developed by the Greek philosophers to explain behavior were those relating to body build. Basically these theories were simple ones that stated that there is a relationship between personality and the body. Fat people were believed to be jolly and outgoing, while thin people were thought to be more reserved, aloof, and unhappy. Some people still believe this today, although many carefully controlled studies have failed to show any such consistent relationship.

Fig. 1–1.   Do overweight people really have more fun? Many psychological studies have shown the opposite to be true.

Fig. 1–2.   This man is a yogi. Through concentration and training he has learned to support his entire body weight on four fingers. How the mind affects the body and vice versa ha[s] been studied by psychologists for many years.

The Mind and the Body

Another question that occupied the attention of philosophers for centuries concerned the relationship between the mind and the body. If there is a change in the body—an illness, for example—does this have an effect on the mind? Or if one is down in the dumps or depressed, does this affect the body? Arguments among philosophers never provided an answer acceptable to all, but as we shall see later in this book, modern psychologists have begun to attack the problem using scientific method. We call this modern version of the problem *psychosomatic medicine,* and there have been some exciting new discoveries about the relationships between mind and body.

Human Nature

Another attempt by philosophers to explain man's behavior centered around debates over human nature. Is man born good or bad? Some believed that man is born good and that if he becomes bad it is because of the influences of society. Others took the opposite view. Man is by nature selfish, greedy, jealous, and aggressive, they said, and it is the job of society to teach him to overcome these unfortunate tendencies.

Such limited views of the nature of man not only represented the personal observations of the philosophers involved but also the times in which they lived. If we look at such theories in a historical context today, we know that philosophers living in a period of war or social turmoil frequently took the view that human nature is bad, while those living in peaceful times felt man is by nature good and innocent.

Few modern psychologists talk about human nature at all. We know the concept is an unscientific one and that there are very few generalizations that apply to all mankind. We cannot say that men are "by nature" aggressive, warlike, jealous, or competitive. There are too many cultures in which such behavior is unknown. This is not to say that heredity has nothing to do with behavior or that all behavior is determined solely by one's environment. It simply means that such behavior as that mentioned previously cannot be considered a part of "human nature" because it does not appear in all human beings.

SCIENCE AND HUMAN BEHAVIOR

The first attempts to apply scientific method in studying human behavior took place in the late 1800s in Europe. German psychologists interested in "the mind" began conducting experiments in which people were asked to solve problems and then describe how they went about it. The psychologists were looking for answers to such questions as, "What are ideas?" "Are there different kinds of ideas?" and "What mental processes make up the mind?"

It soon became apparent that two things happened rather consistently in such experiments. First, people could not always tell how they solved particular problems, and second, the psychologists could not always agree on how to interpret what people said. Finally, after thirty years of such efforts, an American psychologist said, "Let's forget about studying the mind al-

WHAT IS SCIENTIFIC METHOD?

Any scientist, whether he be a biologist, physicist, chemist, or psychologist uses basically the same method to uncover answers to problems that puzzle him. Almost always he begins by formulating an *hypothesis* (an informal guess or idea) about the problem he is investigating. For example, a psychologist may hypothesize that adolescents rebel against their parents when parents are too permissive in raising their children.

Once the hypothesis is stated in such a way that it can be tested, the scientist sets about to make and record systematic observations that will enable him to accept (prove) or reject (disprove) the hypothesis. To test the above hypothesis, for example, he might attempt to locate two groups of adolescents—one rebellious and the other not. Interviews might then be conducted with their parents to determine methods by which the children were reared, that is, permissive or nonpermissive. When the recorded observations—interviews in this case—have been completed, they are then evaluated to determine if they support the original hypothesis. Usually this evaluation involves statistical or mathematical analysis. Finally, the exact findings are communicated to other scientists.

A significant point to remember is that the scientist does not base his conclusions on intuition, opinion, or belief. Rather they are founded on the observations that he has made under systematically controlled conditions.

together and study something we can see and agree on." He was advocating the study of behavior.

The Behaviorists

John B. Watson was the psychologist who changed psychology almost overnight. He argued that there was no way to study "the mind" scientifically, for we cannot see it or measure it in any way. Therefore, he said, psychologists should study what animals and humans *do*, or in other words, how they behave. Scientists can see behavior, he argued, and they can measure it.

Watson did more than change the subject matter of psychology from the mind to behavior. He believed that almost all behavior is learned and that, because of this fact, psychologists should be most concerned with understanding learning. He was, to put it another way, an "environmentalist." That is, he believed environment is everything and heredity nothing. "Give me ten infants to raise as I please," he once said, "and I will turn them into any kind of adults you like."

Watson also influenced psychology in another important way. He said the psychologist should study the behavior of animals other than man in order to learn more about man's behavior. Although the study of animal behavior was under way before Watson, most psychological studies were conducted with human beings. Watson thought that many experiments could be done more easily with animals than with human beings, however, and before long psychologists by the hundreds were studying animal behavior.

Psychologists today study other things besides behavior. Also, few psychologists believe as strongly as Watson in the influence of the environment. Nevertheless, it can be said that Watson helped greatly to make psychology a science. Furthermore, while there are few strict behaviorists in psychology today, learning is still one of the most important processes under investigation, and animals are included as the subjects of experimental study by a great number of psychologists.

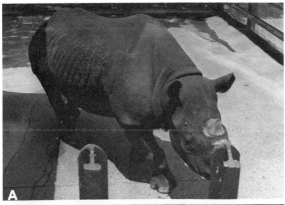

Fig. 1–3. Psychologists study the behavior of animals as well as man. In the top picture, the rhino has learned to touch his horn against a post with a triangle attached to it. When he touches the right post, the psychologist rewards him with a piece of stale bread. The psychologist is trying to find out how long it takes the animal to learn and whether it can remember over long periods.

Freud and Psychoanalysis

While Watson was a giant in the history of psychology, Sigmund Freud, an Austrian physician, looms every bit as large. Unlike Watson, Freud was not particularly concerned with making psychology scientific. He was concerned with understanding the causes of mental illness.

Until Freud's time, it was generally believed that mental illnesses were caused either (1) by the devil or (2) by some physical ailment. Freud showed that such illnesses often could be traced back to an unfortunate emotional experience early in one's life. He developed a method or technique for treating such illnesses called *psychoanalysis*. Basically, psychoanalysis involves talking about one's experiences and feelings in early life while the analyst interprets or explains their meaning. Dreams, similarly, are often described while the analyst interprets them. Freud believed that dreams do have meanings and that they can be important in understanding the causes of personality problems or mental illness.

Later in the book, in the section on knowing who you are, we shall discuss Freud's ideas and psychoanalysis in much greater detail. It is important here to remember Freud as one of the men who was most important in the development of modern psychology.

WHAT PSYCHOLOGISTS DO

If we were to look at the type of work psychologists are doing today, this is what we would find. Some psychologists are employed in industry, working on such problems as how to improve the morale and motivation of factory workers. Others work for the National Aeronautics and Space Administration (NASA), where they collaborate with engineers in the design of new instruments for spacecraft. Still others are employed in research centers, where they study how the brain functions, how children learn to speak, or the effects of drugs on learning complicated tasks. Some work in schools, where they counsel students with emotional problems or difficulties in learning. Still others are employed by the military services to help improve race relations or reduce drug use.

Psychology, then, is a complex field which involves the study of almost every aspect of behavior in both humans and animals. In fact it is customary today to define psychology as the "science of behavior." We call it a science because psychologists use the same methods as those employed by the biologist, physicist, and chemist. How these methods are used to study psychologi-

An Experimental Psychologist at Work

Fig. 1–4. Experimental psychologists don't normally work in a bull ring, but this one is dramatically demonstrating how psychologists have learned to control behavior. A tiny radio-controlled electrode has been implanted in the bull's brain. As the animal begins to charge, the psychologist presses a button on the radio, and the bull comes to a fast stop. Other psychologists have been investigating the effects of chemicals on behavior. We know that so-called instinctive behavior can be changed by injecting chemicals into the brain. Cats can be made to be terrified of mice, for example, after exposure to certain chemicals.
Can the behavior of man be altered in similar ways? The answer is yes, but we still need much greater knowledge of the human brain before we understand exactly how this occurs.

cal problems is discussed in the next chapter. Before going on to that, however, we want to look briefly at some of the special areas within psychology, and at the relationship between psychology and other sciences.

Experimental Psychology

The experimental psychologist usually works either in a college or university or in a research laboratory. He conducts experiments with humans or with animals to learn answers to questions about emotions, thinking, vision, hearing, motivation, and a number of other topics. Sometimes he uses very complicated scientific equipment, including computers. In other cases his experiments may be conducted with almost no equipment at all.

Clinical Psychology

Unlike the experimental psychologist, the clinical psychologist is concerned with the diagnosis and treatment of emotional and behavioral problems such as mental illness, delinquency, mental retardation, alcoholism, marriage adjustment, and so on. Clinical psychologists usually work in mental hospitals, institutions for the mentally retarded, mental health clinics, or prisons. Many are also employed by the United States government in Public Health Service hospitals or the Veteran's Administration.

Fig. 1–5. The psychologist uses psychological tests to understand the problems of those who seek his services. In this picture an intelligence test is being administered to a student who is trying to decide on a career.

Fig. 1-6. *Human engineers and industrial psychologists working in the space program had some difficult questions to answer concerning man's probable behavior under conditions of low gravity as on the moon. Could he use tools? Would he be able to sleep? How would he estimate the size and distance of objects? We know the answers to many of these questions now but a great deal of research on man's behavior was required before he took his first hesitant steps on the moon.*

The School Psychologist

School psychologists are usually employed by a single school or a school system to counsel disturbed pupils and their parents, to identify the gifted, to assist with the testing and evaluation program, and to diagnose special problems such as retardation. Through the use of psychological tests, the school psychologist can often help the student decide on a program of study, pick a vocation, or even determine which college to attend.

Psychology in Industry

The industrial psychologist deals with almost any industrial situation in which human problems are involved. He or she may develop special tests for selecting workers, or revamp work conditions so as to improve morale, or even make suggestions concerning new products. Some industrial psychologists measure consumer attitudes toward certain products and work with advertisers in planning campaigns to sell products. Others, called "human engineers" work with industrial, electrical, or aeronautical engineers in the design of new machines.

These are some of the specialized areas within which psychologists work. There are others as well, but these examples should serve to show that psychology is a complex field including much more than simply the treatment of those with mental or emotional problems.

Psychology and Other Sciences

Broadly speaking, modern science can be divided into two main parts: the physical sciences and the social sciences. The physical sciences include such fields as biology, physics, and chemistry, while the social sciences include history, economics, and political science or government. Psychology is considered a "behavioral science" along with sociology and anthropology. While psychology is most closely related to these latter two fields because they deal with behavior, it is also closely related to the social sciences and to certain of the physical sciences as well.

Why the Physical Sciences Are Important to Psychology

From fields such as chemistry and biology the psychologist is able to gain an understanding of how the body functions. Since behavior is frequently dependent upon what occurs within the brain or nervous system, for example, his study of human physiology is of great importance. Genetics, another branch of biology, is also important to the psychologist in learning about the roles of heredity and environment in such things as intelligence, personality, and mental illness.

Medicine and Psychiatry

Psychiatry is similar to clinical psychology in many respects. They both are concerned mainly with mental illness and less serious emotional problems, and with the diagnosis and treatment of such disorders. The psychiatrist, however, is an M.D. and is trained in medical school, while the clinical psychologist usually has a Ph.D. (Doctor of Philosophy) degree. Psychologists receive their training in universities, and while they are also professional persons, they do not prescribe medicine or use treatments that are physical in nature.

The Social and Behavioral Sciences

We mentioned above that psychology, as one of the behavioral sciences, is closely related to the social sciences of history, economics, and political science. Economics and political science deal with specific aspects of modern life, while history seeks to clarify the development of man through time. The behavioral sciences, on the other hand, deal with the behavior of modern man.

Anthropology is a field that is concerned mainly with the study of primitive man—his family life, social organization, use of tools, and so on. For those interested in human behavior, anthropology is an extremely important field. One reason is that anthropology helps us overcome ethnocentrism, the tendency for a person raised in a particular culture to be centered on that culture. An example will help to make the meaning of ethnocentrism clear.

When we are born and raised in the American culture, the values, motives, aspirations, and other characteristics of that culture tend to color our view of the behavior of people in other cultures. Competition is so much a part of our own culture, for example, that we may think all human beings are competitive. The fact is, however, that in some human groups competition is virtually unknown. Similarly, warfare seems to be so much a part of

Fig. 1–7. Anthropologists study the behavior of primitive people such as these Masai women in Tanzania. An understanding of their customs and habits, as well as those of people living in other parts of the world leads to the conclusion that human behavior is largely learned.

the history of many countries that we may believe it to be a universal part of human life. Anthropologists tell us, however, that there are cultures in which warfare is totally unknown.

One of the most valuable lessons anthropology has for the psychologist is that there are great differences in human behavior from culture to culture. Evidence gathered from the four corners of the world for the last fifty years shows clearly that the behavior of man is dictated largely by the culture in which he lives and by relations among people within that culture.

Sociology is another field of great importance to the psychologist. Groups and the influences of groups on the individual constitute the subject matter of sociology. Thus, because man is a social being and almost invariably lives his life as a member of various social groups, the findings of sociology are invaluable in understanding behavior.

Getting It All Together

Our discussion of the relationships between psychology and the other sciences indicates that the dividing lines between these fields are not as clear-cut as one might expect. There is considerable overlap among them both in terms of what they study and the methods of research used. The sociologist, for example, is interested in understanding the human group, while the psychologist is concerned mainly with the individual. But the psychologist uses findings from sociology concerning groups, social organizations, and the products of culture to help him understand the group setting

---

WHAT TO EXPECT FROM PSYCHOLOGY

If psychology is to be of any practical use, it should help one understand his own behavior and the behavior of people around him. All of us make certain assumptions about behavior even before studying psychology. We may assume, for example, that people will not like us if we behave in certain ways. Such assumptions are built up through our contacts with other people, and in some cases these assumptions are correct. In other cases, they are incorrect and often result from our individually limited experiences. Psychology helps us correct some of our incorrect assumptions and provides us with an objective basis for understanding ourselves and others.

It should be emphasized, however, that one should not expect too much of psychology. The student may be impressed by how much we do know about behavior, but he should realize that psychology is just emerging from its infancy.

No psychologist would pretend that we know most of the answers to the difficult questions in this field. We know the answers to many questions and have a good foundation for discovering answers to many others, but in its present state of development it would be a mistake to expect psychology to provide all the answers to all the questions concerning human behavior.

Another point to remember is that a little knowledge is a dangerous thing. Students sometimes feel they can offer advice concerning emotional and other human problems after they have taken a psychology course. But every student should understand that one course does not qualify him as an expert on the majority of complex human problems. Should a friend approach you seeking your help with an emotional problem, encourage him to get expert professional guidance. A good place to begin is with your school counselor.

in which the individual behaves. The sociologist, on the other hand, learns how individuals affect groups and their organization and functioning.

Behavioral scientists today realize that most human problems are exceedingly complex. To understand crime, for example, or poverty, or war, one must look not only at the affected individuals but at the groups in which they live as well as their history, their economies, their religious beliefs, their values, and so on. Thus a new approach to understanding human problems has developed as scientists have become aware of the limitations of their own individual fields. This approach is interdisciplinary. In other words, it uses knowledge gained by scientists in a number of different disciplines, both the physical and social sciences, to explain complex human behavior.

CHAPTER SUMMARY

1. Psychology is one of several sciences concerned with the study of man's behavior. The two main goals of the field are to (1) predict behavior and (2) control or regulate behavior. If we could not predict behavior at all, we could not live together in an orderly society.

2. Whether we like it or not, our behavior is controlled in many ways every day. When the psychologist speaks of controlling behavior, he is thinking in terms of learning enough about the causes of such problems as crime and mental illness so that they may be eliminated.

3. The first attempts to understand human behavior were made by philosophers as long ago as the time of the ancient Greeks. One early theory held that there was a relationship between body build and personality. Thus fat people were thought to be happy and outgoing, while thin people were thought to be more unhappy and withdrawn. We know today that simple theories such as this are incorrect.

4. The early philosophers were also interested in the relationship between mind and body. Does the mind affect how the body functions in a direct way? Does the functioning of the body have an effect on one's mind? Modern psychology is still concerned with such questions and we call the contemporary version of this problem *psychosomatic medicine.*

5. Another problem that concerned philosophers over the centuries centered around debates over human nature. Is he (man) by nature competitive, jealous, aggressive, and warlike? We know today that there are many cultures in the world in which such behavior is unknown. Thus when we see such behavior we know it must be learned rather than a part of man's inherited nature.

6. Scientific psychology began in the late 1800s, when German psychologists conducted experiments to learn about the "mind." Such experiments, however, were really not very scientific, and it was not until an American psychologist, John B. Watson, advocated the study of behavior that psychology began to grow rapidly. Watson felt that most behavior is learned, and the study of learning became central to the work of the behaviorist. Watson also strongly urged that psychologists study the behavior of animals, for he felt that an understanding of animal behavior could better help us to understand the behavior of humans.

7. Sigmund Freud was mainly interested in uncovering the causes of mental illness. Until Freud's time it was believed that such illnesses were caused either by the devil or some physical disease. In his work with the mentally ill, however, Freud showed that such illnesses could often be traced back to an unfortunate emotional experience early in one's life. By using psychoanalysis—a method he developed which involves talking about one's experiences and feelings in early life—it was discovered that such illnesses frequently disappeared.

8. Modern psychologists work in a wide variety of settings. Some are employed by colleges and universities, others by agencies of the federal government. Still others work for the United States military services or in mental hospitals or prisons. Psychology today involves the study of almost every aspect of behavior in both humans and animals.

9. There are many specialized areas of work within psychology. Four of the best known are (1) experimental psychology, (2) clinical psychology, (3) school psychology, and (4) industrial psychology. The experimental psychologist conducts research in many areas such as learning, motivation, personality, and problem solving. The clinical psychologist does diagnostic work and therapy with the mentally ill, mentally retarded, or with cases involving personal adjustment. School psychologists counsel students, help plan programs, and administer psychological tests. The industrial psychologist deals with almost any industrial situation in which human problems are involved. He may help design machines, recommend motives to stress in advertising, or study how to improve workers' morale.

10. Psychology is one of the behavioral sciences, along with sociology and anthropology. All three behavioral sciences are closely related to the social sciences of history, political science (or government), and economics. In addition, the physical sciences, such as biology and chemistry, are of great importance to the psychologist. Psychiatry is similar to clinical psychology in many respects, since both are concerned with the causes and treatment of mental illness. The psychiatrist is a physician (M.D.), however, while the clinical psychologist usually has earned the Doctor of Philosophy (Ph.D.) degree.

11. The behavioral sciences of psychology, sociology, and anthropology are similar in that they all deal with the behavior of man. The psychologist, however, is concerned with behavior of the individual, while the sociologist is concerned with group behavior. The anthropologist studies both the individual and group behavior of primitive man. The newest approach to the study of behavior —the interdisciplinary approach—uses knowledge gained by scientists in a number of different disciplines. Each discipline has something important to contribute to our understanding of that most complicated organism—man.

Important Terms
from This Chapter

psychology	behaviorist	behavioral sciences
behavior	psychoanalysis	psychiatry
John B. Watson	experimental psychology	anthropology
human nature	clinical psychology	sociology
Sigmund Freud	school psychology	ethnocentrism
scientific method	industrial psychology	interdisciplinary

Answers to Self-Test:

1. F	6. T	11. T	16. F
2. F	7. T	12. T	17. T
3. T	8. F	13. F	18. T
4. T	9. T	14. F	19. T
5. T	10. T	15. T	20. T

Additional Readings
to Help You Learn More

Birenbaum, A. and Sagarin, E. *People in Places: The Sociology of the Familiar.* New York: Praeger Publishers, 1973. Students will find this entire book extremely interesting. A paperback book, it deals with attempts to understand everyday experiences such as why people feel embarrassed in social situations, the social psychology of the gift, and subway behavior.

Kagan, J. and Havemann, E. *Psychology: An Introduction,* 2nd Edition. New York: Harcourt, Brace, Jovanovich, 1972. Chapter 1, ''The Scope and Goals of Psychology,'' tells exactly what psychologists attempt to do and how they go about it.

Longstreth, L. *Psychological Development of the Child,* 2nd Edition. New York: The Ronald Press Company. 1974. Chapters 1 discusses freedom, dignity and man in addition to the determinants of behavior.

Munn, N., Fernald, L. and Fernald, P. *Introduction to Psychology,* 3rd Edition. Boston: Houghton-Mifflin Company, 1972. Chapter 1, ''Psychology and Science,'' discusses the nature of psychology and scientific inquiry. It talks about the differences between common sense and the use of scientific method in the study of human behavior. Chapter 2, ''Methods of Research,'' includes a discussion of such things as naturalistic observation, independent and dependent variables and the problems of adequate controls in research. Chapter 22, ''Historical Perspective,'' is a very complete and concise discussion of the history and development of psychology.

Resnick, W. and Sachs, H. *Dynamic General Psychology: An Introduction.* Boston: Holbrook Press, 1971. Chapter 15, ''The Applications of Psychological Knowledge,'' is an interesting discussion of how we use the psychological knowledge we have learned. It discusses applied psychology, psychology in industry, and in the military services as well as pseudoscientific psychology.

Ruch, F. and Zimbardo, P. *Psychology and Life,* 8th Edition. Glenview, Ill.: Scott, Foresman and Company, 1971. Chapter 1, ''Unraveling the Mystery of Man's Behavior,'' is a very good discussion of the nature of psychology and its goals.

Wertheimer, M. *Confrontation: Psychology and the Problems of Today.* Glenview, Ill.: Scott, Foresman and Company, 1970. Section 6, ''Human Control over Human Behavior,'' discusses the debate over whether we should or should not control human behavior.

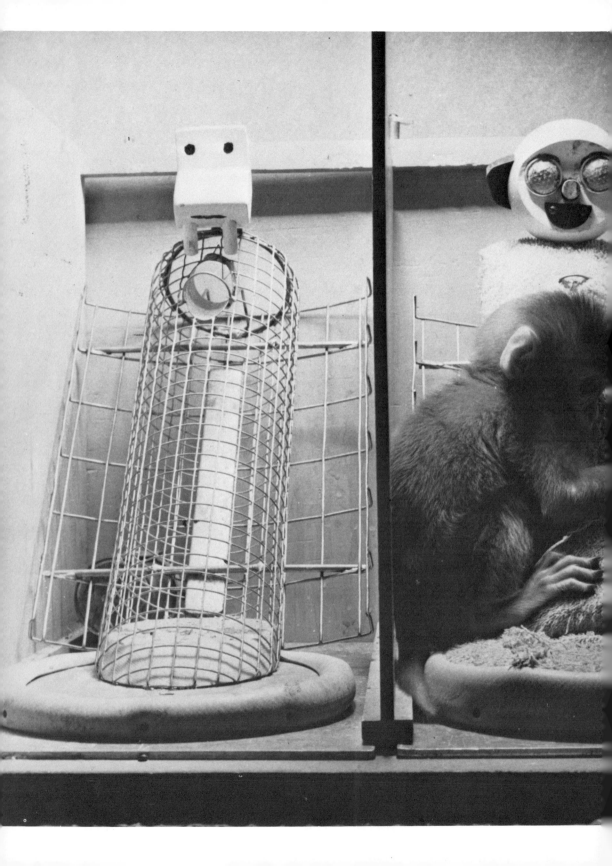

2

If
Psychologists
Are
So
Smart . . .?

In the last chapter we learned that psychologists are mainly concerned with predicting how people behave and with controlling or changing certain kinds of behavior. In particular we would like to be able to change behavior that leads to such human problems as crime, mental illness, drug addiction, and alcoholism. Among other things, we would also like to be able to help eliminate war, teach children to read more easily, improve relationships in marriage, and eradicate poverty. These are certainly admirable goals, but one may ask why it has taken so long for psychology to come up with the answers and why in fact many of these problems remain unsolved? If psychologists are so smart . . . why can't they give us the answers now?

In this chapter we will look at how psychologists go about solving the mysteries of human behavior: What methods do they use? What are the difficulties they face? Why does it take so long to come up with answers?

HUMAN BEHAVIOR IS COMPLEX

One certainly does not need a psychologist to tell him that human beings are very complicated organisms. But just how complicated they are does not really hit us until we begin to think of all the things that affect behavior. Obviously the environment determines to a great extent how we behave; we know that certain kinds of behavior are appropriate in school, still others are appropriate in church, and others are proper on dates or on other occasions where we are out for a good time. The situation in which we find ourselves, in other words, has a great deal to do with how we behave.

But it is not just the situation or the environment alone that determines behavior. Different people in the same situation do not necessarily behave in exactly the same way. Thus we can see that certain characteristics of the individual also are important in determining behavior. The person's intelligence, his personality, the state of his health, his emotions, and other factors all influence behavior.

It is not only the situation in which the person finds himself and characteristics of that person that determine behavior. Other people affect our behavior as well. We do not behave the same way when we are alone as when other people are present. Furthermore, our relationships to other people differentially affect our behavior. For example, we behave differently with friends than with strangers or enemies.

We can see then that to make accurate predictions about behavior requires a great deal of understanding of the many factors that influence behavior. These factors are called *variables* by the psychologist.

Variables in Psychological Studies

The behavior that the psychologist is interested in studying is generally called the *dependent variable* in any psychological investigation. The variable (or variables) that affects the behavior in question is called the *independent variable.* For example, if we want to understand how intelligence affects children's ability to learn to read, we would call learning to read

---

WHAT ARE INDEPENDENT AND DEPENDENT VARIABLES?

In any psychological experiment the investigator manipulates or changes something systematically (the independent variable) in order to study the effects of this on some aspect of behavior (the dependent variable). For example, an investigator interested in the effects of different levels of motivation on how quickly an animal learns might deprive animals of food for varying lengths of time. One group of animals might not be allowed to eat for four hours, for example, while another group is not fed for eight hours. Following the deprivation period the animals are given a task to learn and are rewarded with food when they respond correctly. In this experiment the independent variable is the length of the deprivation period. The dependent variable is speed of learning. The dependent variable, in other words, *depends* upon or is related to changes in the *independent* variable.

the dependent variable and intelligence the independent variable. To avoid confusion, let's look briefly at some actual psychological studies and at the variables under study.

Blue Is Beautiful

Some German psychologists have recently been interested in the effects of colors (independent variable) upon the child's mental performance (dependent variable). To study this they gave intelligence tests to children in rooms painted light blue, yellow, yellow-green, or orange. These were colors the children said they thought were "beautiful." Other children were tested in rooms painted with "ugly" colors—black, brown, and white. The children tested in the "beautiful" rooms were found to make higher scores on the intelligence tests than children tested in the "ugly" rooms.

In another study one group of children played in brightly colored, attractive rooms each day for six months while another group played in a conventional kindergarten. At the end of six months, children in both groups were given intelligence tests, and again the bright colors seemed to raise intelligence. As in the first study mentioned above, the room color was the independent variable, and the child's score on the test was the dependent variable.

It seems that these studies have clearly shown intelligence to be affected by the colors of rooms in which children play or in which they are tested. Great! If so we should be able to make all children smarter by painting school rooms bright colors. But wait—we said human behavior is complicated and that psychologists face many obstacles in trying to find answers to their questions. Before rushing to paint all school rooms blue, orange, yellow-green, and other bright colors, let's take a closer look.

First of all, we know that although two things may appear to be related, they are not necessarily related. For example, higher test scores in the studies mentioned previously appear to be related to room colors. But are they? Is it possible that the person giving the tests in the brightly colored rooms was friendlier than the person testing in the dull rooms? We do not know. Were the children tested at different times of the day? It is possible, for example, that children were tested in the rooms with bright colors in the morning while children in the other rooms were tested later in the day. Would this make a difference?

Another question we have to ask about these studies concerns the tests used. Were both groups of children given the same test? If not, that may account for the difference. How reliable were the tests? In other words, if we gave the same children the same tests again on a later day, would they make the same scores? It is possible that the intelligence tests used in these studies were not very reliable and that if they were given again no differences would be found between the groups of children.

These then are examples of some of the difficulties psychologists face in even the simplest of studies. Finding answers to questions concerning behavior that appear very simple may in fact turn out to be difficult and tedious. As we will see in the examples of other research studies below, this is more often the case than not.

EXAMPLES OF OTHER PSYCHOLOGICAL STUDIES

Many different research methods are used by the psychologist. Some methods, such as those mentioned previously, involve work in a laboratory. They are examples of what the psychologist calls "experimental method." Other methods involve treatment procedures for the mentally ill or the use of psychological tests. Still others utilize observation of natural or real-life situations. Each method has advantages and disadvantages, and the one chosen to study a particular problem is determined by both the advantages of that method and the special problem under study.

After examining several recent interesting psychological studies, we will summarize the various methods used by psychologists and talk briefly about their advantages and disadvantages.

Some Monkeys Don't Love Their Babies

Human love, and particularly love of a mother for her child, is one of the strongest human emotions. Is such love instinctive? If not instinctive, how is love learned? Why don't all mothers love their children? What happens to children who are not loved? These are questions that have been studied by the psychologist, but it is very difficult, or in some cases impossible, to perform experiments with human mothers and their children. We cannot raise some children in isolation, for example, while others are raised by their mothers. For reasons such as these, animals are often used as subjects in psychological studies.

Monkeys are certainly not people, but they are the highest form of animal life with which we can perform certain experiments. Furthermore, the baby monkey resembles the human infant in that it shows affection toward its mother at a very early age. Generally the mother monkey returns this affection in a way that helps the young monkey prepare for the social life that is normal for this kind of animal. But what happens if the baby monkey has no mother?

Psychologists at the University of Wisconsin studied this question by raising young monkeys alone in cages from birth until they were several months old. During this time, of course, food and water were provided, and the cage was cleaned by remote control. But during this isolation period, the baby monkey saw no other living creature, not even a human hand. Obviously moral considerations would prevent this kind of experiment from being conducted with human infants.

Inside the cage, the baby monkeys were provided with two substitute "mothers." One of the substitutes consisted of a wire mesh tube and a wooden block at the head. This was called the "wire mother." The other was made from a block of wood covered with sponge rubber and cloth. This was called the "cloth mother." Both "mothers" are shown in Fig. 2–1.

Either of the "mothers" could be fitted with a nursing bottle, so some of the babies were fed on the wire mother and others on the cloth mother. Regardless of where they were fed, however, the psychologists found that all monkeys spent more time clinging to the cloth mother. Apparently, then,

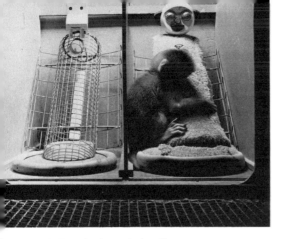

2-1a.   Cloth and Wire "Mothers"
ng monkeys preferred the soft, cloth-covered
ther," even though they were fed on the wire
ther." How was the behavior of the young monkey
ted by being raised in this artificial environment?

Fig. 2-1b.   Mother monkey and baby normally spend a
great deal of time together. The caressing and cuddling
by the mother creates an affectionate bond between the
two.

2-1c.   When baby monkeys are raised together,
without a natural mother, they cling together like
nese twins. If they are separated from each other,
/ "cry" until they can be together again.

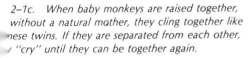

Fig. 2-1d.   Raised without a natural mother, the baby is
terrified of anything new and different. It cannot face
other monkeys nor human beings.

there is an unlearned tendency in baby monkeys to seek comfort with something resembling a natural mother even though feeding is not associated with that object.

What were these monkeys like when removed from isolation at the end of several months? How did they behave toward other monkeys? The psychologists made some startling observations. At first the isolated monkeys were terrified of others. They simply crouched in a corner of the room submitting meekly to the attacks of others. They did not learn to play with the others nor show any of the social behavior typical of normal monkeys. In fact, the danger of their being killed by the others was so great that they had to be removed and again placed by themselves.

Later, when they had grown to full adult size, the monkeys raised in isolation were again introduced into a situation where other normal monkeys were present. They were still terrified, but whereas before they had cowered in fright, they now became vicious attackers. Some of them launched suicidal attacks on large adult males, and in other cases they attacked smaller juveniles—an act almost never seen in normal monkeys.

As adults, those monkeys that had been unloved and isolated as infants were themselves unloving, disturbed, and delinquent. Females raised in isolation became very bad mothers themselves. Denied normal monkey affection in her early life, the mother denied affection to her own infants and, in fact, was often so brutal that the effects were devastating to her infant. Human mothers, the psychologists note, also sometimes deny affection to their offspring, and the "battered baby syndrome," as it is called by physicians, is an all too frequent occurrence. Monkey mothers who are unloved as infants seem to find it difficult to love their own infants. Human mothers who are unloved as children may also make very poor parents.

This experiment, as we have seen, was conducted with monkeys because similar experiments could not be performed with human infants. To study the effects of an unloving mother on human infants, we would seek out such mothers and observe their behavior. Through the use of interviews with the mothers, we would attempt to determine if a lack of love in their own childhood might be responsible for their lack of affection toward their own children. A major problem with such a study, however, is that we have to take things as they are—we cannot manipulate or control variables in such a way as to study their effects. Also, people are not always truthful in such studies, nor is there a way of actually discovering the truth.

Sometimes "natural" experiments involving humans occur, and while psychologists cannot create such experiments, they can study the results after the fact. Let's take a look at two such "natural experiments" in which

Fig. 2-2a.   This six month old monkey was raised in isolation from birth. It shows intense fear and never develops the social behavior characteristic of young monkeys.

Fig. 2-2b.   Normal monkeys raised by natural mothers explore the world and each other. Playfulness is characteristic of their behavior and gradually as they grow older they become less attached to their mother.

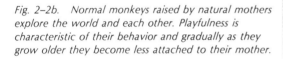

Fig. 2-2c.   Another monkey raised in isolation cannot give up its artificial mother. It has learned to cling to the cloth substitute and shows no interest in adult females.

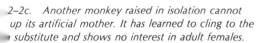

Fig. 2-2d.   When several monkeys are raised together from infancy without natural mothers, they cling together in a line. They do not show the fear of other monkeys that is seen in infants raised alone.

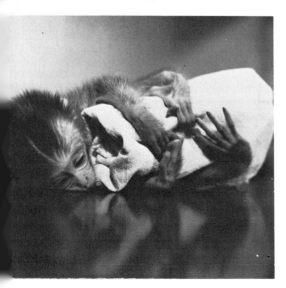

IF PSYCHOLOGISTS ARE SO SMART . . .?   **33**

children grow up apart from other humans or in the company of animals.

Wild Children

We have seen that monkeys who are raised in isolation never develop the behavior typical of adult monkeys raised by their own mothers. Such experiments with humans, as we have noted, are obviously impossible. Nevertheless, the question of what humans would be like if they grew up apart from other humans is a fascinating one.

Those who believe in "human nature" contend that certain behavior in humans is unlearned and characteristic of all humans wherever they may live. Thus aggression, warfare, competition, jealousy, and so on are believed by some to be just part of "human nature." Furthermore, those who believe in "human nature" generally also believe that it can't be changed.

If certain behavior is in fact, characteristic of all humans and unlearned, we would expect humans who grow up alone or those raised by animals to show such behavior. The fact is that such children show very little of what we think of as "normal human behavior."

A number of years ago two girls were found in India living in a cave with wolves. One of the girls was estimated to be between two and four years of age and the other eight or nine when they were discovered. Their behavior could in no way be described as human. They ran about on all fours and in fact had heavy calluses on both hands and knees from such locomotion. They lapped up milk from a dish in the manner of lower animals, and they had little communication other than growls and deep-throated noises. Taken in by missionaries, they eventually were taught to use utensils for eating, to walk upright, and to use about 100 words, but they never progressed in their behavior beyond the level of a normal three-year-old child.

Another case, reported in France, involved a boy who had apparently grown up alone in a forest. Those who discovered him reported he could run as fast as a deer, but, like the two girls in India, he could not talk; nor did he show much other behavior that could be described as human. A psychologist took the boy in and worked with him intensively for five years before giving up. He did manage to teach the boy to wear clothes, to eat at a table, and to speak some words. But he was never able to teach him more than the very young normal child is able to learn.

"Natural experiments" such as these help us to understand that human behavior is not determined by any inherited "human nature." We learn to be human beings by being raised in the company of other humans. This does not mean that any animal could learn to behave as a human by simply being treated and raised as if it were human. We will see in the next two chapters that man is more than simply a naked ape. He has certain biological capabilities that make it possible for him to acquire what we consider normal human behavior. But he must be raised in the company of other humans if he is in fact to develop such behavior.

While natural experiments are helpful to the psychologist in providing clues about the causes of certain behavior, they are not entirely satisfactory. In such "experiments," the behavior is often reported by untrained and unscientific persons and thus may not be very reliable. Furthermore, the small number of cases involved means that we must be very cautious in drawing conclusions.

A far more preferable way of studying behavior, as we have seen, is to conduct an experiment in which we can control events. But we have also seen that there are some problems that cannot be studied in this way. Nevertheless, there are other methods used by the psychologist to explore the problems of behavior. One of these involves the use of *systematic observation*.

As in the so-called natural experiments described above, the psychologist does not make things happen when he uses systematic observation. He simply takes them as they come. But unlike the natural experiments, in which results are often reported by untrained observers, systematic observation is carried out by trained psychologists using scientific method. The following is an example of this method as it has been used to explore the possible link between heredity and criminal behavior.

The Mystery of the "Bad Chromosome"   2013958

Chromosomes are thin threads of genetic material inherited from the parents. They contain chemical instructions for the growth and reproduction of every living cell in the body. Physical traits such as sex, eye color, hair color, and height are controlled by these heredity messages. In each cell of the normal body there are 46 chromosomes, and two of these, called "X" and "Y" determine the individual's sex. Cells in a normal woman have two X chromosomes, while each cell in a normal male has one X and one Y chromosome.

About nine years ago a sensational murder case hit the newspapers in France. A man charged with an exceptionally violent and brutal murder was examined and found to have an extra Y chromosome. No one knows what caused this, but his attorney claimed the man was innocent by reason of insanity due to the extra chromosome. He argued that the defendant had no

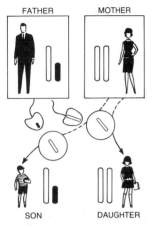

FATHER MOTHER

SON DAUGHTER

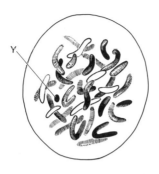

Fig. 2–3. The chromosomes shown here are magnified about 3600 times. The "y" chromosome determines male sex as shown in the diagram. The father determines the sex of the child, for only he contributes a "y" chromosome, but in some cases the extra "y" seems to be related to extreme height, aggressiveness, and mental retardation.

control over his actions or judgment and therefore should be found not guilty. Not long after this, other murderers tried in the United States and Australia were also found to have extra Y chromosomes and pleaded innocent because of insanity.

A study of the available scientific data by geneticists, psychologists, lawyers, and others led to the finding that one out of about 550 men is born with an XYY chromosome pattern. But these scientists said that while some XYY men do seem to develop behavior problems, most develop normally. The only characteristic XYY men seem to show rather consistently is a tendency to extreme tallness. Most of them in fact are over six feet tall.

The initial study of the possible link between XYY chromosome patterns and crime then, did not conclusively prove a connection. But only eleven cases in the entire world were known at that time. More recent studies, based on a much larger number of cases, have reopened the question.

Obviously we cannot conduct an experiment in which we control the number of chromosomes a person is born with. What can be done, however, is to locate a large number of men with abnormal chromosome patterns and compare their behavior to normal men. This is what a number of investigators, including psychologists, set out to do.

Some of the earlier reported cases of XYY males suggested that not only violent behavior and extreme tallness resulted from the abnormality, but mental retardation as well. Thus investigators began looking for men with an extra Y chromosome among tall, retarded inmates of institutions for criminal offenders. More than 100 of them were discovered in four years.

Although there were exceptions, most of these men had manifested episodes of extreme violence in the past. Some of the most renowned murderers of our time, in fact, have been found to have extra Y chromosomes.

A Case History

One patient with the XYY chromosome pattern will serve to illustrate the behavior observed in some of the men with this abnormality.

A 26-year-old man with an extra Y chromosome was found by psychologists in an institution for the criminally insane. His mother reported that he was uncontrollable even in early childhood. In fact, she finally tied him to a tree while doing her outside chores so that he would not harm himself and others. When he started school at age 6, he caused so much trouble his parents were asked to remove him. When he returned to school at age 7, he beat up other children and was a constant disciplinary problem. When he was 10, he was placed in a boarding school for disturbed children. Since that time he has been in institutions of one kind or another. He frequently escaped and his favorite pastime was that of killing chickens from neighboring farmyards by cutting off their heads.

At the age of 20, the patient was committed to a mental hospital because of his increasingly abnormal behavior. Some years later he was transferred to a hospital for the criminally insane after he nearly killed an attendant and another patient. In this institution he was regarded as the most difficult person to manage.

The patient never had any real friends, and his violent behavior was unpredictable and impulsive. He has only borderline intelligence, and he has shown no signs of progress despite years of treatment. He is six feet, seven inches tall.

XYY and Violence—Truth or Fiction?

One case like the one above does not prove that an extra Y chromosome is somehow linked with a tendency toward violent criminal behavior. In fact, as we mentioned previously, there are normal men who possess the extra chromosome and who never show such behavior. But if there is a link between the two, we would expect to find a greater percentage of criminals with this abnormality than noncriminals.

Some twenty investigations of the frequency of XYY chromosomes in criminals have now been completed. Of the 4,293 male criminals examined, there were 61 with the chromosome abnormality (1.4 per cent). This frequency is 15 times that found in newborn males and in normal adult males and almost 3 times as great as the frequency observed among male mental patients. Such a difference would be expected by chance less than 1 out of 50 times. Thus there appears to be rather convincing evidence of a link between the XYY chromosome pattern and violent, criminal behavior.

However, more work needs to be done before we can state conclusively that the extra Y chromosome predisposes men to violent aggressive behavior. As things stand now, we know that not all such men are abnormally aggressive. Furthermore, the vast majority of violent crimes are committed by men without the extra chromosome.

HOW PSYCHOLOGISTS FIND THE ANSWERS

We have examined several examples of psychological investigations which illustrate the different research methods used by psychologists as well as some of the problems faced in such research. Not all of the methods have been illustrated, but we have seen that experimental method can be used to investigate such problems as the effects of colors on mental performance. In another experiment, as we have seen, animals were used to study certain experiences in infancy and their effects on later adult behavior. The study of wild children is an example of the method of systematic observation, as is the study of the XYY chromosome abnormality. So-called clinical methods are also used to investigate certain problems in psychology and, while space does not permit the inclusion of a detailed example at this point, we will examine a number of studies using clinical methods later in the book. Now that we have examined some examples of actual psychological research, we need to summarize the methods and discuss briefly their advantages and limitations.

Advantages of Experimental Method

The experimental method is generally preferred by psychologists above other methods mainly because one has greater control over the variables involved. In using this method, as we have seen, the experimenter decides what he wants to study and then he creates a situation in which the effects of specific variables he is interested in are isolated from the effects of other variables. In the study of the effects of room colors in mental performance, for example, two groups of children were studied. One group was tested in the bright colored rooms, and the other in the "ugly" rooms. The first group is called the *experimental group* and the second the *control group.* Those in the experimental group were exposed to the variable under

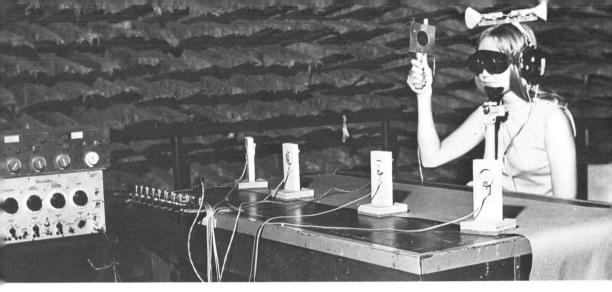

Fig. 2–4. *Use of experimental method often involves elaborate scientific equipment. The studded walls of the room shown here are designed to absorb sound. In this experiment, the girl is asked to point toward the source of a noise. First she is blindfolded then spun around in the chair. The experimenter next makes one of the speakers "beep" and she tries to indicate the direction from which it came. Such experiments could help the blind to find their way better by sound.*

WHAT IS A CONTROL GROUP?

In an experiment, the investigator *controls* or holds constant all variables except the one in which he is specifically interested. For example, if he is trying to learn whether reviewing silently is an aid to memory, he might begin by selecting two groups of people. Those in each group must be as similar to those in the other group as possible—same ages, sex, intelligence, and so on. Both groups are then given the same material to learn. But members of the *experimental group* are told to read the material and then to close the book and review silently what they have read. The other group, the *control group,* is simply told to read the material. Both groups are then tested to see how much they can remember.

If only one group was used and told to read and review silently, there would be no way of discovering whether reviewing aided memory. Only by comparing the memory of the "review" group (experimental group) with a comparable group *not reviewing* (control group) could the experimenter discern whether or not reviewing aided recall.

---

investigation—the brightly colored rooms. Those in the control group, tested in the other rooms, provided a base line for evaluating the effects of the bright colors. If only one group of children had been used in the study and given tests only in the colored rooms, there would be no way to determine the effects of the colors. By comparing the performances of experimental and control groups, as we learned, the investigators concluded that brightly colored rooms do enhance mental performance.

The problem of adequate controls in experiments is a difficult one, and psychologists must be constantly on guard against the possibility that unknown, and therefore uncontrollable, variables influence their results. As we learned in the experiment on room colors, it is possible that differences in the treatment of the two groups of children aside from the colors may have been responsible for the differences in performance. We can say that an independent variable affects a dependent variable, in other words, only when an experiment is conducted in such a way that no other variables except the independent variable could have had an influence.

One of the limitations of experimental method is that it cannot be used to study certain problems. Human infants cannot be raised in isolation, for example, nor can we administer dangerous drugs to human subjects. In such

---

EXPERIMENTAL CONTROLS AND THE PLACEBO EFFECT

Physicians sometimes give "sugar pills" to patients with imaginary complaints. The patient, of course, is told that he will feel better after taking the "medicine." Frequently in such cases the patient does secure temporary relief, but soon he is back asking for additional treatment. Pills such as these, which cause no physiological change, are referred to as "placebos," and the temporary relief they provide is the result of suggestion. The patient believes he will be helped, and therefore he *feels* better temporarily.

Placebo effects sometimes occur in psychological experiments as well. When testing new drugs for mental patients, for example, we must be careful to administer the actual drug to one group while giving a placebo to a comparable group. Since the placebo looks and tastes like the real drug, any differences in the behavior of the two groups must result from the effects of the real drug. Without the placebo we would have no way of determining whether changes in behavior resulted from the drug, or simply as a result of "suggestion."

---

cases, animals are often used. This, of course, is the reason baby monkeys were used in the experiments on love. Such an experiment could not be performed with human infants. But there is a drawback to the use of animals in such situations. Animals are not humans, and their behavior may not be comparable to human behavior in all cases. Therefore, while such experiments are not without value, we have to be cautious in generalizing the findings to humans.

There are other limitations in the use of experimental method as well. Some problems cannot be investigated experimentally because of their very nature. We cannot study the behavior of people in large mobs or crowds, for example, because it is not feasible to control variables affecting such behavior in laboratory situations. Furthermore, we know that the experiment itself may produce effects on behavior. People simply do not always behave the same way in a laboratory as in a real-life situation. To get around such difficulties with the experimental method, systematic observation is often used.

Advantages of Systematic Observation

If we want to study the effects of mother love on human infants or whether a chromosome abnormality such as male XYY is related to criminal behavior, experimental method cannot be used. In cases where the nature of the problem makes experimental study impossible, the psychologist often goes into the field and makes observations of events as they occur. The serious difficulty with this type of research is that it is less objective and precise than research conducted with the experimental method. In addition, when the psychologist must rely on the reports of untrained observers as in the studies of wild children, the disadvantages are especially great.

The advantages of systematic observation, of course, lie in the fact that the behavior occurs under natural conditions rather than in the unnatural

Fig. 2–5. In using systematic observation, the psychologist observes behavior under controlled conditions. In this picture an investigator is studying the development of thinking or concept formation in children.

conditions of the laboratory. Real-life or natural situations produce real-life or natural behavior, and we never need to worry that the behavior we are observing is somehow being affected by the very fact of our observing, or the situation in which it occurs.

The method of systematic observation includes not only observation of behavior as it occurs, but also the use of interviews or questionnaires. Thus, for example, if we wanted to learn about how mothers from different social backgrounds disciplined their children, we might select a sample of mothers to be interviewed on this subject. As with direct observation of behavior, however, there are drawbacks or limitations to the use of interviews and questionnaires. For example, people do not always tell the truth in interview situations. But to discover answers to certain kinds of problems, interviews are often the only means we have.

How Are Clinical and Testing Methods Used?

From experience in treating the mentally ill, we have learned a great deal about personality, motivation, and emotion. Freud, for example, developed a theory of personality based on his attempts to discover the causes of certain kinds of abnormal behavior. Among other things, his experiences led him to emphasize the importance of the first few years of life in later adjustment.

Fig. 2–6. *Clinical methods, including the use of psychological tests, are often used to study behavior. Here the psychologist (on the right) is conducting group therapy—a method of treatment in which several emotionally ill persons are helped by talking about their problems together in a group. As he helps them recover, he frequently develops hypotheses about behavior which can be tested experimentally.*

The clinical psychologist uses psychological tests of various kinds to help him understand the nature of problems faced by his patients. There are tests of intelligence, aptitude, personality, adjustment, interest, and so on. Together with a case history, these help the psychologist make a diagnosis of the problem, and the diagnosis in turn suggests appropriate courses of action for dealing with it.

Clinical and testing methods often help us develop hypotheses about behavior that are later subjected to experimental study or systematic observation. Thus there are two advantages that such methods provide. *First,* they are in themselves a valuable source of knowledge about behavior, and *second,* they provide ideas for experimental study or systematic observation.

If Psychologists Are So Smart . . .

We turn now to the question raised at the beginning of this chapter. If psychologists are so smart, why are so many questions about behavior unanswered? Why can't they give us the answers now? Why does it take so long to unravel the mysteries of human behavior?

As we have seen, human behavior is extremely complex. There are few simple cause and effect relationships that can be demonstrated. Our behavior is determined by the situations in which we find ourselves, by individual differences in such things as personality and intelligence, by the effects that other people have on us, and by our heredity and other biological factors. It is all these things in interaction that determines behavior. In other words, it is the combination of all these factors working together that influences or affects behavior. Coupled with the fact that psychology is a young field (less than 100 years old), this in part explains why it is not easy to give answers to questions that may appear simple.

Another difficulty, as we have seen, is that there are limitations to the research methods we have at hand. Some problems cannot, for a variety of reasons, be studied using the experimental method. Furthermore, the results of those that can be studied experimentally often must be qualified or hedged because of the effects which experiments themselves sometimes produce on behavior. Systematic observation has its drawbacks, as noted previously, in that we cannot control events; we simply have to take things as they are. Finally, as with the others, clinical and testing methods present difficulties. No psychological test is perfect, and all have limitations. In addition, while the treatment of people with mental or emotional problems may help us to understand something about normal human personality, we have to be cautious in generalizing to normal people. In other words, theories of human behavior developed through work with the mentally ill may not be completely valid in explaining the normal personality.

Despite the youth of psychology, the complexity of human behavior, and the drawbacks to our research methods, we are making progress. Certainly we know a great deal more about behavior now than did the philosophers of centuries past. But it will be a slow, tedious process before we can say that the science of psychology has all the answers to the problems of human behavior.

CHAPTER SUMMARY

1. Human beings are very complicated organisms. Their behavior is affected by the situation in which it occurs as well as by characteristics of the behaving person such as his personality and intelligence. In addition, other people affect our behavior. We do not behave the same way when alone as when in the presence of other people. We do not behave the same way in the presence of friends as in the presence of enemies or strangers.

2. In scientific investigations of behavior, the factor we study is called the *dependent variable*. The factor that affects the dependent variable in question is called the *independent variable.* [In a study of the effects of room colors on mental performance, for example, the room colors constituted the independent variable and mental performance (scores on the intelligence tests) was the dependent variable. The investigators, in other words, were interested in how room colors affected mental performance. They changed or altered the colors to determine if test scores were affected by this.]

3. We know that even though two things appear to be related, they are not necessarily related. In the study of the room colors on test performance, children tested in brightly colored rooms made higher scores. But to conclude that there is a relationship between room color and test scores, we have to insure that other factors were not responsible. [Were the children all given the same test at the same time of day, and by the same examiners, for example? If not, the conclusion that bright colors improve mental performance may be incorrect.]

4. Several different research methods are used by the psychologist. Some involve work in a laboratory and are experimental in nature. Others involve observation of natural or real life situations. [The study of maternal love in monkeys is an example of experimental method. Some infant monkeys were raised from the time of birth until several months of age in total isolation. Other infants were raised in the normal way by their natural mothers. The two groups of monkeys were then compared as to the effects of these experiences on adult behavior. Monkeys raised alone were at first terrified of others but later showed violent aggressive behavior. Female monkeys raised alone seemed unable to show love toward their own infants when they became mothers.] Experiments [such as these] with animals are conducted because similar experiments with human infants cannot be carried out.

5. Sometimes "natural experiments" involving humans occur, and while psychologists cannot create such experiments, they can study the results. Examples of such "experiments" involved so-called wild children raised by animals or totally alone. From these we learn that human behavior is not determined by any inherited human nature. We learn to become human by being raised in the company of other humans.

6. When experiments cannot be conducted, the psychologist often simply observes events as they occur. The use of the method of systematic observation is seen in the study of XYY chromosomes in some male criminals. [Such men, for unknown reasons, are born with two Y chromosomes instead of one as in the normal male. By using the method of systematic observation, a group of such males was located in institutions for the criminally insane and their behavior compared to that of normal males. The results suggest that there is a link or relationship between the extra chromosome and violent aggressive behavior.]

7. There are three basic research methods that the psychologist uses to unravel the mysteries of human behavior: experimental method, systematic observation, and clinical and testing methods. Each has advantages and disadvantages. By using experimental method we can control what occurs [an advantage]; but not every problem can be studied experimentally [a disadvantage]. Further, the behavior of human subjects is sometimes affected by the very fact of its being studied

in a laboratory [another disadvantage]. Systematic observation involves the study of behavior under natural or life-like conditions [an advantage]. However, we cannot control what occurs when we use this method [a disadvantage]. Also, when interviews are conducted under this method, we know people are sometimes untruthful and we have no way of discovering the truth [another disadvantage]. Finally, clinical and testing methods are used to study behavior. But while tests allow us to measure certain kinds of abilities or characteristics [an advantage], all tests are subject to error [a disadvantage]. Furthermore, while clinical methods are especially useful in the study of abnormal people, they are less valuable and in some cases, impossible to use with normals [another disadvantage].

8. A number of things have made it difficult for psychologists to discover answers to many of the problems of human behavior. *First,* and probably most important, is the complexity of behavior. *Second,* psychology is a young field with a short history [less than 100 years]. *Finally,* there are limitations to the research methods we use. Despite these difficulties, we have made a great deal of progress in understanding behavior, and we expect to make a great deal more progress in the years ahead.

Important Terms from This Chapter

variable	reliable	natural experiment
dependent variable	instinctive	systematic observation
independent variable	experimental method	chromosome
clinical methods	experimental group	affect
testing methods	control group	effect

Additional Readings to Help You Learn More

Buss, A. *Psychology: Man in Perspective.* New York: John Wiley and Sons, 1973. Chapter 2, "Research and Theory," is a very good discussion of the research methods used by psychologists and some of the difficulties they encounter in the use of these methods.

Harlow, Harry F. "Love in Infant Monkeys." *Scientific American Offprints,* No. 429. San Francisco: W. H. Freeman and Company. Discusses Dr. Harlow's experiments.

Harlow, Harry F. "The Nature of Love." *Bobbs-Merrill Reprints,* P–642. Indianapolis: Bobbs-Merrill Company. Students will find this experimental psychologist's discussion of the nature of love particularly interesting.

Part II.

COMING OF AGE
IN AMERICA

Becoming Human

chapter 3

We have seen that one does not automatically become "human" by virtue of having been born of human parents. Children reared in isolation from other human beings, of course, must eat, sleep, drink, and breathe. But it is the fact of being raised by other humans that gives our behavior a distinctly human character. Human behavior, in other words, is largely learned and thus reflects the environment in which we grow up and live. If this were not true, we would expect to see human beings behaving in very much the same way all over the world. But what strikes us most about humans, in contrast to animals, is the great variability in their behavior.

This does not mean that animals are incapable of learning or that all members of a species behave in exactly the same ways. We know, for example, that chimpanzees and other animals raised in zoos do not behave in precisely the same ways as their counterparts in the wild. Also, while we stress the importance of the environment in determining human behavior, this is not to say that hereditary factors are without importance. We know, in fact, that there is a complex interaction between heredity and environment that determines behavior.

CAN CHIMPANZEES LEARN TO TALK?

If the behavior of humans were determined by the environment alone, it should be possible to teach other animals to behave as humans by raising them as we raise human children. Several psychologists have attempted this but without a great measure of success.

In the first of such studies, two psychologists decided to see if they could discover what similarities and differences would result if a human child and a chimpanzee were reared under the same conditions. They obtained a seven-and-a-half-month-old female chimpanzee named Gua and kept her in their home as a part of their family for nine months. The psychologists' son, Donald, was a few months older than the chimpanzee.

During the experiment, Donald and Gua were treated in very similar ways. Both wore diapers and shoes. Both slept in cribs at night and were taken for rides in the same baby buggy. When affection was shown to one, affection was also shown to the other. They were, in other words, treated very much alike, so that any differences in their behavior could be largely attributed to their different heredity.

For the first months of the experiment, the chimpanzee developed more rapidly than the child and showed superiority in learning to eat with a spoon, drink from a glass, and open doors. Their behavior was also similar in many respects. Both showed affection toward their "parents," and both missed the parents when they were left with a baby-sitter. As the experiment progressed, however, Donald's ability to use language developed, and he began to surpass Gua in virtually every aspect of behavior. Language, as we will see in the next chapter, is a prime factor that differentiates human behavior from the behavior of other animals. Furthermore, language is dependent upon the unique structure of the human brain.

In the first experiment of this type, Gua learned to respond correctly to about 70 commands, but she never learned to speak. In a later experiment by another psychologist, a chimpanzee was given intensive speech training, but after three years the animal could repeat only three sound patterns. Other psychologists, who believed that the chimpanzee's vocal apparatus is not appropriate to the production of human speech, decided to try sign language. Training with this chimpanzee began when she was one year old and continued for the next three years. During this time she lived in a completely equipped house trailer with access to children's toys and other play equipment. She heard no spoken words during this time, and at the age of four years could use about 85 signs properly.

Some psychologists have suggested that such experiments should be carried out over longer periods of time. More intensive training, they say, will produce a larger vocabulary and behavior more closely approximating that of a human. To this we can only say, "Good luck." We doubt that such experiments would be any more successful than previous attempts. The reason for this is that we know that the human brain differs in some important respects from those of other animals. We need not go into the details here, since they will be discussed later in the book. It is enough to say that no animal brain has a capacity for language development even remotely approaching that of a normal human adult. Furthermore, it is human heredity that determines this capacity.

Thus we can see that while human behavior is largely learned and reflects the environment in which one lives, it is not this alone that determines human behavior. Without the biological endowment of man, no amount of exposure to a human environment can produce behavior characteristic of the normal human. In other words, human behavior is determined both by man's biological endowment and human society.

We know that there are actually three sets of principles important in understanding behavior at any given age. These principles pertain to heredity, growth or maturation, and environmental influences. In this chapter our concern is with understanding how these three factors interact to shape behavior.

WHAT DO WE INHERIT?

Genetics is the branch of biology that studies the transmission of physical characteristics from parents to children through the chemical determiners of such characteristics—genes. Strictly speaking, it is correct to say that behavior cannot be inherited directly. But physical characteristics that are known to be genetically determined, such as the structure of the brain, may definitely influence behavior. Intelligence, for example, appears to depend in part on specific characteristics of the brain. In certain kinds of mental retardation, the brain never develops to full normal size, and individuals with such underdeveloped brains are always seriously retarded. Within the normal range of intelligence, however, we are not so sure of the role of heredity.

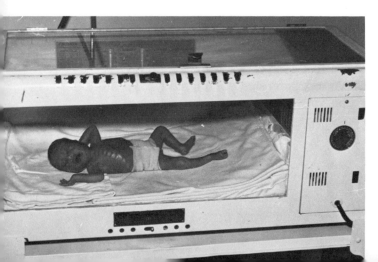

Fig. 3–1. Differences in behavior are seen even in newborn infants. Some cry a great deal while others sleep almost continuously. Later behavior as children and adults undoubtedly reflects these early temperamental differences as well as differences in the influences of the environment.

Even though behavior cannot be directly inherited, the *behavioral geneticist* studies how behavior may be influenced by genetic factors. Before reviewing some of this work in behavior genetics, we first need to examine some of the principles of genetics. Then we will discuss how genetic and environmental factors interact in determining physical and psychological characteristics.

Genes and Chromosomes

As we learned in the last chapter, each cell in the human body, except the sex cells, possesses 46 rod-shaped structures (23 pairs) called chromosomes. The sex cells (ova or sperm) contain only one chromosome from each pair, or a total of 23. In certain abnormal conditions there may be more or fewer chromosomes (as in XYY), and it is also worth mentioning that drugs such as LSD may cause scrambled, broken, or disarranged chromosomes.

Along the chromosomes are the genes—the chemical determiners of structure. No one knows exactly how genes operate to determine structure, but we do know they are composed of DNA (deoxyribonucleic acid), RNA (ribonucleic acid), and proteins. DNA appears to be the most important substance involved in the transmission of characteristics.

We cannot see human genes, but through breeding experiments with animals, geneticists have been able to map gene locations in certain species with considerable accuracy. At one point on the chromosome of fruit flies, for example, is the gene that determines eye color; at other points are located genes that determine the arrangement of facets in the fly's compound eye. On a single chromosome there may be hundreds of genes, each of which determines one aspect of the physical makeup of the animal. In the opposite member of each pair are genes at exactly the same location that influence the same characteristic.

Both genes concerned with any particular characteristic determine its nature. Let us pretend that only two kinds of genes determine your eye color, blue or brown.* If we pretend that there are only two genes for eye color, there are three possible combinations—both brown (BB), both blue (bb), or one brown and one blue (Bb). In this case the gene that determines brown eyes (B) is said to be *dominant.* That is, whenever it is present, the eyes are always brown. The gene that determines blue eye color (b) is said to be *recessive.* Thus we can see that while there are three possible gene combinations in this case (BB, Bb, or bb), there are only two possible physical differ-

*Actually it is a little more complicated than this.

ences in appearance. Eyes are either brown or blue in color, although some people with brown eyes carry genes for blue eyes. When the "brown" gene (B) is present, in other words, it always overrides the effects of the "blue" gene (b).

This example of how eye color is determined helps us understand why children need not necessarily resemble their parents in physical characteristics. If two parents with brown eyes both carried genes for blue eyes (Bb), we would expect some of their children to have blue eyes. In fact in this case, one out of four children would be expected to have blue eyes. The reason for this is that when a child is conceived, each parent contributes one chromosome of each pair of chromosomes to the new child. Thus if the mother has brown eyes but carries genes for both brown and blue eyes (Bb), a chromosome containing either gene could be contributed to the child. The same is true of the father. In such a case three out of four children would be expected to have brown eyes while one would have blue eyes.

Not all characteristics influenced by genetic factors are determined by genes that act in the manner just described. In some cases two genes may interact in such a way as to create a characteristic intermediate between the two extremes. Thus two genes for fur color (black and white) in some animals may produce an intermediate gray color. Also, most physical characteristics are determined by more than a single pair of genes. Some are apparently determined by the interaction of many pairs.

To complicate things still further, we cannot speak of heredity without taking into account the environment in which that heredity is expressed. Because of this we need to define the term "environment" and examine how heredity and environment interact.

THE OLD QUESTION—HEREDITY OR ENVIRONMENT?

In everyday use the term *environment* refers to the physical surroundings in which one lives. From a psychological point of view, however, this use of the term is inadequate. Two children may live in the same physical surroundings, but the forces that shape their behavior may be very different. If they happen to be brothers of different ages, for example, the environment of one includes an older brother, while the environment of the other includes a younger brother. Each brother has been subjected to certain experiences that differ from the experiences of the other.

The most useful definition of environment is one that takes into account all of the influences that have shaped the individual since conception.

Thus we can see that no two individuals ever have exactly the same environments—not even identical twins who grow up in the same house.

Both heredity and environment contribute to all behavior, and we know that these two factors interact in such a way that the influence of one is dependent upon the contribution of the other. Any single hereditary factor operates differently under varying environmental conditions. Conversely, environmental conditions differ in their relative influence on any characteristic as a function of the hereditary factor involved.

If we think of what happens when we plant seeds in a garden, the interaction between heredity and environment becomes clear. Suppose we plant two genetically identical seeds in different soils (same heredity—different environments). The seed planted in rich soil grows into a healthy vigorous plant. But the other seed, planted in poor soil, is stunted and unhealthy. Now suppose we plant two genetically different seeds in identical soils (different heredity—same environment). One grows into a healthy plant, and the other is sickly. The effect of heredity, in other words, is determined in part by environment, and at the same time the effect of environment is in part determined by heredity.

When we understand that heredity and environment interact so that the effect of one depends on the other, we no longer ask questions such as "How much does heredity have to do with intelligence?" There is no single answer to such a question but many answers, depending on which hereditary and which environmental factors are involved. By the same token, when someone says 80 per cent of intelligence is determined by heredity and 20 per cent is determined by environment, we know there is no scientific basis for such a statement.

HOW TWINS HELP US UNDERSTAND HEREDITY

Certain characteristics such as mental illness, mental retardation, and even musical genius seem to run in families. If we examine close relatives of the mentally ill, for example, there is a higher incidence of mental illness than among unrelated persons. Similarly whole families, including parents and children, are sometimes found to be mentally retarded. Also, if we look at the family trees of such famous musicians as Bach (see Fig. 3–2) we find a large number of outstanding musicians. This seems to suggest the possibility that such characteristics are inherited.

However, while members of the same family and close relatives are similar in heredity, they also tend to be exposed to similar environmental

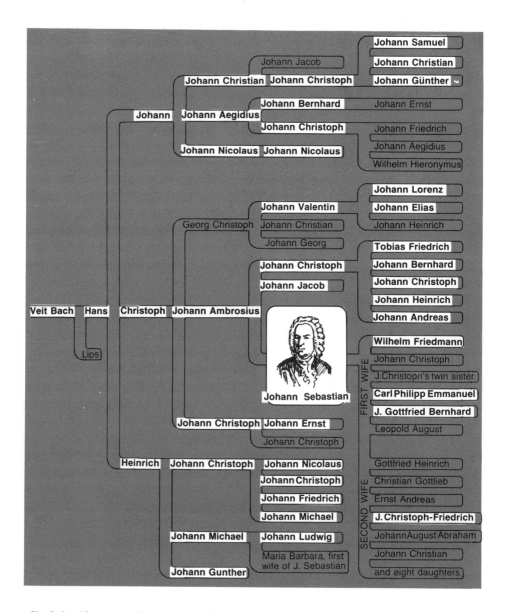

Fig. 3–2.   The names shown in heavy black print are known to have been excellent musicians. However, the presence of a large number of musicians in this family does not prove that musical talent is inherited. We know that growing up in such families also has a lot to do with learning to become a musician.

influences. Thus, because the two factors of heredity and environment are so closely intertwined, we cannot draw any conclusions. Because a particular behavioral characteristic is more common among closely related persons than among those less closely related, this does not prove such a characteristic is inherited. Living in a similar environment is just as likely an explanation.

Identical twins are useful to the behavioral geneticist because any differences between them must reflect differences in environment alone. Such twins are born from a single ovum and have exactly the same chromosomes and genes. When we observe differences in such things as intelligence or height and weight, we know these differences reflect environment.

How similar are identical twins? The answer to this question depends on the characteristic involved. In general, twins are very much alike in height, less alike in weight, and still less alike in intelligence. But even though they are less alike in psychological characteristics such as intelligence, as a general rule they are more alike in such characteristics than are two other brothers or sisters. One might suspect, then, that heredity has a great deal to do with intelligence, since identical twins are more alike than those with less similar heredity. However, the environment of twins raised together tends to be more similar than the environment of two brothers or two sisters. Twins tend to dress alike, go more places together, and to be treated alike by parents and friends. Thus the fact that they are more alike in intelligence than nontwins undoubtedly reflects both their identical heredity and the greater similarity of environmental influences.

How Alike Are Separated Twins?

Identical twins raised apart tend to be less alike in such things as intelligence than twins raised together. But at the same time, they are more alike in intelligence than two other brothers or sisters raised together. This seems to suggest that heredity is more important than environment in intelligence. But we have to ask how different were the environments of the separated twins?

In the few studies that have been conducted with separated identical twins, the environments of each pair tended to be somewhat similar in such things as years of schooling, education of the foster parents, and so on. Thus although raised in physically different environments, their environments were similar in factors that relate to intelligence. In the few cases where twins were exposed to very different environments, they were less alike than brothers or sisters raised together. In one case, one twin received fourteen years more schooling than the other, and they were substantially different in intelligence. What does this all mean? It means that even with identical heredity, two people can be very different in intelligence when exposed to different environments.

INSTINCTS

Instincts are inherited patterns of behavior common in many animals. Certain species of birds build the same type of nests regardless of whether or not they have ever seen other birds engaged in nest building. Other birds migrate at certain times of the year over thousands of miles. Squirrels, chipmunks, and other animals store quantities of food during part of the year to carry them through seasons when there is no food. Still other animals, such as bears, hibernate for several months of each year. These are all examples of instincts.

Psychologists who study instincts are interested in discovering three main things about them. First, what causes the behavior to begin—what triggers it? Second, what factors control the behavior? Third, can the instinct be changed? Many different instincts have been studied, but we will look at only one to illustrate these points.

Salmon migrate from their birthplaces in shallow streams to the sea and then back again to the same stream in which they hatched. Not all salmon complete the migration successfully, but most of them do; and psychologists have spent a great deal of time studying their behavior.

Fig. 3-3.   The number of instincts in lower animals seems almost without limit. Here a male South Pacific skag regurgitates food for the female and her young. Note the distinctive nest which is characteristic of this species.

Migration apparently begins when the salmon reach a certain size and become sensitive to light. The fish seek to avoid the bright light of the shallow stream and begin swimming to deeper and darker water. When they finally reach the ocean, they stay in the general vicinity of the mouth of the river, because the river waters are less salty and contain more oxygen. They remain in this area for two to three years.

When the salmon becomes sexually mature, its metabolism changes, and it needs more oxygen. Thus it swims again into the river from which it originally came and continues to swim against the current until reaching one of the headwaters. There it lays or fertilizes eggs and dies. The fact that salmon usually return to the stream where they hatched is apparently determined by a sensitivity in the fish to the odor of the water in that particular stream.

The "mysterious" behavior of the salmon, then, is not so mysterious after all. The need to avoid light begins the process; the need for oxygen keeps the fish near the mouth of the river; an increased need for oxygen causes the animal to return to the river; and the odor of the water causes the fish to seek out a particular stream—often the one in which it was spawned.

Are There Human Instincts?

In the past, almost all human behavior was believed to be instinctive. Today, however, most psychologists seldom use the term "instinct" when discussing human behavior. The reason for this is that we cannot find behavioral patterns in humans that appear to be inherited. Not all human mothers care for their infants in the same way, for example, and certainly not all mothers love their children or even want children. Thus the old idea of a "maternal instinct" has gone out the window. Maternal behavior in many other species does appear to be unlearned, in that it varies little from female to female. This does not mean that all animal mothers behave in exactly the same ways, or that learning cannot alter the behavior—in the last chapter we saw evidence that female monkeys raised alone make very bad mothers. But it does suggest that learning is relatively unimportant in such behavior. In human mothers, on the other hand, learning seems to be the most important factor that determines maternal behavior.

Instincts are either nonexistent or less important in all higher animals, including man, because they are unnecessary. In lower animals they play an important role—they have survival value both for the individual and the species. If it were not for instincts, in other words, many animals would not survive. Humans have less need for instincts because of their greater intelligence. Human survival depends upon our ability to think, plan, and solve problems—not upon a behavioral pattern that is influenced by heredity.

GROWTH AND MATURATION

The discussion of instincts does not imply that all human behavior is learned. We know, for example, that learning has little to do with such behavior as walking or with control of the bladder or bowel although toilet training involves some degree of learning. In fact, learning seems to be less important in the determination of most behavior early in life. It becomes more important as the individual grows older.

Physical growth is regulated from within the body and occurs in an orderly, patterned way. As the individual grows, behavior appears that is clearly dependent upon the development of underlying physical structures such as the nervous system and brain. When we see behavior that appears in all members of a species at about the same age, this strongly suggests that such behavior is a result of physical growth or maturation.

Walking and Talking

Almost all children go through the same stages of behavior that precede walking, and they do so at about the same ages. Furthermore, we see the same behavior in children living in other cultures. Because of such uniformity we assume that such behavior depends mainly upon growth; the alternative would be to assume that all parents in all cultures raise their children in the same ways, and we know this is not the case.

One psychologist studied children in the Hopi Indian tribe who spend much but not all of the first few months of life strapped on their mother's back. When removed from the cradleboard, however, these children walked at about the same age as non-Hopi children. Such behavior has to be accounted for by growth rather than by learning or practice.

Much the same thing can be said of talking. Of course children learn a specific language, but they cannot learn any language before parts of the brain and nervous system develop fully. Talking is dependent upon growth or maturation just as is walking. This is not to say that learning or practice has nothing whatsoever to do with such behavior. Recent evidence suggests that infants totally prevented from moving their limbs in the first months of life do not walk at the same age other children do. By the same token, exercise of vocal cords probably must precede talking.

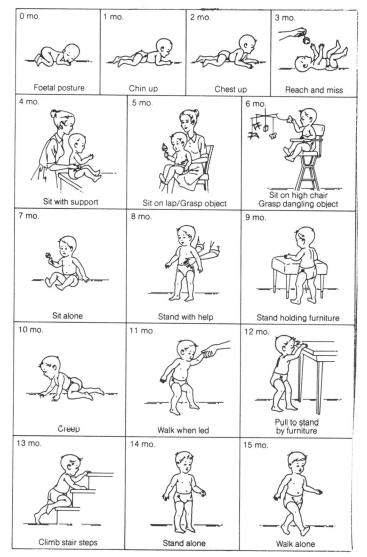

0 mo.	1 mo.	2 mo.	3 mo.
Foetal posture	Chin up	Chest up	Reach and miss

4 mo.	5 mo.	6 mo.
Sit with support	Sit on lap/Grasp object	Sit on high chair Grasp dangling object

7 mo.	8 mo.	9 mo.
Sit alone	Stand with help	Stand holding furniture

10 mo.	11 mo.	12 mo.
Creep	Walk when led	Pull to stand by furniture

13 mo.	14 mo.	15 mo.
Climb stair steps	Stand alone	Walk alone

Fig. 3–4. Ninety-five per cent of all children raised normally go through these stages at about the ages shown.

What Can We Say for Sure about Maturation?

There are several lessons that psychological studies of early behavior provide. *One* is that older children require less training to achieve certain behavior than younger children. The older the child, the easier he is to toilet train, for example. *Second*, when behavior is dependent upon reaching a

Fig. 3–5. Studies of these children in an orphanage in Iran show that walking is not totally due to growth or maturation. All of them are above three years of age and yet only a few can stand or walk. As infants they were kept in cribs that almost completely prevented moving the legs. Unlike Navajo or East Asian babies who are removed from the cradleboard much of the time when awake, these children had almost no opportunity to exercise their legs as infants.

certain stage of growth or maturation, early training will have little effect on the behavior. For example, all children must go through roughly the same stages before walking, and attempts to speed this up will have little effect. *Third,* training before the child is mature enough to develop certain behavior will fail. Children cannot be toilet trained before a certain age no matter what the parent does. *Fourth,* behavior that builds on developing behavior is most easily learned. When a child learns a language, for example, his first words are likely to be those that fit in most readily with his spontaneous babbling. *Finally,* training given before maturational readiness may do more harm than good. Attempts to toilet train before a certain age may cause frustration and delay actual training.

GROWTH AND MATURATION IN ADOLESCENCE

We have seen that in early childhood the appearance of certain behavior is clearly dependent upon the growth of underlying structures. The child does not walk or talk before the nervous system reaches a certain stage of maturity. But one might also ask if certain behavior is dependent upon the growth changes that take place at adolescence. Is interest in the opposite sex so dependent? What about the feelings of awkwardness and insecurity expressed by so many young people? Why are so many adolescents rebellious against parental and other adult authority figures? Does this have anything to do with the physical changes that take place in adolescence? Before attempting to answer such questions, we first have to understand exactly what physical changes take place in the body.

Hormone Changes

Six glands located in different parts of the body are called *endocrine* or *ductless* glands because they secrete chemical substances called hormones directly into the blood. We need not discuss all of them here, but three of these are especially important in adolescence.

The *pituitary gland* is located at the base of the brain. It secretes hormones that not only control the physical growth rate of the body but also regulate two other glands—the *adrenals* and the *gonads* (sex glands). Between nine and twelve years of age in girls and between eleven and fifteen in boys, the pituitary begins secreting hormones which stimulate both the gonads and adrenals. These glands in turn, secrete hormones which result in a number of rather rapid physical changes in the body. Boys grow in height as much as four inches a year, and girls may grow almost this much.

Other changes that occur include development of primary and secondary sex characteristics. *Primary sex characteristics* involve the reproductive organs themselves, while *secondary sex characteristics* are those other characteristics that distinguish mature males and females. These include development of breasts and pubic hair in girls, and changes in the voice, development of a beard, and pubic hair in boys. In addition to these physical changes, there are increases in blood pressure and heart rate, metabolic rate decreases, and there is an increase in the activity of oil and sweat glands.

Differences in Growth

Not all boys and girls grow at the same rate during adolescence. Both are about the same size until age 11, when girls begin to develop rapidly in both height and weight. Two years later boys surpass girls, and they maintain a height and weight advantage for the rest of their lives. However, we are speaking of the "average" boy or girl in this case. Some boys mature earlier than the average girl, while a few girls mature later than the average boy. There is an overlap in the growth rates of the two sexes, in other words.

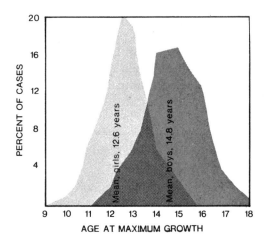

Fig. 3–6. The chart shows that the average girl achieves maximum growth two years before the average boy. But note that some girls mature later than the average boy, and some boys mature earlier than the average girl.

What happens to the boy or girl who is out of step with his or her age mates? We know that late-maturing boys tend to have stronger feelings of rejection and are more concerned with being socially accepted than boys who mature early. Boys who mature early, on the other hand, are more self-confident and independent. Early-maturing girls may feel too grown-up and uncomfortable around their age mates, but by the time they reach high school these feelings disappear. Late-maturing girls, on the other hand, tend to feel insecure and uncomfortable with age mates in much the same way as late maturing boys.

There are other differences in growth that influence adolescent behavior as well. The body does not necessarily grow in a uniform way. One part of the body may be out of step with the others. The arms and legs may suddenly elongate, for example, or the nose and chin may develop prominently. Thus some adolescents may appear and feel awkward and uncomfortable.

Another problem experienced by some adolescents is obesity. Being overweight can result from metabolic or hormonal disorders, or it can stem from psychological problems such as insecurity and unhappiness. In the latter case, overeating provides some feeling of relief from loneliness or feelings of inadequacy. Needless to say, however, being overweight creates more problems than it solves.

Behavior and Adolescent Growth

Unlike behavior development in infancy and childhood that appears to depend directly on changes in the body, very little adolescent behavior seems so directly related to maturation. In other words, what we are saying is that changes in the body tend to indirectly influence adolescent behavior. Growth hormone, for example, determines how large we grow, and in our society a person eight feet tall is likely to be regarded as a freak. Thus the way in which others react to a person this tall may influence his personality and behavior; but the excess of growth hormone, of course, does not have a direct influence. The adolescent girl who is "too tall" or the boy who is "too short" may feel anxious and uncomfortable. They may feel rejected by their peers and defiant of their parents. But such behavior does not stem directly from changes in the body. It is the perception by such adolescents of themselves relative to others, as well as the reactions of other people, that determines such feelings.

Even sexual behavior, including interest in the opposite sex, is not so closely tied to physical maturity as one might think. Hormones secreted by the testes or ovaries appear to influence behavior, but the evidence suggests that these hormones more directly influence the sexual behavior of lower animals than man. Female mammals other than humans show a cyclical behavior that is clearly dependent on ovarian functioning. Such animals are sexually receptive only at specific periods during the so-called estrus cycle. Female humans, on the other hand, do not generally show behavior so clearly related to the menstrual cycle.

As further evidence that human sexual behavior is less closely tied to gonadal functioning, we can compare results of castration in lower animals and man. Removal of the ovaries from a female rat results in an almost immediate ending of normal adult sexual behavior. In the human female after removal of the ovaries or following menopause (the ceasing of ovarian functioning), sexual behavior may decrease, remain the same, or increase. Human sexual behavior is not as closely related to the functioning of the sex glands as is the sexual behavior of lower animals.

Cultural Differences in Adolescence

There is another large body of scientific information which tends to confirm the assertion that adolescent behavior is not directly determined by changes taking place in the body. This is information contained in studies of adolescent behavior in other cultures. From such studies we know that adolescence is not universally a period of storm and stress. Rebellion, demands for independence, feelings of insecurity and anxiety, worries about appearance and so on, are not typical of the behavior of adolescents all over the world. Of course, all adolescents do experience the physical changes in the body described previously, regardless of where they live. But reactions to these changes are frequently quite different from those in our own culture.

In the next chapter we will discuss adolescent behavior again, particularly in terms of the social context in which it occurs. As we shall see, such an approach is really the key to understanding what some people regard as the "problem" of adolescent behavior.

With this brief look at some of the problems of adolescent growth, we turn our attention now to the last of three factors that determines human behavior—socialization.

LEARNING TO BE HUMAN

If we observe the behavior of human infants in different cultures, we see great uniformity. Virtually all children go through the same stages in learning to walk, all are motivated at first only by biological needs, and all are similar in the development of emotions. There are differences of course, but what strikes us most about the behavior of human infants is its uniformity.

If we compare the behavior of five-year-old children to that of infants, we see that differences in behavior are much more apparent among the older children. Furthermore, comparing the behavior of adolescents or adults with five-year-old children reveals even greater differences. In other words, behavior is most similar among very young children and becomes less similar with increasing age.

Learning is the main factor responsible for the great variability in adult human behavior. It is not the race, sex, or physical type to which the individual belongs by heredity that determines behavior. Rather it is the cultural group in which the individual is raised—the traditions, attitudes, and points of view he learns—that most significantly influence his behavior.

The differences we see in the behavior of human beings in different cultures and even within the same culture are due largely to a process we call *socialization*. Socialization involves learning accepted and approved ways of behaving. When a child has been socialized, he has learned to behave in accordance with customary ways of behaving that are typical of the group in which he was raised; he has become "human."

MALE AND FEMALE BEHAVIOR

To understand how behavior is shaped through socialization, we can begin by examining male and female behavior. In our culture the two sexes can be rather clearly differentiated in terms of behavior that is considered appropriate to each. Men, for example, seldom cry; women cry more easily. Women are thought to be more emotional, while men are regarded as less easily upset. Men are expected to take the initiative in courtship, while women play a more passive role. And certain activities are regarded as masculine or feminine in our culture. Knitting and crocheting are almost completely feminine in character, but hunting and fishing are typical recreational pursuits of men. We do, of course, see some men who knit and some women who hunt and fish, but for the most part such activities tend to be identified with either men or women. In addition, many occupations are typically associated with one sex or the other. We find very few young women enrolled in engineering courses in college, for example, and very few young men enrolled in home economics.

With the advent of women's liberation, we are beginning to see some changes in sex roles in our culture. But for the most part, activities typically associated with one or the other sex change very slowly. One reason for this

Fig. 3–7. Beauty is only skin deep, but nevertheless, this man in New Guinea wants to appear attractive. Wearing make-up on the face and necklaces are feminine characteristics in our culture. In many other cultures however, such characteristics are masculine.

is that the process of socialization begins very early in life. We see little girls playing house and feeding, bathing, and dressing dolls, while we see little boys playing with electric trains and Erector sets, and engaging in games of cops and robbers or cowboys and Indians. Such activities are encouraged by the parents.

Recent studies by this psychologist have found that by the time girls enter the first grade they have learned rather clearly what is expected of girls. We asked both boys and girls in the first and third grades what they wanted to be when they grew up. First grade girls, almost without exception, spoke of becoming nurses, teachers, or housewives. Boys, on the other hand, talked of becoming firemen, astronauts, professional football players, and so on.* It was not until the third grade that we began to hear boys expressing more realistic occupational aspirations. What is expected of girls in our culture, then, must be communicated at an earlier age than is the case for boys. Furthermore, the prescribed role for girls seems to be much narrower than that for boys.

The differences in the behavior of boys and girls in our culture appear so early and are so consistent that we may be inclined to think they are dictated by the biological differences between the sexes. Thus the interest in dolls we see in little girls may be attributed to a "maternal instinct," and the "snips and snails and puppy dogs' tails" interests typical of boys may be attributed to biological characteristics of males.

If such differences in behavior and interests were actually due to the biological differences between the sexes, we should see such differences in all cultures. The fact is, we do not.

Margaret Mead's Research

Margaret Mead is a famous anthropologist who spent considerable time studying behavior in New Guinea and Samoa. Her work in New Guinea is of special interest here, since she found three tribes on that island whose behavior differs from that observed in the United States.

In one tribe, the behavior of both sexes would be considered feminine by our standards. Men as well as women tend to be unaggressive, cooperative, and responsive to the needs of others. In this tribe an ideal marriage consists of a "mild, responsive man married to a mild, responsive woman." In courtship, neither men nor women are expected to take the initiative. Both, however, can initiate courtship.

*Some boys of course, *do* become firemen, astronauts or professional football players. The point is that most do *not*, and that these aspirations tend to be less realistic than those expressed by girls at the same age.

In another part of the island she found a tribe whose sex roles would be considered masculine by our standards. Both men and women are ruthless, aggressive individuals in whom tenderness and gentle behavior are an absolute minimum. In this tribe the ideal marriage consists of a violent, aggressive man married to a violent, aggressive woman. Courtship is a violent, passionate affair, with both men and women being equally aggressive.

In a third tribe the social roles for the two sexes are reversed by our standards. That is, men are emotional and home-oriented, and women are dominant, impersonal, and businesslike. In marriage the woman runs the family, and the man plays a passive role. In courtship, women are the aggressors. They initiate action and seek out men they desire. Men, on the other hand, are reluctant and coy.

Thus in the research of Margaret Mead we see three societies in which male and female roles differ from our own. If the behavior of men and women were dictated solely by biological differences, we would expect to see men and women behaving in much the same way all over the world. The fact that we see wide variations in sex roles suggests that such behavior is largely learned through socialization.

We do, of course, see some behavior that may be attributable to the biological differences between the sexes. In all cultures men are more likely to be involved in activities requiring greater physical strength. Women, on the other hand, are more likely to be engaged in activities concerned with the family and home because of biological differences related to bearing children and nursing the young. Except for these differences, however, we cannot account for differences in temperament or many interests in terms of biological factors.

How Does Socialization Occur within the Family?

The family is the most important group where socialization is involved. We do not come in contact with our entire culture. Rather, certain aspects of that culture are transmitted to individuals through groups with

Fig. 3–8. Children all over the world learn to behave as adults by identifying with adults. Here young Japanese children help with the family gardening business.

which the individual is affiliated. The family, of course, is one of these groups.

Infants are born into an already existing group—the family—which has customary ways of behaving, accepted values, attitudes, and so on. These customary ways of behaving and thinking are referred to as *social norms*. Every family has innumerable social norms related to many different aspects of life. Some of these norms are found in other families within the same culture, and some are unique to the particular family involved.

There are many social norms related to eating, for example, so that in a particular family in our culture the evening meal may be served at exactly 5:30 P.M., with all members expected to be on hand. Food is served in a particular order, and everyone is expected to eat the food in that order. In other families, some of these norms may exist, but there may be other norms that are quite different. This fact becomes quite clear when we examine social norms in different socioeconomic groups within our society.

In any particular family there are also social norms related to how one dresses, the language one uses, how one reacts to relatives, what is proper masculine and feminine behavior, and so on. It is also apparent that some of these norms are of much greater importance to the family than others. Thus behavior that deviates from some norms is not considered very serious, while deviation from others is viewed as very serious and consequently is dealt with harshly.

In other words, we see that social norms not only exist within every human group, but also that each group uses punishment of one form or another to insure that all members conform to the various social norms. Punishments, of course, vary depending upon the age of the group member and also the norm involved. Furthermore, it is clear that the child learns to conform not only because of fear of punishment, but because conforming behavior brings the approval and recognition of the parents. Since we have been discussing male and female behavior to illustrate socialization, it should be helpful to examine how that behavior is shaped in a family in our own culture.

Early in life parents make no attempt to insure that children conform to social norms relating to masculine or feminine behavior. Boys play with dolls, and girls frequently climb trees and play baseball. As the boy grows older, however, he is given toys thought to be appropriate for boys, and the girl is given toys appropriate for girls. If the boy persists in playing with dolls beyond a certain age, mild punishments may be applied or the doll taken away. If the behavior continues, he may be ridiculed and called a sissy. If the girl persists in climbing trees beyond a certain age, she may be called a tomboy.

Slowly the behavior of boys is channeled into what is considered by family members to be an appropriate direction. The same is true of girls. Thus the behavior exhibited by the older child and the adult depends to a great extent on the specific family group in which he or she was raised. Age mates and peer groups are also of considerable importance in determining the behavior of the older child and adult.

By grasping the idea that socialization takes place primarily in the intimate face-to-face relationships within the family, and that each family has social norms to which its members conform, we can see how cultural influences shape behavior and why there are individual differences in behavior within cultures.

Socialization, of course, is not the whole story. We are not just passive slaves to the environment, whose behavior is shaped this way or that because of family or other group pressures. Specific characteristics of the individual may determine that certain social norms are adhered to while others are ignored. No person is ever a mirrorlike reflection of all the social influences to which he or she has been exposed. Differences in temperament or intelligence determined by heredity affect one's response to family and other group influences.

CHAPTER SUMMARY

1. Human behavior is largely learned and thus reflects the environment in which we grow up and live. In contrast to other animals, adult human beings vary greatly in their behavior in different parts of the world.

2. Early in life human behavior does not substantially differ from that of other higher animals. However, as the child grows older and learns language, he' begins to surpass other animals in almost every aspect of behavior. No animal brain even remotely approaches the normal human brain in its capacity for language development. Without the biological endowment of man, no amount of exposure to a human environment can produce behavior characteristic of the normal human.

3. We inherit physical characteristics from our parents through genes—the chemical determinants of such characteristics. Genes are located on chromosomes found in each cell of the body. Sex cells contain 23 single chromosomes and other cells contain 46, or a total of 23 pairs.

4. On a single chromosome there may be hundreds of genes, each of which determines one aspect of the physical makeup of the individual. In the opposite member of each pair are genes at exactly the same location that influence the same characteristic.

5. Some genes are called *dominant* because they override the effects of other genes, which are referred to as *recessive*. Thus children do not always resemble their parents in physical characteristics. Both parents may have brown eyes, for example, but carry recessive genes for blue eyes. Some of their children would be expected to have blue eyes because of the presence of recessive genes in the parents.

6. Both heredity and environment contribute to all behavior, and we know that the influence of one is dependent upon the contribution of the other. Hence any single hereditary factor operates differently under varying environmental conditions. Furthermore, environmental conditions differ in their relative influence on any characteristic as a function of the hereditary factor involved.

7. Identical twins help us understand heredity and environment because any differences between them must reflect environment; such twins are exactly alike in terms of heredity. When identical twins are raised in different environments, they tend, on the whole, to be more alike than other brothers or sisters raised together. However, when there are great differences in the environments, identical twins are substantially different in intelligence and other characteristics. This means that even with identical heredity, two people can be very different when exposed to different environments.

8. *Instincts* are inherited patterns of behavior common in many animals. Instincts are either nonexistent or less important in higher animals, including man, because they are unnecessary. In lower animals they have survival value. But human survival depends on one's ability to think, plan, and solve problems—not upon a behavioral pattern influenced by heredity.

9. Some human behavior, especially early in life, is not much influenced by learning. Walking is one type of behavior that seems to depend mainly upon growth or maturation. We know this because children in all cultures go through the same stages in walking, and at about the same age.

10. A number of bodily changes take place during adolescence. The pituitary gland stimulates growth through production of growth hormone. The adrenal and sex glands produce hormones that bring about the development of both primary and secondary sex characteristics. Adolescent behavior tends to be indirectly influenced by these bodily changes; how you compare yourself to others and how others react to you are the primary determinants of behavior.

11. Infants born in different cultures are very similar in behavior. But as the individual grows older, his behavior tends to become more variable. We know that it is the cultural group in which the individual is raised that mainly determines behavior. The differences we see in the behavior of human beings in different cultures are due largely to a process we call *socialization.*

12. Socialization is the process which involves learning accepted and approved ways of behaving. Girls develop "feminine" behavior and boys develop "masculine" behavior largely because of differences in socialization. But socialization is not the whole story. We are not simply mirror-images of family and other group influences. Our heredity and stage of growth determine how we respond to such influences.

Important Terms
from This Chapter

heredity	dominant	hormones
environment	recessive	pituitary
maturation	identical twins	primary sex characteristics
genetics	instincts	secondary sex characteristics
behavioral geneticist	adolescence	socialization
genes	endocrine glands	social norms
chromosomes	gonads	

Additional Readings
to Help You Learn More

Hayes, K. and Hayes, C., "The Intellectual Development of a Home-Raised Chimpanzee." *Bobbs-Merrill Reprints.* Indianapolis: Bobbs-Merrill Company, P–149. Beginning students will find this paper particularly interesting.

Jersild, A. "Studies of Children's Fears." *Bobbs-Merrill Reprints.* Indianapolis: Bobbs-Merrill Company, P–181. An elaboration of the fears that children have and how they develop.

Premack, D. "Language and Chimpanzee?" *Bobbs-Merrill Reprints.* Indianapolis: Bobbs-Merrill Company, P–787.

Hilgard, E., Atkinson, R. and Atkinson, R. *Introduction to Psychology,* 5th Edition. New York: Harcourt, Brace, Jovanovich, 1971. Chapter 4, "Adolescence and Adulthood," is a good discussion of the nature of adolescence, bodily changes during adolescence, and problems faced during the adult years.

Morgan, C. and King, R. *Introduction to Psychology.* New York: McGraw Hill Book Company, 1971. Chapter 2, "Behavioral Inheritance," is an extremely good discussion of the nature-nurture issue, also known as the heredity-environment controversy.

Psychology Today: An Introduction, 2nd Edition. Del Mar, Calif.: CRM Books, 1972.

Chapter 2 in this book deals with instinctive behavior and is particularly relevant to the present chapter.

Stone, L. and Church, J. *Childhood and Adolescence,* 3rd Edition. New York: Random House, 1973. Chapter 1, "The Birth of a Baby," and Chapters 10 and 11 on adolescence are particularly relevant to the present chapter.

People: More than Naked Apes

We have seen that human behavior, from birth to death, is the joint product of social and biological factors. Furthermore, these two factors interact in such a way that the contribution of one is clearly dependent upon the other. It is not just being raised in a human environment that makes us human. Nor is it our biological inheritance that automatically dictates the development of human behavior. Rather, it is both of these things together that make human behavior unique on this planet.

Some writers, in attempting to explain behavior, have stressed man's "animal nature." Despite cultural achievements and impressive technological advances, they say, beneath it all man is little more than a naked ape. Wars take place, according to this point of view, because man is territorial. He fights to secure and hold territory just as many other animals do. He lives in groups that are similar in many respects to the groups in which other primates live. His sexual behavior, as well as other motivated behavior, is similar to that of apes. On and on they go, stressing similarities that are frequently superficial in nature.

As we will learn in this chapter, man is not simply a naked ape whose animal nature dictates fundamental patterns of behavior. His behavior is determined in extremely significant ways by the groups in which he lives. But as we shall see, these groups function in ways that are quite unlike those of any animal.

Animal and Human Societies

Almost all humans live in societies consisting of a population of both sexes and all ages. Such societies are organized to keep the group members alive, to reproduce new members and turn them into useful adults, to produce goods and services, and to maintain order. Individuals within a society tend to share a number of common beliefs, attitudes, and ways of behaving.

The term *society* refers to the organization of the largest groups within which humans live; the term *culture* refers to the content or products of society. Knowledge, beliefs, art, morals, law, and customs or habits are all part of culture. Society and culture are closely related. There is no culture without a society and, at least for man, there is no society without a culture.

Man, of course, is not the only animal to live in societies. A number of "social animals" such as ants, bees, termites, and monkeys also live in organized groups. Some ants, for example, live in societies consisting of thousands of members, each of whom carries on specialized activities. Some are involved only in breeding, others with nursing the young, still others with providing food, and so on. But an important question is, do these specialized activities come about in the same way as the division of labor we see in human societies? The answer is no.

Fig. 4–1. *Members of animal societies such as these baboons can often be differentiated in terms of status or influence. Unlike status in most human groups however, differences in physical strength are primarily responsible for the differences in animal status.*

Scientific studies of insect societies have shown that their organization depends upon chemical "signals" given off by individual insects. Excretion of one chemical causes alarm in others, still another chemical causes exchange of food particles, and so on. Furthermore, we know that the behavioral differences we see are largely determined by the biological structure of individual insects. The queen, for example, is quite unlike the worker ant, and the worker is quite different from the soldier. The behavior of such animals, in other words, is determined by their biological makeup, not by learning.

This does not mean that animals such as ants or bees are incapable of learning. It simply means that learning tends to be relatively unimportant because it is not transmitted from one generation to the next. Each insect must learn for itself.

Human Communication

The crucial factor that makes human societies different from those of animals is language. More basically, it is man's ability to use symbols that sets human societies apart. It is also this symbolic ability that makes it possible for man to produce a culture, while animals do not. A *symbol* is simply one thing that stands for something else. Human language or communication is symbolic in nature. The sounds we make have no meaning in themselves—they stand for something else, and we must learn the meaning of sounds. Unlike the communication of other animals, it is the learned symbolic nature of man's communication that is unique.

In a limited way, animals can learn to respond to symbols. One psychologist trained chimpanzees to obtain food from a machine called a "chimp-o-mat." They had to work for different-colored poker chips which could then be exchanged, like money, for food. Some colors were worth more food than others, and when shown these chips, the chimps often responded by extending their lips and smacking them as they did when they were offered grapes. However, the psychologist discovered that while the poker chips acquired some symbolic value for the chimps, unless they could be turned in almost immediately for food, work would cease.

Humans, it should be remembered, save and collect things with symbolic value regardless of whether they can be exchanged immediately. Furthermore, humans often save things with no exchange value whatsoever. Thus a lock of hair or a program from the school dance frequently become keepsakes.

In these examples of the use of symbols, we see one of the most fundamental differences between human behavior and the behavior of other animals. Because of the unique symbolic character of human language, man can originate concepts or abstractions that are totally beyond the capabilities of lower animals. Before they acquire language, for example, children cannot be motivated by concepts such as honesty, religion, patriotism, and duty. Nor can they be motivated over long periods of time to reach goals that are only of symbolic value. The acquisition of language is basic to both of these aspects of motivation.

Some Other Differences between Animal and Human Behavior

Because of the relative lack of ability to use symbols, lower animals are limited in their behavior largely to the immediate situation. This limitation, as one psychologist has noted, involves both time and space. The chimpanzee lives in the present. He can solve problems using sticks as tools (such as reaching out with a stick to pull food into the cage) but only when the sticks are close to the problem situation. If they are moved to the rear of the cage, they often are no longer seen as potential tools, even though the chimp may have used them before.

Still another limitation in the behavior of animals is a relative inability to work cooperatively. Animals can and do work cooperatively in some situations: Wolves, lions, and wild dogs, among others, hunt together in a pack. One animal may visibly show itself in order to drive the quarry in the direction of another predator hidden in tall grass. But such cooperative behavior is determined by inherited mechanisms or instincts rather than by plans or goals laid out and comprehended by the group.

Human culture, then, consists of beliefs, values, ideas, and ways of behaving that we share with others and that are transmitted through language from one person to another and from one generation to another. Animals do not have cultures mainly because of their very limited ability to use symbols. And while many other animals live in societies in which there is a division of labor, such behavior is not learned but rather is based upon innate biological characteristics of the animals.

HUMANS IN GROUPS

In addition to being a member of a particular society, individuals in complex societies such as our own also usually belong to many other groups and organizations. The high school student, for example, is a member of a

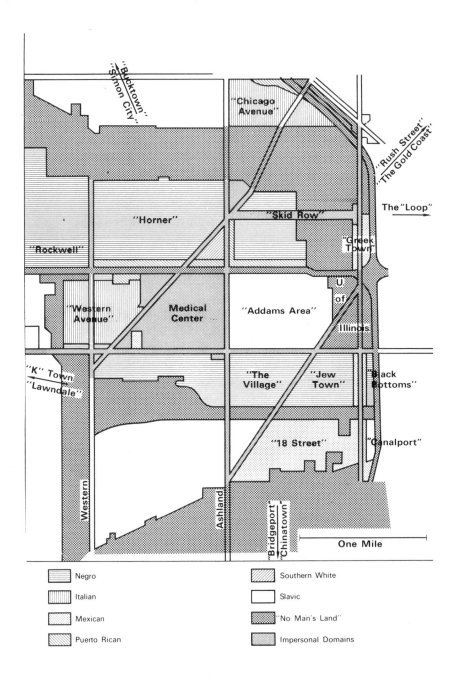

Fig. 4–2. The West Side of Chicago, once the territory of Al Capone, is now divided into a number of smaller territories or "turf" occupied by rival street gangs. This does not mean that a territorial motive is the basis for human aggression, however. Not all are territorial, and some human cultures are even known to reject ownership and possession of goods.

family, may belong to a special interest club, an athletic team, and other groups. The businessman not only has his family but may belong to social organizations such as a lodge or country club, the Chamber of Commerce, a church group, and so on. In addition, most people also associate with a number of small, informal groups of close friends.

How is behavior affected by membership in such groups and organizations? Long ago psychologists discovered that we do not behave the same way when we are alone as when we are with others. One of the earliest experiments on how we are affected by others attempted to find out if people work better alone or in a group. Some subjects were given arithmetic problems and other tasks which they were to do in the presence of others working on the same tasks. Other subjects were given the same problems but asked to work on them alone. It was found that while people do more work in a group, the quality of that work is not equal to work prepared alone.

Other experiments have been done to determine if it is easier to learn alone or in a group. In general, these experiments have shown that learning by oneself is superior to learning in a group situation. One psychologist has said that learning is inhibited in group situations, but performance, or displaying what we know, is enhanced. He suggests that ideally students should study alone in isolated cubicles and then take examinations on stage in the presence of an audience. The score on the exam, he says, would be beyond the student's wildest dreams, provided he had thoroughly learned the material.

What Factors in Group Structure Affect Our Behavior?

We know today that it is not simply the physical presence of other people that affects our behavior. Our relationships to the others present are even more important. Are the other people strangers to us? Are they friends or rivals? Do we feel comfortable around them? What kinds of attitudes do the other people have toward the situation—negative or positive? These are all key factors that affect our behavior in group situations.

One psychologist has summarized the factors or variables that affect our behavior in group situations. Some of these pertain to the individuals involved, others pertain to the task or problem faced, and still others pertain to the setting or situation. For example, how we behave in group situations is affected by characteristics of those present. How old are they? Are they all of one sex or both sexes? How much education have they had? Are they of the same race or different races? What about religious differences? Are they friends of ours or enemies? Are they strangers?

The task or problem at hand also affects the behavior of people in groups. Is the task new or familiar? Is it easy or difficult? Have those present handled problems like this before? Furthermore, the setting or situation in which the group finds itself affects behavior. We do not behave the same way in church as on a date. Certain behavior, in other words, is appropriate in some settings and inappropriate in others.

All of these factors together determine our behavior in group situations. Thus it is not simply the number of people present, or whether they are friends, or the setting in which they find themselves that influences behavior. It is all these things that combine to determine how people behave in groups.

What Are Groups?

This may seem to be a simple question to answer. A group, you may think, is simply a number of people gathered together in one place. But for the psychologist, this is an inadequate answer that does not help us understand how our behavior is affected in groups.

Social situations range from those that consist of perfect strangers all the way to those consisting of members of tightly knit groups, with varying degrees of established relations between the two extremes. For the purpose

Fig. 4–3. Groups differ in a number of characteristics. Some are small but still "formal" in the sense that leaders are officially designated and rules are written. (A high school football team would be an example of such a group). Others are informal friendship groups such as the English girls shown attending a "pep rally." Some are quite small such as the three men shown below who play golf together on weekends. Although there are no written rules in these smaller, informal groups, members typically share some common ways of behaving (social norms). Furthermore, they can be differentiated in terms of status and roles within the group.

of understanding how behavior is affected by others, it is very important to distinguish between temporary social situations on the one hand and tightly knit groups on the other.

Temporary social situations are those in which the participants do not have positive or negative ties to one another. A crowd attending a football game would be an example, as would be a number of people waiting for a train or plane. Students attending a class constitute another example of a temporary social situation, even though the class may last several months.

Regardless of whether a social situation is temporary or of a group nature, it produces differences in the behavior of individual participants. As we have seen, even the mere presence of others engaged in the same activity affects behavior. But the effects of temporary social situations on our behavior tend to be determined mainly by the task or problem at hand, or the situation itself. The effects of group situations, on the other hand, are determined mainly by mutual ties, expectations, mutual loyalties, and commitments among the participating members.

Definition of a Group

When we observe a group of any kind in real life and follow its activities for a time, we can see consistent relationships among the group members. Members can be differentiated in terms of status or social position relative to others in the group. The leader occupies the highest status in the group, and being a leader involves behaving in particular ways toward other members of the group and toward those outside the group. This is his role in the group.

Another thing that we observe in all groups is the tendency for group members to develop standards of behavior or customs that we referred to in the last chapter as social norms. Norms consist of beliefs or values that affect the conduct of individuals in group situations. Thus when we say one "conforms," we are referring to the tendency to behave in line with the social norms in the group to which the individual belongs.

Groups, then, may be defined as social units with two or more members that can be differentiated in terms of status and the roles they play within the group. Furthermore, groups always possess a set of norms or standards that affect the behavior of individual members.

Groups are formed when individuals with some common problem or motive come together to solve such a problem or satisfy a motive. In the process of acting together, individuals become differentiated in terms of their status and role in the group. And when individuals interact with one another, they tend to develop common or shared ways of behavior. These are social norms. Such groups, of course, do not spring into existence ready-made, nor are they unchangeable.

Are There Different Kinds of Groups?

There are obviously many different kinds of groups that fit the definition above. Some are large, such as the Unites States Army; while others, such as a students' ski club, may be quite small. Some are formal, in that they have elected officers and written rules; while others are simply loose collections of individuals who get together once in a while for social purposes.

Psychologists usually distinguish between informal and formal groups. *Formal groups* are those that have written rules and regulations that govern members' behavior. Also, in such groups there are officials or officers who are elected or appointed. In *informal groups,* on the other hand, there is no written code of conduct, and there are no elected or appointed officers. Nevertheless, whether the group is formal or informal, all groups have members who can be differentiated in terms of status and roles, and all have social norms that affect the behavior of members. In addition, all group members have some motivation in common and tend to behave differently in group situations than when alone.

REFERENCE GROUPS

In large complex societies such as our own, individuals seldom belong to just one group. Simultaneously a person may be a family member, a leader in a friendship group, a student at a school, a member of an ethnic or racial group, a church member, and so on. Each of these different groups may have different social norms and the individual may have different statuses and roles in each. When a person relates himself psychologically to a group, that group becomes his reference group; the social norms that exist in that group influence or determine his behavior.

We can see that groups of which we are a member do not necessarily serve as reference groups. On the other hand, we do not have to be a member of a particular group for that group to serve as a reference group. For example, an adolescent may be a member of a particular family, but the social norms of that family do not necessarily determine his behavior; for example, he may instead identify with the varsity squad he hopes to join. The social norms of the varsity squad are the standards by which he behaves.

The concept of reference group is a particularly useful one in understanding many of the problems of adolescence in our society. Frequently adolescents find themselves members of two or more groups with conflicting social norms. In the family, for example, there are frequently parental standards concerning how late one may stay out, what nights of the week one can date, and so on. Often these norms conflict with those of one's teen-age friendship group. In such cases, the friendship group often serves as one's reference group. The teen-ager often rejects or defies the parental standards when they conflict with the standards of his or her friends.

Adolescent Groups

The adolescent in our society is caught between childhood and adulthood. Physically mature but still dependent on the parents, the adolescent is neither boy nor man, girl nor woman. Parents often react to adolescents in very inconsistent ways. On some occasions the youth may be told, "You're not old enough to do that"; at other times, he or she is told, "Grow up and

Fig. 4–4. Social norms regarding dress and hair length have changed drastically in adolescent groups over the past 10 years. Long hair is now the norm for male adolescents and the boys shown here are considered nonconformists. Who knows what the future style will be?

TEENAGER'S COMPLAINTS ABOUT THEIR PARENTS

How many of these do you agree with?

Problem	Percentage of Students Who Acknowledge Problem *		
	Boys	Girls	Total
Afraid to tell parents what I've done wrong	18%	19%	19%
Parents too strict about my going out at night	16	19	18
Parents too strict about family car	24	9	16
Family always worried about money	15	15	15
Parents too strict about dating	8	17	13
Parents interfere in my choice of friends	10	15	13
Parents nag about studying	16	10	13
Parents hate to admit I'm sometimes right	13	13	13
Parents too strict about dates on school nights	10	13	12
Wish parents would treat me like a grown-up	10	14	12
Parents interfere with spending money I earn	15	7	11
Parents play favorites	8	12	10

* The percentages are not additive, because one student may make several complaints.

act your age." Typical complaints about parents include being "too strict about my going out at night," "too strict about the family car," "always worried about money," "too strict about dating," "interference in my choice of friends," and so on. It is no wonder, then, that adolescents seek out others with the same problems.

We have seen that humans form groups when there is some common motivation that can be satisfied only in concert with others. Adolescents, feeling that no one understands them, seek out others with the same feelings.

"THE GROWN-UP PROBLEM"
ART BUCHWALD

There has been so much discussion about teen-age problems that the grown-up problem is practically being ignored. And yet if you pick up a newspaper, you realize grown-ups are responsible for some of the most serious problems this country has ever faced.

For example, 60 percent of all crime in the United States is committed by grown-ups.
The birth rate among grown-up women is four times that of teen-agers.
The divorce rate is double.
The purchasing power of grown-ups almost exceeds that of teen-agers.
Grown-ups are responsible for more daytime accidents than any other age group.

The source of these statistics is sociology Prof. Heinrich Applebaum, B.A., M.S., L.L.D., Y.E.H., Y.E.H., Y.E.H., who told me in an exclusive interview that his studies showed grown-ups were drifting farther away from society all the time. "The average grown-up," Prof. Applebaum said, "feels his children don't understand him. The more time he spends with them, the less they communicate with him. So the adult feels isolated, insecure, and misunderstood. In defense he seeks out other grown-ups who feel the same way he does. Pretty soon they form gangs, go to the theater together, hold cocktail parties and dances, and before you know it you have a complete breakdown of the family."

"Why do you think grown-ups are constantly rebelling against their children, Professor?"

"I guess it's an age-old old-age problem. You have parents wanting to break away and yet not having the nerve to cut the ties completely. Grown-ups are afraid to stand up to their children, so they rebel against society instead."

"Do you think teen-agers could in some way be responsible for the behavior of their parents?"

"I definitely do," the Professor said. "Grown-ups try to emulate teen-agers. They want to do exactly what teen-agers do, which is to drink, smoke, and drive fast cars. If teen-agers didn't do these things, their parents wouldn't. For every bad adult in America, I'm sure you'll find a bad teen-ager somewhere in the background."

"Where do you think the trouble starts?"

"In the home. Teen-agers are too rough on their parents. They're always criticizing them for listening to Frank Sinatra records and reading **Holiday** magazine. Teen-agers don't have any patience with their mothers and fathers. They can't understand why their parents like Doris Day and Rock Hudson movies or what they see in Cary Grant. If teen-agers spent more time at home with grown-ups and tried to understand them, I don't think you'd have half the trouble that you have in the United States today."

"Do you mean teenagers should spend more time at home with their parents?"

"Of course. Grown-ups need security. They want to know where their children are. They want the feeling they belong. Only teen-agers can give grown-ups this feeling."

"Professor, have you found any homes where grown-ups are leading healthy, normal, secure lives, thanks to the attention they've received from their loving teen-age children?"

"We haven't yet. But we've been looking only a year. These surveys take time."

Together with others experiencing the same problems, the adolescent is more comfortable and secure. He or she is somebody, at least in the eyes of close friends.

The most important groups in terms of understanding teen-age behavior are the informal friendship groups or cliques. As in any other group, common ways of behaving come into existence as the individuals continue

---

COMMON PROBLEMS OF TEENAGERS

YOUTH'S BILL OF RIGHTS

1. Stand by us, not over us. Give us the feeling that we are not alone in the world, that we can always count on you when we are in trouble.
2. Make us feel that we are loved and wanted. We want to love you, not as a duty but because you love us.
3. Train us by being affectionately firm. You really will achieve more with us through patient teaching than punishment or preaching. Say "No" when you feel you have to, but explain your rules, don't merely impose them.
4. Bring us up so that we will not always need you. Teach us how to take on responsibility and become independent of YOU. We will learn this faster and better if you will let us question you, your ideas and standards.
5. Don't act shocked when we do things we shouldn't. It is going to take us time to learn how to grow into life properly.
6. Try to be as consistent as possible. If you are mixed up about what you want from us, why shouldn't we be mixed up, too, in what we give you?
7. Don't try to make us feel inferior. We doubt ourselves enough without your confirming it. Predicting failure for us won't help us succeed.
8. Say "Nice Work" when we do something really well. Don't hold back the praise when we deserve it. That's the way to spur us on.
9. Show respect for our wishes even if you disagree with them. Respect for you will flow naturally from your respect for us.
10. Give direct answers to direct questions. But don't give us more than we ask or can understand. When YOU don't know, say so, but find someone for us who does know.
11. Show interest in what we're doing. Even though by your standards our activities may not be important or interesting, don't reduce them in our eyes by your indifference.
12. Treat us as if we are normal, even when our conduct seems peculiar to you. All of God's children have problems. That doesn't mean we're all problem children.
13. Sometimes all of us run into serious emotional difficulties. Should that happen, obtain for us professional counseling. It isn't always easy for boys and girls to

---

understand themselves or know just what they want. That's why there are specialists in personal adjustments and vocational selection.

14. Teach us by example. "What you are speaks louder than your words."
15. Treat each one of us as a person in his own right. Children are people, not carbon copies of grownups. Treat all children in your care fairly; that is, as of equal value to you. That is how we will learn to respect the rights of other people and to treat them fairly.
16. Don't keep us young too long. We want a chance to prove what we can do as soon as we are ready to give proof. Don't hold us back by love which over-protects and paralyzes.
17. We need fun and companionship. Help us share our interests and happy feelings with groups of friends. Give us time to be with them and make them welcome when they come to visit.
18. Make us feel that our home belongs to us. We are AT LEAST as important as the furniture. Don't protect "things" at our expense by making us feel like intruding bulls in a china shop.
19. Don't laugh at us when we use the word "love." The need to love and be loved starts early (and never ends). Getting romantic is merely setting to soft music the eternal desire to belong to someone and have someone belong to us.
20. Treat us as junior partners in the firm. Democracy starts at home. If you want us to be worthy successors to you, take us into your confidence, and let us help you in managing *our* school, and *our* community.
21. Make yourself an adult fit for a child to live with. Prove to us "it ain't so" that parents are the worst persons in the world to have children, or that teachers are precisely the people least suited to teach. Show that home and school are not simply places where children learn how to get along with disagreeable adults.
22. Prepare us to lead *our* lives, *not* yours. Find out what *we* can do or *we* want to be before you force us beyond our capacity or make us become what *you* want us to become.
23. Give us the right to a major voice in our own lives. Decisions that will affect our whole future should be made *with* us, not *for* us. We have a right to our kind of future.
24. Let us make our own mistakes. To make wise decisions takes experience. That means we have to try ourselves out and find out for ourselves. We can only learn from our own actions—not yours.
25. Permit us the failings of average children, just as we permit you the failings of average parents. Let us both break the rules sometimes. We can grow only at our own rate, which means in easy stages. We want to become the best we can become, but we would not be human if we were perfect. (White House Conference on Children and Youth).

to interact. Perhaps most striking in adolescent groups is the conformity we see in matters of dress and grooming. In 1965, long hair and sideburns became popular among adolescent males. Blue jeans, open shirts, and sandals became almost literally the uniform of the teen-ager. To the older generation these fashions appeared sloppy, and in many schools there was an attempt to set rules for hair length. Perhaps largely because of the opposition by adults, these fashions became almost universal.

Such fashions constitute social norms, and to remain a member in good standing of a particular group one must conform to the norms of that group. If we want to be accepted by those important to us, we must behave according to the social norms they accept. This means not only dressing "properly," but also using the language or slang customarily used by group members. In some adolescent groups it may also mean using drugs or committing crimes.

Drugs and Adolescent Groups

Such words as "acid," "speed," "smack," "joint," and others are now commonplace in American slang. In the 1960s, with the rise of the hippie movement, the use of drugs became increasingly prevalent among many American teen-agers. At first drug use occurred mainly in the slums or ghettos of large cities. But with alarming rapidity drugs began to find their way into the suburbs and into the schools and homes of middle-class and well-to-do adolescents. Adults reacted with alarm, and the government instituted crash programs to wipe out the problem. But the more intense these attacks and programs became, the more the problem seemed to spread.

How can we account for the spread of drugs in our society? Has the moral fiber of adolescents changed? Does it reflect a breakdown in American family life? Are drug users emotionally disturbed? Undoubtedly there are many factors responsible, and it would be an oversimplification to say that drug use is due simply to this or that. We can say, however, that certain characteristics of adolescents and adolescent groups in our society tend to make drug use more likely at that age.

We have already seen that many adolescents feel insecure and anxious. Gravitating together and forming cliques is a natural result of such feelings. In the group, the individual feels accepted and comfortable. And if he is to remain a member of the group, he quickly learns to conform to norms or standards of behavior important to group members. Some adolescents feel a need to show others that they are hip, with it, or cool. To some this means driving recklessly, or doing other inherently dangerous things. In the past, drinking by adolescents demonstrated that they were grown-up or cool.

COMMON PROBLEMS OF TEENAGERS

Problem	All Boys	All Girls	All 9th Graders	All 12th Graders
Want people to like me more	47%	60%	55%	52%
Want to make new friends	45	56	52	46
Get stage fright before a group	46	59	54	47
Want to gain (or lose) weight	49	56	54	51
Wish I were more popular	36	47	50	32
Seldom have dates	48	39	50	32
Have a "crush" on a friend of the same sex	34	47	48	29
Do things I later regret	38	43	42	36
Can't help day dreaming	29	41	35	34
Worry about little things	26	44	32	40
Feel I'm not as smart as others	30	37	36	28
Want to improve my posture and body build	42	33	40	32
Concerned about improving my figure	7	41	26	21
Want to get rid of pimples	33	33	31	33
Don't have a girl friend (or a boy friend)	41	30	38	30
Need to develop self-confidence	31	40	33	41
Ill-at-ease at social affairs	26	25	26	23
Easily excited	14	32	23	23
Trouble keeping my temper	27	38	34	32
Often feel lonesome	16	24	19	20
Easily hurt	19	39	28	30
Hesitate to assume responsibility	21	15	16	19
Want to discuss my personal problems	19	29	24	27
Should I go steady?	19	25	20	22
Unsure of myself	20	26	21	26
How far should high school students go (on a date)?	24	26	24	24
Bite my nails	26	24	28	23

Smoking also, since it was forbidden by adults, was a way of showing others that one was "with it." Today, although secret drinking and smoking still occur among many teen-agers, such behavior is more generally accepted than it was. Schools may still forbid smoking by students, and parents may disapprove of drinking, but such behavior is more widespread and is not regarded so seriously as in the past. In other words, much of the kick has been removed from such activities.

Drugs, however, are another story. Every teen-ager has heard of the dangers of drug use. An overdose can kill you, and you can be arrested and thrown in prison for even possessing drugs. For some adolescents, because of these very real dangers rather than in spite of them, drug use has become attractive. Using drugs has become a way of showing one is not afraid of anything. Drug use in some teen-age groups has become a social norm. To join such a group or to remain a member, one must use drugs.

What about Soft Drugs?

Some argue that so-called soft or nonaddictive drugs should be legalized. Others argue that there is nothing wrong with using marijuana, since one cannot be addicted. These arguments, however, fail to take into account the facts discussed above.

In some adolescent groups, smoking marijuana is a way group members have of showing one another how hip or cool they are. Suppose one of the group members gets hold of heroin or cocaine? On a dare, perhaps, or to show one is not chicken, other group members are induced to try it—to experiment. Since these drugs are even more dangerous in terms of their effects and the consequences if caught, some teen-agers mistakenly feel that trying them really does demonstrate nerve. In fact, it takes more nerve for a teen-ager to defy friends and group pressures by leaving the stuff alone.

One of the problems with marijuana and other nonaddictive drugs is that within the social context of some adolescent groups they are likely to lead to the use of more serious drugs. Legalization of soft drugs may seem like a simple solution, but we suspect that for some teen-agers, it would increase still more the attractiveness of hard drugs.

Crime and Delinquency in Adolescent Groups

In the discussion above we have pointed out that teen-age drug users are not necessarily emotionally disturbed or sick. Nor are they ignorant of the dangers of drugs. Consequently, attempts to deal with the problem through psychiatric treatment or through information programs do not always succeed. In the same way we can say that teen-agers who shoplift or who commit other crimes are not necessarily emotionally disturbed.

Just as using drugs in some teen-age groups becomes a way of showing others that one is hip, ripping off businesses by shoplifting or other criminal acts are sometimes ways of conforming to social norms. When those in an adolescent group seek to demonstrate to each other that they have nerve or guts, petty thievery or vandalism may be the result. When such a social norm develops, one cannot join such a group or continue to be a member without conforming.

To understand how normal teen-agers from "good" backgrounds sometimes wind up in jail or as drug addicts, we need to take a closer look at conformity and nonconformity.

CONFORMITY AND NONCONFORMITY

When we call someone a nonconformist, we usually mean that he or she is behaving in different ways from most people. Nonconformity, in other words, implies deviating in some way from the accepted standards of society. But in fact there are very few nonconformists in the sense of totally doing one's own thing. Most people conform to the social norms of one group or another, even though they may not appear to do so. The hippie or the commune member may be a nonconformist in terms of American society as a whole, but he or she is usually very much of a conformist within his or her own group. The terms "conformity" and "nonconformity," then, imply vari-

Fig. 4–5.   The subject in this experiment is #6 from the left. He doesn't know that the others present have been told in advance how to behave.

ation in behavior relative to some standard or social norm. In other words, there has to be a standard or social norm to conform to or deviate from.

Psychologists have spent a great deal of time studying the nature of pressures for conformity in various social situations. We know today that even in temporary social situations in which we have no ties to the others present, there are strong pressures to conform. A psychologist named Asch demonstrated this very nicely in a series of experiments. The task in these experiments was to judge which of three lines presented on a separate card seemed equal in length to a standard line on another card.

A subject was selected and asked to report at a certain time to the room in which the experiment was to be conducted. When he arrived he found several other strangers waiting to participate in the same experiment. Unknown to the subject, however, the other individuals had agreed in advance to cooperate with the experimenter. When the experimenter arrived, all present entered the room and were asked to take seats. The experimenter had instructed his confederates to be sure that the subject took a seat next to the end of the table. The instructions were given and those present were asked to make their judgments one at a time. The actual subject in each case was the next to the last person to judge.

All present were in agreement on the first two trials and selected the correct line. On the third trial, however, and on 12 out of the 18 trials in the experiment, the confederates had been instructed to select an *incorrect* line. The purpose was to see if the subject involved would also select the incorrect line or if he would judge correctly. The subject, of course, was in the position, on 12 of the trials, of being the only person who disagreed in a group of seven to nine people.

The experimenter found that 37 per cent of the incorrect judgments of the group were accepted by the subjects. Furthermore, a large majority of the remainder who responded correctly apparently were made extremely uncomfortable by the situation, even though they did not go along with the group. When these subjects were later placed in the situation alone, however, their judgments were correct with less than one per cent error.

In this experiment we can see that even in social situations where the others present mean nothing to us and when the task involved is relatively unimportant, there are strong pressures to conform. We don't want to be different, and if we *do* differ from the group, it makes us feel very uncomfortable. Think of how much greater the pressures are to conform when we are with people that mean a great deal to us. We want to be accepted by them, and we run the risk of being rejected or ridiculed if our behavior departs from that acceptable to the group.

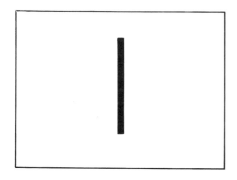
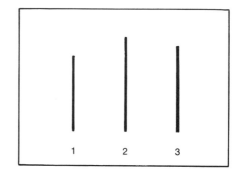

Standard line   Comparison lines

Fig. 4-6.   Cards used in Asch's experiment.
The subject is asked to pick from the three lines on the right, the one most equal in length to the line of the left.

Adolescents sometimes find themselves in a position similar to that of the subject in the previous experiment. Such instances bring the individual face to face with a choice between being different and risking rejection by one's friends, on the one hand, or following paths he believes right, on the other. If faced with a choice of using drugs or losing friends, some teen-agers choose to use drugs. If faced with a choice of shoplifting or risking ridicule by the people most important to him, other teen-agers shoplift. It is as simple as that. Such individuals do not have to be mentally disturbed or ignorant of the risks, although in some cases they may be.

WHAT DOES THIS MEAN TO YOU?

First of all, by understanding your own needs and problems and those of other adolescents, you are in a position to understand why acceptance by others is so important. And with some knowledge of how groups function, you can be aware of how group pressures can sometimes force adolescents to participate in activities which, under other circumstances, would not be in accordance with their own personal value systems. The vast majority of teen-agers, of course, never find themselves in such positions. Drug use, stealing, and other antisocial behavior is still characteristic of only a minority of adolescents. Still it is important to recognize the hard fact that one may face some extremely difficult choices—choices between friends and doing what one believes is right.

Chapter Summary

1. Most humans live in societies consisting of a population of both sexes and all ages. The term *society* refers to the organization of the largest groups within which humans live. The term *culture* refers to the content or products of such organizations. Knowledge, beliefs, art, morals, law, and customs or habits are all a part of culture. Society and culture are closely related. There is no culture without a society and, at least for man, there is no society without a culture.

2. Man is not the only animal to live in societies. A number of social animals, such as ants, bees, termites, and monkeys, also live in organized groups. In such societies, however, the specialized activities of individual members are determined by their biological makeup rather than learning. The crucial factor that makes human societies different is man's ability to use symbols.

3. Human communication is symbolic in nature. The sounds we make have no meaning in themselves; they stand for something else, and we must learn the meaning of sounds. It is the learned symbolic nature of human language that is unique. Because of this symbolic nature of his language, man can originate concepts or abstractions that are totally beyond the capability of lower animals.

4. Because of the relative lack of ability to use symbols, other animals are limited in their behavior to the immediate situation. Still another limitation in the behavior of animals is a relative inability to work cooperatively. When we do see cooperative behavior, it is determined by inherited mechanisms or instincts rather than by plans or goals laid out and comprehended by the group.

5. Most humans belong to many groups other than just the societies in which they live. Such groups affect behavior in different ways.

6. How we behave in group situations is determined by the characteristics of those present, the task or problem faced, and the setting or situation in which we find ourselves.

7. Human social situations range from those consisting of gatherings of strangers to tightly knit groups. Temporary social situations are those in which participants do not have positive or negative ties to one another. In groups, however, members can be differentiated in terms of social position within the group and the roles they play. In addition, group members always tend to develop standards of behavior or customs referred to as *social norms.*

8. Reference groups are those to which a person relates himself psychologically. Groups of which we are a member do not necessarily serve as reference groups, however, nor do we have to be a member of a particular group for that group to serve as a reference group. The concept of reference group is particularly useful in understanding adolescent behavior.

9. Adolescents often feel that no one understands them. Caught between childhood and adulthood, they are frequently treated in very inconsistent ways by parents and other adults. Informal friendship groups or cliques form at this time because membership in such groups seems to satisfy needs and motives that cannot be satisfied elsewhere. Such groups, then, serve as reference groups, and the behavior of adolescents is determined by the social norms that develop in these groups.

10. In some teen-age groups the use of drugs or the committing of illegal acts such as shoplifting have become social norms. To join such groups or to remain a member, one must engage in these activities. Thus it is very possible for "normal" teen-agers from "good" homes to wind up in jail or addicted to drugs. Such individuals are often brought face-to-face with a choice between not wanting to be different on the one hand, or following paths he believes right, on the other.

Important Terms
from This Chapter

society	differentiate	informal group
culture	status	reference group
symbol	role	clique
group	social norm	conformity
temporary social situation	formal group	nonconformity

Additional Readings
to Help You Learn More

Asch, Solomon E. "Opinions and Social Pressure," *Scientific American Offprints,* No. 450. San Francisco: W. H. Freeman and Company. Discusses in detail Dr. Asch's famous experiments on the effects of others on our behavior.

Doby, J., Boskoff, A. and Pendleton, W. *Sociology: The Study of Man in Adaptation.* Lexington, Mass.: D. C. Heath Company, 1973. Chapter 4, "Basic Organization and Functioning of Human Societies," discusses the fundamental problems of human societies and how societies are organized.

Hilgard, E., Atkinson, R. and Atkinson, R. *Introduction to Psychology,* 5th Edition. New York: Harcourt, Brace, Jovanovich, 1971. Chapter 22, "Social Psychology," discusses such things as attraction between persons, group membership and individual behavior and how attitudes and opinions are changed.

Johnson, R. *Aggression in Man and Animals.* Philadelphia: W. B. Saunders Company, 1972. In Chapter 2, "Biological Factors — 1. Territory, Social Dominance, and Ecology," Dr. Johnson discusses the similarities and differences between aggressive behavior in human beings and other animals.

Lorenz, Conrad Z. "The Evolution of Behavior," *Scientific American Offprints,* No. 412. San Francisco: W. H. Freeman and Company. Deals with some of this famous Nobel prize winner's ideas about the development of animal and human behavior.

Mussen, P. and Rosenzweig, M. *Psychology: An Introduction.* Lexington, Mass.: D. C. Heath Company, 1973. Chapter 3, "Conformity," discusses the nature of conformity, who conforms, and why.

Psychology Today: An Introduction, 2nd Edition. Del Mar, Calif.: CRM Books, 1972. Chapter 34, "Drugs and Drug Therapy," presents an expanded discussion of the problem of drugs and drug addiction.

Ruch, F. And Zimbardo, P. *Psychology and Life,* 8th Edition. Glenview, Ill.: Scott, Foresman and Company, 1971. Appendix D, "Drug Use and Abuse," is an excellent discussion of the nature of addicting and nonaddicting drugs and their effects on personality.

Wertheimer, M. *Confrontation: Psychology and the Problems of Today.* Glenview, Ill.: Scott, Foresman and Company, 1970. Section 2, "Conformity, Compliance and Integrity," discusses some of the most interesting research that has recently been carried out on the effects of social pressures on our behavior.

Part III.

LEARNING:
A PAINLESS PRESCRIPTION
(Almost)

chapter **5**

What
We
Know
about
Learning

No topic in psychology is more important than learning. It is true that some behavior early in life is determined mainly as a result of maturation or growth. But we have also seen that as the individual grows older, virtually all of his or her behavior is learned. Socialization, as we noted, is essentially the process of learning to be human. Furthermore, we know today that emotions are largely learned and also that many human motives are learned. In addition, attitudes and skills must be learned. Finally, it is apparent that all human knowledge is learned and passed from one generation to the next through a unique system of learned communication.

Learning may be defined as the process through which behavior originates or is changed through training or experience. Thus changes in behavior due simply to growth or maturation are ruled out by this definition. Also, changes in behavior that result from fatigue, disease, or the effects of drugs are excluded. The definition also excludes unlearned or innate responses such as reflexes or instincts.

The study of learning is not only important in understanding human behavior in general; it will be of great help to you in becoming a better student. For these reasons, in this chapter and the next, we will discuss the exact nature of learning and the conditions under which it occurs. Is motivation necessary for learning? Do we learn better through rewards or punishments? How can we learn more efficiently? These are questions that are as important to you as to the professional psychologist.

Do We Learn through Association?

Suppose we begin by performing a simple experiment. I will say a word and you say the first word that comes into your mind. Ready? Table . . .; Up . . .; Black . . .; Hot. . . .

Let me try to guess what your responses were. To the word "table," you responded "chair"; to "up," you responded "down"; to "black," "white"; to "hot," "cold." Perhaps not all of your responses were exactly these, but chances are they were pretty close. Why is it that most people think of "chair" when someone says "table," or "white" when someone says "black"? Philosophers long ago felt that such associations are learned because of contiguity, similarity, or contrast.

Contiguity simply means that when two ideas, objects, or events occur together in time or space, they tend to become associated. *Contrast,* on the other hand, refers to the notion that opposites tend to be associated, while *similarity* means that similar things tend to be associated.

Philosophers also believed that associations tend to be strengthened through repetition. The greater the number of repetitions, the stronger the association. We know today that while association is an important part of learning, it is not simply association alone that is responsible for learning. Nor does repetition alone strengthen associations. Something else is involved, and that something else is reward or reinforcement.

Cats in a Puzzle Box

To study how animals learn, a psychologist named E. L. Thorndike many years ago built a puzzle box for cats. In order for the cat to escape from the box, it had to do three things. First, one of the bolts holding the door in

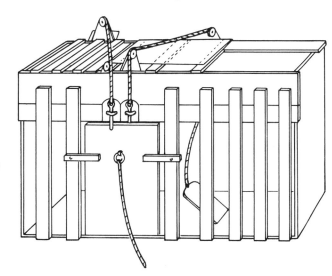

Fig. 5–1. The puzzle box used by Thorndike to study learning. Cats placed inside must learn to step on the pedal, pull a rope, and turn a bar before they can escape.

place had to be removed by pressing on the pedal inside the cage. Second, the other bolt on the door had to be removed by pulling on a suspended rope in the cage. Finally, one of the two bars outside the door had to be turned vertically. When all three things were done, the door opened.

How do cats learn to escape from such a complicated box? Thorndike thought they learned through trial and error. When he placed a hungry cat inside the box for the first time, it tried to squeeze between the bars. Then it clawed and bit at the bars. It kept doing these things until by accident it clawed at the rope inside or stepped on the pedal. Again trying to squeeze between the bars, it turned one of the small bars holding the door, and the door opened. When it escaped, it ate from a dish placed close to the cage.

When again placed back in the cage, the cat did much the same thing. After repeated sessions, however, Thorndike noted that the cat's behavior had changed. Frequently, immediately after being placed in the box it stepped on the pedal and pulled at the rope. Escape took much less time. After many trials, the cat escaped almost immediately. It spent no time on wasted effort. It had learned to do only those things that led to escape.

How did the animal learn? Thorndike thought that through trial and error, associations or bonds were established between the sight of the rope or pedal and pulling the rope or pressing on the pedal. These associations, he thought, were established not simply because of repetitions but because of rewards and punishments. When the cat pulled the rope or pressed the pedal, in other words, it was rewarded by escaping from the box and eating. When it tried to squeeze between the bars or when it clawed the bars, no reward was forthcoming.

In this simple experiment we can see several important ideas about the nature of learning. First, Thorndike thought that learning is gradual and

Fig. 5–2. *Before conditioning begins, the unconditioned stimulus elicits or brings about the unconditioned response. This is unlearned. By presenting conditioned and unconditioned stimuli together, the conditioned stimulus eventually brings about the conditioned response—the response formerly made only to the unconditioned stimulus. This is learned.*

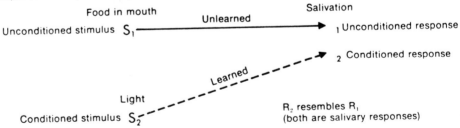

Food in mouth   Salivation

         Unlearned

Unconditioned stimulus S_1 ⟶ ₁ Unconditioned response

₂ Conditioned response

Learned

Light

Conditioned stimulus S_2 R_2 resembles R_1
(both are salivary responses)

that it comes about through trial and error. Those responses or actions that lead to reward are gradually learned, in other words, while those that are not rewarded or punished, are not learned. We can also see that motivation must have something to do with learning. It is only those actions that are followed by rewards that are learned, while punishments have the opposite effect. Finally, we can see that Thorndike had an idea about the nature of learning itself. He thought it involved associations or bonds between stimuli and responses. *Stimuli* are simply things in the environment that activate the senses, while *responses* are actions or movements. In this experiment, the sight of the bar or pedal was the stimulus, while pulling the rope or pressing the bar was the response.

SIMPLE LEARNING AND CLASSICAL CONDITIONING

Thorndike's work was a great step forward in helping us to understand learning. But it left a great many questions unanswered, and we also know that he was not quite correct in some of his conclusions. The work of a Russian, Ivan P. Pavlov, helped to provide additional knowledge about learning, and the work of others has corrected some of Thorndike's erroneous conclusions.

Pavlov was studying digestion in animals when he observed something that puzzled him. Dogs salivated or drooled when food was placed directly in their mouths, but they also salivated when someone entered the room carrying food. Perhaps you have done the same thing when you are hungry and someone calls you for dinner. Sometimes your mouth begins to water when you just think about food. At any rate, Pavlov could understand that food placed directly in the mouth chemically arouses the taste sense organs on the tongue. When the sight of food causes salivation, however, this must be learned.

A number of experiments were conducted to discover how such responses are learned. In these experiments a dog was restrained in a harness

Fig. 5–3. Pavlov used this apparatus to study conditioning in the dog. Saliva secreted from the dog's mouth runs down a tube and the amount is recorded on the instrument shown at the left.

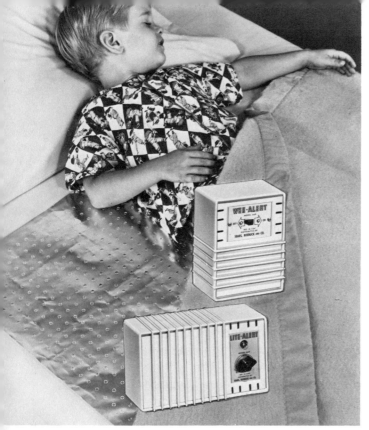

Fig. 5–4. A conditioning device used to cure bed wetting. Sold by Sears, Roebuck Co., this device has an alarm system which sounds when the pad under the child gets slightly wet. It wakes him up, and he becomes conditioned to wake whenever the need to urinate occurs at night.

as shown in Fig. 5–3. A minor surgical procedure exposed part of the salivary gland so that secretions from this gland could be accurately measured.

Pavlov noticed that salivation occurred each time the dog saw food and shortly before it tasted the food. Therefore, he thought, the response of salivating to the taste of food might become attached to the sight of food because the sight of food always closely precedes the taste of food in the mouth. If this were true, the response of salivating to the sight of food could be attached to still another stimulus that preceded this.

To see if this happened, he flashed a light and then about half a second later placed food directly in the animal's mouth. At first, salivation occurred only when food was placed in the mouth. After several trials, however, the dog began to salivate when the light was flashed. The animal had learned that food was always presented shortly after the light flashed. Pavlov called this process *conditioning.*

How does conditioning occur? Pavlov believed that there are some responses that occur naturally; that is, they are unlearned. Salivating to the taste of food in your mouth, for example, is a response that does not have to be learned. The stimulus that causes such a response is the taste of food.

Other stimuli may become connected to certain responses, however, if they precede such responses closely. For example, we learn to salivate when we see food, because eating that food usually occurs shortly thereafter.

The process of conditioning, then, involves substituting one stimulus for another. The new stimulus to which the response becomes attached is called the *conditioned stimulus.* A response made to that stimulus is called a *conditioned response.* The stimulus which originally caused the response is the *unconditioned stimulus,* and the response to that stimulus is known as the *unconditioned response.*

All this may seem complicated, but it really is not. And in terms of understanding learning, it is of great importance. Watson, the American psychologist whom we discussed in the first chapter, thought Pavlov had hit on the key to all human learning. He carried Pavlov's work further and demonstrated that even some human fears may be acquired through conditioning.

How Fears Are Conditioned

Watson reported the now famous case of Albert, an 11-month-old boy who had almost no fears prior to the experimental study. Repeated tests were conducted to see what stimuli would evoke a fear response in the child. It was found that only loud noises and falling caused crying and other evidence of fear. Before the experiment, the child had no fear of animals or other objects and, in fact, he played happily with a white rat for many hours.

At the beginning of the experiment, Albert was suddenly presented with the white rat with which he had played happily earlier. As he reached for the rat, however, a bell rang behind his head, making a very loud noise. This caused a startled reaction, although he did not cry. As he reached for the rat again, however, the bell again rang loudly and this time Albert jumped visibly and whimpered.

A week after the first experimental session, Albert was again presented with the rat. This time he was somewhat hesitant in reaching for it, and when he finally touched it, he withdrew his hand quickly. Several additional conditioning trials followed. Each time the rat was presented, the loud bell rang behind the child's head. Finally, the rat was again presented without the loud bell. This time Albert began to cry immediately.

For a long time after the conditioning, the child continued to show signs of fear toward the rat. Watson found that this fear had even *generalized* to other white, furry objects. A white rabbit and even a white glove were capable of causing fear. Finally, the fear was eliminated through *recondition-*

Fig. 5–5. Most human fears are learned and can be unlearned. The average person in our country is frightened of bees but not this 16 year-old fellow. He raises bees as a parttime job while attending school and has not been stung since he was a child.

ing. The rat was presented at meal times and at a safe distance. Gradually the rat was moved closer and closer to the child, and as the association grew between the rat and eating food, the rat could finally be placed on a table next to Albert without any signs of fear in the child. The loud bell, of course, was not rung during reconditioning.

Some Principles of Conditioning

In these two examples of conditioning, we can see that in order for a response to become conditioned, the new or conditioned stimulus must always be presented with or followed by the unconditioned stimulus. Thus in the experiment with Albert, the loud bell (unconditioned stimulus) was sounded just as the rat (conditioned stimulus) was presented. The pairing of conditioned and unconditioned stimuli in such experiments is called *reinforcement.*

Reinforcement is obviously a vital part of the conditioning process. If Pavlov had simply flashed the light without ever giving the dog food, the response of salivating would never have become associated with the light. If Watson had simply shown Albert the white rat without ever ringing the bell, no fear of the rat would have been conditioned.

When reinforcement ceases, the conditioned response begins to weaken. In the experiment with Albert, repeatedly showing the white rat without ringing the bell caused the conditioned response of fear of the rat to diminish. This is called *extinction.*

Another point is that in the experiment we saw that the fear response generalized to other stimuli aside from the white rat (conditioned stimulus). Thus a white rabbit or white furry glove also tended to cause the fear response. This is known as *generalization.*

Now that we have some understanding of the basic principles of classical conditioning, we are ready to look at another kind of conditioning that is even more important in terms of understanding human learning.

WHAT IS OPERANT CONDITIONING?

Classical conditioning is unlike much of the learning we encounter on a day-to-day basis. The responses made in this kind of conditioning do not accomplish anything, since the reinforcement is presented regardless of the response made by the animal. In most learning, the responses we make are instrumental in determining certain effects or results. We are often rewarded or we avoid punishment as a consequence of what we do. Behavior that is spontaneous and that produces some result that would not otherwise occur, is called *operant behavior.* The procedure through which such behavior is learned is called *operant conditioning.*

To study operant conditioning, a psychologist named B. F. Skinner built an apparatus like that shown in Fig. 5–6. This apparatus is now known as a *Skinner box.* On one wall of the box is a lever or bar connected to a food delivery device outside the cage. When the bar or lever is pressed, a small pellet of food is automatically dropped into a food cup inside the cage and close to the bar.

Operant conditioning in this device generally occurs in the following way. A hungry rat is placed in the box and immediately begins to explore the new surroundings by standing on its hind legs, sniffing, and moving around.

Fig. 5–6. In this device the rat learns to press a bar for food. Here he has one paw on the bar while he grabs the pellet of food that has come down the chute. Sometimes the food delivery mechanism is set so that the rat must press several times before eating. Note the similarity between this behavior and that of people playing slot machines.

WHAT GAMBLERS DON'T KNOW ABOUT OPERANT CONDITIONING

It's a fact that you cannot win when you put money in slot machines or "one-armed bandits." Why then, if this is true, do people put several million dollars each year into them? They do it because the owners of such machines understand how reinforcements can be used to shape behavior. Instead of "paying off" every time the handle is pulled, these machines pay off at irregular intervals. Studies of animal behavior have shown that animals will work harder if reinforcement occurs intermittently. In a Skinner box, for example, the number of bar presses per minute goes up when the box delivers food after several responses have been made. The rat does not know when he will be "paid." He only knows that if he keeps pressing the bar, sooner or later food will come. People playing the "slots" know the same thing. What they don't know is that the machines are set to retain a certain percentage of the money they put in. If they play long enough, they cannot possibly win.

In one of these movements, the bar is pressed and a pellet of food is delivered. Often the first time this happens the animal does not see the food, and it continues to explore the box. Sooner or later, however, the food is discovered and eaten. Following this, in one of the animal's exploratory movements, the bar is again pressed, and food is delivered. Again the animal may not see the food immediately, but in a short time it discovers and eats it. The next time the animal presses the bar, however, it seizes the food immediately and then again stands on its hind legs near the bar. Coming down, the animal again presses the bar and immediately eats the food. Now the animal spends more time close to the bar and food cup. Shortly after eating, the animal again presses the bar and is fed. Now we see the rat quickly alternating between pressing the bar and eating. It has been conditioned to press the bar for food.

Some Conclusions about Learning

This example of learning a simple lever pressing response tells us much about operant conditioning and the nature of human learning as well. We can see that motivation plays an important role in the learning process. If the rat was not hungry, its movements around the box would be fewer, although curiosity is another motive in this situation. The movements the rat

Fig. 5–7. *"Boy, have I got this guy conditioned! Every time I press the bar, he drops in a piece of food!"*

makes around the box are important, for if the animal did not make a response that was reinforced, it would not learn.

We can also see that reinforcement is of great importance in the learning process, as it was in classical conditioning. Reinforcement in this case simply means that the animal reaches a goal that satisfies or reduces a need. The reinforcement in the Skinner box was the pellet of food delivered each time the bar was pressed. Unless the pellet of food was given, the animal would not learn.

Another principle in this example is that learning is a gradual process.

We noted the same thing in the puzzle box experiment reported earlier and in Pavlov's studies of classical conditioning. We do know, however, that some learning occurs much more rapidly than this.

Finally, if reinforcement is withdrawn in this situation, extinction occurs, just as it does in classical conditioning. In other words, once the animal has learned to press the bar, we can eliminate that behavior simply by disconnecting the food delivery mechanism. The animal does not stop pressing the bar immediately, of course, but it does slow down and eventually pays no attention to the bar at all.

In the following example, we can see that the principles of learning discovered in operant conditioning experiments have many applications in real life. They can even help us understand how some children learn to be "spoiled."

Fig. 5–8. Children are sometimes "spoiled" by their parents who unwittingly reinforce unpleasant behavior. To quiet the child they give into his demands, but at the same time they increase the probability that this behavior will occur again.

How Some Children Learn to Be Spoiled Brats

Suppose while shopping a child wants his mother to buy him a particular toy, and she refuses. The child then screams and cries until finally the mother gives in and buys him the toy. What can we predict about the child's future behavior? We can predict that the next time the mother refuses the child's demands, he will again scream and cry. The mother, without realizing it, has reinforced this behavior, and the child has learned to make these responses whenever the mother refuses his demands.

From studies of operant conditioning, we know that conditioned responses become stronger with additional reinforcements. Again, if we apply this principle to our example above, we can predict that the more times the child's behavior of screaming and crying is followed by reinforcements, the

---

HOW BEHAVIORAL ENGINEERING TECHNOLOGY IS USED TO TRAIN ANIMALS

If you are ever unlucky enough to find yourself unarmed and threatened by a big, angry male wolf, what would you do?

It is not likely you would have the courage, but what you ought to do in such a spot is lie on your back and bare your throat, as if inviting the wolf to bite the most vulnerable place.

That is the advice of Dr. Leon Smith, a comparative psychologist—that is, a psychologist who specializes in the learning processes of animals.

"Lying on the back and exposing the throat is the attitude and signal of submission among wolves and other canines," Smith said.

"It's almost impossible for a dominant animal to attack a properly submissive and fawning one," he said.

Smith admitted that such an act of submission would take more courage and coolness than most people would be able to summon, but he himself put his theory to the test.

He went into a cage with a cross male wolf and when the animal growled threateningly, Smith lay down and bared his throat.

"The wolf touched my throat with his teeth, in the typical canine caress," the psychologist said.

"I wasn't bitten, but I was almost scared to death."

Understanding and using signals animals use to communicate is part of the system Smith has developed to work with animals.

He calls his system "behavioral engineering technology," or BET for short, and is using it to train the dangerous Hokkaido bears at the Japanese Village and Deer Park here.

Smith says all the animals he has ever worked with, right down to goldfish

---

and chickens, have a lot more intelligence than they are given credit for.

In fact, he admits he was once conned by a chicken. . . .

He was teaching a bantam rooster to walk a tightrope.

The idea was for the chicken to walk the rope, hop up on a platform at the end, turn around, and walk back to where he began. Then he would get his reward —some food.

The rooster, in a hurry for his prize, first learned he would get it even if he only put one foot on the platform instead of both feet. Then he learned he could get away with skipping the platform altogether.

"In 30 minutes that bantam was only walking a third of the way across the tightrope before coming back to claim his reward," Smith said. . . .

According to Smith, it was not generally realized how smart most animals really are until a method of training called "operant conditioning" came into use just before World War II.

"BET is a variant of operant conditioning, and the great thing about it is that it makes use of instantaneous rewards without any punishment—no punishment ever," Smith said in an interview.

Immediate reward and absence of punishment are two BET basics, but there is more to it than that.

He governs temperature, for instance. To train the Hokkaido bears he keeps the temperature in their cages at 50 degrees Fahrenheit. To bears from Japan's far northern island that is ideal.

An important part of BET is control of the animals' weight, according to Smith and his chief assistant, his wife, Rebecca.

"Toko, one of the Hokkaido bears here, learns fast and performs with greatest precision when he weighs about 220 pounds," Smith said.

"When he gains a few pounds, say only to 235, Toko gets a little unreliable. He goofs off."

At the Deer Park, Smith directs the bear training from an electronic console behind barred doors and a heavy glass window.

With console buttons he raises and lowers the doors to the individual bear cages, all of which open into the training room behind the glass, and controls the sound, light and temperature in which the bears are taught. He also uses a pushbutton to dispense the meat pellets that are the bears' rewards.

"Training animals with pushbuttons is a piece of cake," Smith said. "With buttons you can shape an animal's behavior just as a sculptor shapes clay."

Smith says punishment has no place in animal training because it retards it, and even stops learning altogether. Even so, it is fundamental in training animals for many circus and theater acts.

"Punishment creates anxiety, and no anxious animal, any more than an anxious child, can learn well," the psychologist said. . . .

more likely this behavior is to occur when the child's demands are not satisfied.

We have also seen that when reinforcement ceases, the response diminishes and finally stops altogether. Thus we can predict that if the mother stops reinforcing the undesirable behavior, the frequency of such behavior will diminish and finally stop.

How Animal Trainers Use Operant Conditioning

Animal trainers often teach tricks in much the same way the mother described above taught her child to have tantrums. The difference lies in the fact that animal trainers do this deliberately, while the mother was unwittingly conditioning her child.

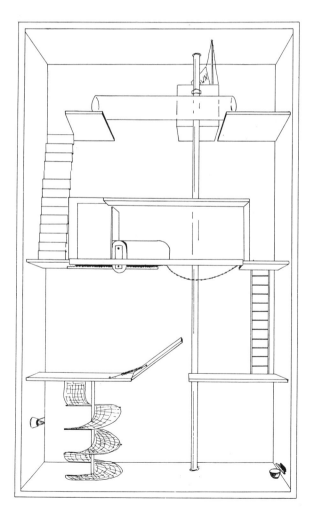

Figure 5–9. Barnabus - the College Educated Rat
Using the apparatus shown at the left, Barnabus enters on the first floor. When a light goes on he mounts a spiral staircase to a platform. Then he runs to another platform by pushing down a raised drawbridge and then crossing it. From here he climbs a ladder, summons a car by pulling an attached chain hand-over-hand, pedals the car through a tunnel, climbs a flight of stairs, runs through a tube, steps into a waiting elevator, and celebrates his progress by raising a flag. Raising the flag starts the elevator, on which Barnabus now descends to the ground floor where he is rewarded.

Suppose an animal trainer wants to teach a seal to play the first few notes of the "Star Spangled Banner" on a set of musical horns. If he waits until the seal actually plays the tune before giving reinforcement, he is likely to wait a long, long time. What he does is to make the correct responses occur by carefully using reinforcement and a method we call the *method of approximations.* This method involves reinforcing behavior that gradually becomes more and more like the final desired behavior.

First of all, the seal is deprived of food to make sure it has the motivation necessary for learning. Then a new stimulus, such as a Halloween clicker or "cricket," is used as a reinforcement. This stimulus becomes a reinforcement by associating it with another reinforcement, such as food. The trainer throws the seal a piece of fish, and at the same time sounds the clicker. He

Fig. 5–10. Animal trainers use reinforcement to shape the behavior of many different species. This Siberian tiger has been trained to "sit" until the trainer gives a signal to return to its stand.

does this repeatedly until it becomes clear that the clicker is a signal to the seal that food is coming. The clicker is referred to as *secondary reinforcement*, because it does not directly reduce an animal's need. Secondary reinforcement is often used in operant conditioning because it can be given at the exact moment the desired response occurs. We know this is important because the longer the time between a response and reinforcement, the slower will be the learning. Secondary reinforcement can often be given immediately, while the short delay between a response and receiving food results in slower learning. Once it is clear to the trainer that the clicker has become a secondary reinforcement, the training begins.

The trainer waits until the seal makes some slight movement in the direction of the horns, and when this occurs he sounds the clicker and throws the seal a piece of fish. The next trial, the trainer waits until the seal moves slightly closer to the horns and then he reinforces the behavior. The procedure is repeated over and over until the seal is quite close to the horns. Now the trainer waits until the seal's mouth is close to one of the horns before giving the reinforcement. On the next trial he may wait until the seal touches one of the horns, and finally he reinforces only a blowing response. Now he begins to train the animal to play the notes in proper sequence, and the same procedure just described continues. Behavior is gradually shaped in the desired direction by administering reinforcement for closer and closer approximations of the final desired behavior.

The method of approximations can be used to teach any number of unusual responses to animals. Some psychologists have taught rabbits to play basketball and chickens to play a toy piano. B. F. Skinner has even taught pigeons to play Ping-Pong. The principles we have discussed here are sufficient for any student to try his hand at operant conditioning of his or her pet dog, or any other animal.

CONDITIONING HUMAN BEHAVIOR

Humans can be conditioned using the same principles as those employed by the animal trainer. One psychologist, for example, conditioned the use of certain words by a subject. Whenever the person referred to himself in conversation, the psychologist nodded in approval and said, "Mm-hmm." He was reinforcing any self-references by the subject. As the conversation went on, it was clear that the subject talked more and more about himself. He did not know, of course, that the psychologist was deliberately reinforcing only self-reference comments.

BIOFEEDBACK: HOW WE CAN LEARN TO CONTROL BODY FUNCTIONS

By Michael T. Malloy
© Knight Newspapers

COLD. Snow. An icy wind blowing across my fingers. I imagined all those things, and pretty soon the needle on the temperature gauge began to swing downward: 92 . . . 91 . . . 90 . . . and finally 89.

I turned myself mentally around. Now I imagined a blast of hot air on my fingers, heat waves dancing above my hand, the metal sensor taped to my fingertip getting hot. The temperature gauge moved upward: 90 . . . 91 . . . 92 . . . 93.

Through will power and imagination I was controlling the temperature of my hand. A short time ago I would have "known" this was impossible. But the impossible is becoming commonplace as scientists hook up ordinary people like myself to gadgets that feed back information about skin temperature, blood pressure, heartbeat, brain rhythms and other biological functions previously believed to be beyond our conscious control.

Biofeedback, as the process is called, already has demonstrated that we can exercise uncanny control over "involuntary" activities if we have some way—a dial, a bell, or a flashing light—to tell us just what those bodily functions are doing when we try to bend them to our will.

Heart patients in Baltimore have been trained to speed or slow their heartbeat to smooth out irregularities in its rhythm. They do it by watching colored lights that monitor the actions they are trying to control.

Patients in Boston have been trained to lower their high blood pressure with the help of a monitor that beeps and flashes a light whenever the pressure inches downward.

Rats in New York have been trained to change the rates at which their kidneys function and to blush one ear while turning the other pale.

Experimental subjects in many places have been trained to raise or lower the temperature of their hands or of small patches of their skin.

It is impossible to detect with our own senses the operation of a single one of our billions of nerve cells. But the "firing" of such a cell can be made to ring a bell if a sensitive detector is attached to the tiny bit of muscle that the nerve controls. With this kind of feedback, thousands of people have swiftly learned to fire a single nerve cell so expertly that they can make it imitate fancy drum rolls and flourishes.

The best known example of biofeedback is the readily demonstrated ability that most of us have to alter the ebb and flow of electrical activity in our brains. This has given rise to a great deal of seemingly supernatural hokum about "alpha waves."

But it may be the most exciting technique in the long run, because the brain regulates our thoughts, emotions and all the actions of our bodies. The prospect of consciously regulating one's own brain has led some biofeedback researchers to talk about ushering in a "golden age of the mind."

All this evidence stretches the imagination. If kidney function can be hurried by the mind, why can't the growth of cancer cells be slowed? Or the hardening of arteries? Or the growth of fear? Or the conception of babies? Or . . . or . . . or . . . ?

"There's a great deal of baloney ground into the meat," cautions Dr. John Basmajian, who pioneered the training of isolated nerve cells. "You're dealing with enthusiasts in biofeedback, with a motley crew. Yesterday it was transcendental meditation, today it's biofeedback, tomorrow it's acupuncture."

Coming down to earth, biofeedback is still mostly an exciting demonstration of potential rather than fact. "We've established that we can do these things," says Dr. Bernard T. Engel of his success at training the Baltimore heart patients. "But there's a long way to go before you could call it a treatment . . . A therapy has to be more than something that one guy in the whole world can do."

The principles of operant conditioning have been used to teach emotionally disturbed children to talk, to sit quietly, and to respond to questions. In hospitals for the mentally ill, these same principles have been used to teach "normal" behavior to extremely disturbed patients. Such patients are not cured by operant conditioning, but in some cases patients who refuse to wear clothes or who refuse to eat, for example, can be helped to show more normal behavior. Similarly, in institutions for the mentally retarded, very seriously retarded patients have been toilet trained and taught other behavior that in the past was impossible to teach.

In our chapter on mental illness and mental health, we will discuss in more detail how conditioning is employed with emotionally disturbed people. Here we will only give one example of such techniques; an example of how operant conditioning is used to treat abnormal fears.

Three psychologists recently investigated how operant conditioning might be used to eliminate an intense fear of snakes in several young adults. These fears, called *phobias,* were so severe that the affected individuals were quite restricted in their activities. Some were afraid of going for a walk; others were afraid of gardening, and so on because of the possibility of encountering snakes.

The patients were divided into four groups that were matched for their degree of fearfulness. Those in the first group watched a film in which children and adults handled a large harmless king snake. These subjects had been previously trained in deep muscle relaxation, and they could stop the film whenever they became uncomfortable. The film was then reversed to the beginning of the disturbing sequence, and they relaxed. This process continued until the situation that provoked the fear now provoked only relaxation. The patient, in other words, was conditioned to respond to situations that initially produced fear with relaxation. Relaxation and tension, it should be noted, are incompatible. One cannot be both relaxed and tense at the same time.

Patients in another group imitated the behavior of a live model as the model engaged in progressively more fearful activities with the snake. The subjects were gradually guided through such activities as touching the snake while wearing gloves, then with a bare hand, holding the snake, and finally letting the snake loose in the room. In a third group, patients were asked to imagine scenes that made them uncomfortable or afraid. At the same time they were trained in deep relaxation. As the patients learned to imagine a fearful scene and at the same time to relax, they were gradually asked to imagine increasingly fearful scenes while relaxing. Over several sessions, their fear of snakes diminished.

Patients in the fourth group served as a control and were given no special training. They did not improve. All the other patients showed improvement; their fear of snakes diminished. Those that had participated with the live model showed the greatest improvement. Almost all overcame their fear of snakes, and a follow-up investigation later showed that these fears did not return.

How Are Superstitions Learned?

How do people learn that certain days are unlucky, or that finding a four-leaf clover brings good luck, or that walking under a ladder or seeing a black cat brings bad luck? The principle of reinforcement, which we discussed previously, is clearly responsible.

In experiments designed to study how superstition is learned, pigeons were confined in small cages. Regardless of what the birds did, at regular intervals food dropped into a food cup attached to the cage. Six of the eight pigeons tested clearly developed "superstitious" behavior. One bird learned to make two or three counterclockwise turns about the cage between reinforcements. Another learned to toss its head repeatedly. And still another learned to make pecking or brushing movements toward the floor.

In another experiment, pigeons were trained to peck at an orange light. When they did so, food was presented in the food cup at irregular intervals. However, for four minutes of each hour a blue light appeared in

Fig. 5-11. *Superstitious behavior not only involves the learning of superstitions, but also ways of avoiding "bad luck." Witch doctors in many parts of the world perform ceremonies to ward off "evil spirits" as this one in Borneo is doing.*

place of the orange. Some pigeons developed a negative superstition of the blue light—they felt it was bad luck. Others developed a positive superstition —they felt it was good luck. Some, in other words, responded with more rapid pecks at the blue light than at the orange. Others learned to avoid it. The important thing, of course, was whether or not reinforcements were presented while the blue light was on. If no reinforcements occurred, the animal learned to avoid the light. If it was reinforced while the light was on, increased pecking resulted.

Human beings learn superstition in much the same way. If a bad storm occurs on Friday the thirteenth, that is taken for evidence that this is an unlucky day. If one has good fortune shortly after finding a four-leaf clover, that results in learning that such clovers bring good luck. Also, when we have already learned a superstition, we tend to be especially watchful for evidence to confirm the superstition. If one believes that black cats bring bad luck, he is likely to be especially sensitive to any event that can be interpreted as unfortunate.

PUNISHMENT

At the beginning of this chapter, we mentioned that Thorndike believed rewards and punishments to have opposite effects. Reward strengthened learning, while punishment was believed to weaken or eliminate learned responses. Such a view is still widely held by the general public, but psychological studies of learning have shown this belief to be inaccurate.

To study the effects of punishment, one psychologist using a Skinner box trained two groups of rats to press a bar in order to obtain food. After all the animals had learned the response, the food delivery mechanism was disconnected. Neither group could now secure food by pressing the bar. For those in one group, however, each time they pressed the bar, the bar slapped down hard on their paws. They were punished for making a response that had previously been rewarded. The punishment was administered for only the first ten minutes of the first day. Thereafter, bar presses were not punished, but no food was forthcoming either.

For both groups, the number of bar presses was recorded, and it was found that by the end of the second day, they were the same. In other words, punishment operated to *suppress* or *inhibit* the learned response. As long as punishment was applied, the response did not occur. But when punishment ceased, the response reoccurred. This suggests that punishment does not eliminate learning; it operates only to suppress learned responses temporarily.

From other studies, we know that many factors determine the effectiveness of punishment. Stronger punishment seems to work better than weaker punishment, but the strength of the learned response is also a factor. Very strong tendencies to respond are often not eliminated by punishment.

What does this all mean? It means that rewards and punishments do not have equal and opposite effects on learning. It also means that punishment may be effective in temporarily inhibiting undesirable responses, if other more desirable responses can be made through which the person or animal may satisfy a motive. The child, for example, may learn to ask his mother for cookies, if this behavior is reinforced while taking cookies without permission is punished.

The most effective way of eliminating responses is through the process of extinction—that is, by withdrawing reinforcement. If we want to eliminate undesirable behavior, we must insure that such behavior is not reinforced.

Why is it that prisons are notoriously ineffective in changing the behavior of those confined? Punishment, it is hoped, will teach the criminal the error of his ways. But we have seen that punishment alone—even very strong punishment—does not necessarily eliminate learned behavior. When released from prison, the criminal often commits other crimes and this behavior is reinforced. In other words, he may escape detection for a time while spending his ill-gotten gains. Socially desirable behavior, at the same time, may not be reinforced. The released prisoner may be unable to find a job or otherwise satisfy his needs. The result is that a very substantial portion of released offenders again commit crimes and are returned to prison. How can we change this behavior? What is the most effective way of preventing criminal behavior in the first place? With your new knowledge of the principles of learning, you should have some ideas.

CHAPTER SUMMARY

1. Learning is defined as the process through which behavior originates or is changed through training or experience. Changes in behavior due to maturation are ruled out by this definition. Similarly, behavior changes that result from fatigue, disease, or drugs are eliminated. Finally, the definition excludes unlearned or innate responses such as reflexes or instincts.

2. Thorndike demonstrated that while learning involves association, there is more to it than that. Studying how cats learned to escape from a puzzle box, he concluded that, through trial and error, bonds or associations are formed between stimuli and responses. Furthermore, he thought that responses leading to reward are learned, while those leading to punishment are eliminated.

3. Pavlov, a Russian physiologist, discovered a very simple type of learning which is now called *classical conditioning*. The process of conditioning involves substituting one stimulus for another. A new stimulus (the conditioned stimulus) evokes a response (conditioned response) which in the past was evoked by a different stimulus (unconditioned stimulus). The response formerly made to the unconditioned stimulus is called an unconditioned response. You can remember these terms by reminding yourself that the *un*conditioned response is an *un*learned response.

4. Classical conditioning occurs through reinforcement. That is when the conditioned and unconditioned stimuli are presented together, or when the conditioned stimulus is presented slightly before the unconditioned stimulus, the response becomes attached to the new stimulus. Presenting the two stimuli close together is the reinforcement. When reinforcement ceases, the response begins to weaken until it finally stops altogether. This process is called *extinction.*

5. Operant conditioning is different from classical conditioning in that reinforcement depends upon the animal's responses. If the animal does not make the proper response, no reinforcement is forthcoming. In classical conditioning, reinforcement is presented regardless of what the animal does. Behavior that is spontaneous and that produces some result that would not otherwise occur is called *operant behavior.*

6. From the example of learning a lever pressing response in a Skinner box, we can draw several conclusions about learning. Motivation plays an important role, for if the animal did not move about making various responses, none could be reinforced. Reinforcement is also important, for only those responses are learned that are closely followed by reinforcement. In operant conditioning, reinforcement is something that reduces or satisfies a need. Thus a pellet of food for a hungry animal is a reinforcement.

7. Animal trainers often use a technique called the *method of approximations* to train animals. This method involves reinforcing behavior that gradually becomes more and more like the final desired behavior. So-called secondary reinforcements are typically used in such training because they can be given at the exact moment the desired response occurs. This is important because the longer the time between response and reinforcement, the slower will be the learning.

8. Operant conditioning has been used with humans as well as animals. In hospitals for the mentally ill, severely disturbed patients have been taught "normal" behavior through operant conditioning. Similarly, the behavior of severely retarded patients can be changed in many ways through operant conditioning.

9. Reinforcement and punishment do not have equal and opposite effects on learning. Punishment seems to temporarily inhibit responses, but when the punishment ceases, the responses again reoccur. The most effective ways to eliminate undesirable behavior seem to be through extinction; that is, the withdrawal of reinforcement.

Important Terms
from This Chapter

learning	similarity	response
association	contrast	stimuli
contiguity	E. L. Thorndike	Ivan P. Pavlov

classical conditioning   reconditioning   B. F. Skinner

conditioned stimulus   reinforcement   Skinner box

unconditioned stimulus   extinction   motivation

conditioned response   operant conditioning   method of approximations

unconditioned response   operant behavior   secondary reinforcement

Additional Readings
to Help You Learn More

Haas, K. *Understanding Adjustment and Behavior,* 2nd Edition. Englewood Cliffs, N.J.: Prentice-Hall, Inc., 1965. Chapter 10, "Intelligence, I.Q. and Human Ability," is a good discussion of the nature of intelligence and also I.Q. differences by sex and race.

Skinner, B. F. "How to Teach Animals," *Scientific American Offprints,* No. 423. San Francisco: W. H. Freeman and Company. An excellent article that you will find very interesting.

Skinner, B. F. "Pigeons in a Pelican," *Bobbs-Merrill Reprints,* P-318. Indianapolis: Bobbs-Merrill Company. In this paper Skinner discusses what seems to be almost a science fiction story of a research project that was carried out during World War II on animal training.

Our own eggs

chicken

duck

goose

the next hatching
will be on

Making Learning Easy

chapter **6**

You may have seen advertisements for machines that promise to teach you almost anything while you sleep. "Just turn on the recorder," they say, "and put the speaker under your pillow. When you awake, you will have learned German vocabulary, algebra, high school chemistry, or any other subject of your choice." Bunk! No one has yet invented any machine that teaches you without any effort on your part. Yet the idea of painless learning has so much appeal that unscrupulous promoters are able to bilk thousands of dollars out of gullible people every year.

It may not be possible to learn without expending any effort, but some students seem to go out of their way to make learning as unpleasant and difficult as possible. The football player learns dozens of complicated plays with ease but has a terrible time trying to remember formulas in his algebra class. The cheerleader can remember scores of intricate movements and cheers but cannot recall the dates of important events in her world history course. Why? Why is it so easy to learn some things and so difficult to learn others?

In this chapter we will take a look at what psychology has discovered about human learning. Our goal will be to teach you how to learn the most with the least effort; this should be the goal of every student.

WHAT AFFECTS LEARNING?

There are three major classes or categories of variables that affect human learning. The first of these is about the learner himself. Is he motivated to learn? How intelligent is he? Does he have emotional problems or hangups that affect learning? The second category pertains to the task or material to be learned. How long is it? How difficult? Is it meaningful to the learner? What type of task or material is involved? The final category pertains to the methods of learning. Should learning be distributed over time? How important is knowledge of results? Is it better to be an active learner? Should we try to learn the whole thing or break it down into parts?

You Are the Most Important Factor in Learning

There is little doubt that, regardless of what is to be learned, the person doing the learning is most important. One of the factors as far as the individual is concerned is his or her intelligence. More intelligent people learn more easily than those less intelligent, and they remember what they have learned longer. But is intelligence the only factor, or even the key factor, in learning? For the typical high school or college student, the answer is probably no. To see why this is true, we must take a brief look at intelligence and at how it is measured.

The average person thinks of intelligence as the innate, biological, God-given ability to think or solve problems. But very few, if any, modern psychologists regard intelligence in this way. Most of them reject the idea that intelligence is inborn, unchanging, or determined solely by heredity. Rather, it is considered that intelligence reflects the individual's intellectual capabilities at any given time. Such capabilities reflect both the individual's biological potential and his experiences or training since birth.

What Is the I.Q.?

The *I.Q.*, or *intelligence quotient*, is a score that is calculated by comparing how well one person has done on an intelligence test with others of the same age who have taken the same test. On most tests, the average I.Q. is arbitrarily set at 100. Scores below that number mean that the person has done less well than most others of his age, while scores above 100 mean that he or she has done better.

The I.Q. is not a fixed number, but in fact varies from test to test. For the average person, variations of as much as five points one way or the other

Fig. 6–1.   This is the Stanford-Binet Intelligence Test. Most of the materials shown are used in testing young children. Verbal materials such as vocabulary words are used in testing older individuals.

are not uncommon. For those with emotional problems or reading difficulties, variations can be much greater.

No intelligence test measures only what you were born with, nor is there any possibility of ever constructing such a test. Rather, all tests of intelligence measure what you are capable of at the present time. Although they are designed insofar as possible to minimize the effects of educational opportunities, all tests do reflect education to some extent. Thus people with more education tend to earn higher I.Q.s than people with less education. Furthermore, all intelligence tests reflect verbal ability or the ability to use language. Individuals who are poor readers do less well on such tests than if they could read at a level appropriate for their age.

In addition to these limitations, many tests are relatively unfair insofar as they measure the intelligence of members of minority groups. We need not go into all the details of test construction here: it is sufficient to say that certain kinds of test items or questions are inappropriate within particular cultural subgroups. Also, members of minority groups are often not represented at all or are under-represented in the groups upon which tests are *standardized*. The standardization group for any test consists of a number of individuals who take that test and against which the scores of individuals later taking the test are compared.

Are There Different Kinds of Intelligence?

Some psychologists consider intelligence to be an overall or global ability to think rationally and deal effectively with one's environment. Others argue that while there is such a general ability, there are also other special abilities that are important in certain types of mental activities. Still others hold that intelligence is a collection of a number of different independent abilities.

The evidence seems to support the position that intelligence does consist of both general and specific factors. The specific factors involved appear to relate mainly to abilities to use language on the one hand and numbers on the other. Some people seem to have greater quantitative or numerical ability than others, while not necessarily being more intelligent overall. Others tend to be superior in language or verbal ability while at the same time tending to have less quantitative ability. Usually the differences between these two kinds of intelligence are not very great within the same person: in some people, though, there are substantial differences in verbal and quantitative abilities.

What Does This Mean to You?

First of all, it is important to remember that intelligence is only one of many factors that determines ease or difficulty in learning. We know that there is not a perfect relationship between intelligence and academic achievement. Less intelligent people frequently make better grades than those more intelligent. Nevertheless, students sometimes worry that their I.Q.s are not high enough.

You may have seen charts indicating that the average intelligence of college students is 120. Does this mean that an I.Q. above 120 guarantees success in college while an I.Q. below that figure guarantees failure? Not at all. As we will see in the next section, motivation is of tremendous importance in determining success or failure in college, as it is in high school.

By the same token, this does not mean that intelligence is unimportant, or that scores on intelligence tests (I.Q.s) have no value. Certainly some people are not sufficiently intelligent to tackle college level work. This does not imply that these people are somehow less worthy than those who attend college or that they cannot lead successful and productive lives. It simply means that they should pursue careers other than those that require a college education.

For those students having difficulty in one or more of their courses, the guidance counselor or school psychologist should be of help. Usually the counselor will take a look first at the student's study habits. Very frequently these are the source of the problem. Often, however, the student is poorly motivated or has negative attitudes which interfere with his or her performance. In some cases, his preparation for certain courses has been inadequate. If it is apparent that the difficulty does not lie in any of these areas, psychological tests—including an intelligence test—may be used. In a small number of cases, low intelligence may be responsible for poor academic performance. In such a case, the person usually has other assets which the counselor can identify and use in guiding the individual toward a worthwhile and satisfying career.

HOW IMPORTANT IS MOTIVATION?

As we saw in the last chapter, there is little or no learning that takes place without motivation. Learning in animals is usually motivated by their biological needs. The rat learns to press a bar in a Skinner box when it is motivated by hunger and rewarded with food. The seal learns to play a set of musical horns when it is rewarded with a piece of fish.

Human learning is generally not motivated by incentives or goals that are directly related to biological needs. The math teacher does not reward us with food when we learn to solve algebra problems. The social science teacher does not give us cookies for writing an essay on the Magna Carta. Two types of goals or incentives are generally most important in the type of learning that takes place in school—those intrinsic in the material learned, and those extrinsic to the material.

When we learn to do something simply because of the satisfaction or pleasure we get in doing it, we are motivated by an *intrinsic incentive*. On the other hand, when we learn something because of an external reward, we are motivated by an *extrinsic incentive*. If we read a book because of an interest in the subject matter, we are motivated by an intrinsic incentive. If

Fig. 6–2. This child is motivated to learn by an intrinsic incentive. He doesn't regard this kind of learning as unpleasant or even difficult, yet school work is often unpleasant when we are not properly motivated.

we read a book only because it is required in a given course and because we want to pass the course, we are motivated by an extrinsic incentive. Grades are examples of extrinsic incentives.

In general, we can say that learning through the use of intrinsic incentives is superior to learning through extrinsic incentives. When the student takes a course that he enjoys for its own sake, he is likely to learn a great deal more than if he simply takes the course in order to satisfy a requirement for graduation. But what about those courses we have to take but in which we have little interest and/or little ability? Here it helps to keep in mind that doing as well as possible may be important in terms of long-range goals. The grade average we need to enter college may suffer if we goof off in a course because we do not like it. The good job we hope to get after graduation may depend on what we learn in that course, whether it be English, math, or something else. It helps to recognize that we generally like those subjects in which we have ability and in which we do well. When we have lesser ability for a particular subject, we tend to dislike it and to spend less of our study time on that subject. The good student recognizes that he or she has to spend more time studying those subjects that are disliked or in which he or she has less ability.

Praise and Sarcasm in the Classroom

Just as it is normal for us to like some courses and not others, it is normal to like some teachers and dislike others. Unfortunately, many students seem to believe that they are somehow punishing disliked teachers when they refuse to study the material in their courses. In the long run, of course, it is not the teacher who suffers.

Why are certain teachers disliked? Psychological studies have shown that in some cases it is because they scold or use sarcasm in trying to motivate students. One psychologist divided 106 younger students into four groups that were matched for intelligence and arithmetic ability. For 15 minutes each day for 5 days, the children were given practice in addition, and their progress over that period was rewarded. One group served as a control group in a separate room and heard no comments from the teacher about their performance. The other three groups were together in the same room during the experiment. Regardless of the scores actually achieved on the addition problems, one group received constant praise, another group constant scolding, and the third group was simply ignored.

The children in the praised group were called by name, told they were doing good work, and encouraged to do even better. Children in the scolded group were also called by name but were criticized for their "poor work," "careless mistakes," and "lack of improvement." Children in the ignored group received no comments regarding their work.

In this study, children in the praised group showed the largest gains, while those in the scolded group were second in order of improvement. The ignored group showed some improvement but not significantly greater improvement than those in the control group. In terms of the effect of praise or scolding over several days, the praised group continued to improve, while improvement in the scolded group tended to level off.

Scolding or sarcasm may be better than ignoring the student, but praise or encouragement seems to have the most beneficial effect on classroom learning. Furthermore, sarcasm or scolding may turn some students off so that their dislike of the teacher is translated into no work for that teacher.

Just as you will almost certainly have to take some courses in which you have little interest, it is just as likely that you will have some teachers you dislike. This is especially true if those teachers use sarcasm or ridicule in dealing with students. In these cases you will want to remember that what you learn or do not learn may be important to you in terms of what you hope to achieve in the long run.

Emotions and Learning

There is little doubt that intellectual efficiency is affected by emotions. The student who is insecure and anxious because of an unpleasant or disturbing situation at home, for example, often has difficulty in school, both in learning and in remembering what he or she has learned. Difficulties in learning in school may also stem from emotional disturbances and worry caused by the school situation itself; anxiety about a test may be so great that even if the student knows the material well, his ability to remember it may be severely impaired.

Anxiety in the school situation may stem from many sources: too much emphasis on competition, an overemphasis on grades, or failure and the feeling of frustration that stems from failure. One psychologist conducted an experiment in which he studied the amount of time spent daydreaming by students following success or failure. In many cases, failure did not inspire the student to make greater efforts: he simply spent more time daydreaming. Success, on the other hand, reduced daydreaming and at the same time improved performance and efficiency.

Most of us experience failure from time to time. The simple fact of recognizing that other people also fail occasionally is often of help in overcoming the frustration and despair of failure. The one rule to follow when one fails is "take action." Find out what went wrong. If you failed a test, ask the teacher to go over the test with you. Try to determine if your study habits were inadequate. Can the teacher suggest some additional things you might read that would be of help? Learning to overcome failure or poor performance is one of the most important lessons for any student to learn.

If you do have emotional problems which seem to be dragging down your work in school, do not be hesitant about approaching the school counselor or psychologist. He or she is there specifically to help students with just such problems.

LEARNING AND THE MATERIAL TO BE LEARNED

At the beginning of this chapter we pointed out that it is not only characteristics of the learner that affect learning, but also the nature of the material to be learned. Are some kinds of things learned more easily than others? What about the length of the task—how does that affect learning? Are items in the middle of a list easier or harder to learn than those at the ends? These are all questions that have been studied by psychologists interested in human learning.

In the nineteenth century, a psychologist named Ebbinghaus was one of the first to study such things as how the length of the task affects learning and remembering. He memorized both short and long lists of meaningless

Fig. 6–3. The subject must trace along the line as rapidly as possible. The difficulty of the task is increased since he sees the star reversed in the mirror.

three-letter syllables. These are called *nonsense syllables,* and they are often used in such studies because they are about equal in difficulty. If real words were used in such studies, some would be more easily learned and remembered than others.

Ebbinghaus found that while longer lists required a greater number of practice trials to learn, retention for them was greater. He also discovered that the number of practice trials required to learn a list of syllables increases more rapidly than the length of the material to be learned. If seven syllables can be learned in one trial, learning twelve syllables requires seventeen trials, and learning sixteen syllables requires thirty practice trials.

Another early discovery was that when we try to learn material in a list it is easier to learn items at the beginning and the end than it is those in the middle. In fact we know today that items at the beginning of a list are the easiest to learn, while items at the end are learned with only slightly greater difficulty. The position of maximum difficulty is just past the middle of the list. This is called the *serial position effect.*

Other investigations have studied the ease or difficulty of learning meaningful versus nonmeaningful material. If we compare the number of practice trials required to learn a list of nonsense syllables with the number of trials needed to learn a meaningful sentence with about the same number of sounds, there is no doubt that learning the nonsense syllables is much more difficult. The importance of these studies lies in the fact that to make learning as easy as possible, the material should be as meaningful as possible to the learner. One psychologist points out that dates and names of persons should not be memorized as isolated bits of information. Instead they should be incorporated into larger units of understanding.

Of greater significance, perhaps, than the nature of the material to be learned are the methods one uses to learn. In some respects these are even more important to the student than characteristics of the learner because he or she has more control over them. You can consciously decide to use this or that method because it saves time and you learn more. For these reasons, most of the rest of this chapter is concerned with how to study and remember what you learn.

HOW TO STUDY

In seventeen years of teaching college and university students, this psychologist has not seen more than a handful of people fail because they were not sufficiently intelligent to learn. Students who fail in college or in high school almost always either do not study at all or are so poor in study habits that they learn practically nothing. Sometimes the failing student will say, "I can't understand it—I studied, but I still failed." Typically, when such students say they have "studied," what they mean is that they have casually read their book and/or their class notes. They don't recognize the fact that effective studying means one has to be an active learner.

Be an Active Learner

When a student relaxes in a chair, opens his book, and merely reads the assignment through from beginning to end, he or she is using *passive learning*. *Active learning* involves attempting to commit the lesson to memory through recitation, through self-testing, or through outlining.

Psychologists have been interested in discovering how much time should be devoted to reading versus recitation* and also in determining how

---

*The term "recitation" means to read first and then to try and recall silently or aloud what you have read.

early in the study period recitation should begin. In one experiment, the same amount of study time was involved in all conditions. The amount of time devoted to reading, however, varied from 20 per cent to 100 per cent, and the amount of time devoted to recitation varied from 0 per cent to 80 per cent. The results of the experiment showed that regardless of the type of material, more learning occurs when a large proportion of the time is devoted to recitation. In addition it was found that recitation should begin early in the learning process; the student should not wait until all of the material has been read before beginning to recite.

If you have one hour to study, approximately 15 minutes should be spent in reading the material and 45 minutes in trying to remember what you have read. Obviously if the material is too long to read in just 15 minutes, you will have to devote more than one hour to the study of that material. As we noted previously, this doesn't mean that you should read for the first 15 minutes and recite for the next 45. Rather, the time should be broken up into short periods of reading and longer periods of recitation.

How to Pick a Book Apart

Many students do not know how to read a book. They can read, of course, but they do not know how to tackle a book in the most systematic fashion. The worst way to read is to open the book to the assignment and then read silently all the way through from beginning to end.

The smart student who wants to learn the most in the shortest possible time does the following. He or she leafs through the entire assignment from beginning to end in order to get a general overall idea of the subject matter concerned. He or she also pays attention to the author's organization of the material. Most chapters in textbooks, for example, are divided into several major parts with minor parts under each.

Now the student begins to read. He or she reads the first section, paying attention initially to the section title, since the author uses that to tell you what the section is about. As the student reads, he tries to see what the major point is that the author is trying to get across. Often only one point is expressed in a section, with most of the section devoted to elaborating that point and giving examples of it.

After finishing the section, the student closes the book and tries to remember in his own words the main point or points of the section. Some students find it more helpful to write this down, while others recite silently. Still other students find it helpful to jot down notes in their own words as they go along.

Two things are important to remember here. First, do not try to remember everything you read. Generally this is not only unnecessary but impossible. As we mentioned above, often there is only one major point expressed in a single section—that is the point you want to remember. Second, do not try to remember the author's exact words—paraphrase the point and put it in terms you understand. You will remember the material much better if you do this.

After finishing the first section, use the same tactics to learn the second, third, and so on. In other words, read short sections, try to determine the main points expressed, put those points in your own words, close the book and try to remember the points.

One final thing to note before moving on. When you read, read everything. Some students ignore tables, graphs, and illustrations. This material, however, is placed in a text for good reasons. Usually it elaborates on the points that are written in the various sections. They are intended to better help you understand the material. Do not ignore them.

Pay Attention!

Some students behave in class as they do when reading a book. They relax, make no effort to remember, and as a result, often make poor grades. The number one rule in class is "Pay attention." Number two is "Take notes."

When we say, "Pay attention," we mean more than just listening to what the teacher says. You should try to pick out the main points being emphasized just as you do when reading a book. As in a book, many teachers give only a few major points in each class but spend a great deal of time elaborating on the points and giving examples. They do this to help you understand.

As in reading a book, do not try to remember everything you hear in class, and do not try to write everything down. Try to write down the main points in your own words. You will find this easier to remember than if you try to remember the exact words of the teacher. At times, of course, you will be told to learn something exactly, but in most classes you are only expected to learn the sense of what is being said.

If you do not understand something, raise your hand and have it clarified then and there. If you still do not understand, talk to the teacher after class. Most teachers, you will find, react favorably to sincere students who are interested in learning.

Finally, keep an organized notebook and review your notes as soon as you can after class. There should be a separate section in your notebook for each class, or separate notebooks. Each day you attend class, jot the date down, and then write down what the teacher says he or she will cover that day. As the class goes on, write down the main points in your own words. Do not try to write everything. It is unnecessary in most cases and if you do, you will be so busy writing that you will miss much of what is said.

Should You Distribute Your Learning?

Some students make a point of cramming for tests or exams. They wait until the night before the test and then try to read everything that has been assigned since the last test. This may be better than not reading the material at all, but it is certainly not much better.

Psychologists have conducted many investigations of massed versus distributed learning. *Massed learning* means that only one time interval is available for learning. When learning takes place over several time intervals, we call this *distributed learning.* If you have six hours of time available for study, is it better to study six hours straight (massed learning) or should the study time be broken up into smaller periods (distributed learning)? If the latter is better, how short should the study periods be? Is it better to study one hour a day for six days or three hours a day for two days?

In terms of learning the kinds of material required in school, there is no question but that distributed learning is superior to massed learning. This does not necessarily mean that you have to study every subject every day. It does mean that you will learn more and remember it better if you space your learning periods. Class notes, however, should be reviewed on a daily basis, and as soon after class as possible.

How long or short should your study periods be? No one can tell you exactly, but they should be long enough to overcome warm-up periods and short enough to avoid fatigue. In most cases a warm-up period is necessary during which the student gets set to learn. During this time the student is orienting himself toward what he has covered and what he still has left to do. It may only take a few minutes, but if you only plan to study for 15 or so minutes, most of your time will be spent in warming up. For most students, study periods of between one-half and one hour are ideal.

You should remember that distributed practice does not involve more work or time than massed practice. You will spend the same amount of time studying under either system, but the payoff will be much greater when you space out your study. Also, it should be pointed out that cramming just before a test, when no study has preceded it, is different from an intensive review of the material the night before the test, when you have previously learned the material. Such a review, following distributed practice, yields better results than distributed practice with no review. Both of these methods, in turn, are superior to massed practice or cramming.

How to Take a Test

The best word of advice in taking tests is "Be prepared." If you have read your book as was suggested earlier, and spaced out your learning periods, and taken adequate notes which you reviewed, taking the test should be no problem. There are a few other things that you should do too. Find out as early as possible when tests are to be given and what they will cover, as well as what type of test they will be. By knowing when tests will occur and what will be covered, you will be able to judge how much time you will have to spend on the material and how it should be spaced. By finding out whether the test will be essay or objective (true-false or multiple choice) you can adjust how you study accordingly. The main difference in taking essay and objective tests is that you have to organize your answers on an essay test. Thus when you study for an essay test, you should try to recall in outline form what you know.

In the final review for a test you should go over your notes and the textbook, but only to see if you can remember the main ideas and important details. You should not try to reread the entire material assigned for the test, but only those parts you have trouble remembering. In this connection, it is sometimes helpful to look at section titles and try to remember what is discussed in that section. Some students also find it helpful to sit down with a friend also taking the class and ask each other questions from the class notes or book. This is helpful only if both of you have already learned the material and if you are prepared to be serious and not fool around.

When you get into the examination room, do not choke up. Take time to read over the instructions and the entire test before you begin to write. If it is an essay test, take a few minutes to plan your answers before writing. Try to think of how the answer should be organized so that it makes sense. Sometimes it helps to begin by answering those questions to which you are positive you know the answers. Do not get bogged down on a question you find difficult and spend too much time struggling. On the other hand, try to answer every question. Even if you are not sure, write something. This is also good advice when taking objective tests. Do not fail to answer any questions, and if you do not know the answer, guess. Sometimes teachers will take off points for guessing; in this case, answer only those questions you are sure of. In most tests, however, guessing is not penalized; but you definitely are penalized if you leave the question unanswered.

Some final words of advice: Watch your time. If the examination lasts one hour, and you have four essay questions to answer, you should spend 15 minutes on each. Before you begin writing you should roughly calculate how much time you have for each question. Do not wind up short at the end of the exam with several questions unanswered. That will cost you for sure. Also, when you write try to be as legible as possible and watch your spelling. Don't be shot down by the *halo effect;* poor handwriting and spelling influence a teacher's judgment of your work whether they realize it or not. This halo effect often causes a teacher to underrate what you have said.

Some Other Tips for Good Students

We have seen that some students do not study at all, and they usually make poor grades. Others spend a great deal of time at the books and also make poor grades. Still others spend a relatively small amount of time studying and wind up with excellent grades. It is not necessarily true that these students are more intelligent than the others, and in fact we know that this is usually not the case. Rather, such students have generally learned how to get the most out of the study time they have available. In addition to doing the things already mentioned, these students schedule their time; they do not dribble it away. By making out a time schedule for each day, you are able to organize your time so that you get the maximum out of each hour. You do not spend more time studying than you should, and you have more time left for activities other than study.

Good students also generally study in the same place or places each day. The ideal place for study is one that is quiet, well lighted, and uncluttered. Teen-agers often kid themselves into thinking that they can study while listening to the hi-fi. Psychologists know that loud music and serious study do not mix. If you want to study and listen at the same time, you are either going to learn less or have to spend more time at the books than you would otherwise.

WHAT HAPPENS WHEN WE FORGET?

Have you ever played the old game "telephone"? A group of people sit in a circle and one person whispers a story to the person seated next to him. That person then is supposed to whisper the exact story to the next person, and so on around the room. The last person then recites aloud the story exactly as he heard it. Often the story reported by the last person is hilariously different from the story that began with the first person. Somehow as the story passed from one person to the next, it changed in context, and many of the details disappeared.

What happens in this game illustrates some important things about human memory. When we forget, it is not only the amount of information that decreases, there tend to be changes in the substance or meaning of the information as well. Furthermore, we know that forgetting is most rapid in the period immediately after learning and much less rapid thereafter.

Ebbinghaus, the German psychologist we discussed earlier, was the first to construct a curve representing the course of forgetting. As shown in Figure 6–4, the amount we can remember drops very rapidly at first. One day after learning something, we have forgotten much of it. Two days after learning we have forgotten still more, but not as much as we forgot the previous day. You will note that after the second day, however, much less forgetting occurs.

Several factors or variables affect the shape of forgetting curves. How rapidly the curve drops is determined in part by the way we measure forgetting. If we measure it in terms of how much we can recognize, there is a relatively slight drop over time. If we measure it in terms of recall, however, the drop is much greater. In other words, if we are given a test such as true-false, or multiple choice in which we only have to recognize or pick out the correct answer, we do much better than if we have to recall answers from

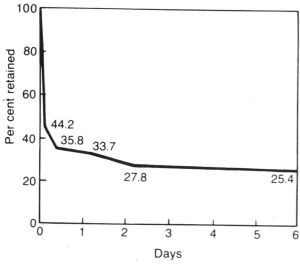

Fig. 6–4. Ebbinghaus' Curve of Forgetting This forgetting curve was constructed using the saving method and is based on the learning of nonsense syllables.

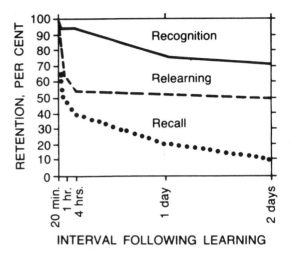

Fig. 6–5. Retention curves as a function of method of measurement.

scratch, as on an essay test. Furthermore, if forgetting is measured in terms of how long it takes us to relearn something, the drop is less than if measured through recall, but more than if measured by recognition. Three such curves are shown in Figure 6–5.

How we measure forgetting is not the only thing that affects the shape of forgetting curves. Such things as the meaningfulness of the material, the methods of learning, and other factors also influence forgetting. Ebbinghaus's curve, shown in Figure 6–4, is based on the number of nonsense syllables he could remember over a period of six days. He learned a list of

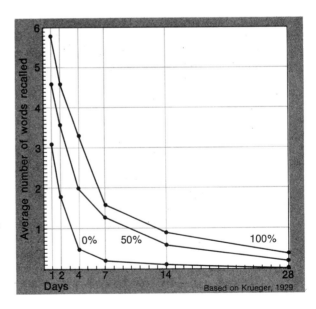

Fig. 6–6. Overlearning Effect Subjects who had already memorized a group of words were divided into groups which either practiced the words again for the same amount of time it had taken them to learn the words originally (100%), practiced the words for half the time it took to learn them originally (50%), or did not practice at all (0%). The 100% group recalled about twice as many words on each of six later tests, though by the 28th day, recall was very low for all groups.

such syllables and then on successive days relearned the list. You will note that in the first few hours after learning he had forgotten almost 60 per cent of what he had learned. Forgetting was much less rapid after that.

Is it true that we always forget 60 per cent of what we learn within a few hours of learning it? The answer is no. Although we do forget more in the period right after learning and less as time goes on, it is not true that we always forget more than half of what we learned in the first few hours after learning. If we plotted a curve for the amount retained after learning a list of meaningful words, the drop would be much less great in the first few hours, although the shape of the curve would generally be the same. Even in learning nonsense syllables, however, different methods can be used so that the amount of forgetting is not so great. One of those methods studied by Ebbinghaus is called overlearning.

What Is Overlearning?

When we learn something beyond the point of mere mastery, this is called *overlearning*. For example, suppose it takes five repetitions to commit a particular list of words to memory. Instead of repeating the list five times, what would happen if we repeat it ten or twenty times? Ebbinghaus discovered that overlearning significantly improves memory. In other words, the curve shown in Fig. 6–6 would not drop nearly as much initially. The greater the overlearning, the greater the amount retained. The lesson for the student is to improve memory by overlearning. When you have reached the point where you can remember the material, spend some additional time studying it. You will forget much less than if you only learn the material to the point of mere mastery.

Mnemonic Devices

So-called memory experts use a number of tricks or gimmicks to help them remember. One such expert appearing on a television show had each member of the audience (about 100 people) stand up and introduce themselves at the beginning of the show. At the end of the show he had each person in the audience stand up, and he called out the person's name. How could he remember the names of 100 people when he heard them only once? It took practice to develop the feat, but he also used a mnemonic system. As each person stood up he tried to note to himself something unusual about that person. "Mr. Brown has a big nose"; "Mrs. Smith is wearing a funny hat"; and so on. Instead of just trying to remember the name, he also tried to remember something odd or unusual about the person.

We all use mnemonic devices even though we may not have heard them called that. Almost everyone knows the sentence that begins "Thirty days hath September ... " If we can remember that verse, we can easily remember the months that have only thirty days. And this is easier than trying to memorize the names of the months with thirty days and those with thirty-one (or 28). Medical students remember a sentence that goes "On Old Olympus Towering Top, A Finn And German Brewed Some Hops." This helps them remember the names of the twelve cranial nerves. The name of each nerve is associated with the first letter in each word—On=olfactory, and so on.

When we have to memorize, mnemonic devices can be very helpful. There is nothing at all wrong with using such devices. But they cannot be used to remember very complicated material, and they should not be used to remember material that you do not first understand.

Theories of Forgetting

Because we do not know exactly what happens in the brain when we learn, we cannot say exactly how forgetting occurs. Several theories of forgetting have been developed. One of these, called the *theory of disuse*, holds that we forget when we do not use particular skills or when we do not recall certain memories periodically. The basic idea is that when we learn something, connections are formed between cells in the brain. When we forget, these connections between cells gradually fade away much as the contrail made by a jet in the sky fades away.

One major problem with this theory is that there sometimes is an increase in the amount we can remember shortly after learning. The forgetting curve does not always drop in the period after learning. It may go up and then down. Another problem with the theory is that time is considered to be the major factor causing forgetting. But, as one psychologist has noted, time itself causes nothing to occur. An iron bar left out in the rain rusts through time. But does the bar rust because of time? No, time simply provides an opportunity for other things to happen.

A better theory holds that we forget mainly because the learning of new material interferes with the recall of the old. Thus this is known as the *interference theory,* and it is based upon what we know about *retroactive inhibition.* When we study Spanish and then study French, what effect will the study of French have on our ability to recall the Spanish? We know that we will not remember as much Spanish as we would have had we followed the study of Spanish with the study of math or some less similar subject. The

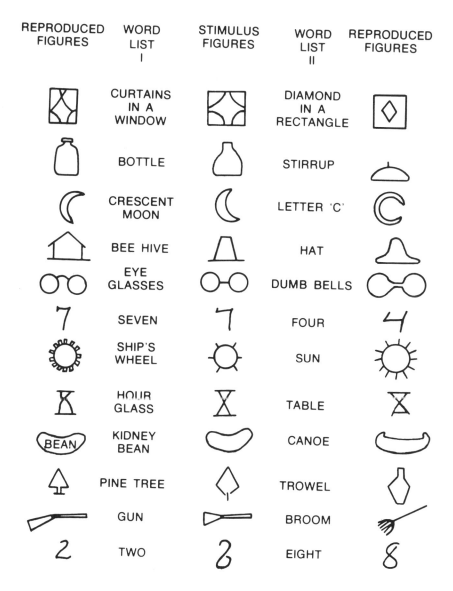

REPRODUCED FIGURES	WORD LIST I	STIMULUS FIGURES	WORD LIST II	REPRODUCED FIGURES
	CURTAINS IN A WINDOW		DIAMOND IN A RECTANGLE	
	BOTTLE		STIRRUP	
	CRESCENT MOON		LETTER 'C'	
	BEE HIVE		HAT	
	EYE GLASSES		DUMB BELLS	
	SEVEN		FOUR	
	SHIP'S WHEEL		SUN	
	HOUR GLASS		TABLE	
	KIDNEY BEAN		CANOE	
	PINE TREE		TROWEL	
	GUN		BROOM	
	TWO		EIGHT	

Fig. 6–7 How memory of shapes is affected by what they are called. One group of subjects was shown the figures in the middle column, together with the words shown on the left of the figures. Reproductions of the figures from memory by members of this group are shown on the left. Another group saw the same figures but with the words shown on the right. Note the differences in their reproduction of the figures, shown on the right, as compared with those of the other group.

new learning interferes with the recall of the old, in other words, and this is called retroactive inhibition.

Other evidence that supports the interference theory of forgetting comes from studies of how much we forget while sleeping as compared with how much we forget while awake. In general, we know that much less forgetting occurs while we sleep. To forget the least, in other words, we should study just before going to sleep.

While the interference theory does a better job of explaining why we forget than the theory of disuse, it is not completely satisfactory. It does not account for the small amount of forgetting that occurs when we sleep, nor does it explain why changes sometimes occur in what we recall. Two other theories address themselves to these points.

The *dynamic* or *motivational theory of forgetting* emphasizes the role of anxiety or guilt, among other things. We forget unpleasant things more quickly than pleasant things because of the discomfort or anxiety caused by the unpleasant memories. This theory holds, too, that we tend to remember those things that are of motivational significance to us. Cattle ranchers can often remember, in great detail, transactions involving cattle that have taken place years before. Supposedly this is because they are more highly motivated to remember these facts rather than others.

The final theory of forgetting attempts to account for changes in the content of what we remember rather than simply the amount remembered. This is called the *Gestalt theory,* and it is mainly concerned with memory for forms or shapes. An illustration of this theory is seen in the experiment described in Fig. 6–7. In that study we can see that language clearly has an effect on the way we remember shapes and forms.

To summarize these four theories, we can say that all but the theory of disuse seem to have some merit. Interference or retroactive inhibition clearly affects retention, and we also know that motivation also plays an important role in determining what we remember. In addition, the Gestalt theory is supported by scientific evidence that accounts for certain changes or alterations in memory.

The main reason no theory of forgetting is supported by all the facts seems to be that we do not know what happens in the brain when we learn and when we forget. Until we have more knowledge along these lines, no theory that is completely satisfactory will be developed.

Chapter Summary

1. Three major classes or categories of variables affect human learning. The first of these pertains to the learner himself. The second pertains to the task or material to be learned. The third category pertains to the methods of learning.

2. Regardless of what is to be learned, the person doing the learning is very important. One of the factors as far as the individual is concerned is his or her intelligence. But intelligence is not the only factor involved in learning, nor is it, in many cases, the most important factor. For the typical student such things as motivation to learn, attitudes, and study habits are even more important.

3. Intelligence is not regarded by psychologists as an innate, biological, God-given ability to solve problems. Rather, intelligence reflects the person's intellectual capabilities at any given time. Such capabilities reflect both the individual's biological potential and his experiences or training since birth.

4. The I.Q. or intelligence quotient is a score that is calculated by comparing how well one person does on an intelligence test with others of the same age who have also taken the same test. On most tests the average I.Q. is 100. Scores below that number mean that the individual has done less well than most others his age, while scores above 100 mean he or she has done better.

5. Some psychologists believe that intelligence is an overall or global ability to think rationally and deal effectively with one's environment. Others believe that in addition to a general ability, there are also special abilities that are important in certain kinds of mental activities.

6. We know that there is not a perfect relationship between grades in school and intelligence. Less intelligent people often make better grades than those who are more intelligent. While this does not mean that intelligence is unimportant, it does mean that study habits and other factors are frequently of equal or even greater importance.

7. Motivation to learn is especially important in the classroom. Furthermore, learning that stems from the satisfaction we get in that learning (intrinsic incentives) tends to be superior to learning that results from external or extrinsic incentives such as grades or fear of failure.

8. Some people give up when they fail or do poorly. The important thing to realize is that everyone experiences failure from time to time. The one rule to follow when one fails or does less well than expected is *take action.* Find out what went wrong and attempt to correct it.

9. How easily we learn is determined not only by our characteristics as learners, but also by the material to be learned. We know that meaningful material is more easily learned than nonmeaningful material. We also know that ease of learning is affected by the length of the material and by the position of items in a list of items to be learned.

10. Even more important in many cases than characteristics of the learner and the material to be learned, are the methods of learning used. Good students are active learners. They attempt to commit the material to memory through recitation, self-testing, or outlining. Psychological studies have shown that only about one-fourth of one's study time should be spent reading. Three-fourths should be spent in recitation, that is, in trying to remember what one has read.

11. In class as in reading a book, one should not try to remember everything. The good student attempts to pick out the main points and to remember these in his or her own words. Notes should be kept in an organized notebook and reviewed as soon as possible after class.

12. Learning should be distributed over time. *Massed learning* means that all the time available for learning involves one interval. In *distributed learning,* the student doesn't study longer than under massed learning, but his study time is distributed over a number of shorter periods.

13. Most of what we forget slips away from us in the first few hours after learning. We forget less and less as time goes on. Memory can be improved, however, if we use overlearning. Overlearning means that we learn beyond the point of simple mastery. Once we have learned something we go over it again and again. Each time we do this we are insuring that forgetting will take less of a toll of what we have learned.

14. We seem to forget mainly because new learning interferes with our recall of the old. This is called *retroactive inhibition.* Motivational factors are also known to affect forgetting. We tend to forget unpleasant experiences more quickly than pleasant ones. Finally, there are changes in the content of what we remember. Thus, forgetting involves more than simply changes in the amount we can recall.

Important Terms
from This Chapter

intelligence	active learning	mnemonic devices
intelligence quotient	passive learning	theory of disuse
intrinsic incentives	massed learning	interference theory
extrinsic incentives	distributed learning	retroactive inhibition
Ebbinghaus	halo effect	dynamic theory
serial position effect	overlearning	Gestalt theory

Additional Readings
to Help You Learn More

Blaine, G. and McArthur, C. *Emotional Problems of the Student.* New York: Appleton-Century-Crofts, Inc., 1961. Chapter 5, "Problems Connected with Study," deals with some of the emotional problems students frequently experience in connection with their studies. Chapter 19, "Student Apathy," discusses a problem that almost every student experiences at one time or other.

Longstreth, L. *Psychological Development of the Child,* 2nd Edition. New York: The Ronald Press Company, 1974. Chapter 12, "Adjustment to School," discusses such things as peer effects on attitudes toward teachers, home effects on school adjustment, and the problem of grading.

Morgan, C. and Deese, J. *How to Study.* New York: McGraw Hill Book Company, 1957. This book, although fairly old now, is still an extremely important and valuable paperback that students will find particularly useful in improving their study habits.

Munn, N., Fernald, L. and Fernald, P. *Introduction to Psychology,* 3rd Edition. Boston: Houghton-Mifflin Company, 1972. Chapter 9, "Learning Efficiently," is an excellent discussion of study techniques and habits, transfer of training and the effects of reward and punishment in learning.

Mussen, P. and Rosenzweig, M. *Psychology: An Introduction.* Lexington, Mass.: D. C. Heath Company, 1973. Chapter 15, "Human Intelligence and Its Measurement," is a detailed discussion of the nature of intelligence and how intelligence is tested by psychologists.

Part IV.

MOTIVES, FEELINGS AND HUMAN BEHAVIOR

chapter 7

Motivation: What Makes Johnny Run?

When we try to explain or understand human behavior, we are often faced with the problem of finding motives. Why did the used car salesman offer us such a good deal on that car? Why can't we get along with our brothers and sisters? Why won't parents let us hang around with a particular crowd? Why does that particular teacher seem to dislike us? When we understand the motives behind behavior we are often in a much better position to understand the behavior itself.

Almost all human behavior is motivated. And one's motives become more numerous and complex as one grows older. Infants and very young children are motivated only by their basic biological needs. From time to time, every human infant must eat, sleep, and drink. But even these motives change as we grow up. We learn to like certain kinds of food, prepared in certain ways, and eaten at certain times. We learn to dress in clothing approved of by those important to us. Thus it is not simply eating that becomes important, but what we eat. It is not simply a matter of keeping warm in the winter and cool in the summer, but wearing attractive clothes that counts.

Not only do motives relating to our biological needs change as we grow older, but we learn new motives as well. One teen-ager may be motivated to work long hours after school so that he can buy a car. Another may be motivated to earn high grades so that he or she will be able to attend college. Still another may move heaven and earth so that he or she will be accepted into a particular high school sorority or fraternity. Regardless of whether behavior is directed toward food, membership in a social group, buying a car, or earning high grades, however, these are all examples of motivated behavior. When we use the term *motive*, then, we are referring to the various kinds of goal-directed behavior that all humans exhibit.

WHAT ARE MOTIVES?

Motives are internal conditions that make us active and that lead us to seek certain goals. Some motives, such as hunger, thirst, and sex, have their origins in the biological functioning of the body. Thus, in part they are inborn or innate. Other motives have no biological basis whatsoever; they are learned. Regardless of the origin of a motive, however, all motives lead to activity which is directed toward certain goals that have become related to the motive through learning.

Motivated behavior has three characteristics. *First,* it tends to occur

DRIVE

INSTRUMENTAL RESPONSE

GOAL

DRIVE REDUCTION

Fig. 7–1. Motivated behavior is cyclical. First a motive or drive is aroused. Then behavior occurs which is intended to satisfy that motive. Finally when the goal is reached, the motive is reduced or satisfied.

in cycles. A motive is aroused from body needs such as the need to drink or eat, or from psychological needs such as the need for companionship. A sequence of behavior then occurs in which the person seeks a means of satisfying that need. Finally, when the goal is reached, the motive is reduced or satisfied. *Second*, motives make human behavior selective. In other words, when we are hungry, our behavior becomes increasingly oriented in the direction of securing food rather than some other irrelevant goal. *Third*, motivated behavior is active and persistent behavior. As a motive becomes stronger, we tend to become more active and more persistent in our efforts to reach a particular goal.

Where Do Motives Come From?

There are two main classes or categories of human motives. Some, as we have seen, have their basis in the biological requirements of the body, and they are inborn or present at birth. These are the *biological motives*. Others are learned in the course of being socialized in a given culture, or they are acquired later in the social groups to which we belong. These are the *social motives*. All motives affect behavior in the same way regardless of their origin; they all lead to goal-directed behavior.

The biological motives are those that reflect bodily needs. Such needs are unlearned, and they are found in all human beings. Among them are hunger, thirst, sex, sleep, elimination, respiration, avoidance of pain, and avoidance of extremes of heat and cold. Psychologists have been mainly

Fig. 7–2. The hunger motive is inborn. But what we eat, and when, and where, is learned. Thus all motives, even those that stem from bodily needs are influenced by learning.

158

interested in two things concerning such motives: (1) what is their biological basis and (2) how does learning affect the way in which they are satisfied? When we are hungry, is this because of the contractions of the empty stomach or because of changes that take place in the blood? How do we learn to prefer some foods rather than others? Is it natural to eat three meals a day rather than two or four?

For the high school student it is not so important to know what psychologists have discovered about the biological bases of such motives. It is more important to be aware that while such motives exist in every human being, many of them are satisfied in very different ways; it is this fact that differentiates the biological motives of humans from those of animals. Although, man, like other animals, must eat to live, learning determines the kind of behavior we exhibit when hungry. We want certain food, prepared in certain ways, and we prefer to eat with certain people, although these factors have little or no relationship to satisfying the hunger motive. The same thing may be said of most other biological motives. The human sex drive, for example, involves more than simply seeking out a member of the opposite sex. If this were not the case, almost any member of the opposite sex would serve to satisfy human sexual desires. But humans go through a complicated courtship, often suffering a great deal of anguish, before selecting a suitable mate. We look for a person who comes up to the expectations of our family and friends. We want someone who has about the same educational background as ourselves, someone who likes the same things, and someone of an appropriate age. In short, selecting a mate in human society for satisfaction of our sexual needs alone is not the usual case.

The Puzzle of Curiosity

Is curiosity a motive? Do animals learn to be curious? Is man the most curious of all animals? These are questions that have been studied by psychologists in a variety of experimental situations.

To prove that curiosity is a motive in the same sense that hunger and thirst are motives, three things must be demonstrated. *First*, it must be shown that animals will work for long periods of time with only the satisfaction of curiosity as a reward. *Second*, the satisfaction of curiosity must produce learning just as food causes the hungry animal to learn responses leading to food rewards. *Third*, we must be sure that no other motives than curiosity produce this behavior.

One psychologist built a box with two small windows on one side in order to study curiosity in monkeys. The two windows were covered with

Fig. 7–3. The monkey in this experiment gets no reward for solving the puzzle other than satisfying his curiosity.

small hinged doors so that they could be pushed open from the inside. One of the doors was painted yellow and the other blue, but the yellow door was always locked. By pushing open the blue door, the monkey could look out of the box for 30 seconds. After 30 seconds, the door was closed, and the monkey had to push on it again in order to look out.

In the first experiment, monkeys pushed at the blue door for 20 days. In another experiment they pushed at the correct door for some 57 days. In another study, the psychologists investigated the kinds of things to which monkeys might be attracted. Sometimes when the monkey pushed at the blue door it got to watch another monkey. In other cases it could look at a bowl of fruit or a toy electric train running around on a small track. In still other cases, opening the door afforded only a look at an empty room.

In terms of the number of times the monkey pushed open the correct door it was discovered that the strongest reward was the sight of another monkey. The electric train ran a close second, with food next, and the empty room last.

These experiments show that monkeys have a strong curiosity motive. Such motivation is apparent in very young monkeys and in other higher animals as well. It is apparently inborn, and some psychologists feel that the strong curiosity motive in higher animals is responsible for the extensive early learning that contributes to their success as a species.

Man, as we might expect, also has a strong curiosity motive which is apparently inborn. One psychologist studied how human infants react to patterns of various complexity such as shown in Fig. 7–4. He discovered that they most frequently turn their eyes to the most complex of these patterns. Curiosity is not limited to infants and small children; it is apparently a strong motive in adults as well. All we have to do is think of the amount of time humans spend watching each other. In a contest with a monkey, there is no doubt about the outcome. For higher animals, including man, it is probably incorrect to say that curiosity killed the cat!—curiosity is probably the main thing that kept the cat alive.

Fig. 7–4. Infants between 3-9 months of age were shown the diagram above. Psychologists found that they looked first at the more complex figures on the lower right. Why do you think they did this?

HOW STRONG ARE THE VARIOUS MOTIVES?

It is sometimes said that survival is the strongest human motive. Some argue that man has only a thin veneer of civilization and that this is easily stripped away to reveal his basic animal nature. The evidence offered to support this contention frequently appears convincing. One has only to think of the survivors of an airplane crash that became stranded in deep snow in the Andes Mountains during the winter of 1972. That group of survivors resorted to cannibalism in order to exist when their food supplies were exhausted. In another incident often used as evidence that survival is basic, over 400 people were either burned or trampled to death in a nightclub fire in Boston in the 1940s. The panic occurred when hundreds of people stampeded to a small number of exits in order to escape the rapidly spreading fire.

But if survival is really the fundamental human motive, how do we explain such behavior as that of the Catholic priest in a German concentration camp who voluntarily took the place of another man who was to be sent to the gas chamber? How do we explain the behavior of the soldier who threw himself on a hand grenade in order to save the lives of his buddies? How do we account for the mother who lost her life when she rushed back into a burning house to rescue one of her children? Are these only exceptions to the general rule, or is there no general rule at all?

These questions have puzzled psychologists for a long time and have led to the development of a number of theories about human motivation. One theory, held by the psychologist Maslow, is that there is a hierarchy of needs. According to this theory, basic needs or motives must be satisfied before the next higher order of needs become important to the individual. Thus, hunger and thirst must be satisfied before such safety needs as storing food for the future begin to affect behavior. Safety needs in turn must be satisfied before the individual becomes motivated to affiliate with others in groups, and so on. When all other motives have been satisfied, according to this theory, the individual becomes concerned about self-actualization. *Self-actualization* refers to the achievement of one's potential. If a person is musically talented, for example, he becomes self-actualized through achievement in the field of music.

While there is some evidence that substantiates Maslow's theory, there is also evidence that tends to contradict it. Learned motives—those toward the top of the hierarchy—in some cases are more important in determining behavior even though fundamental motives are unsatisfied. We cannot say then, that starving people will do anything in order to secure food.

By the same token, we cannot say that survival is the most fundamental human motive.

SOME EXAMPLES OF HUMAN MOTIVES

In thinking about motives we can see that some, such as hunger and thirst, occur in all human beings regardless of the culture in which they live. Others, such as sex, are seen in all cultures, but not necessarily in all individuals. Still others, such as aggressiveness and the desire to acquire possessions, are seen in some cultures but not in all. Finally, there are some motives that are highly personal in nature—they occur only in a very small number of individuals.

Aggression

Warfare has been so consistent in human history that some people think it reflects a fundamental part of human nature. There are, however, some human groups in which warfare is unknown. On the other hand there are human groups that almost continually engage in warfare. Is aggression the main motive responsible for war? The answer appears to be no. Among

Fig. 7–5. How is aggression learned? We know that the social groups with which we affiliate determine how aggressive behavior is manifested. These young men in Thailand have learned to fight with their feet.

American Indians we know that wars were generally conducted for the purpose of acquiring horses, while certain African tribes often engaged in war to acquire slaves. Even in so-called civilized wars, the main motives for fighting do not usually include aggression. In World War II, for example, a study of attitudes toward the enemy was conducted by the United States Army. It was discovered that hatred of the enemy actually was less the closer the individual soldier was to the front lines. Many different motives, then, are responsible for wars. Aggression is not seen in all human groups, and even in those groups where aggressive motives are common, such motives do not appear to be the primary causes of war.

How is aggression learned? Psychologists know that the social groups with which we affiliate are mainly responsible for aggression. All human groups have rules to limit the kinds and direction of aggression that may be expressed. Such rules vary from society to society, as well as among family groups within any particular society. Thus we know that, to understand aggressive behavior, we must look at the culture in which the individual was raised and particularly at the social groups with which he is and has been affiliated.

The Need to Be with Others

We have seen that almost all human beings live in groups. The extent of association with others, however, varies greatly from culture to culture and within the same individual at different times in his or her life. In some cultures, people live in small family groups almost totally isolated from others. In other cultures, the individual is affiliated with much larger numbers of persons in groups. Minimal family grouping, however, does occur in all cultures, and experimental studies by psychologists suggest that the need to be with others (*affiliation*) is the result of early infantile and childhood experiences. Since the human infant is absolutely dependent upon others for a long period of time, satisfaction of both biological and social motives comes to be related to the presence of other human beings.

The need to be with others varies from time to time, depending upon events in the environment. When human beings are faced with some kind of external threat, there is an increased desire to be with other people. And we have seen that particularly in adolescence there is an increased need to associate with others. The old saying "Misery loves company" seems to be appropriate here. We might also extend it by saying that the more miserable one feels, the greater is the need to be with others facing the same problems. This is not always the case, of course, but adolescents who particularly feel that no one understands them are more likely to seek out the company of others with similar feelings.

The Need to Acquire

Ours is a society in which the acquiring of material possessions is an important motive for most people. "Keeping up with the Joneses" means that if our neighbor buys a new car, we have to buy a new car. Status and self-esteem often seem to depend on how many possessions we can call our own. But just as aggression and the need to be with others vary from culture to culture, so also does the need to acquire possessions. In some cultures there is almost no private ownership of property, while in others almost every blade of grass has its individual owner. Among members of one Indian tribe on the west coast of Canada, acquiring possessions for their own sake is unimportant. Rather, it is how much one can acquire and then destroy that counts. Among people living in Western Samoa there is very little interest in acquiring possessions at all. In fact many Samoans feel perfectly justified in taking anything they find in someone else's house, particularly if that person is a relative. They know that person will not mind; in fact, he expects it.

Fig. 7–6. What is everybody trying to hit? Look closely and you will see that it's the "jackpot." Acquisitive motives in a society such as ours are extremely important, but in other societies they are much less important and even non-existent.

Many young people in our culture have rejected the strong emphasis on materialism and the so-called work ethic. Instead of doing things because they lead ultimately to a good job and material wealth, they emphasize doing one's own thing, period! In other words, instead of worrying about the future, the emphasis is on activities that broaden and deepen experience now. The guy or gal, for example, may decide to join the Peace Corps rather than attend college—at least for the present. This trend within American culture has been called the counter-culture, because it runs counter to the mainstream beliefs in work and sacrifice for the future. There are two aspects to this counter-culture. One emphasizes a desire to build a better society, while the other emphasizes a quest for self-indulgent pleasant experiences.

Money, Money, Money

Acquiring money is an important motive in American society for many people. But we have to ask if higher wages or other material benefits are as important in business and industrial situations as motives relating to security, the opportunity for advancement, being treated with respect, or doing a good job. Business executives and supervisors have discovered that industrial workers are not motivated mainly by their weekly paycheck or other material incentives. One psychologist found that among workers who changed jobs only one-third were unhappy with their former pay. Other reasons for changing jobs were given by two-thirds of those who quit. And when those who were satisfied with their jobs were asked why, only 15 per cent mentioned wages as the reason.

Those who believe that people work only to make money are incorrect. We know that people will not necessarily do more work in order to earn more money. It is not that money is unimportant in terms of motivating those who work, but rather that—when one's pay is within certain limits—other motives become more important.

WHAT ARE PERSONAL MOTIVES?

Personal motives are often variations of other motives widely seen within a particular culture. In our culture, as compared with many others in the world, the need for achievement is particularly strong. But the need to achieve varies from individual to individual in a highly personal way. One individual may strive for goals beyond his capabilities, while another person may do just the opposite. Success in high school for some is represented by an outstanding record of high grades. For others, however, success means simply getting by with the least effort.

What a person expects to accomplish is determined by the culture in which he lives, the groups with which he is affiliated, his personality characteristics, and by previous experience. Many different experiments have been conducted by psychologists to discover how these various factors affect the level of aspiration.

Success, Failure, and the Level of Aspiration

Suppose we give a person a number of addition problems to solve and tell him he has only five minutes to work. We then ask him to estimate how many problems he thinks he can solve correctly within that period. When he finishes we compare his estimate with his actual performance. Then we repeat the procedure several times. Did he think he could solve more than he actually did, or was his estimate too low? We know that some people consistently overestimate their future performance, while others consistently underestimate. Still other subjects quickly adjust their estimates of future performance so that they are in line with past performance. When this happens it illustrates that previous experience often affects one's level of aspiration. We know, for example, that failure in school often leads to a lowering of aspiration levels. Thus a high school student who hopes to study engineering in college may lower his aspirations after failing several math courses. However, we also know that failure does not inevitably cause the individual to lower his goals. Not all students who hope to study engineering abandon that hope after failing in math. Some persist and eventually succeed through greater efforts. Others persist and eventually fail. But we can see in this that level of aspiration is not determined solely by actual performance.

Groups have a great deal to do with determining the goals we set for ourselves. This was very nicely demonstrated by one psychologist who told college students that their scores on a simple test were either above or below high school, college, or graduate students' scores on the same test. When they were again given the chance to work at the test, those told that they were below high school students increased in performance most. Those who were told they had done better than graduate students decreased the most. Thus it is apparent that in setting our own level of aspiration, we often relate ourselves to various groups and adjust our performance accordingly.

How Personality Determines Our Goals

The goals we set for ourselves are determined not only by previous experience or group influences but by personality characteristics as well. As one famous psychologist has said, "Self-esteem equals success over pretensions." In other words, it is not simply how good a person thinks he is with regard to some quality, but how good he wants to be that counts.

In terms of setting personal goals or ambitions, we behave in ways that help us maintain our self-esteem at the highest possible level. In one study students were asked, "What business or profession do you realistically think you are most apt to go into?" It was discovered that while a student might ideally like to become a surgeon, corporate lawyer, or millionaire, he or she generally scaled down his goals to what he considered to be within the range of possible achievement. Thus each of us selects goals in line with how we assess ourselves. By being selective, we are able to achieve personal goals and thus maintain favorable opinions of ourselves.

WHAT CAUSES FRUSTRATION?

Frustration occurs when something interferes with or prevents the satisfaction of a motive. Sources of frustration may be either in the environment or within ourselves. Regardless of the source, however, anything that interferes with the satisfaction of a motive causes frustration and leads to feelings of tension and anxiety.

Environmental sources of frustration may be either physical or social. Physical sources of frustration may involve losing our car keys when we are planning to go on a date. They may involve injury to someone we love, pens that refuse to write, or noise when we are trying to study. Sometimes a lack of something can be frustrating; a lack of rain is often frustrating to the farmer.

Social sources of frustration exist for all of us almost from the time of birth. From the beginning, the infant is often fed on an arbitrary schedule, which means that at least part of the time the hunger motive is frustrated. *Sibling rivalry,* or rivalry between two children in the same family for the attention and affection of the parents, is another common social source of frustration in childhood. During adolescence parents often cause considerable frustration. We may want to hang around with particular people, but our parents object. We may want to go out on dates during the week, but our parents will not allow this.

Fig. 7–7a. Frustration can be caused by the environment as for example when that environment makes for continual poverty.

Fig. 7–7b. In other cases frustration may stem from being too small to accomplish what we want. This basketball player will make the team after he grows a little taller. Until then he will be frustrated.

Not all people are subject to the same sources of frustration. A black American may not be able to get a desired job because of discrimination. A person from a wealthy family may never know the frustration experienced by someone from a poor family. But for all of us, rich or poor, black or white, Christian or Jew, there are social sources of frustration with which we must learn to cope.

Frustration sometimes is also caused by things within us that prevent the satisfaction of certain motives. Physical handicaps may be extremely frustrating to the affected person. Often an unattractive appearance, low intelligence, or physical weakness can be sources of frustration. The boy who is still physically small in high school may be frustrated by his inability to make the school's athletic teams. The adolescent girl troubled with acne may find these skin blemishes very frustrating if they prevent her from getting dates.

Superior intelligence or outstanding ability in some field, such as athletics, lessens the probability of frustration when one is motivated to achieve status and acceptance by others. The reverse, of course, is also true. The lack of any ability that helps improve status and acceptance increases the probability of frustration. High abilities, of course, do not guarantee acceptance, nor does the lack of ability necessarily mean that the individual will not be accepted by others. We all know of some very intelligent people who are unable to establish satisfactory relationships with others, and we also know many average people who get along very well with others. Individual abilities simply constitute one set of characteristics that must be considered in connection with potential internal sources of frustration.

How Do We React to Frustration?

People vary greatly in their reactions to frustration. One person takes constructive steps to overcome an obstacle, while another simply daydreams about success. One individual becomes aggressive in the face of frustration, while another becomes apathetic. Some people seem to have very little

Fig. 7–8. Sometimes the reaction to frustration is so severe that mental illness results. The patient is suffering from schizophrenia.

ability to overcome even the smallest frustrations, while others appear to have an almost unlimited capacity for overcoming all obstacles.

The amount and length of frustration one can endure without falling apart or becoming mentally ill is referred to as *frustration tolerance.* What factors determine frustration tolerance? We know that such things as an unsatisfactory home life as a child and a history of mental or emotional disorders make it more difficult for the individual to withstand the pressure of frustration. Emotional immaturity, loss of emotional support through death of a parent, and even poor health conditions lower the individual's resistance to frustration.

Individuals not only differ in overall frustration tolerance, but there are differences within each of us from day to day as well. Some days we are able to overcome minor frustration with ease, while on other days we react to frustration with unusual annoyance and tension. In some girls the wide swing in hormonal balance during the menstrual cycle accounts in part for increased edginess before the beginning of menstruation.

The intensity with which we experience frustration is affected by many different things. Interference with the satisfaction of strong motives leads to greater frustration than is the case with weaker motives. If we can easily overcome the source of the frustration, or if we can find substitute goals, we generally experience less frustration. We also know that frustration sometimes is cumulative. Several frustrating events in a row lead to greater feelings of frustration than if only one event is involved. In addition, we know that an individual with a history of emotional instability is less likely to withstand the effects of frustration than one with a history of good mental health. Finally, the closer we are to completing a task or securing a goal, the greater is the frustration when we are prevented from doing so.

Reactions to frustration are not always aimed directly at removing the source of the frustration. They sometimes involve distortions of reality that are designed not to solve the problem but to protect us against reality. Such reactions are referred to as "defense mechanisms," and we will discuss these in the section on adjustment later in the book.

WHAT IS CONFLICT?

Conflict occurs when there are two or more motives present at the same time and the satisfaction of one interferes with or prevents the satisfaction of the other. A girl going to a dance has to choose between two boys who have asked her; a boy wants to try out for two sports but finds that they both take place at the same time. Conflicts may be minor and resolved easily, or they may be of great importance and resolved only with considerable difficulty and discomfort. Psychologists have classified conflicts into three categories: approach-approach, approach-avoidance, and avoidance-avoidance.

Approach-Approach Conflicts

When we are forced to choose between two attractive goals, we experience an *approach-approach* conflict. An example of this kind of conflict is choosing one of two desserts, or choosing between two attractive outfits to wear on a date. Such conflicts are generally resolved rather easily. We may hesitate before choosing apple pie or ice cream, but such hesitation is generally only momentary.

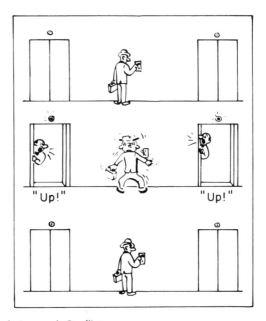

Fig. 7–9. Approach-Approach Conflict

As two goals become more alike in attractiveness, however, or the choice becomes more important, indecision increases and the length of the hesitation period increases as well. Furthermore, the discomfort or tension we experience increases. When the girl has to choose between two boys who have asked her out, each of whom are attractive to her and whom she likes equally well, the period of indecision is likely to be long; and she is likely to feel very uncomfortable until the choice is made. If she is much more attracted to one boy than the other, the choice can be made quickly and with little discomfort.

Avoidance-Avoidance Conflicts

Sometimes we find ourselves caught between the devil and the deep blue sea—in other words, we are forced to choose between two unattractive goals. We may have to take one of two unpleasant and difficult courses in order to graduate. Or we may be told to clean our room or else mow the yard. Unlike the approach-approach conflicts discussed previously, *avoidance-avoidance* conflicts generally result in longer hesitation and also a tendency to avoid making the choice if possible. The student faced with choosing between two difficult courses may think about dropping out of school. The one faced with cleaning his room or mowing the lawn may try to sneak out of the house.

Approach-Avoidance Conflicts

Another fairly common type of conflict we all face involves both attractive and unattractive goals at the same time. Such conflicts result in simultaneous attraction and repulsion. The girl may want to go to the dance but not with the boy who asked her. A child may be attracted by the water at the beach but afraid of being knocked down by the big waves.

When we feel attracted and repelled at the same time, this is called *ambivalence,* or an *approach-avoidance* conflict. Such feelings are not uncommon in all of us. We are taught that children should love and respect their parents. Religion teaches us the value of brotherly love, and we all know quotations such as "Love thy neighbor as thyself" and "Do unto others as you would have them do unto you." Unfortunately, human relationships are seldom either all love or all hate. Most of our relationships with other people involve ambivalent feelings. Parents can be extremely annoying at times even though we love them. They do not always deserve our love and respect, even as we do not always deserve theirs. Furthermore, in a competitive culture such as our own, hostile feelings toward those with whom we must compete are common.

Most of us are not severely troubled by such feelings. When parents annoy us, we can express our feelings without feeling guilty. When someone frustrates us, we can express our anger and hostility. Usually when such feelings are expressed or ventilated, they subside. For some people, however, the expression of hostility and anger is impossible. When we find a person with a severe inability to recognize and express such feelings, we often find an individual with an emotional disturbance or mental illness. In such cases the person is often faced with a severe approach-avoidance conflict.

Some psychologists believe that understanding how people react to conflict is of great importance in understanding mental illness. When conflict is severe and prolonged, they think, the resulting anxiety or tension causes the breakdown of behavior. In the section on adjustment later in the book, we will explain how this comes about.

CHAPTER SUMMARY

1. Motives are internal conditions that make us active and that lead us to seek certain goals. Some motives such as hunger, thirst, and sex, have their origins in the biological functioning of the body. Others are learned in the process of being socialized, or in the groups with which we affiliate; examples are aggression, acquisitiveness, and the need to be with others.

2. Motivated behavior has three characteristics. *First*, it tends to occur in cycles. *Second*, it is selectively oriented toward certain goals. *Third*, it is active and persistent.

3. There are two main classes or categories of motives. The biological motives are inborn or present at birth; they reflect bodily needs; and they are found in all human beings. The social motives are learned; they have no biological basis; and they may exist either in virtually every human being or in only a very small number of persons.

4. Even though the biological motives exist in every person, they are frequently satisfied in very different ways. For example, learning determines the kind of behavior we exhibit when hungry. We prefer certain kinds of food, prepared in certain ways, and we prefer to eat with certain people, although these factors have little or no relationship to satisfying the hunger motive. The same thing may be said of other biological motives, such as sex.

5. Curiosity is a strong motive in higher animals, including man. Animals can and do learn to make responses which lead to no other reward than satisfaction of curiosity. The curiosity motive is probably responsible for the extensive early learning that contributes to the success of many species.

6. Questions about the relative strengths of certain motives have led to the development of a number of theories of motivation. According to Maslow, basic needs or motives must be satisfied before the next higher order of needs becomes important to the individual. In certain cases, however, less basic motives are more important in determining behavior even though more fundamental motives are unsatisfied.

7. Aggression in the form of warfare is unknown in many human cultures, and even in those cultures where warfare occurs, motives other than aggression are usually involved. We know that aggression is often learned in the social groups with which the individual affiliates. It is not an unlearned motive.

8. The need to be with others is found in almost all humans, even though the extent of association with others varies from culture to culture. This need or motive is probably learned in early childhood as a result of the long period of absolute and complete dependency upon others for the satisfaction of needs.

9. The need to acquire possessions also varies widely from culture to culture. In some there is almost no ownership of private property at all, while in others virtually every blade of grass has its owner. We know that in work situations, motives other than the desire for money are of primary importance even in our own culture.

10. Personal motives are variations of other motives widely held in a culture. The need to achieve, for example, varies from person to person in a highly individual way. The goals we set for ourselves are determined by our culture, the groups to which we belong, our personality, and our previous experience.

11. Frustration occurs when something interferes with or prevents the satisfaction of a motive. Sources of frustration may be either in the environment or within ourselves. Our ability to withstand the effects of frustration is called *frustration tolerance.*

12. Conflict occurs when there are two or more motives present at the same time and the satisfaction of one interferes with or prevents the satisfaction of the other. Psychologists have classified conflicts into three categories: approach-approach, approach-avoidance, and avoidance-avoidance.

Important Terms
from This Chapter

motive	aggression	frustration tolerance
biological motive	affiliation	conflict
social motive	counter-culture	approach-approach
Maslow	personal motive	approach-avoidance
hierarchy	level of aspiration	avoidance-avoidance
self-actualization	frustration	ambivalence
	sibling rivalry	

Additional Readings
to Help You Learn More

Kagan, J. and Havemann, E. *Psychology: An Introduction,* 2nd Edition. New York: Harcourt, Brace, Jovanovich, 1972. Chapter 11, "Frustration, Conflict and Abnormal Behavior," is an excellent discussion of the nature of conflict and frustration.

McClelland, D. "N Achievement and Entrepreneurship: A Longitudinal Study." *Bobbs-Merrill Reprints,* P-670. Indianapolis: Bobbs-Merrill Company. This paper is a discussion of some of Dr. McClelland's extremely important ideas about the nature of achievement motivation.

Readings in Psychology Today, 2nd Edition. Del Mar, Calif.: CRM Books, 1972. "How to Quit Smoking" is a good discussion of some of the techniques that actually work in helping one to quit.

Schachter, S. "Some Extraordinary Facts about Obese Humans and Rats." *Bobbs-Merrill Reprints,* P-800. Indianapolis: Bobbs-Merrill Company. This paper deals with why some rats and certain human beings become fat.

Emotions: The Bitter and the Sweet

In our culture, adolescence is perhaps the roughest time of life as far as emotions are concerned. Feelings of inferiority are common: the adolescent is often oversensitive to criticism; he or she is easily embarrassed, moody, giggly, and worried. Why are the teens such a problem period? How do emotions affect the body? How do emotions develop? What can we do to better cope with emotional problems? These are all questions that have been studied by psychologists.

In this chapter we will examine the nature of emotions, how they help us, and how they hurt us. We will also take a brief look at normal emotional behavior and the role of emotions in abnormal behavior. Finally, we will talk about emotional problems in adolescence and how to handle them.

THE NATURE OF EMOTIONS

Emotions are similar to motives in that they often make us active and lead to goal directed behavior. When we are angry, we want to do something that will relieve the anger. We lash out at someone with verbal abuse; or if we cannot, we slam doors or yell at younger brothers or sisters. When we are afraid, we try to avoid the source of our fear. On a day we are scheduled to give an oral report in school, we may become "sick," or think of excuses to get out of it. Emotions differ from motives in that they do not stem from biological needs as do some motives. Also, emotions typically depend upon our awareness of the significance of a situation, and thus they involve thinking.

Emotions are reflected in facial expression and other kinds of bodily response as well as in internal or physiological changes. We smile or scowl, laugh or cry when we experience emotion. Our hearts beat more rapidly, the pupils of our eyes dilate, our palms may sweat, and we may feel butterflies in our stomachs. Furthermore, there are three dimensions along which emotions vary: These are tension-relaxation, pleasantness-unpleasantness, and attention-rejection. When we experience an emotion such as fear, for example, the feeling involved ranges from mild to such a degree of intensity that it dominates our behavior. When we are angry, we may be only slightly miffed or so mad that we lose control of ourselves. This is the dimension of tension-relaxation.

Emotions also vary in terms of whether they are pleasant (love) or unpleasant (anger). In addition, some emotions cause us to attend to something (fear), while others cause us to turn away (disgust). We know also that emotions make both behavior and experience more selective as they become more intense. The terrified person can think of nothing but his fear. He cannot eat, he has difficulty in sleeping, and he finds it difficult to carry on his normal daily routine. The old saying "love is blind" also very nicely illustrates how strong emotions make behavior and experience selective. When we love someone, we have great difficulty in seeing their faults. Often when we fall out of love we are amazed at the unpleasant things about the person that we did not notice before.

We also know that other people affect our emotions. T.V. comedies frequently are accompanied by canned laughter—a sound track of people laughing which is added to the film after it is completed. Producers do this because they know that people laugh more when they hear other people laughing. Joy, of course, is not the only emotion that is contagious. When other people are afraid, we also are often frightened. In fact we know that panic frequently spreads in situations that are unclear, and in which only a few people were frightened at first. President Roosevelt was aware of this in the Depression of the 1930s when he made the famous remark, "The only thing we have to fear is fear itself."

How Does the Body React in Emotion?

We all know that certain changes take place in the body when we experience emotion. The lover loses his appetite, trembles, and perspires when he sees the girl of his dreams, and he may become tongue-tied when

Fig. 8–1. Other people clearly affect our emotions. If the people around us are happy and excited, we tend to experience these same emotions. And if others are sad or depressed we also feel down in the dumps.

he is near her. The high school student called on to give an oral report in front of his or her class may feel queasy in the stomach, tense, and jumpy. The soldier going into combat for the first time often feels sick to his stomach; his heart pounds, his palms sweat, and his mouth is dry. These are feelings we have all experienced to a greater or lesser degree on many occasions.

When we experience a strong emotion, the body reacts in a number of ways: heart rate increases; breathing becomes more rapid; the mouth and throat become dry; muscles become tense and often tremble; the pupils of the eye enlarge; blood pressure goes up and the amount of blood in various parts of the body changes; the amount of sugar in the blood increases; digestion ceases; and we perspire. In addition to these changes, the adrenal glands secrete adrenalin which helps the blood clot more quickly, increases blood sugar, and elevates blood pressure.

What causes these changes in the body to occur? They are brought about by a part of the nervous system which is largely concerned with the control of involuntary functions of the body. This is the autonomic nervous system, and we will discuss it in greater detail in the next chapter. Here it is sufficient to note that most of the internal organs of the body are controlled or regulated by the autonomic nervous system. One part of this system, for example, speeds up the heart while another part slows it down. Under normal circumstances we cannot voluntarily control this nor any of the other bodily changes that occur in emotion.* This fact has made it possible to develop a machine that detects lies—the polygraph.

How the Polygraph Detects Truth and Lies

The *polygraph*, or lie detector, is simply a machine that measures various changes in the body when we experience emotion. Usually changes in heart rate, blood pressure, breathing, and perspiration are measured. These changes, you will recall, all occur involuntarily. For most people, when they tell a lie there are very slight changes that occur in heart rate and the

*We can learn to control such functions, however, through use of a new technique called "biofeedback."

Fig. 8–2. The polygraph (lie detector) detects truth from lies by measuring certain physiological changes that take place within the body as the person answers questions put to him by the examiner.

183

other functions just mentioned. When the embezzler is asked if he took a certain sum of money, his internal organs often give him away.

Can the lie detector be fooled? For most people, the answer is no. There are some individuals, however, who never develop a normal conscience. They are able to lie, with a straight face, so to speak. In other words, when they lie there are no changes in their internal organs. The polygraph record looks the same as one from a person telling the truth. For this reason, as well as others, results of a polygraph test are not admissable as evidence in court.

How Do Emotions Develop?

We are not born with all the emotions we experience as adults. Very young infants react to any form of sudden stimulation with aimless thrashing of the limbs and crying. Stimuli such as pain, being restrained, loud noises, or falling do not evoke clear-cut different emotions. It is not until the infant is about three months of age that we can see the emotions of delight and distress in addition to the generalized excitement seen earlier.

Between three and six months of age, distress becomes differentiated into anger, disgust, and fear. By the end of the first year of life, delight is differentiated into elation and affection. By eighteen months of age, jealousy and affection for children as well as adults can be seen. By two years of age, delight has been differentiated so that the child also expresses joy.

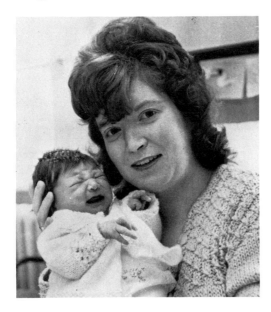

Fig. 8–3. Young infants tend to react to any form of sudden stimulation with generalized distress. It is not until much later that we can identify a number of clearly defined emotions such as joy, jealousy, and affection.

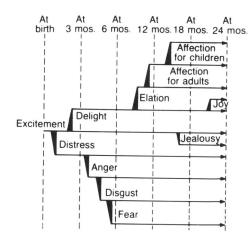

Fig. 8–4. *Differentiation of Emotions in Childhood*
This chart shows the average ages at which the appearance of various emotions occurs. Note the transition from simple excitement initially to a variety of specific emotions at a later age.

The development of emotional behavior is shown in Fig. 8–4. As in walking, you will note that there is a pattern of emotional development which is roughly the same in all children. Emotions such as laughing, crying, and smiling appear in all children at about the same age regardless of whether they have had the opportunity to see or hear these emotions in others. We know that even in deaf-blind children, emotional development is very similar to that in the child with normal vision and hearing. This strongly suggests that the differentiation of human emotions is largely determined by growth and maturation. Even facial expressions in emotion seem to be influenced very little by learning.

Learning does influence the expression of emotions in certain ways. How to cry is not learned, but when and where to cry are definitely influenced by learning. Men in our culture seldom cry, while women cry much more easily. In France, men cry much more easily than do men in the United States. By the same token, crying is observed in all very young children, but the situations that cause crying in older children are largely learned. In particular, strange places and persons produce the largest increase in the frequency of crying as the child grows older.

How Emotions Help Us

Emotions are both a boon and a curse to mankind. In some cases, strong emotions help us to survive. In other cases, strong emotions are involved in mental illness and even in some physical illnesses. Let's look first at the beneficial effects of emotions.

Fig. 8–5.   How do emergency situations affect emotions? Strong emotions help us use our maximum strength and remain active for long periods. They also lessen our sensitivity to pain. Here, although it may not look like it, several young men are rapidly trying to push a car out of the way of a fire.

When we face an emergency situation, the physiological changes that accompany emotion help us in three ways. *First,* we are able to use our maximum strength for short periods. *Second,* we are able to remain highly active over a longer period of time than is generally possible. *Third,* we are less sensitive to pain when we experience strong emotions such as fear or anger.

From time to time we read newspaper accounts of a person who carries a refrigerator or some other heavy object from his house during a fire, only to discover some time later that he can no longer even lift the object. Strong emotions such as fear or anger enable a person to use his maximum strength for short periods. When the emotion fades away, one's physical strength is also reduced.

Strong emotions also make it possible to engage in physical activity over longer periods of time without becoming tired. The person who is intensely afraid may be able to go long periods without sleep. He may be able to do heavy physical work without fatigue. The man who finds his home on fire may carry out half the furniture and then help the firemen to put out the blaze without any feeling of fatigue.

In addition to helping minimize fatigue, strong emotions also reduce pain. A person injured in an automobile accident may be completely unaware of the injury until some time later. Occasionally we even hear of people who have broken limbs or suffered some other serious injury without any awareness of pain at the time.

The football or basketball player also benefits from the physiological changes produced by emotion. Athletes often are so psyched up for big sports events that they engage in strenuous physical activity without feeling fatigue. Pain from injuries in athletic contests is often not felt until the event is over. In addition, the pain from bumps and bruises seems to be greater when the individual's team loses.

But while every coach tries to get his team up before a big event, he knows that there is a real danger in getting them too far up. The football team coming into the biggest game of the season may be so intensely anxious about winning that they cease to work together as a team. For a football team, fumbles and broken plays often reveal the intense emotions early in the game. As everyone settles down, plays begin to click and running backs seem to have an easier time hanging onto the ball.

What we are saying, then, is that there seems to be a relationship between the intensity of emotion and effectiveness of action. Strong emotions help us in dealing with emergency situations—stronger emotions may make effective action more difficult or even impossible. The football team often does a better job if members are somewhat tense about the game than if they are relaxed and overconfident. Some of the biggest upsets in sports have undoubtedly occurred because the favorite team took winning for granted.

HOW EMOTIONS HURT US

Many physicians believe that one out of every two patients they see is suffering from an illness related to mental or emotional problems. This does not necessarily mean that the complaints of such people are imaginary or all in their minds. It means that mental or emotional problems have in some way contributed to their illness.

In some cases, we know that emotional problems produce physical complaints that are completely imaginary. In other cases, these problems contribute to an illness that is physical in nature—they make it worse, in other words. In still other cases, emotional problems actually cause a genuine physical illness. These illnesses are called *psychosomatic reactions.*

How can emotional problems cause a genuine physical illness? To understand how this happens, we have to remember that very strong emotions produce great physiological changes in the body. The autonomic ner-

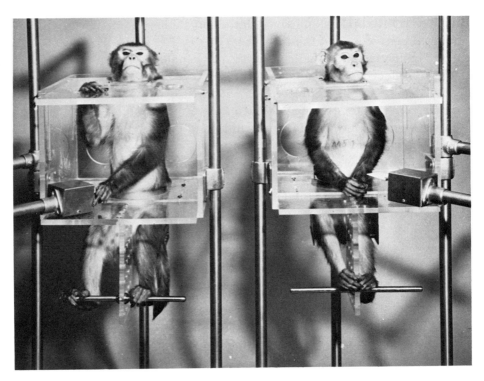

Fig. 8–6. Avoidance Behavior And Ulcers
In this experiment eight monkeys were divided into pairs and placed in the chairs shown above. They were then given shocks every 20 seconds for a total of 6 hours. The monkey on the left, however, could avoid the shock for both by pressing the lever at least once every 20 seconds. Both animals received the same number of shocks but only the one who could control them developed ulcers as a result of the stress.

vous system increases heart rate, blood pressure, and respiration among other things. In the well-adjusted person, strong emotions soon wear off, and the body returns to normal. In some people, however, strong emotions do not wear off and the body remains in an uptight condition. It is almost as if these people are continually angry or frightened. Like an engine that is run at full speed or wide open, something is bound to give sooner or later. And that is exactly what happens—the body, or part of it, breaks down.

Why is it that some people remain continually tense even when there seems to be nothing to account for this? Strong emotions in lower animals typically last only a short time. The cat frightened by a dog reacts intensely while the dog is around, but when the cat escapes or the dog leaves, the emotion disappears and the cat's body returns to normal. Human beings, however, not only react to things physically present with emotion, but also to symbols of these things that they carry in their minds. Thus a stimulus for fear or anger need not be present to create intense emotions. An idea or a memory may be just as effective as some concrete visible stimulus in producing emotion. A man who becomes angry at the office may continue to be angry when he arrives home that evening. He may continue to react as if the anger-producing stimulus were physically present, and this reaction may last for days or even months.

The fact that humans have the ability to symbolize events and react to these emotionally increases the potential for psychosomatic illnesses in humans as compared with other animals. This fact does not explain why some people develop these illnesses and others do not. To answer this question we have to look at some of these illnesses and the kinds of people who have them.

The Psychosomatic Reactions

Physical illnesses that have their origins in emotional disturbances affect many different parts of the body. There are skin reactions such as hives or acne, skeletal reactions such as backaches or cramps, respiratory reactions, high blood pressure, ulcers, and even constipation. We need not go into detail about all of these, but two—ulcers and high blood pressure—can help us understand how such illnesses develop. A very important point for the student to remember in connection with all of these disorders is that they are not necessarily psychosomatic in nature. Each and every one of them can be caused by an organic disturbance in the body. A kidney infection, for example, can cause high blood pressure. Respiratory disorders such as asthma can be caused by allergies. But when the physician can discover no possible organic basis for these illnesses, he may begin to look for an emotional cause.

What Are Ulcers?

Perhaps the most common type of psychosomatic reaction is the peptic ulcer. Sometimes known as "Wall Street stomach," ulcers are holes in the lining of the stomach or intestine. They are caused by an excessive secretion of gastric juices stimulated by emotional stress.

When we look at the typical ulcer patient, we get a good idea of the causes of such reactions. The ulcer patient is usually a male in his forties or fifties, hard-driving and independent. Frequently he is an executive with great responsibilities which require long, hard hours of work. But are ulcers

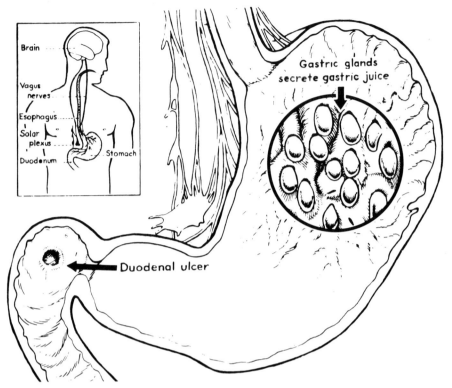

Fig. 8–7. Development of Ulcers
The ulcer is actually a hole or wound in the lining of the stomach or intestine. Excessive secretion of gastric juices stimulated by emotional strain is responsible in the large majority of such illnesses.

simply the result of hard work? From treating such patients, psychologists know they are not.

The man who develops ulcers, more often than not, is a person who does not recognize his strong emotional needs to be dependent upon others. To him the most important thing is self-reliance and independence, but underneath it all he is a person who desperately needs others. We know this is true because in treating such patients, psychologists usually find that once dependency needs are recognized and satisfied, the ulcer disappears.

What Causes High Blood Pressure?

Many patients who suffer from high blood pressure have great difficulty in expressing anger or hostility. For most of us, when something happens that makes us angry we are able to express it. We shout, stamp around, tell somebody off, or kick a chair. Thus expressed, the anger subsides. The person unable to express anger is like a volcano ready to erupt. But the eruption never occurs, and the body remains in a tense state. High blood pressure is often the result, and unless the person learns to express his anger, the condition does not disappear.

Why is it that certain emotions or feelings cause some people so much trouble? Why can't a person recognize that he or she has certain feelings and accept them? For answers to these questions we need to look more closely at the nature of emotional experience and at how people learn to express and control emotions. We will focus our attention particularly on common emotional problems that occur during adolescence.

EMOTIONAL PROBLEMS OF ADOLESCENCE

While very few adolescents are troubled with high blood pressure or ulcers, there are some lessons to be learned from such illnesses that help us to understand emotional problems in general. The *first* of these is that emotions or feelings are not always conscious. We are not always aware that we have certain strong feelings. *Second,* in the ulcer patient or person with high blood pressure, we can see that in order for the problem to be solved (or the illness cured) the person must not only come to understand himself and his feelings, he has to accept the fact that he has certain feelings.

Why is it that some emotions or feelings are unconscious? Freud, the physician who developed psychoanalysis, felt that feelings become unconscious because of anxiety—a feeling of apprehension, dread, or foreboding. We will discuss the unconscious mind in more detail in the chapters on adjustment. At this point it is sufficient to be aware of the fact that emotions may be unconscious and affect our behavior without our realizing it.

Two kinds of feelings cause people in our culture more problems than any others—those related to aggression and those related to sex. We have already seen that some people cannot express anger or hostility. They get mad, of course, as we all do. But they cannot show their anger. In many cases this is because they were severely punished for aggressive behavior as children. Earlier we noted that every society has rules for the expression of hostility. In some families, however, anger on the part of a child toward a parent or toward a brother or sister is punished by the withdrawal of love. The parent reacts to the child's anger with severe rejection. Each time the child becomes angry, then, it causes so much anxiety that he or she becomes unable to express this emotion.

Sexual feelings in some individuals also cause great anxiety. Often, like anger or aggression, sexual behavior is severely punished during childhood. Parents teach their children that the nice boy or girl simply does not do certain things. If sexual behavior is punished by rejection on the part of the parents, sexual feelings may result in severe anxiety and feelings of guilt.

Most adolescents do not have unconscious feelings of hostility, nor do they have severe anxiety concerning sexual feelings. Nevertheless, problems in handling hostility and sexual impulses are common during this period of one's life. For this reason we shall take a few minutes to look at these two problem areas.

How to Deal with Hostility

Most of us would change certain things about ourselves if we knew how to go about it. "I fly off the handle too easily," one person says. Another person says, "I get mad over things that aren't really important." Such comments, of course, indicate awareness of hostile feelings, and this is the first step in handling such feelings in a mature way. Comments like these also indicate that we sometimes do not feel quite in control of such feelings.

It helps to recognize that many other adolescents feel very much the same way, and that these are normal feelings at this age. It also is important to be aware of the fact that anger or hostility is perfectly justifiable in many situations. In fact, it would be abnormal not to feel anger in situations where we are frustrated or disappointed. As we mentioned earlier, the healthy person recognizes that he or she has certain feelings and he or she also has some understanding of why these feelings exist. In addition, such a person is able to express these feelings without guilt or anxiety.

When we feel angry, the expression of anger is highly desirable from the point of view of our adjustment and mental health. This does not mean that we go around blowing our tops over every small thing that goes wrong, or that we physically attack those who make us angry. In fact, all of us encounter situations in which we cannot express anger in an unlimited way. The man who tells off his boss may lose his job. The student who calls the teacher names may be suspended. The boy who swears at his father may regret it.

But even in situations where we have to control anger, there are constructive ways to express feelings. Talking things over with a close friend often helps. Daydreams in which we tell him off often help to reduce hostility. Even physical activity such as jogging or using a punching bag can help. The important thing is to find some way of relieving the anger rather than letting it build up inside us.

Dealing with Sexual Feelings

Just as it helps to recognize that anger and hostility are normal feelings, so also it is important to recognize that sexual feelings are normal in the sexually mature young man or woman. Unfortunately, in many people such feelings evoke embarrassment, guilt, anxiety, and even fear. Particularly in young people raised in strict, perfectionistic homes, sexual impulses in adolescence are likely to be the source of great concern and worry.

One of the reasons sexual feelings cause problems among adolescents in our society is that there exists a period of several years between sexual maturity and marriage. In other cultures where marriage occurs close to the time of sexual maturity, these problems are typically unknown. For many adolescents in our society there is a dilemma—sexual urges exist, but society in general frowns on the satisfaction of such urges until marriage. At the same time, sex is made attractive and even glamorous in movies, T.V., and magazines. We read that more and more people are having sexual relations prior to marriage. But is this true, we have to ask ourselves, and if it is, among what groups and what kinds of people is it true?

One of the problems for the adolescent, then, is in judging what is normal and what is acceptable. Most people do not talk about their own intimate sexual experiences or thoughts. Even when they do, we have little basis for judging the truth of the matter. Perhaps the most important thing to recognize is that the boy or girl who has a strong opinion of himself or herself will avoid behavior that is seen as inconsistent with that opinion. As one psychologist has noted, "The girl who thinks of herself as master of her behavior, who takes pride in being a person who cannot be used by others, and who feels that being used for someone else's pleasure is beneath her dignity and standards, is unlikely to indulge in behavior that would injure her concept of herself." Similarly, he says, "The boy who thinks of himself as a responsible person of honor and integrity, who feels contempt for preying on weaker or less knowledgeable people, who takes pride in the honesty of his dealings with everyone, is unlikely to attempt to persuade any girl to engage in activities that might expose her to injury or criticism."*

Understanding the psychological aspects of sex is an important part of becoming emotionally mature. Love and physical sex are not the same; men and women differ in their psychological makeups insofar as the physical aspects of sex are concerned. In the chapter on love and dating later in the book, we will discuss these differences in greater detail.

*Thomas F. Staton, "The Emotions and Sex Education for Adolescents," *Understanding Adolescence,* Edited by James F. Adams. Boston, Mass.: Allyn and Bacon, 1973, p. 287.

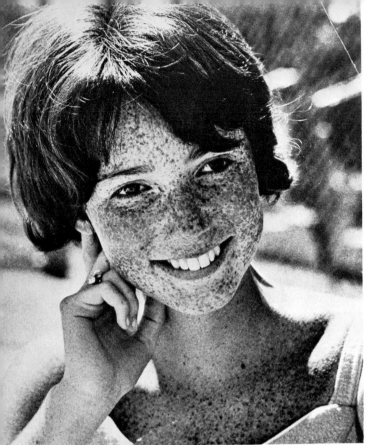

Fig. 8–8. Worries about appearance are very common during adolescence. But what seems to be a defect at one age is often seen as an asset later. This girl has just been voted "America's Most Beautiful Freckled Teenager."

Feelings of Inferiority

Adolescents frequently feel inferior to others of the same age for a number of reasons. Girls often feel they are unattractive—their hips are too big, their hair is the wrong color, their complexions are bad, and they are not as popular as others in their class. Boys often feel they are too small, or not strong enough, or too homely. Sometimes feelings such as these are the starting point for a vicious circle. The person who feels others do not like him, avoids contacts with others. Because he or she does this, they tend to have fewer friends, and this verifies the original feeling.

Feelings of inferiority are more common in adolescence than at other times in life because the individual often is unsure of himself in his relations with others. New situations arise which the person has not had to face in childhood. "How should I behave?" "What if I make a mistake and other people laugh at me?" Self-confidence tends to develop with experience. As one encounters the same situation over and over again, one begins to feel more comfortable in that situation—more poised and more confident of doing the right thing. Feelings of inferiority tend to diminish in most people as new social situations become more familiar.

Another reason adolescents often feel inferior is that they have unrealistically high standards; they want to be perfect. Failure or falling short is the inevitable result of setting such high standards. Recognizing and accepting shortcomings or faults is an important part of becoming emotionally mature, just as is recognizing one's strong points or assets.

One of the important lessons about human behavior that every young adult has to learn is that we cannot judge other people by what appears on the surface. It may seem to us that we are the only ones with problems. Other people seem so attractive, so poised and sure of themselves—surely they cannot have the same worries we do. Psychologists know, however, that most people do a great job of concealing their emotions. The person who appears assured and confident may be shaking on the inside. The ones we envy for their good looks and personality may in fact envy us. When we realize that most other people our age have the same problems and worries as we do, it often helps one to overcome feelings of inferiority.

Other Emotional Problems in Adolescence

Moodiness, embarrassment, and self-consciousness also tend to be characteristic of a large number of young adults in our society. To some extent these problems are related to those we discussed previously. Feeling blue or depressed often stems from falling short of high standards we set for ourselves. Self-consciousness and embarrassment often occur when we find ourselves in new and unfamiliar situations. But just as feelings of inferiority tend to diminish as unfamiliar situations become familiar, so also do we tend to become less self-conscious in such situations. Speaking in front of a group, for example, is something that most people feel uncomfortable about. We often admire the polished, confident public speaker addressing a large group. But we fail to understand that his or her confidence and poise have developed out of long experience. Rather than avoiding situations in which we feel uncomfortable, we should look on them as challenges. Only by gaining experience in such situations can we develop the emotional maturity we so greatly admire in others.

Some Final Tips

Several points in the preceding discussion are worth re-emphasizing. First, it is important to understand and accept one's emotions. By understanding why we feel angry or why we feel guilty, we are in a better position to deal maturely with such feelings. Furthermore, it is important to be able to accept ourselves as human beings with faults and frailties. No one is perfect, even though they may seem to be. This does not mean that we do not try to change undesirable characteristics. It simply means that we try to set reasonable and achievable standards for ourselves.

A second point worth remembering is that we should learn to get along with our emotions instead of fighting them. As one psychologist has noted, "Bottling up our feelings or trying to deny them can only get us into trouble."* By recognizing that other people have similar feelings and that we are not somehow worthless and inferior because of such feelings, we are better able to deal with them.

It is also important to remember that, to some extent, emotional maturity comes with experience. Feelings of inferiority, embarrassment, and self-consciousness tend to diminish as we gain more experience in a variety of social situations. We should not avoid new situations but instead enter into them with the knowledge that in the long run we will be happier and healthier individuals.

We also know that a greater breadth of experience helps one keep things in perspective. What seems like the end of the world today may be relatively or totally unimportant ten years from now. Because of the limited experience of adolescents, the apparent significance of events is often blown all out of proportion to their real significance. It helps, therefore, to try to see things that upset us in terms of how important they will be to us in the long run. It also helps to keep a sense of humor. The person who can laugh at himself has discovered perhaps one of the most important ways of reducing negative feelings.

Finally, it is important to try and find constructive ways to express our feelings. By talking with a friend or counselor about our worries, anger, disappointments, and even loves, we can better understand and deal with them.

CHAPTER SUMMARY

1. Emotions are similar to motives in that they often make us active and lead to goal directed behavior. They differ from motives, however, in that they do not

*James C. Coleman, *Personality Dynamics and Effective Behavior.* Chicago, Ill.: Scott, Foresman and Co., 1960, p. 329.

stem from biological needs. Also, emotions typically depend upon our awareness of the significance of a situation, and thus they involve thinking.

2. There are three dimensions along which emotions vary: tension-relaxation, pleasantness-unpleasantness, and attention-rejection. Emotions can be intense or weak; they can be pleasant, like love, or unpleasant, like anger, and they can cause us to pay attention to something as in fear or to turn away as in disgust.

3. Emotions are reflected in facial expression and bodily response as well as in internal or physiological changes. When we experience a strong emotion, the body reacts in a number of ways: heart rate and respiration increase; muscles tense; the mouth and throat become dry; blood pressure goes up; digestion ceases; and the adrenal glands secrete adrenalin. These changes in the body are regulated by the autonomic nervous system, and we normally cannot voluntarily control them.

4. The lie detector measures changes that occur in the body when we experience emotion. Since these changes occur involuntarily, when we lie the internal organs of the body often give us away. People who do not develop a normal conscience, however, are often able to lie without being detected. For this reason and others, polygraph tests are not admissible evidence in court.

5. Very young infants do not show the variety of emotions we see in older children and adults. Generalized excitement tends to be the response to any emotion-producing stimulus. Other emotions appear as the child grows older, and the pattern of emotional development is very much the same in all children. Learning seems to be important only in determining when and where certain emotions will occur.

6. Emotions help us react to emergency situations by enabling us to use maximum strength for short periods. They also help us to remain active over longer periods than is normally possible. We are less sensitive to pain when we experience a strong emotion such as fear or anger.

7. Emotional problems sometimes create imaginary illnesses or contribute to an already existing illness. In other cases they can cause illnesses which are physical in nature. Such illnesses are called *psychosomatic reactions,* and ulcers and high blood pressure are typical examples.

8. Two kinds of feelings or emotions tend to cause people more problems than any others—those related to anger or aggression and those related to sex. Some people, often because of certain experiences in childhood, cannot express anger or hostility. Such feelings are frequently unconscious and result in emotional problems for the person. Other people experience severe anxiety and guilt over sexual impulses or urges. Recognizing that anger and hostility are normal feelings, as are sexual feelings in the mature young man or woman, often helps to eliminate these feelings as sources of worry or fear.

9. Adolescents also frequently suffer from feelings of inferiority, embarrassment, and self-consciousness. Sometimes these feelings stem from unrealistically high standards one sets for oneself. In other cases these feelings occur when we face new or unfamiliar situations. Setting reasonable and achievable standards for ourselves often helps in the first case. In the second, as we gain more experience in a variety of social situations, we tend to become more self-confident and assured.

10. In terms of emotional maturity, it is important to understand and accept one's emotions, set reasonable standards for ourselves, express our feelings, and seek out new social situations in which we can develop competence. We should also try to keep things in perspective and maintain a sense of humor.

Important Terms
from This Chapter

emotion	autonomic nervous system	psychosomatic reactions
tension-relaxation	involuntary	unconscious
pleasantness-unpleasantness	polygraph	anxiety
attention-rejection	physiological changes	inferiority

Additional Readings
to Help You Learn More

Adams, J. *Understanding Adolescence: Current Developments in Adolescent Psychology,* 2nd Edition. Boston: Allyn and Bacon, Inc., 1973. Chapter 1, "Adolescents in an Age of Crisis," is a down-to-earth discussion of the personal concerns of adolescents and the problems they face in today's world. Chapter 11, "The Emotions and Sex Education for Adolescents," deals with such topics as "romance, love and exploitation."

Schachter, S. and Singer, J. "Cognitive, Social and Physiological Determinants of Emotional State." *Bobbs-Merrill Reprints,* p. 553. Indianapolis: Bobbs-Merrill Company. This is an extremely important discussion of the factors that influence the expression of various emotions.

Psychology Today: An Introduction, 2nd Edition. Del Mar, Calif.: CRM Books, 1972. Chapter 17, "Emotion," deals with the lie detector, the physiology of emotion and various theories of emotion.

Readings in Psychology Today, 2nd Edition. Del Mar, Calif.: CRM Books, 1972. "When Fear is Healthy," teaches us that fear is not always a bad thing.

Part V.

PERCEIVING THE WORLD
AND
GETTING THE MESSAGE

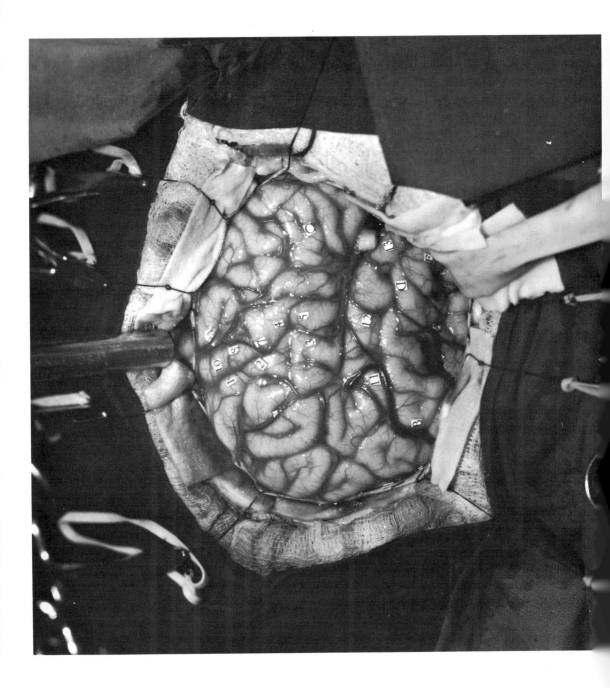

Beneath the Skin

chapter **9**

In trying to understand why people behave as they do, psychologists not only look at the behavior itself but also at what takes place within the body. When we learn something, how is this registered in the brain? Why don't we remember everything we learn? Why are some people more intelligent than others—how do their brains differ? What causes us to fall asleep? Why do we dream? How do glands affect our behavior?

At this point no one can answer all of these questions. We do know the answers to some, however, and we are well on the way to finding answers for others. In this chapter we will talk about the nervous system, its parts, and the brain in particular. We will also take a brief look at hypnosis and at the nature of sleep and dreams. Finally, we will expand on our earlier discussion of glands and behavior.

THE MYSTERIOUS NERVOUS SYSTEM

When you prick your finger, what happens? Obviously, you say, it hurts. But where does it hurt? In your finger, you say; but this time you are wrong. When you prick your finger, it hurts in your brain. Nerve endings in the finger send impulses into your brain when they are stimulated. If you blocked those nerves by cutting them or deadening them with drugs, your finger would not hurt, no matter how much you pricked it. The reverse is also true. Sometimes people with amputated limbs complain of pain in the absent parts. This is called *phantom pain*, and it occurs when the brain receives impulses from the nerves that used to go to the missing limbs.

Nerve impulses are actually electrochemical in nature, so that the nervous system is somewhat like an electrical wiring network that ties or connects the various parts of the body together. Each nerve cell is like a small battery with a combined conducting wire. When one of these cells is stimulated, it fires or discharges an impulse, which in turn stimulates adjacent nerve cells and causes them to fire.

Some nerve cells are grouped into fibers, much like a cable. What goes into your brain when you see with your eyes is not a picture, but nerve impulses. In some respects this is similar to a coaxial cable for T.V. What is transmitted in television is not a picture, but electricity. Furthermore, if the optic nerve is damaged, no impulses get through to the brain, and the person is blind.*

The nervous system consists of the brain, the spinal cord, and a network of nerves that run to every part of the body. Basically the system operates to integrate or regulate all of the specialized organs and systems of the body. Without the nervous system, we could not move any part of the body; we could not read, nor feel pain, nor think. In fact, life itself would cease, since the nervous system controls heartbeat, respiration, and other vital body functions.

The basic building blocks of the nervous system are the individual nerve cells called *neurons.* To understand how the nervous system works, we have to begin by examining how these specialized cells work.

What Are Neurons?

The term *neuron* is the technical term used to refer to nerve cells. As noted above, the entire nervous system is composed of neurons grouped together in fibers or clustered together as in the brain. These cells differ from others in the body in that they can generate and store tiny electrochemical charges much like a battery. It is not quite correct to say that the nervous system is simply an electrical system, but we need not go into the detailed differences here.

When a neuron is stimulated, it fires or discharges a nerve impulse, which in turn causes other neurons to fire. Thus an impulse that begins in a neuron located in the finger, jumps or moves from one neuron to another

---

*Some of the examples used here are from the book *The Big Ball of Wax* by Shepherd Mead (N.Y.: Ballantine Books, 1954).

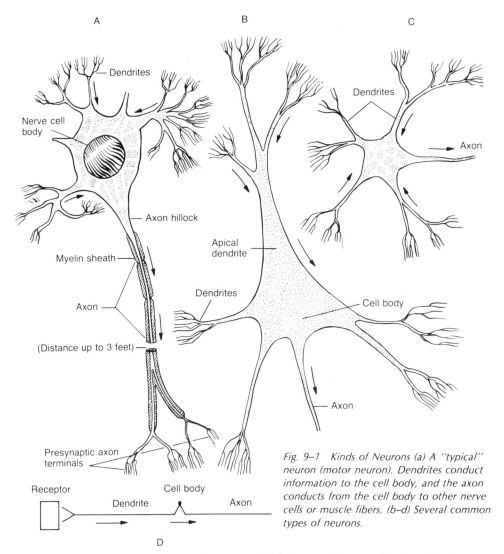

A

Dendrites

Nerve cell
body

Axon hillock

Myelin sheath

Axon

(Distance up to 3 feet)

Presynaptic axon
terminals

B

Dendrites

Apical
dendrite

Dendrites

C

Dendrites

Axon

Cell body

Axon

Receptor

Dendrite

Cell body

Axon

D

Fig. 9–1 Kinds of Neurons (a) A "typical"
neuron (motor neuron). Dendrites conduct
information to the cell body, and the axon
conducts from the cell body to other nerve
cells or muscle fibers. (b–d) Several common
types of neurons.

until it ends up in a particular part of the brain. We say the impulse jumps,
because there is a gap between neurons called a *synapse,* and it is across this
synapse that the nerve impulse must move. Again, the technical details of
how this occurs are unimportant for our purposes. The main thing to remember is that there is a gap (synapse) between cells across which the nerve
impulse has to travel.

There are several different kinds of neurons. One kind, called *sensory
neurons,* conducts nerve impulses only toward the brain or spinal cord.
Others, called *motor neurons* conduct impulses away from the brain and

toward muscles or glands. When we step on a tack or prick our finger, sensory neurons carry the message to the brain. When we move our arms, motor neurons carry the message from the brain to the muscles in our arms.

What Are the Main Parts of the Nervous System?

The human nervous system is divided into two parts that have different functions. One part, the *central nervous system*, regulates or controls voluntary activities, and it includes certain parts of the brain and spinal cord which we will discuss later. When we make any voluntary movement, such as writing or speaking, the central nervous system is involved. The other part, the *autonomic nervous system*, regulates or controls involuntary activities such as heartbeat and respiration. It includes parts of the brain and spinal cord aside from those in the central nervous system.

You might remember what the autonomic nervous system does by remembering the word "automatic." This part of the nervous system, in other words, controls the automatic functions we need to stay alive. We don't have to think about breathing or making our heart beat; the autonomic nervous system does this for us automatically.

The autonomic nervous system is divided into two parts or branches. One branch is called the *sympathetic* division and the other is the *parasympathetic* division. Each organ of the body controlled by the autonomic nervous system has both sympathetic and parasympathetic connections. These two branches have opposite functions. The heart, for example, beats more rapidly when the sympathetic division is activated. The parasympathetic division, on the other hand, operates to slow the heart down.

Psychologists used to think that the two parts of the nervous system were quite separate—in other words that we could not learn to control such things as heartbeat or blood pressure. Recent experiments, however, have shown that through operant conditioning, such functions can be voluntarily controlled. Some people have even learned to raise the temperature of the skin on one hand while at the same time lowering the temperature of the other. This is done by controlling dilation and constriction of the blood vessels—something normally controlled by the autonomic nervous system.

The practical importance of this recent discovery is enormous, because we know that abnormal functioning of the autonomic nervous system is often involved in such things as heart disease, ulcers, and other ailments. If people suffering from such diseases can be taught to control blood pressure or heart rate, it would be a tremendous step forward in eliminating these diseases.

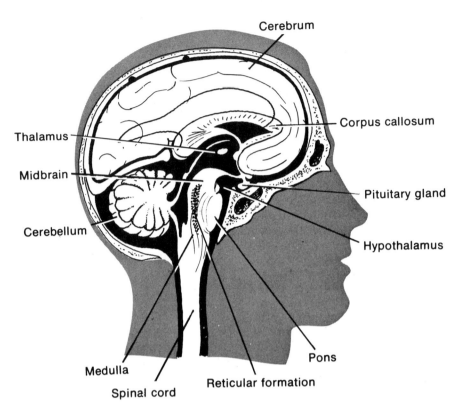

Fig. 9–2 Major Parts Of The Human Brain. This side view of the brain shows the major anatomical and functional parts. The two cerebral hemispheres are connected through the corpus callosum, while the lobes of the cerebellum are connected through the pons.

How Does the Brain Work?

The human brain is perhaps the most complex of all the organs of the body. In some respects it is like a computer, but it is more complicated than the largest computer ever built. For centuries men believed that the brain functioned as a whole—that such functions as vision and hearing were not located in a particular part of the brain. Today we know this is not true, but while we know what many different parts of the brain do, there are still many other questions about the brain that no one can answer yet.

Different Parts of the Brain

The human brain has three major parts: the cerebral cortex, the cerebellum, and the medulla. The *cerebral cortex* is mainly concerned with higher mental functions such as thinking, while the *cerebellum* is concerned with helping us maintain our balance or equilibrium. The *medulla* is actually an extension of the spinal cord, and it has parts which regulate all of the vital functions of the body, such as heartbeat and respiration.

In human beings, the cerebral cortex is much larger than the other parts of the brain. Among simpler animals, the cortex is smaller in comparison to the rest of the brain. What does this mean? It means that less of man's brain is devoted to running the body. More of it is available for thinking and problem solving. It is not this alone, however, that makes human beings more intelligent than other animals. An important factor is the size of the brain relative to the size of the body. We will return to this in a moment. At this point, we want to find out more about what the cerebral cortex does.

If you look at the map of the cerebral cortex shown in Fig. 9–3, you will notice that areas for vision, speech, and hearing are clearly marked. Also indicated on the map are the sensory and motor areas. What do these areas

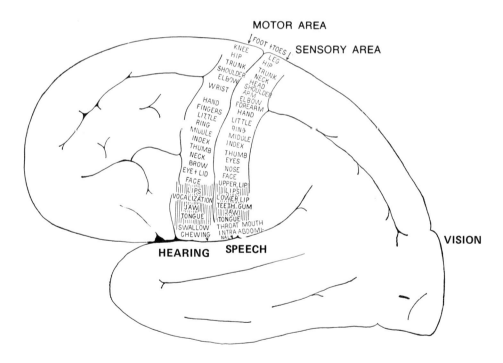

Fig. 9–3. Organization of the Sensory and Motor Areas. Side view of the left hemisphere showing organization of sensory and motor areas, as well as areas involved in speech, hearing, and vision.

do and how do they work? As you might expect, the vision area receives nerve impulses that travel along the optic nerves from the eyes. This area is involved in interpreting or making sense out of the pattern of nerve impulses it receives. If damaged, the individual is blinded, even though the eyes and optic nerves are intact.

The hearing area receives and interprets nerve impulses from the ear located on that side of the head. Here it should be noted that Fig. 9–3 shows only one-half of the cerebral cortex. The cortex is divided into two hemispheres that are connected by a complicated sheath of nerve fibers called the *corpus callosum.* More about that later.

Part of the speech area shown is responsible for controlling the muscles involved in speech. When we talk, nerve impulses originate in this part of the brain and travel to muscles in the mouth and throat. Damage to this part of the brain would make it impossible to speak.

The motor area controls the various muscles in the body which we can move voluntarily. When we move our arm, for example, nerve impulses originating in one specific part of this area travel down the spinal cord, along nerve fibers in the arm, and finally terminate in the muscles. An interesting fact about the motor area is that the left side of the body is controlled by the right side of the brain, and vice versa. When we move our right leg, the motor area on the left side of the brain is responsible. If the motor area is damaged, the individual is either partially or totally paralyzed, depending upon the extent of the damage.

The sensory area receives nerve impulses from specialized nerve cells in various parts of the body. When a part of the body is stimulated, nerve impulses from that part of the body are sent to the sensory area. If this part of the brain is damaged, we have no feeling in the affected parts of the body.

Computers, the Brain and Thinking

No one knows exactly how or even where in the brain, thinking occurs. As we mentioned earlier, there are some similarities between the human brain and computers. But the human brain is infinitely more complex than the largest computer ever built. Also, the brain operates through electrochemical impulses while the computer is totally electrical in nature. There are other differences as well. Computers can solve mathematical problems much faster than the human brain; one machine solved a problem involving 9 million mathematical operations in 150 hours. It would have taken a single mathematician 1,500 years to solve the same problem.

Before we become too impressed with, or even frightened of, comput-

Fig. 9–4   Is the computer like the human brain? In some ways yes and in others, no. The brain is more complex than the computer but the computer can solve some mathematical problems much faster than the brain. Further, the computer is an electrical instrument while the brain is basically electrochemical.

ers, it should be pointed out that no one has yet discovered how to teach a computer to compose a masterpiece. Shakespeare's *Hamlet* and Beethoven's *Ninth Symphony* are beyond the capabilities of even the most sophisticated computer today, and probably always will be. One reason, of course, is that neither Shakespeare nor Beethoven nor modern scientists understand what constitutes creative genius, and hence we are unable to duplicate it in a computer. In a sense, then, the computer can be thought of as a giant moron, useful to us as a calculating machine, but hardly a threat to the potential of the human brain.

One more point deserves mention before going on to the general question of intelligence and the brain. You will note in Fig. 9–3 that no functions are indicated for the large frontal area of the cerebral cortex. Even when this part of the brain is destroyed or damaged, the person's behavior does not appear to be drastically affected. Nevertheless there is evidence that in such cases the person's ability to deal with abstract concepts is diminished.

We believe, then, that the frontal areas of the brain are vital in the kinds of thinking or problem solving that require abstraction. As we noted in an earlier chapter, concepts such as "God," "morals," "duty," and "honesty" are beyond the capabilities of even the most intelligent animal. These are abstract concepts, and the fact that humans can evolve such concepts probably is dependent in large measure on the frontal areas of the brain. This does not mean that thinking occurs only in the frontal areas or that animals other than man cannot think. It simply means that abstract thinking in humans very much involves the frontal areas.

Intelligence and the Brain

We mentioned earlier that intelligence seems to be related to the size of the brain in comparison to the size of the body, rather than brain size alone. Some animals, such as the elephant, have much larger brains than man. But the elephant's body is also larger. This means that most of the brain tissue in animals such as the elephant must be concerned with running the body—regulating heartbeat, respiration, and so on. After these functions are taken care of, little brain area remains to be devoted to thinking or problem solving.

In humans as a species, there is little relationship between brain size

Fig. 9-5 This little girl has "Down's Syndrome," or "mongolism." No one knows what causes it, but her brain has been affected by an extra chromosome with which she was born. She is mentally retarded.

and intelligence. Those with larger brains are not necessarily more intelligent than those with small brains. In some types of mental retardation, the brain is abnormally small and intelligence is markedly affected. But within the range of normal human beings no one has ever shown intelligence and brain size or weight to be related.

In the past some people believed that there was a relationship between intelligence and the number of wrinkles or convolutions on the surface of the brain. But while it is a fact that every human brain is wrinkled, there is absolutely no basis for believing that the more wrinkles you have on your brain, the more intelligent you are. One of the puzzling things about the brain, in fact, is that no features have yet been identified by which we can distinguish genius from average intelligence.

How Do We Remember?

We are only now beginning to unlock the secrets of human memory. For a long time we have known that memories are not located in specific parts of the brain; a large number of neurons in widely separated parts of the brain seem to be involved in the memory of single events. How this occurs, no one knows. We do know that chemical changes take place in neurons when we learn something, but we are just beginning to understand what these changes are. Interestingly enough, some of the most important recent scientific information has come from studies of memory in simple flatworms called planaria.

Planaria are interesting organisms for several reasons. *First,* like other simple animals, they are capable of learning. *Second,* when cut in half, each half regenerates or grows again into a complete organism. As shown in Fig. 9–6, the tail half grows a new head and the head half grows a new tail.

Three psychologists performed the following experiment: Several planaria were conditioned to constrict in response to a flash of light. While they

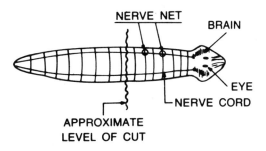

Fig. 9–6 *Planaria regenerate when cut in half. The tail grows a new head and the head grows a new tail.*

were being trained, the light was flashed and then they were given a tiny electric shock. This procedure was repeated several times until each animal learned to respond to the light. Following this all animals were cut in half and allowed to grow again into complete animals. The new animals were then tested to see if they would respond to the flashing light.

The most remarkable results were obtained. Not only did those animals which had grown a new tail remember, the ones that had grown a new head remembered as well! In these organisms, then, learning must take place throughout the entire nervous system rather than just in the brain.

An even more remarkable experiment followed the first. Planaria were conditioned using the procedure described above. Then these organisms were ground up and fed to untrained planaria. You guessed it! The untrained animals responded to the flashing light just as if they had been trained.

As you might expect, this experiment caused considerable excitement among psychologists. How could it be explained? Would it work with higher animals? Did it mean that learning could be chemically transferred from one animal to another? Could learning be given like a pill?

Earlier in the book we mentioned that body cells contain DNA (the hereditary substance), RNA, and protein. On the basis of the experiment discussed above and others, we now think that RNA is somehow involved in memory. There must be chemical changes that take place in RNA molecules when an animal learns something. Exactly what this process is or how it occurs, we do not know.

In other experiments, RNA has been extracted from the brains of trained laboratory rats and injected into the brains of untrained rats. As in the planaria, there is some evidence that memory can be transferred from one rat to another in this way. It is too early to even suggest that this might be possible in human beings—furthermore, it does not work very well in laboratory rats.* Nevertheless, these experiments have given us some idea of how memory occurs in the brain, and they form the basis for a great deal of additional research on this fascinating topic.

Are Two Brains Better than One?

Earlier in this chapter we noted that the cerebral cortex is divided into two halves, or *hemispheres*. These hemispheres are connected by a large

---

*Some psychologists think it doesn't work at all. They have repeated these experiments but have not found the same results.

nerve tract called the *corpus callosum*. Until recently we did not know exactly what the corpus callosum did nor what would happen if it were cut. Some recent experiments have provided a few answers, but in fact they have actually raised still more questions about how the brain works.

For most of us, the left side of the brain is dominant. This means that we are right-handed, and also that the speech area of the brain is located in the left hemisphere. In left-handed people, speech is sometimes controlled by the right side of the brain and sometimes by the left. At any rate, if the left side of the brain tends to be dominant in most people, why do they need a right side—what does this part of the brain do?

One psychologist, Dr. Robert Sperry, has spent a great deal of time studying this problem. Of particular interest to him was a man whose corpus callosum had been surgically cut in an effort to reduce epileptic fits. This man had, in effect, two brains with no connection between the two.

When told to raise his hand or bend his knee, the man could respond only with the right side of his body. He was not paralyzed on the left side, but the right side of his brain did not understand language! When the man was blindfolded, he could not even tell what part of his body was touched if it happened to be on the left side. When he was asked to pick up a number with his left hand and then indicate the number with his right hand, he could not do it. Clearly, in this man one side of the brain did not know what was happening in the other.

As Dr. Sperry notes, with the passing of time this man became more

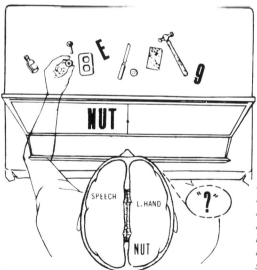

Fig. 9–7. Names of objects flashed to left half field can be read and understood but not spoken. Subject can retrieve the named object by touch with the left hand, but cannot afterwards name the item nor retrieve it with the right hand. (What we see in the left half of each eye is sent to the left half of the brain, and vice versa).

and more two men. His left hand kept doing things the right hand deplored. He once threatened his wife with his left hand while his right hand tried to come to his wife's rescue. Furthermore, it became apparent that while the right side of the brain is not stupid, it is speechless and illiterate—it simply does not understand language.

The corpus callosum, then, obviously keeps the two halves of the brain in touch with one another. Learning in one half is transferred to the other through this structure, since when it is destroyed both halves of the brain learn independently. We will have to await the results of further experiments before we can answer some very puzzling questions about the illiterate, nonspeaking half of the brain.

WHAT IS THE EEG?

The *EEG*, or *electroencephalograph*, is a machine that records or measures the electrical activity of the brain. Neurons, as we mentioned earlier, can build and store tiny electrical charges. The millions of neurons in the human brain continually produce electrical pulsations known as *rhythms*. When the EEG is used to study these rhythms, electrodes are attached to the scalp and they feed the electrical discharge from the brain through wires to a machine which amplifies and records it. Fig. 9–8 shows the machine and Fig. 9–9 shows an EEG record.

When the eyes are closed and the person is awake, the brain pulsates about ten times each second. This is known as the *alpha rhythm*. When the

Fig. 9–8. The Electroencephalograph (EEG) measures electrical activity within various areas of the brain. It is used to detect epilepsy and brain tumors, and to study such things as dreams.

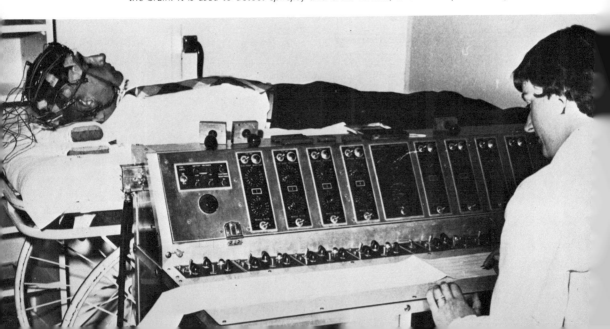

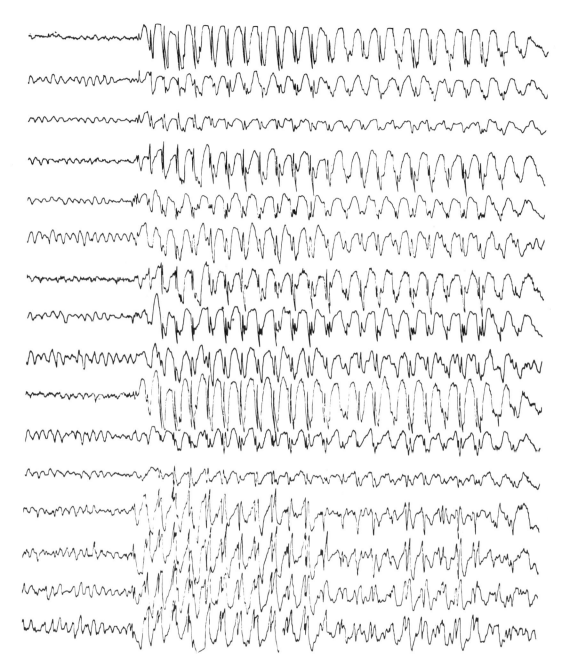

Fig. 9-9   The Electroencephalogram (EEG) record shown here was taken from a patient with epilepsy. In this case the record was made when the patient was breathing deeply (hyperventilation). Hyperventilation in such cases alters the oxygen content of the blood and results in the abnormal discharge of cortical neurons.

eyes are open, the pattern of electrical activity in the brain changes, as it does when the person thinks about the solution to a problem or answer to a question. Brain rhythms, however, do not reflect different kinds of thought processes.

In some people the electrical activity of the brain is disturbed or abnormal from time to time, and neurons discharge wildly. When this occurs the individual suffers a seizure or fit, and the condition is called *epilepsy.* Epilepsy can be inborn, or it can be caused by a severe injury to the brain. In most cases the seizures can be controlled by a physician who prescribes medication. People with epilepsy are in no way abnormal in personality, nor does the condition affect intelligence. The EEG is a useful machine in that it can detect epilepsy even in the absence of seizures. It is also useful in experiments on sleep.

Sleep and Dreams

Even when we sleep, the brain never actually shuts down completely. The pattern of electrical activity changes, however. We know that sleep actually occurs in four distinct stages. These stages of sleep range from very light to very deep, and they are reflected in changes in the electrical activity of the brain as shown in Fig. 9–10.

We know that dreams occur only in about 25 per cent of the total sleep

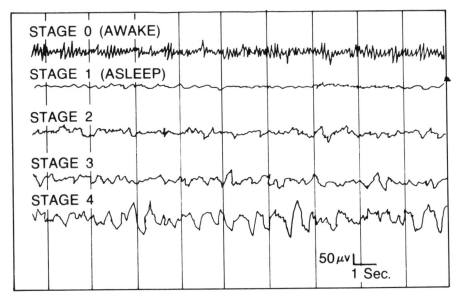

Fig. 9–10. Sleep occurs in four distinct stages as this record shows.

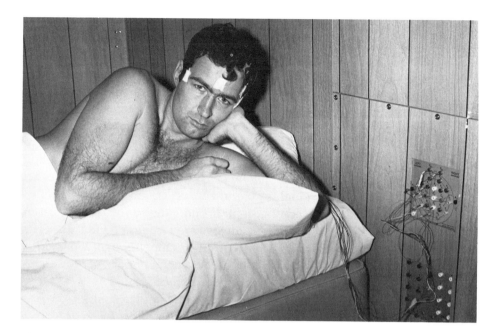

Fig. 9–11   Electrodes taped to the head of the man are attached to an EEG that traces brain waves and eye movements during sleep.

period each night. In addition, we know that dreaming occurs only during stage 1 of sleep and that little dreaming occurs in the first hour. How do we know this? We know it because one psychologist discovered that when people dream, their eyes move rapidly! Even though the eyes are closed when we sleep, eye movements can be detected by placing electrodes on the eyelids. In the sleep laboratory, whenever the eyelids of a sleeping person move, he or she is awakened; the person usually reports they had been dreaming. Waking the same person at times when the eyes are not moving almost always brings forth the report of no dreams. The rapid eye movements that occur when we dream are called *REMs*, and investigators are now convinced that there are three distinct states that occur in daily cycles—wakefulness, REM sleep, and NREM sleep. *NREM sleep* is that period when there are no rapid eye movements.

Why do the eyes move when we dream? Why do we dream? Are dreams necessary? What do dreams mean? Some psychologists believe that eye movements reflect the content of dreams. One person awakened in the middle of a dream reported he had been watching a Ping-Pong match. His eye movements while asleep had been moving rapidly from side to side. In other cases the evidence is not so clear. Small infants for example, show

REMs while asleep, but we do not believe very young infants dream. Dreams seem to depend upon remembered perceptions.

In terms of why we dream and whether or not dreams are necessary, there are two important ideas. First, Freud thought that dreams protect sleep. According to him, unconscious feelings are responsible for many dreams. These feelings are expressed in dreams, he thought, in disguised form; and since they are disguised, the person is able to satisfy them even while asleep. Thus he distinguished between what actually occurs in a dream and what this means to the person. If the person's true unconscious feeling were reflected as such in the dream, he would wake up. By being expressed in disguised form, the individual is able to remain asleep.

Not all psychologists today accept Freud's theory of the nature of dreams—in fact, we know some of his ideas were wrong. Dreams do serve a purpose, however, since some strange things happen when a person is prevented from dreaming. This brings us to the second important idea about why we dream and whether or not dreams are necessary.

In one laboratory, people were prevented from dreaming. How was this done? Simple—they were awakened every time REMs were detected. What happened to these people? *First,* if people were prevented from dreaming one night but allowed to dream the next night, the amount of time spent dreaming the second night increased greatly. *Second,* if people were prevented from dreaming for as many as five nights in a row they became irritable, anxious, and they had difficulty in concentrating. As soon as they were allowed to dream again, these feelings disappeared.

It seems that when people are prevented from dreaming, pressure to dream builds up. Dreams, then, must be a way of blowing off steam while we sleep. We cannot quite say that Freud was right in his belief that dreams protect sleep, but modern psychologists believe that a certain amount of dreaming each night is nevertheless a necessity.

What Is Hypnosis?

In some respects hypnosis seems to be similar to sleep. Often to hypnotize a subject, he is told that he feels drowsy or sleepy. We know that there are stages in the hypnotic state ranging from very light to very deep as well. Furthermore, the word *hypnosis* is derived from the Greek word for sleep (*hypnos*). But we know today that the hypnotic state is not one of sleeping but waking. If we compare the EEG of brain activity during hypnosis with that during sleep, they are not the same. The EEG of a person under hypnosis looks very much like that of a person wide awake.

If hypnosis is not sleep then, what is it? For now, the best we can say is that it is an artificially induced state of heightened suggestibility. According to the psychologist Ernest Hilgard, hypnotized people show the following characteristics: (1) The subject does not like to initiate activity—he or she waits for the hypnotist to tell them what to do; (2) The person's attention becomes more selective under hypnosis. That is, if the hypnotist tells the subject to listen only to his voice, the subject pays no attention to other voices; (3) Reality testing is reduced—the subject, for example, may pet an imaginary rabbit in his lap; (4) The subject will enact unusual roles—for example, re-enacting his own behavior at a much younger age; (5) Hypnotic subjects often react to suggestions that they will not remember what they did while hypnotized.*

There are a number of other questions often asked about hypnosis: (1) Who can be hypnotized? Apparently almost anyone, even though some people are much easier to hypnotize than others. Also, most people become better hypnotic subjects with practice; the more times a person is hypnotized, the shorter the time required to become hypnotized and the deeper the trance. (2) Is hypnosis dangerous? The hypnotic state itself is not in the least bit dangerous. The danger in hypnosis occurs when it is used by an untrained person. Suggestions that the subject feels no pain, for example, may lead the subject to expose himself to injury. (3) Can a hypnotized person be made to do things he would not normally do? The answer to this is both yes and no. Most people will not normally pretend to be a chicken or a duck, but under hypnosis they often will. On the other hand, if told to put his hand into a cage containing a poisonous snake, the hypnotized subject usually refuses. (4) Does hypnosis have any practical uses? The answer to this is a definite yes. Major surgery can be performed on a hypnotized subject without his feeling any pain; teeth can be extracted; and even babies born. In the latter case, childbirth is often safer under hypnosis because anesthesia administered to the mother often physiologically affects the baby as well.

GLANDS AND BEHAVIOR

Now that we have some basic understanding of the nervous system and how it works, we will take a brief look at the endocrine glands and how they affect behavior.

*E. Hilgard, R. Atkinson, and R. Atkinson, *Introduction to Psychology*, 5th ed. New York: Harcourt, Brace, Jovanovich, 1971.

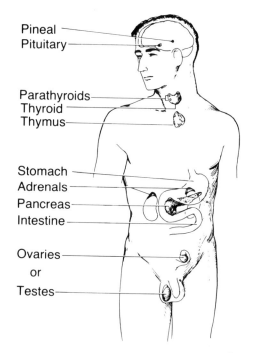

Fig. 9–12 *The Endocrine Glands. Location of the various endocrine glands in the body. The six recognized glands are shown as well as two suspect endocrines—the thymus and intestine. Function of the pineal, if any, is unknown.*

Pineal
Pituitary

Parathyroids
Thyroid
Thymus

Stomach
Adrenals
Pancreas
Intestine

Ovaries
or
Testes

There are two types of glands in the human body—*exocrine* or *duct* glands, and *endocrine* or *ductless* glands. The duct glands secrete their products directly into body cavities or onto the surface of the body. The salivary glands and the sweat glands are examples.

The endocrine or ductless glands secrete their products, called *hormones*, directly into the blood. There are six endocrine glands located in different parts of the body. These include the (1) pituitary, (2) thyroid, (3) adrenal, (4) pancreas, (5) parathyroid, and (6) sex glands or gonads.

The *pituitary* gland, located at the base of the brain, is sometimes called the "master gland" because it exercises control over three others—the adrenals, thyroid, and sex glands. Hormones produced by the pituitary stimulate these other three glands to produce their own hormones. The hormones produced by these glands, in turn, affect the production of hormones by the pituitary. Thus there is a two-way interaction between them. If the adrenals produce insufficient adrenal hormones, the pituitary produces a hormone which in effect tells the adrenals to get to work. Adrenal hormones in turn tell the pituitary, "We are working—take it easy." Thus the pituitary slows down its production of hormones which stimulate the adrenals.

In addition to producing hormones which stimulate the three glands mentioned above, the pituitary also secretes hormones which regulate growth and other body functions. Undersecretion of growth hormones, for example, causes dwarfism, while too much growth hormones causes gigantism.

The *thyroid* produces a hormone called "thyroxin" which regulates or controls the basal metabolism of the body. If too little thyroxin is produced the person becomes sluggish, easily tired, and often gains weight. Too much thyroxin, on the other hand, causes overactivity, excitability, and lose of weight. Among children, severe underproduction of thyroxin can cause mental retardation, cretinism in particular. This used to be a frequent cause of mental retardation, but it is seldom seen today since it is easily diagnosed and treated.

The *adrenal* glands are divided into two parts. One part secretes hormones that play an important role in the use of salt and carbohydrates by the body. Injury to this part of the gland results in death unless the patient is properly treated with adrenal hormones. Furthermore, it is this part of the adrenals that is stimulated by the pituitary. The other part of the gland secretes adrenalin, and as we noted in an earlier chapter, adrenalin plays an important role in emotional behavior. Heart rate, blood pressure, and other body functions are affected by adrenalin. An important point in connection with this part of the adrenal glands is that stimulation of it occurs through the autonomic nervous system. Thus it is not a true endocrine gland, since all the others are stimulated to produce their hormones through chemical changes in the blood.

The *pancreas* secretes insulin, which helps to maintain a proper level of sugar in the blood. Diabetics suffer from a condition in which insufficient insulin is produced by the pancreas. The injection of insulin corrects this condition and causes blood sugar to remain within normal limits.

The *parathyroid* glands produce a hormone which is vital in the use of calcium by the body. Undersecretion of this hormone causes death through an involuntary spasm of the muscles. The normal functioning of nerve cells also is dependent upon the hormone produced by this gland, since these cells work properly only when the amount of calcium in the blood is within certain limits.

The *sex glands* (ovaries or testes) begin to produce their hormones as a result of stimulation by the pituitary at about age 13 in girls and somewhat later in boys. Androgen, the male hormone, and estrogen, the female hormone, are related to the development of secondary sexual characteristics and to some extent, sexual behavior, in the mature adult. As we noted in an earlier chapter, however, human sexual behavior is not nearly as closely tied to the functioning of the sex glands as it is in lower animals. Human sexual behavior is in large part learned and thus independent of the effects of the sex hormones.

CHAPTER SUMMARY

1. The nervous system consists of the brain, spinal cord, and a network of nerves that run to every part of the body. Basically, the system operates to integrate or regulate all of the specialized organs and systems of the body.

2. Neurons, or nerve cells, are the basic building blocks of the nervous system. These cells are grouped together in fibers or clustered together as in the brain. They differ from other cells in the body in that they can generate and store tiny electrochemical charges much like a battery. When a neuron is stimulated, it fires or discharges a nerve impulse which in turn causes other neurons to fire. There is a gap between nerve cells called a *synapse,* and it is across this synapse that nerve impulses move from one cell to the next. Sensory neurons conduct impulses toward the brain, while motor neurons conduct impulses away from the brain and toward muscles or glands.

3. The nervous system is divided into two main divisions. The central nervous system, consisting of parts of the brain and spinal cord, controls voluntary activities. The autonomic nervous system controls involuntary activities. The autonomic nervous system has two branches—sympathetic and parasympathetic. Each organ of the body controlled by the autonomic nervous system has sympathetic and parasympathetic connections. One of these stimulates the organ in question while the other slows it down—thus they have opposite functions.

4. The human brain has three main parts—the cerebral cortex, the cerebellum, and the medulla. The cerebral cortex is mainly concerned with higher mental functions such as thinking, while the cerebellum helps us maintain our balance and coordination. The medulla, or brain stem, contains centers which regulate vital body functions such as heart beat.

5. In the cerebral cortex are specialized areas responsible for vision, speech, hearing, the movement of muscles, and the sensing of stimulation in various parts of the body. The cortex is divided into two halves or hemispheres connected by a large nerve tract called the corpus callosum. The left side of the body is controlled by the right side of the brain and vice versa.

6. No one knows exactly how or where thinking occurs in the brain, but there is some evidence that the frontal areas of the cortex are involved in the use of abstract concepts. Man seems to be more intelligent than other animals in part because of a larger brain compared to the size of the body, and a large cerebral cortex. Brain size or weight alone, however, are not related to intelligence except in some kinds of mental retardation in which the brain is abnormally small.

7. Memory apparently involves large numbers of cells in the brain, and recent research also suggests that RNA is somehow involved in the storage of memory. Learning that takes place in one half of the brain is transmitted to the other half through the corpus collosum. When this structure is cut, both halves of the brain may learn independently. In most people the left half of the brain is dominant. Speech or language centers are located there, and there is some evidence that the right half of the brain is illiterate.

8. The EEG or electroencephalograph is a device that measures electrical activity in the brain. Neurons in the brain pulsate rhythmically about ten times a second in the normal person. Epilepsy, a condition in which the electrical activity of the brain is disturbed, can be detected with the EEG. The EEG has also been used to study sleep.

9. The brain never shuts down completely even when we sleep. The pattern of activity changes, however, and we know that sleep actually occurs in four distinct stages. These stages, ranging from very light to very deep, are reflected in changes in the electrical activity of the brain. Dreams occur only in about 25 per cent of the total sleep period each night. We know this because rapid eye movements (REMs) occur when we dream and these are observed only in light sleep, which is about one quarter of total sleep. No one knows for sure why we dream or what dreams mean.

10. In some respects hypnosis seems similar to sleep. We know it is not, however, because the EEG of a hypnotized person is exactly like one who is wide awake. In itself, the hypnotic state is not dangerous. It can be extremely dangerous in the hands of an untrained person however.

11. There are two types of glands in the body—exocrine or duct glands, and endocrine or ductless. Exocrine glands secrete their products directly into body cavities or on the surface of the body. Sweat glands and salivary glands are examples. Endocrine glands secrete their products—hormones—directly into the blood. There are six known endocrine glands: pituitary, thyroid, adrenal, pancreas, parathyroid, and sex glands.

Important Terms
from This Chapter

phantom pain	parasympathetic division	EEG
nerves	cerebral cortex	alpha rhythm
neurons	sensory area	hypnosis
nervous system	motor area	thyroid gland
synapse	planaria	adrenal gland
sensory neuron	DNA	pancreas
motor neuron	RNA	parathyroid gland
sympathetic division	corpus callosum	nerve impulse
	R. Sperry	

Additional Reading
to Help You Learn More

Dement, W. and Kleitman, N. "The Relation of Eye Movements During Sleep to Dream Activity: An Objective Method for the Study of Dreaming." *Bobbs-Merrill Reprints,* P-87. Indianapolis: Bobbs-Merrill Company. This is an expanded discussion of some of the material presented in this chapter.

Groch, J. *You and Your Brain.* New York: Harper and Row, 1963. Extremely well-written and very easy to understand, this book on the nervous system and the brain was written for laymen.

Hilgard, E., Atkinson, R. and Atkinson, R. *Introduction to Psychology,* 5th Edition. New York: Harcourt, Brace, Jovanovich, 1971. Chapter 7, "States of Awareness," deals with sleeping and dreaming, hypnosis, meditation, and the effects of drugs. Students will find it particularly interesting.

Kagan, J. and Havemann, E. *Psychology: An Introduction,* 2nd Edition. New York: Harcourt, Brace, Jovanovich, 1972. Chapter 8, "Heredity, Glands and the Nervous System," contains a discussion of how the glands affect behavior that is particularly appropriate to this chapter.

Morgan, C. and King, R. *Introduction to Psychology.* New York: McGraw Hill Book Company, 1971. Chapter 19, "Brain and Behavior," is a very good discussion of the biology of learning and memory, the physiological drives, and drugs and behavior.

Olds, J. "Pleasure Centers in the Brain." *Scientific American Offprints,* No. 30. San Francisco: W. H. Freeman and Company, deals with some fascinating research on the effects of stimulating various brain centers.

Readings in Psychology Today, 2nd Edition. Del Mar, Calif.: CRM Books, 1972. "Who Believes in Hypnosis?" is the discussion by Dr. Ted Barber of the nature of hypnosis which students will find fascinating.

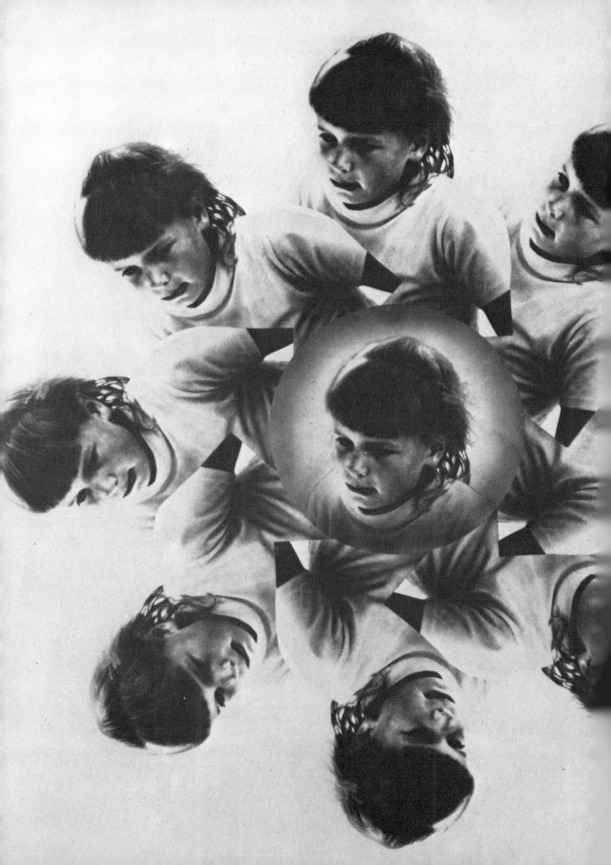

Perception

chapter 10

Everybody knows there are only five senses—vision, hearing, taste, touch, and smell—right? Wrong! In the human body there are probably as many as twenty different senses, each one of particular importance to us. For example, have you ever heard of the "otolith organs"? You have two of them in your head, and without them you would flop around like a fish washed up on a beach. They help us maintain our balance.

Everybody also knows that seeing is believing—in other words, that our senses always give us an accurate picture of what is happening around us. Right? Wrong again! Sometimes our senses give us very bad information about the world, and we have to ignore them because we know they are not telling us the truth. Magicians often take advantage of our senses by presenting us with illusions. In other words, things are not always what they seem to be. Furthermore, did you know that we see the world upside down? That's right—the image of the world around us is upside down in our eyes. We have never seen it any other way, of course, so we manage very well.

Is it possible—even theoretically—that a person without eyes could see, or a person without ears could hear? Is it possible to see light or hear sound when we are in a completely dark, soundproof room? This time the answer is yes. Psychologists are at work now on a system that might permit blind people to "see" through their skin. And it is also possible that someday totally deaf people will hear again with artificial ears. In addition, we can very easily show how one can see light or hear sound when there is no light or sound present.

These are some of the things we will talk about in this chapter. What are the senses? How do they work? Can we believe what they tell us? How does the way we look at things affect the way we behave? Let's begin by examining the senses and how they work.

THE HUMAN SENSES: KEYS TO THE WORLD AROUND US

The sense organs are composed of specialized nerve cells that enable us to be aware of changes in the external environment or within our bodies. Everyone is familiar with the five senses mentioned earlier: vision, hearing, touch, smell, and taste. Not many people however are aware of the fact that the sense of touch is actually four different senses: pressure, heat, cold, and pain. Nor are very many people aware that there are a number of senses located inside the body, in muscles, tendons, and joints. Whenever we move a part of the body, we are aware of it because those senses send neural impulses or messages to the brain.

All of the sense organs operate in very much the same way; they simply convert various kinds of physical energy—light, sound, pressure—into neural impulses. Each sense organ is particularly sensitive to one form of energy. For example, light striking cells located at the back of the eye causes those cells to discharge nerve impulses along the optic nerve to the brain. But this doesn't mean that cells in the eye respond only to light, or that light is the only stimulus that can cause visual sensations.

If you are struck in the eye by a ball, or if you suffer a blow to the head, you "see stars." In other words, you "see" flashes of light. What happens here is that the physical blow to the eye stimulates nerve cells to discharge impulses, and these are transmitted to the visual area of the brain. A blow on the head often causes nerve cells in the visual area of the brain to discharge, and thus you also experience a visual sensation—"seeing stars."

The kinds of sensations we experience, then, depend not necessarily on the physical stimulus involved or even on which sense organ was activated. Sensations clearly depend on the part of the brain activated. Nerve impulses terminating in the visual area can result only in visual sensations; those terminating in the auditory or hearing area can result only in auditory sensations. Theoretically, it would be possible for us to "see sound" or "hear light"; if somehow the nerve impulses from the ear were short-circuited and wound up in the visual area, we would "see sound," and if impulses from the eyes ended up in the auditory area, we would "hear light."

From this discussion, you should be able to tell how one might see light in a totally dark room or hear sound when there is no sound. If we stimulated the visual part of the brain while a person was in a totally dark room, that person would experience visual sensations. Similarly, if we stimulated the auditory part of the brain, the person would hear sound. How could we do this? It could easily be done with tiny electrodes touched to nerve cells on the surface of the brain. Nerve cells can be stimulated to discharge or fire by an electrical stimulus. In fact, surgeons operating on the brain often use such techniques to study how the brain functions.

You should also be able to tell from this discussion how a totally deaf person might hear again or how a totally blind person might see. If the blindness or deafness resulted from damage to the ears or eyes, and not to the auditory or visual areas of the brain, we should be able to construct artificial ears or eyes. In other words, we would need to build a device that converted sound or light into neural impulses and then transmit these impulses directly into the appropriate part of the brain. No scientist would even begin to pretend that this is possible today or even in the foreseeable future. There are other possibilities, however, such as teaching the blind to "see" with the skin. We will return to this shortly, but first we must take a closer look at vision.

Fig. 10–1. Below is a diagram of the thin photosensitive surface of the eye—the retina. Note that the rods and cones are in the layer cells farthest away from the front of the eye.

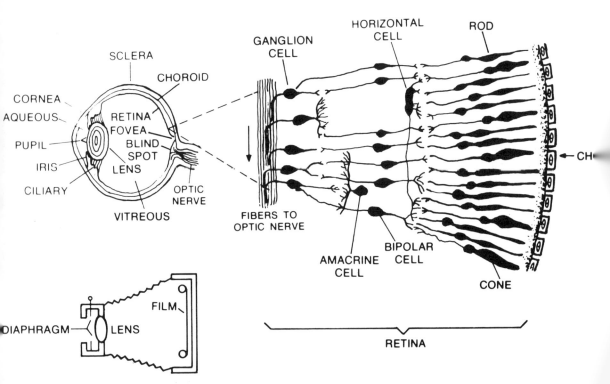

How the Eye Works

The human eye is the finest light-sensitive organ in the world. Some physical instruments, or the eyes of other animals, may be better for detecting certain things, but none can match the human eye for its range of abilities —sensitivity to light, color discrimination, and sensitivity to detail.

In terms of sensitivity to brightness, the human eye can detect differences ranging from the brightness of the sun to a very dim star. Sensitivity to detail is so great that it can detect a black line one-quarter of an inch wide at a distance of one-and-a-half miles. Finally, the human eye can differentiate some 20,000 colors and if we consider various tints and shades, the possible discriminations run as high as 350,000.

The eye, as shown in Fig. 10–1, consists of a number of different parts. There is a tough outer layer which helps protect it and maintain its shape. The part sensitive to light is called the *retina*, and this is the innermost layer. Light reaches the retina by first passing through the cornea, then the pupil, and finally, the lens which focuses the light on the central part of the retina.

In some respects the eye is like a camera. Both have shutters (the eyelid in the human eye) which can prevent light from entering. Furthermore, the opening through which the light enters can change size; the *iris* or colored part of the eye does this. In addition, light in both camera and the eye passes through a *lens* which reverses the image so that it is focused upside down on a light sensitive surface (*retina* or film).

But there are many differences between the eye and camera. The inside of the eye is filled with a thick clear liquid, not air as in the camera. Also, light is focused both by the cornea and lens in the eye, but only by the lens in the camera. In addition, the lens in the eye changes shape in order to focus the light, while in the camera the lens moves back and forth. There are other differences as well. For example, we know that the eye is constantly moving and that when movement stops completely, the image on the retina fades quickly away.

The light sensitive layer of the eye—the retina—is quite different from film in a camera. We need not go into all the differences here, but it is important to know that the retina contains two different kinds of structures that enable us to see not only black and white but colors as well. These are the rods and cones.

If we magnify the retina and examine the structures it contains, we notice that some are long and thin while others are shorter and thicker. The former, called *rods,* are much more numerous than the latter, the *cones.* The rods are responsible for night vision, while the cones are the receptors for day vision. At night, the cones become relatively inactive and we cannot see colors. This is because the cones need more light than the rods to function properly. At night, when there is less light, we see largely with the rods, and because of this we cannot see colors. Some people of course, cannot see colors at all, or see only some colors; they are color-blind.

What Is Color Blindness?

It is surprising that it was not until about 1800 that people became aware of color blindness. Surely there were color-blind people before that time. But even today there are color-blind people who do not know they are color-blind. How can this be? How can a person not see certain colors and at the same time be unaware of it?

First of all most color-blind people can see some colors. In fact the average color-blind person sees all colors except red and green. He (and it usually is a male) thinks he can differentiate red and green. This is because he has learned to respond to cues other than hue (red, green, blue, and so on). Color actually has three visible aspects, only one of which is *hue*. The others are *brightness* (how light or dark the color is) and *saturation* (how deep or rich the color is). Thus two colors can be of the same hue—for example, green—but differ in both brightness and saturation. Color-blind persons often learn to differentiate red and green because of differences in the brightness of these colors. In addition they learn that certain objects such as grass are green, while others such as apples are red. But when given a test for color blindness in which both red and green are the same brightness, they cannot tell the difference.

Can color blindness be cured? It cannot, in most cases, because it is an inherited condition which affects the cones. As we mentioned above, very few women are color-blind; in fact, only about one-half of 1 per cent are affected. On the other hand, about 8 per cent of the male population is color-blind. This is because color blindness is genetically determined by a sex-linked recessive gene. If a color-blind man marries a normal woman, in other words, they will have normal children but the daughters will carry the gene for color blindness. If these daughters have sons, the sons will have a 50–50 chance of being color-blind.

What are Illusions?

Illusions are false perceptions of stimuli. If you look at Fig. 10–2 for example, the line on the left looks longer than the line on the right. Yet the

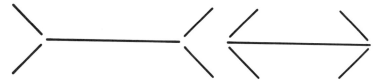

Fig. 10–2. The Müller-Lyer Illusion. Subjects in Western cultures tend to perceive the straight line on the left as longer. However, most subjects in primitive societies do not perceive the illusion.

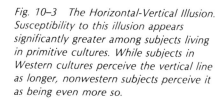

Fig. 10–3 The Horizontal-Vertical Illusion. Susceptibility to this illusion appears significantly greater among subjects living in primitive cultures. While subjects in Western cultures perceive the vertical line as longer, nonwestern subjects perceive it as being even more so.

two lines are exactly the same length, as are the lines shown in Fig. 10–3. An even more surprising illusion is shown in Fig. 10–4. Why are the two faces so different in size? Is one person a dwarf and the other a giant? No. Both men are almost the same size, yet they appear different because they are different distances from the camera that took the picture; the man on the left is much further away. You can see this easily if you look at the diagram of the room shown in Fig. 10–4. Note that the left side of the rear wall is much further away from the viewer than the right side. It does not appear to be, because the rear wall is not rectangular.

Almost all people see the illusion in Fig. 10–4, because they have learned that the walls of rooms are usually rectangular, and they expect them to be. Thus this tells us quite a bit about illusions and about perception in general. We often experience illusions because we have developed certain ideas about how the world is and how it should appear. Perception is not simply the passive recording of information by the sense organs. It is a creative act. In other words, we develop hypotheses about what is out there, and we expect to see the world as we believe it to be.

Fig. 10–4   Distorted Room As Used By Ames. The two faces appear quite different in size, although they seem to be the same distance away.

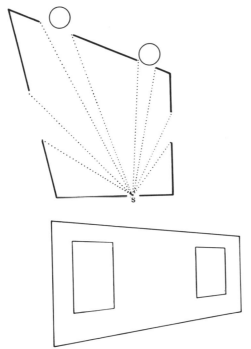

Evidence that this is true comes in part from studies of how people in different parts of the world respond to illusions. If the perception of illusions depended upon certain characteristics of the eye, then all normal-sighted people should perceive the same illusions. The fact is, they do not. We in our culture see the left line in Fig. 10–2 as longer than the right line. But people living in other cultures often perceive these lines as the same length. Thus it is evident that the kinds of experiences we have had, the kinds of things we have come in contact with, affect our perception of the world, and our susceptibility to illusions as well.

"Seeing" with the Skin

Before leaving the topic of vision, we want to look briefly at some fascinating recent experiments which may ultimately lead to the development of new "eyes" for the blind. Several psychologists in California have been exploring how the skin might be used as a communication channel. The "eye" of the system they have developed consists of a television camera which can be moved by the subject being tested to any part of the room in order to locate and identify objects. The image from this camera is transformed and sent to dozens of vibrators mounted in the back of a chair. As the camera is moved, these vibrators respond in a pattern reflecting the televised object. Thus if the camera is focused on an "X," the vibrators reflect the "X" pattern. The subject, in other words, feels this pattern on his back.

A number of totally blind people have been tested with this device and they very quickly learn to identify vertical or horizontal stripes and other simple figures. With practice, many of them have learned to identify a collection of some 25 objects such as a coffee cup, a telephone, and a stuffed animal. Such results, as the psychologists who developed it note, are the basis for cautious optimism about the ultimate possibility of developing a substitute for the visual system. With a sensor that could be mounted on the head and a mobile backpack, the blind person may ultimately be able to move about in his or her environment as easily as a sighted person.

Hearing

Just as the eye is amazing for its sensitivity to light, the human ear is also remarkable for its sensitivity to sound. For example, if an insect one-tenth the size of a mosquito were to jump up and down on your eardrum 3,500 times per second, you could hear it. Yet the distance the eardrum moves in this case is only one-tenth the diameter of a hydrogen molecule! In

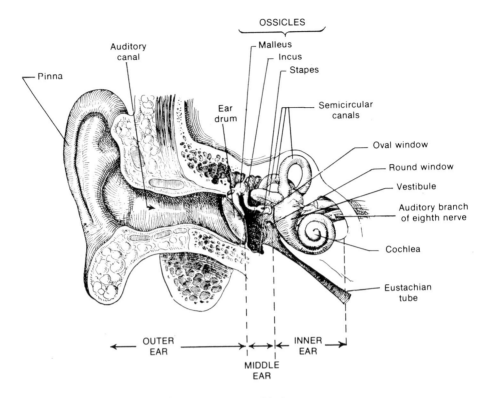

Fig. 10-5 Diagram Of The Human Ear.

fact, if the ear were any more sensitive than it is you could hear the movement of air molecules. Furthermore, the range of sensitivity to sound by the ear is as fantastic as the range of sensitivity to light by the eye.

How does the ear work? We know that the outer part of the ear, the part sticking out from your head, is relatively unimportant in hearing. All it does is to focus sound waves down the tunnel or canal leading to the eardrum. If you look at the diagram in Fig. 10-5, you can see that the true hearing part of the ear is located deep within the bony structure of your skull.

Sound waves travel down the auditory canal and strike the eardrum. Attached to the eardrum are three small bones the smallest in the body sometimes called the *hammer, anvil,* and *stirrup* (because of their shapes). When the eardrum moves, these three bones also move, and they carry the sound waves to a tiny oval membrane located in the *cochlea.* The cochlea is a spiral-shaped hollow structure filled with fluid. When the oval window vibrates the fluid in the cochlea moves, and this causes nerve cells located along a structure called the *basilar membrane* to fire. The basilar membrane is a triangular-shaped structure inside the cochlea. Nerve impulses from the cells located along the basilar membrane are then sent through the auditory nerve to the brain.

There are three dimensions to sound just as there are three dimensions to color. The dimensions in hearing are called pitch, loudness, and quality. *Pitch* refers to how high or low the sound is. *Loudness,* of course, refers to the intensity of the sound, while *quality* refers to how pure the sound is. No one knows exactly how the ear is able to differentiate these three characteristics, although there are a number of theories.

The Other Senses

At the beginning of this chapter we mentioned that there are probably as many as twenty different senses in the human body. We need not discuss all of them here, but a few words about several of them will help to increase our understanding of how complex perception really is.

Taste and smell are sometimes called the *chemical senses* because chemical reactions seem to be involved in some way in their functioning. The sense organs for taste are located on the tongue and also in parts of the mouth. We know that there are only four qualities of taste: salt, sweet, sour, and bitter. In other words, particular organs for taste, the *taste buds* each respond to one and only one taste. If this is true, how can we taste something other than these four qualities? No one knows for sure, but probably because two or more of these different taste buds are activated at the same time.

The sense organs for smell are located in a small region of the nasal cavity. In spite of the relative inaccessibility of these organs, smell is about 10,000 times more sensitive than taste. In fact we can smell some things in concentrations so low that there are no physical or chemical means of measuring them. We also know that smell and taste are somehow related. When we have a cold, for example, this affects the taste of food. No one knows how or why this occurs.

Other senses are located in the skin and deep within the body. The sense of touch, as we noted earlier, is actually four senses: pressure, heat, cold, and pain. Each of these sensations results from the stimulation of different sense organs. Pain is perhaps the most mysterious of the four, since a number of physical stimuli trigger it. Also, we know today that injury is not the only cause of pain, and that the amount of pain experienced is not proportional to the injury. Much more work has to be done, however, before we fully understand this sense and how it works.

Balance and equilibrium result from the operation of sense organs located in the head as well as in muscles, tendons, and joints. Some of the sense organs located within the body are activated when we move. Others respond in the absence of stimulation so that we know the position of our body even though we may not have moved for some time.

On each side of the head in the bony structure of the skull are the *otolith organs* or semicircular canals. There are three canals or hollow structures in each organ, and these canals are in different planes from one another. The otolith organs are filled with a thick fluid that moves whenever the head is moved in any direction. Movement of the fluid in the canals causes hairlike fibers to trigger nerve cells which send impulses to the brain. Without the otolith organs, we would have a difficult time in maintaining our balance.

.Now that we have some understanding of the sense organs and how they work we are ready to turn our attention to perception. As we will see, perception is a process that in part involves the activities of the sense organs. But it is more than that. In part at least, it involves how we interpret or understand the information sent to the brain by the senses.

WHAT IS PERCEPTION?

We are so accustomed to trusting our senses that it is sometimes difficult for the student to understand the nature of human perception. The eye may not be exactly like a camera, but doesn't the eye simply record the world as it is and transmit this to the brain? Doesn't the ear record sound like a tape recorder and send this information to the brain?

As we mentioned earlier in this chapter, perception is not simply the passive recording of information by the sense organs; it is a creative process. We have ideas about "what is out there," and we expect to see the world as we believe it to be. Thus how we perceive the world around us depends not only upon what our senses tell us but also upon ourselves as perceivers. We can say then, that perception is a process that intervenes between the activities of the senses and behavior. It is initiated by the information from the sense organs but not completely determined by it.

One famous psychologist, Wolfgang Köhler, said long ago that perception is a "bi-polar process." By this he meant that perception has two aspects or parts. One part consists of the messages or information sent to the brain by the sense organs. The other part consists of characteristics of us—our personalities, motives, beliefs, values, and even the language we speak.

Does this mean that how we perceive the world depends on what motives we have, or what our personality is like, or whether we speak English, French, or some other language? You bet it does! Not entirely of course, but these factors play a role in all human perception to a greater or lesser degree.

Why Perception Is Important to You

Perception is important to each and every one of us because what we perceive determines our behavior. To illustrate this and also the fact that things such as beliefs influence perception, suppose we perform a simple experiment. Let's assume that we place a small nonpoisonous snake in a cage. We ask several people to come into the room to observe the snake and we tell them that it is a perfectly harmless garden snake. By "accident," we tip over the cage and let the snake escape into the room. How would the people react? A few would be frightened, since some people have a fear of all snakes. Most however, would not react with great fear.

Now suppose we go through exactly the same procedure with a different group of people. The only difference this time is that we tell them the snake is one of the most deadly poisonous reptiles on earth. How do you think they would behave when we "accidentally" tipped over the cage, letting the snake escape? No doubt most people would try to leave the room by the nearest exit, and as quickly as possible.

The same snake was used with both groups. Yet the perception of those in one group was in part determined by their belief that the snake was poisonous, while the perception of the others was influenced by the belief that the snake was harmless. Different perceptions, then, led to dramatically different behavior. Furthermore, we can see that perception is determined by more than the information sent to the brain by the sense organs. Both groups saw the same snake, yet one group perceived it as dangerous and the other as harmless.

Perception in Different Situations

In many cases our perception of the world around us corresponds very closely to the information sent to the brain by the sense organs. If someone holds up a book and asks us what we perceive we say, "A book." Our personality or motives do not influence our perception of clear-cut objects such as this. But not all objects in the environment are this clear-cut. Sometimes we face stimuli in the environment that are unclear or ambiguous. For example, look at the object shown in Fig. 10–6. What do you perceive? Do you think

Fig. 10–6 An Ambiguous Stimulus. Perception of this stimulus is determined more by characteristics of the perceiver than by characteristics of the stimulus.

other people would perceive the same thing you do? The chances are that if we asked everybody in your class what they perceive in Fig. 10–6, we would receive a variety of answers.

Fig. 10–6 is an example of an unclear or ambiguous stimulus, and we know that the perception of such stimuli depends to a greater extent on the perceiver than on the stimuli involved. In other words, when we face ambiguous stimuli, our personalities, motives, values, or beliefs are much more likely to affect our perception than when we face stimuli that are clear-cut.

Does this knowledge have any practical value? Can we make use of it to better understand behavior? The answer is yes. As we will learn in the next chapter, some of the most widely used tests of personality are based on the principles discussed above. The best known of these, the Rorschach test, consists of ten inkblots made by dropping ink on a piece of paper and then folding it over. The result is a symmetrical blot of irregular shape that people perceive in different ways. Ten of these blots make up the test, and the person taking the test is simply asked what the blot looks like—what might it be?

You will remember that the perception of unclear or ambiguous stimuli such as these inkblots tends to be determined more by the perceiver himself than by the nature of the stimulus. What the person "sees" thus gives us an understanding of his personality. We know that people with similar personality characteristics tend to perceive the inkblots in similar ways. Those with different personalities perceive the blots differently.

There are other practical uses for these principles as well. For example, some psychologists have devised ambiguous stimuli which help us measure attitudes. Through what the person perceives, he tells us about certain of his attitudes without even realizing it.

We will return to these and other topics in the next chapter, which deals with personality. In particular we will be concerned with how people perceive one another and how we form impressions of other people. Before going on to that, however, we need to conclude our discussion of perception with a brief overview of the nature of attention.

PAY ATTENTION!

When we are awake, the sense organs of the body send a tremendous amount of information to the brain. Yet at any one time we are aware of only a limited amount of it. If we are listening to our teacher, we are only vaguely aware of people whispering near us. We do not clearly perceive those walking down the hall. We do not notice the temperature of the room. Obviously

Fig. 10–7   Times Square in New York City. Why do some of the signs attract our attention while others do not? Size, movement, and novelty are just three of the reasons.

we have some control over what stimuli become the focal point in our perceptions.

Attention, like perception, can be determined primarily by the stimuli around us or by characteristics of ourselves. Let's take a look first at how stimulus conditions affect attention.

Stimuli that Attract Us

First of all, it is obvious that any sudden change in stimulus conditions attracts our attention. If the lights suddenly go out or if there is a loud crash nearby, our attention is drawn to those stimuli. Whether a particular stimulus attracts our attention, however, is also determined by the background of competing stimuli. A sudden shout in the library or in study hall, attracts everyone's attention, while the same shout at a football game would go unnoticed.

Movement is another stimulus characteristic that attracts attention. When everything else is standing still, one moving object tends to attract our attention. By the same token, when everything else is moving, one object remaining stationary attracts attention.

Size is another characteristic that influences attention. Large objects, in general, are better attention getters than small objects. Repetition is another factor that attracts attention. If we are listening to the radio while we study, we may become unaware of it as we try to learn the material in our book. If the disk jockey lets the needle get stuck in one groove, however, so that the same notes play over and over, we find our attention drawn to the radio. Novelty and high frequency sounds also are examples of stimulus conditions affecting attention. But attention is not determined alone by stimulus conditions.

How We Influence Attention

As noted above, we often control our attention. We consciously decide to pay attention to the teacher or to the football team on the field. But there are also characteristics we have as people that determine our attention as well. For example, when we are hungry we are much more likely to attend to the pleasant smell of food cooking. If we are interested in automobiles, we are much more likely to notice the new models driving down the street. And finally, if we are an average young man, we are much more likely to pay attention to the girls around us, while the average girl is much more likely to notice the boys.

Motives, interests, values, and even personality characteristics are internal factors that determine attention. In some cases our attention is likely to be determined by the stimulus characteristics around us. In other cases, characteristics we ourselves possess determine our attention.

How Advertisers Use Attention

The successful advertiser knows a great deal about the factors that determine attention. If he wants to erect an outdoor sign that will attract attention, he knows it should be large and also involve movement of some sort (for example, moving lights). In addition, novelty is a great help in securing attention. This latter factor is of special importance in an age when we are literally bombarded with advertising.

These principles also hold not only for outdoor advertising but for magazine and television advertising as well. There is much more involved in successful advertising, of course, than simply drawing attention to one's ads. The advertiser designs his ads with knowledge of the motives, anxieties, and frustrations of his audience in mind. For example, have you noticed how many ads are aimed directly at the teen-age billion dollar market? A large proportion of ads for breath mints, deodorants, teeth whiteners, shampoos, hair sprays, nail lengtheners, facial cosmetics, and shaving lotions are clearly aimed at this market. Why? The implication in many of these ads of course, is that brighter teeth or sweeter breath or shinier hair will make you more popular and help you get dates—and attractive ones at that. The reverse implication is that if you ignore these products you are likely to be in big trouble. Next time you watch television or read a magazine, try to see if you can tell who the advertiser is trying to reach and what he is really saying.

CHAPTER SUMMARY

1. The human sense organs are composed of specialized nerve cells that enable us to be aware of changes in the external environment and within our bodies. There are probably as many as twenty different senses, each one particularly sensitive to one form of physical energy such as light, sound, pressure, and so on.

2. The sense organs convert various kinds of physical energy into neural impulses. Thus nerve cells in the eye discharge or fire when stimulated by light. But the kinds of sensations we experience do not necessarily depend on the physical stimulus involved or even the sense organ itself. Sensations depend upon the part of the brain activated by incoming nerve impulses.

3. The human eye is the finest light sensitive organ in the world. No physical instrument or eye of another animal can match the human eye for its range of abilities—sensitivity to light, color discrimination, and sensitivity to detail. The part of the eye sensitive to light is called the *retina*. Light reaches the retina by passing through the cornea, the pupil, and finally, the lens.

4. In some respects the eye is like a camera. Both have shutters, a changeable opening through which light enters, a lens, and finally, a light sensitive surface. The interior of the eye however, is filled with liquid—not air as in the camera. Also, light is focused by both the cornea and lens in the eye, but only by the lens in a camera. In addition, the lens in the eye changes shape in order to focus light while focusing in the camera occurs when the lens moves back and forth.

5. The retina of the eye contains two different kinds of structures that enable us to see not only black and white, but colors as well. These are the *rods* and *cones*. The rods are responsible for night vision, and less light is needed to activate them in comparison to the cones, which function mainly during the day.

6 Color blindness is generally an inherited condition which largely affects males. Most color-blind people can see all colors except red and green. Color has three visible aspects: hue, brightness, and saturation. Color-blind people sometimes learn to differentiate red and green when they are of different brightness.

7. Illusions are false perceptions of stimuli. We often experience illusions because we have developed certain ideas about how the world is and how it should appear. Thus perception is not simply the passive recording of information by the sense organs. It is a creative process. Not all people perceive the same illusions, and this suggests that the kinds of experiences we have had affect our perception of the world.

8. The range of sensitivity of the ear is as remarkable as the range of sensitivity to light by the eye. When we hear, sound waves travel down the auditory canal and strike the eardrum. Attached to the eardrum are three small bones which carry the sound waves to the cochlea, a spiral shaped organ filled with fluid. Movement of the fluid within the cochlea causes nerve cells along the basilar membrane to fire.

9. Taste and smell are called the chemical senses because chemical reactions seem to be involved in their functioning. Other sense organs are located in the skin and deep within the body. In the skin there are actually four senses: Heat, cold, pressure, and pain. Balance and equilibrium result from the operation of sense organs located in the head (the otolith organs or semicircular canals) as well as in muscles, tendons, and joints.

10. Perception is a process with two aspects or parts. One part consists of the information sent to the brain by the sense organs. The other part consists of characteristics of ourselves—our personality, motives, beliefs, values, and even the language we speak. In many cases our perception of the world around us corresponds very closely to the information sent to the brain by the sense organs. This is particularly true in our perception of clear-cut and unambiguous stimuli. The perception of ambiguous stimuli, however, depends to a greater extent on the perceiver than on the stimuli involved.

11. Attention, like perception, can be determined primarily by the stimuli around us or by characteristics of ourselves. In terms of stimulus conditions that attract attention, we know that any sudden change in our surroundings is important. Movement and size as well as repetition and novelty are also important. Motives, interests, values, and even personality characteristics are among the internal factors that determine attention.

Important Terms from This Chapter

perception	color blindness	cochlea
cornea	hue	basilar membrane
retina	brightness	chemical senses
iris	saturation	otolith organs
rods	illusions	semicircular canals
cones		attention

Additional Readings to Help You Learn More

Mussen, P. and Rosenzweig, M. *Psychology: An Introduction.* Lexington, Mass.: D. C. Heath Company, 1973. Chapter 22, "The Creativity of Perception," discusses the nature of perception and how hereditary and environmental factors interact to determine perception.

Psychology Today: An Introduction, 2nd Edition. Del Mar, Calif.: CRM Books, 1972. Chapter 13, "The Senses," enlarges substantially upon the discussion presented in this chapter.

Part VI.

ADJUSTMENT: KNOWING
WHO YOU ARE

Personality

chapter 11

At the beginning of this book, we said that psychologists attempt to predict behavior and that accurate predictions are necessary if we are to change certain undesirable behaviors such as mental illness or criminality. Yet many people, including more than a few beginning students in psychology, believe that behavior is unpredictable. Why? Well, one reason often given is that each individual is unique. He or she has a personality unlike that of any other human being. If this is so, how can one hope to find general principles or laws that would lead to the accurate prediction of what a person might do in this or that situation?

As we will see in this chapter, psychologists are in general agreement that no human personality is exactly like any other. Yet at the same time, scientific studies of personality have shown that, despite uniqueness, it is possible to measure personality characteristics and to make reasonably accurate predictions about behavior based on these measurements.

In this chapter we will examine how personality is studied and measured. We will also discuss a number of theories about the nature of personality. Finally, we will talk about the self and how we defend it against things that threaten our self-esteem.

DIFFERENT IDEAS ABOUT PERSONALITY

If you look at the people around you—those you know in school and in your neighborhood—how would you describe them? Some, you would probably say, are friendly, happy, outgoing, and capable. Others you might call reserved, quiet, moody, and shy. A few might have one or two really striking characteristics. One may be a show-off, always clowning around and making people laugh. Another might be a Don Juan, a ladies' man interested in dating every girl he can.

There is something else you would note also, if you stopped to think about it. There is a certain consistency to personality. Once you know a person well, you expect him or her to behave in much the same way each time you meet. Of course, people have moods. On a particular day, a normally happy-go-lucky person may act down in the dumps. But for the most part when we really know someone well, we can usually predict how she or he will behave. Moods may change from day to day, but personality tends to be rather consistent.

The thoughts expressed above generally reflect what psychologists call a *trait* approach to personality. Theories of personality based on traits utilize a number of dimensions that are assumed to be common to all men and women.

What Are Trait Theories?

Trait theories attempt to describe personality in terms of a limited number of dimensions such as dominance-submission, masculinity-femininity, and introversion-extraversion. These theories assume, for the most part, that such traits exist to a greater or lesser degree in every human personality.

One problem with such theories, of course, is in deciding how many traits or dimensions are required in order to describe personality. Can we account for the differences among people with ten traits, or twenty, or do we need even more? Psychologists disagree on the required number as well as on the traits themselves.

One famous psychologist, Gordon Allport, has said that certain personality characteristics are not found in all people. Thus he believed that while it is valuable to study or describe personality in terms of the traits all people have, we need to go beyond that. He spoke in terms of what he called "cardinal traits," "central traits," and "secondary traits."

Cardinal traits, according to Allport, are those that are seen only rarely, but they are so dominant and obvious that the person is known by the trait and may even be famous because of it. A "Don Juan" or a "Beau Brummel" would be examples. Central traits are those that come most read-

Fig. 11–1   President Kennedy manifested dominant and obvious personality traits that have been called "cardinal traits" by psychologists.

ily to mind when we think about the personality of someone we know. These are the traits, in other words, that might be mentioned in a letter of recommendation. Finally, secondary traits are less conspicuous and less often seen in the person's behavior than central or cardinal traits.

Not all psychologists feel that personality may be best described and understood in terms of traits. Some believe that there are personality *types*.

Are There Different Types of Personality?

There are two rather different approaches to the idea of personality types. One approach is based on the idea that there is a correspondence between body build and personality. The other approach holds that there are different psychological types.

Earlier in this book we examined the notion that personality is related to body build. The first of these theories originated with the Greek philosophers, but there have been many others down through the ages. Put very simply, these theories hold that clusters of traits are associated with body type. Short, fat people, for example, are believed to be dependent, relaxed, and pleasure-loving. Tall, thin people, are believed to enjoy privacy, solitude, and emotional restraint.

We need not go into all of the details about such theories here. It is sufficient to say that they are probably oversimplifications and have limited use in enabling us to predict behavior.

Theories of psychological types assume that people can be placed in this or that category. For example, a well known psychologist, Carl Jung, described personality in terms of introversion and extraversion. Introverts, he believed, avoid people. They are content to spend evenings at home alone reading rather than being with other people. Extraverts, on the other hand, would rather be around other people than by themselves. They are likely to want a job as a salesman or social worker rather than, say, a laboratory technician.

If you think about people you know, you may say, "Well, Jung was right —some people are introverts and others are extraverts." But how many of your friends could you classify into one or the other category? Most people are what we call *ambiverts*. That is, sometimes they are introverted in their behavior while at other times they are extraverts. One problem with such theories, then, is that most people do not fit in nice, neat categories. Furthermore, even for those few who do fit, have you really adequately described his or her personality when you say she or he is an introvert . . . or extravert?

By this time you can see that personality is not as easy to define and explain as you may have thought earlier. In fact, there are many more theories of personality than we have discussed so far. We will not discuss all of them, but we do need to look briefly at Freud's theory before going on to talk about some other aspects of personality. Freud's theory is important because it is more widely known and perhaps more widely used to explain personality than any of the others.

Freud and Psychoanalysis

Sigmund Freud (1856–1939) was a physician who lived in Vienna, Austria. The theory of personality he developed was largely constructed as

Fig. 11-2 Sigmund Freud in his later years.

a result of trying to treat the mentally ill. For the most part he treated the so-called psychoneurotic person, in contrast to the more seriously ill psychotic. We will discuss these forms of mental illness in greater detail in the following chapter. An important point to note here, however, is that before Freud's work it was generally believed that all mental illnesses had a physical basis. In treating patients, however, Freud became convinced that less serious mental illnesses were caused by events or experiences in the individual's life—particularly in his or her early life.

Early in his career Freud employed hypnosis as a means of getting the patient to talk about his or her childhood. The patient was first hypnotized, and then, while lying on a couch, was asked to talk about his early life. Particularly important, Freud thought, was the individual's relationships with his or her parents as well as brothers and sisters.

Hypnosis was abandoned as a technique, however, when Freud found that some patients are very difficult or even impossible to hypnotize. Furthermore he found that another technique, *free association*, worked just as well. In free association the patient lies on a couch and says whatever comes to mind. The psychoanalyst then interprets or explains the meaning of what is said in terms of the individual's current problems. As we learned in an earlier chapter, Freud also believed that dreams were significant in terms of what they revealed about the "unconscious mind." Thus the interpretation of dreams became an important part of psychoanalysis as a treatment for the mentally ill.

Freud developed so many ideas about personality and its formation that we could not possibly discuss all of them in the short space of this chapter. Two parts of his theory, however, are important to summarize. The first of these has to do with the structure or makeup of personality, and the second is concerned with its development.

Freud's View of Human Personality

As we mentioned above, Freud thought that the mind is divided into two parts: conscious and unconscious. Those thoughts and feelings that we can freely verbalize are conscious. Whenever thoughts or feelings make us extremely anxious, however, they become unconscious and cannot be freely verbalized. We may not be aware that we even have such thoughts or feelings. Nevertheless, even though certain ideas or feelings may be unconscious, they still affect our behavior. Unconscious feelings may be reflected in various "symptoms," or even in such simple things as "slips" of the tongue or pen. For example, we mean to say or write one thing, but without realizing it, we say or write just the opposite.

In terms of personality, Freud thought that there are three parts: the id, the ego, and the superego. The *id* consists of those instinctual urges with which the individual is born, according to Freud. This part of personality is concerned only with selfish pleasure. As the individual grows, however, another part of personality develops out of the id: the *ego*. This part of personality is reality-oriented, according to Freud. It tries to satisfy the in-

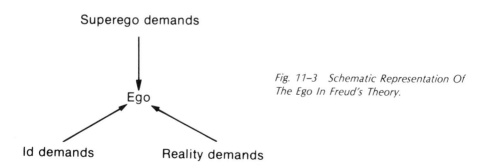

Fig. 11–3 *Schematic Representation Of The Ego In Freud's Theory.*

Fig. 11–4 The superego is formed in part through reward and punishment by our parents. We learn what is right and wrong as we grow up, and these standards become a part of our personality.

stinctual urges of the id but in such a way that the individual does not get in trouble with those around him.

The *superego* is the moral arm of personality. It consists of all of the socially acceptable ways of behaving taught by parents and others. It represents the ideal, and it strives for perfection rather than pleasure. The id, then, might be called the "do" part of personality while the superego could be called the "don't" part.

According to Freud, there is a delicate balance that exists between these three parts of personality. The ego acts as a mediator between the id and superego, and at the same time acts to keep the individual's behavior in line with reality. In some people, if the superego is weak, the person has difficulty with society because he satisfies his own selfish needs without regard for others. In still other people, the superego is so strong that the people are unable to satisfy needs—particularly sexual ones—and they suffer guilt feelings as well.

Freud and the Development of Personality

In the discussion above, we can see some of Freud's ideas about how personality develops. The individual is born with the id, and the ego and superego develop out of it. But there is much more than this to personality development, according to Freud.

Freud assumed that all human beings go through a number of stages

Fig. 11–5 During the oral stage the baby is likely to be much more interested in the bottle than in the animals present. In later personality stages his interests will change.

in personality development. The first of these, the *oral stage*, occurs from birth until about one year of age. During this stage the infant derives pleasure from the mouth. His or her whole world, in other words, revolves around eating. Frustration during this period has consequences for later personality development, according to Freud. Oral sarcasm and argumentation often stem from frustrations and other difficulties during the oral stage.

The *anal stage* lasts from one to three years of age, and during this stage the child goes through toilet training. As in the oral stage, problems during this period may leave a permanent mark on one's personality. Be-

Fig. 11–6 Boys learn to be boys and girls to be girls by identifying with the parent of the same sex. The kind of behavior seen here is much more common in boys than in girls.

tween three and six years of age, the *genitals* become the center of the child's attention, according to Freud. It is during this stage that the boy goes through the Oedipus complex and the girl through the Electra complex.

Without going into great detail, both Oedipus and Electra complexes involve the development of sexual identification. It is during this period in other words that most boys learn they are boys and girls learn they are girls. Basically this involves identification of the boy or girl with the parent of the same sex. Some psychologists believe that homosexuality has its origins in this stage, where in some cases the child overidentifies with the parent of the opposite sex.

This is a very abbreviated, capsule summary of Freud's views of personality. Not all psychologists go along with these ideas, but certainly no one can deny that they have had tremendous impact on psychology as a whole and particularly on theories of mental illness and its treatment.

THE SELF AND HOW WE DEFEND IT

Some theories of personality use the self as the central concept. The *self* is sometimes defined as the feelings, attitudes, perceptions, and evaluations that the person holds about himself or herself as an object. Self-esteem, as we noted in an earlier chapter, is important to all of us. We try to set achievable goals in line with our abilities because to do otherwise (as, for example, setting unrealistically high goals) may lead to failure and a subsequent blow to self-esteem. Furthermore, we know that our interactions with others have a great deal to do with the maintenance or change of self-esteem. We are thus highly selective in terms of who we associate with. We tend to select friends from among those who think well of us and to avoid those who obviously dislike us.

As one psychologist has noted, all friendship is, at least in part, a mutual admiration society. Each person in the relationship helps to maintain the self-esteem of the other. The best example of this is in romantic love and the great intensity with which the mutual admiration is held. Such relationships are surely a great prop to self-esteem.

How do people react to perceived threats to self-esteem? Suppose we fail at something very important to us? Suppose we do something we feel ashamed of? Some reactions, of course, are reality-oriented; we try to change the situation or our behavior in some way. The boy who fails to make the school football team may practice all summer in order to make the team the following fall. The girl who has no dates may try different styles of hair or makeup. In other situations we may compromise or try to find substitutes.

The Defense Mechanisms

Not all reactions to threats to self-esteem are reality-oriented. Sometimes we distort reality in ways not designed to change the situation, but simply to make us feel better. Such reactions are called *defense mechanisms* and, while some people use them more than others, they are observed in the behavior of every human being.

RATIONALIZATION. Perhaps the most common of all defense mechanisms is *rationalization.* When we rationalize, we find logical but false reasons for past, present, or future behavior. These reasons protect us from recognizing and admitting our own weaknesses and shortcomings. The boy, for example, who fails to make the school basketball team because he was not a good enough player, may say, "I didn't really want to be on the team anyway—they're going to have a losing season." The sour grapes attitude reflected in this statement makes rejection from the team easier to take. Also, in such a case the real reason—not being good enough—is unrecognized by the person involved. To recognize and admit the real reason would hurt his self-esteem. Therefore, he rationalizes the situation.

Students often rationalize when they receive poor grades in a course. It makes one feel better to say, "The tests were unfair," or "The teacher didn't like me," or "I didn't need to do well in that class anyway," than it is to say "I am stupid, that's why I made a poor grade," or "I was too lazy to study."

Examples of some of the rationalizations used by students are shown in the following section:

ALIBI-OGRAPHY FOR STUDENTS

What to say—

When you are given an objective test: "It doesn't let you express yourself."

When you are given an essay test: "It's so vague. You don't know what's expected."

When you are given many minor tests: "Why not have a few big ones? This keeps you on edge all the time."

When you are given a few major tests: "Too much depends on each one."

When you are given no test: "It's not fair. How can he possibly judge what we know?"

When every part of the subject is taken up in class: "Oh, he just follows the book."

When you are asked to study a part of the subject by yourself: "Why we never even discussed it!"

When the course is in lecture form: "We never get a chance to say anything!"

When the course consists of informal lecture and discussion: "He just sits there. Who wants to hear the students? They don't know how to teach the course."

When detailed material is presented: "What's the use? You forget it all after the exam anyway."

When general principles are presented: "What did we learn? We knew all that before we took the course."

One point to remember in connection with the defense mechanisms is that one is not aware that he or she is using them. If the person was aware he or she was rationalizing, for example, rationalization would offer no defense to one's self-esteem.

REPRESSION. Another defense mechanism used to protect our self-esteem is *repression*. Freud believed it is through repression that certain feelings or ideas become unconscious. In fact, this was one of the central concepts in his theory of personality.

Whenever we have feelings that make us extremely anxious—particularly those that conflict with what we have learned is "right"—these feelings may become repressed. In an earlier chapter we said that sexual feelings and aggressive impulses often cause anxiety, particularly when one has been severely punished as a child for being aggressive or for showing sexual curiosity. Most people learn to deal with such feelings in a mature way, and consequently these feelings do not evoke anxiety. In some cases, however, these feelings are repressed.

Repression, it should be noted, is not like suppression. When one consciously tries to avoid thinking about certain things, this is suppression. Repression, however, is unconscious. We are not aware of it when it occurs. As in rationalization, if we were aware of repressing certain feelings, there would be no defensive value to the mechanism. Another point to remember is that repressed feelings are not simply forgotten. Furthermore, even though such feelings may be unconscious, they can still affect the individual's behavior. We will examine how this occurs in the next chapter.

COMPENSATION AND OVERCOMPENSATION. When a person feels inferior in certain aspects of his or her behavior, he or she often tries to make up for it by *compensating.* Suppose, for example, that a person is a very poor student. To defend against the feelings of inferiority this arouses, he or she may try to excel in other areas. The boy may put extra effort into becoming a good athlete. The girl may try to become a leader in school social activities. Not all good athletes or social leaders, of course, are compensating. But when a person feels inferior about one aspect of his or her life, he may compensate for these feelings by excelling in another.

Feeling inferior about one aspect of behavior does not necessarily lead to excelling or attempting to excel in another. The poor student may work extremely hard to become a good student. The boy who sees himself as physically weak and who feels inferior because of it, may go in for weight lifting, karate, or some other such physical activity. These are examples of *overcompensation.* This defense mechanism involves protecting self-esteem by excelling in those areas in which the individual feels inferior.

PROJECTION. All of us have difficulty in seeing ourselves as others see us. We have a tendency to emphasize our strong points and to overlook our short-comings. Characteristics we cannot accept about ourselves we often tend to see in others. One psychologist asked a number of college students to rate each other on four undesirable traits: stinginess, stubbornness, disorderliness, and bashfulness. Each subject was also asked to rate himself on these characteristics.

The psychologist found that many of those who were rated by others as high in these characteristics tended not to rate themselves as high. These same subjects, however, tended to rate other subjects as high in the undesirable characteristics. In other words, through the mechanism of *projection* we attribute our own faults or shortcomings to others.

REACTION FORMATION. Sometimes when a person has feelings that make him or her anxious, he or she tends to give strong expression to the opposite feeling. The mother who resents her child may feel guilty and anxious over this feeling. As we all know, "mothers are supposed to love their children." Her feeling of resentment may lead to overprotection of the child. Through her behavior, in other words, she is denying and hiding her true feelings. By being overprotective—that is, excessively concerned about the child's health and safety—she is in effect saying to herself, "See what a good mother I am —see how much I love my child!"

OTHER DEFENSES. The defense mechanisms listed above are only a few of those used by people in attempting to protect self-esteem. Others include identification, regression, fantasy, apathy, fixation, and acting out.

When we *identify*, we assume certain characteristics of an admired person or persons. Identification is particularly obvious in movies or television. We want the hero or heroine to win out, and when they do we feel better because of it.

In *regression* one's behavior becomes more infantile or primitive. By acting less mature, people are sometimes able to avoid situations that threaten self-esteem and/or feelings of self-worth.

Both *fantasy* and *apathy* can also be defense mechanisms. In daydreams we may be the conquering hero, winning the day and the applause. Apathy, on the other hand, often means adopting a do-nothing or an I-don't-care attitude.

Fixation is sometimes used as a defense mechanism in that behavior fails to develop or progress normally. A child may be so overprotected that he or she is afraid of attempting any new activities. When such a child becomes an adolescent, he or she may be so strongly tied to the parents that they find it difficult to establish normal boy-girl relationships at this age.

Finally, *acting out* means that anxiety is reduced by permitting the expression of forbidden desires. Feelings are translated directly into actions. For example, hostility or aggression may be reflected in temper tantrums.

HOW WE MEASURE PERSONALITY

There are many different ways of measuring or assessing personality. Some involve observation of the individual and employing either rating scales or interviews. Still others involve taking samples of the person's behavior—for example, he or she is observed in specially devised situations. More commonly, tests of one sort or another are employed. In some instances, all of these methods are used together.

What Are Rating Scales?

Several different kinds of rating scales are used in personality assessment. Some involve assigning numbers or numerical scores. For example, a teacher might be asked to check one of the following items regarding a student's work: "Of Doubtful Satisfaction (–2); Not Quite Up to Standard (–1);

Satisfactory (0); Superior to Most Students (+1); Exceptionally High (+2)" A number of items similar to this one make up the total scale, and poor characteristics are assigned negative scores while good characteristics are assigned positive ones. The overall score gives some idea of whether the student is above or below average and by how much.

Other rating scales simply involve making a check mark along a continuum of behavior from negative to positive. Still others involve ranking the individual relative to others. The teacher, for example, may be asked: "In comparison to other students you have known, how would you rank this individual in terms of his or her potential for college work? ——In the highest 5 per cent; ——In the highest 25 per cent; ——In the top half; and so on.

Rating scales often have certain shortcomings which limit their usefulness. Sometimes rater bias or halo effects makes them relatively unreliable. The term *"halo effect"* simply means that if the rater perceives the person being rated as good in one area, he or she may rate the person good in all areas. Of course, the reverse is also true; a person perceived as poor in one area is likely to be so rated in all areas.

Letters of recommendation are similar to rating scales in that the person writing the recommendation is usually asked to rate the person he or she is recommending relative to some activity such as a job or college. In asking someone to write a letter of recommendation for you, you should be sure that that person knows you well and knows of any special qualities or skills you have that would enhance your candidacy.

Interviews

Interviews are frequently used to assess personality, and while there are advantages over rating scales in some cases, in other cases they have less value. Basically there are two types of interviews. In one the applicant is asked a set of standard questions. In the other, the interview is open-ended. That is, any questions may be asked that come to mind. For the most part, the former type is more reliable than the latter in that each person interviewed has been asked the same questions. Thus relative comparisons among applicants can be more easily made.

We do not have the space to discuss how one should dress, behave, and answer in an interview situation. Before leaving school however, you should discuss this with your school counselor or some other knowledgeable person. Sooner or later in life you are almost certain to be faced with an interview, the outcome of which may determine an important part of your life.

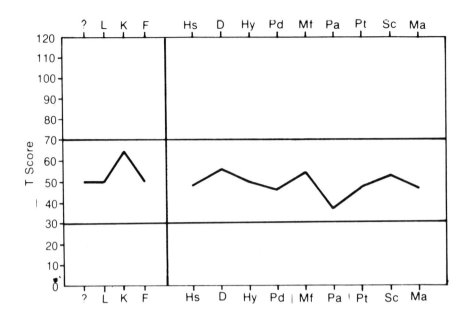

Fig. 11-7.   Above: The Personality Profile of a Normal Adult On The Minnesota Multiphasic Personality Inventory. Below: A "Typical Psychotic Profile" On The Same Test.

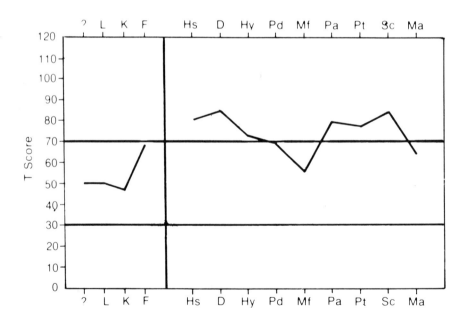

Personality Inventories

Personality inventories are psychological tests designed to measure the inner characteristics of personality—how the person feels about himself, his self-confidence, and so on. Most psychologists feel this information is more useful than information obtained through the use of rating scales or interviews.

There are literally hundreds of such tests. One which has been rather widely used is the California Psychological Inventory. This test consists of 480 items or statements that are answered true or false. For example, one item is "A person does not need to worry about other people if only he looks after himself."

Each statement on the test is related to a scale such as "dominance," "sociability," "self-acceptance," and so on. Forty-six of the items are related to the dominance scale. When you take the test, then, your answers to these items are compared with the answers of a large number of other people who have also taken the test. Some of these people are known to be very dominant, others very submissive. Whether you are judged to be dominant or submissive depends on how your answers compare with theirs.

Usually on such tests a profile of personality is drawn up like that shown in Fig. 11–7. A trained psychologist examining the profile can then write an evaluation of your personality, depending upon the scores you made on each of the scales that make up the test. There are, of course, no right or wrong answers on such tests. There are only differences among people in the way they answer the questions. Such differences reflect differences in their personalities.

The Projective Tests

For most students the most interesting tests of personality are the projective tests. These tests are called *projective* because it is assumed that the individual projects or imposes certain aspects of his personality on the material presented.

You will recall that in our chapter on perception we said how we perceive ambiguous stimuli such as inkblots depends more on ourselves than on the stimuli. In other words, what they look like to us depends to a great extent on our personality, interests, values, and motives.

The most famous of the projective tests is the Rorschach, or inkblot test, named after a Swiss psychiatrist, Herman Rorschach. There are ten inkblots that make up the test, and the person taking it is asked to tell what the blot resembles or what it might be. As in other personality tests, of course, there are no right or wrong answers.

Most people tend to see humans, parts of humans, animals, parts of animals, or anatomical details in the inkblots. There are, of course, many other responses to the blots aside from these. Furthermore, the test is scored not only in terms of what you see but where and how you see it. We need not go into all this here, since it takes a highly trained person both to administer and to score and interpret the test.

The Rorschach is a useful instrument for several reasons. *First,* a trained psychologist learns a great deal more about the individual's personality from the test than he can through an interview or rating scale. *Second,* the test cannot be faked; the individual taking the test cannot fool the examiner by trying to appear different from how he or she really is. This is because he or she has no basis for knowing the meaning of what he or she sees.

The Rorschach is only one of a large number of projective tests. Some involve asking the subject to draw a person. Others ask that he or she make up a story to go with pictures they are shown. In each case, however, the stimulus presented is ambiguous, and it is assumed that the subject projects his or her personality onto that stimulus.

One final word: these tests are not games that can be used to amuse and astound your friends. Furthermore, no trained psychologist would administer one to you just for the heck of it or because you are curious. The tests are scientific instruments designed to probe the mysteries of perhaps the most complex aspect of human beings—the personality.

CHAPTER SUMMARY

1. Theories of personality based on traits attempt to describe personality in terms of a limited number of dimensions such as dominance-submission, masculinity-femininity, and introversion-extraversion. These theories assume, for the most part, that such traits exist to a greater or lesser degree in every human personality.

2. There are two rather different approaches to the idea of personality types. One approach is based on the idea that there is a correspondence between body build and personality. The other approach holds that there are different psychological types such as introversion-extraversion.

3. Freud's theory of personality was developed through his efforts to treat the mentally ill. He thought that the mind is divided into two parts: conscious and unconscious. In addition, he believed that personality is made up of three parts: the id, the ego, and the superego.

4. The id consists of those instinctual urges with which the individual is born, according to Freud. The ego develops out of the id and strives to satisfy the urges of the id in such a way that the person does not get into trouble with those around him. The superego is the moral arm of personality. It represents the ideal, and it strives for perfection rather than pleasure.

5. Freudian personality theory holds that there are a number of stages through which personality develops. These include the oral stage (from birth until one year), the anal stage (one to three years), and the genital stage (three to six years). Each of these stages is important in personality development, according to Freud, and problems in any one of them can permanently affect personality.

6. Other theories of personality use the self as the central concept. The self is sometimes defined as the feelings, attitudes, perceptions, and evaluations that the person holds about himself as an object. Self-esteem is important to all of us, and much of our behavior is aimed at maintaining self-esteem at the highest possible level. This includes the setting of achievable goals, our choice of friends, and even sometimes the distortion of reality involving the use of defense mechanisms.

7. Defense mechanisms are used by all human beings to a greater or lesser extent. One of the most common is rationalization—finding logical but false reasons for past, present, or future behavior. Another defense mechanism is repression. Whenever we have feelings that cause us great anxiety, they may become unconscious through repression.

8. Compensation involves trying to make up for feelings of inferiority in one activity by excelling in another. Overcompensation involves protecting self-esteem by excelling in those areas in which the individual feels inferior. The defense mechanism of projection involves attributing our own faults and shortcomings to others.

9. Sometimes when a person has feelings that make him or her anxious, they give strong expression to the opposite feeling. This is the defense mechanism of reaction formation. Other defense mechanisms include identification, regression, fantasy, apathy, fixation, and acting out.

10. There are many different ways of measuring or assessing personality. Some involve the use of rating scales or interviews. Others include the use of personality inventories—psychological tests designed to measure the inner characteristics of personality. The projective tests employ ambiguous or unclear stimulus materials, such as inkblots. In such tests it is assumed that the individual projects or imposes certain aspects of his personality on the material presented.

Important Terms
from This Chapter

ambiverts	cardinal traits	compensation
anal stage	central traits	ego

Electra complex

extravert

free association

Freud, S.

id

introverts

Jung, C.

Oedipus complex

oral stage

overcompensation

personality inventories

projection

projective tests

psychological types

psychoneurotic

psychotic

rating scales

rationalization

reaction formation

repression

Rorschach, H.

secondary traits

self

superego

trait theories

Additional Readings
to Help You Learn More

Buss, A. *Psychology: Man in Perspective.* New York: John Wiley and Sons, 1973. Chapter 25, "The Self," discusses such things as roles, self-esteem, body image and various theories of the self.

Munn, N., Fernald, L. and Fernald, P. *Introduction to Psychology,* 3rd Edition. Boston: Houghton-Mifflin Company, 1972. Chapter 17, "Personality," gives a brief history of personality types as well as various other theories of personality.

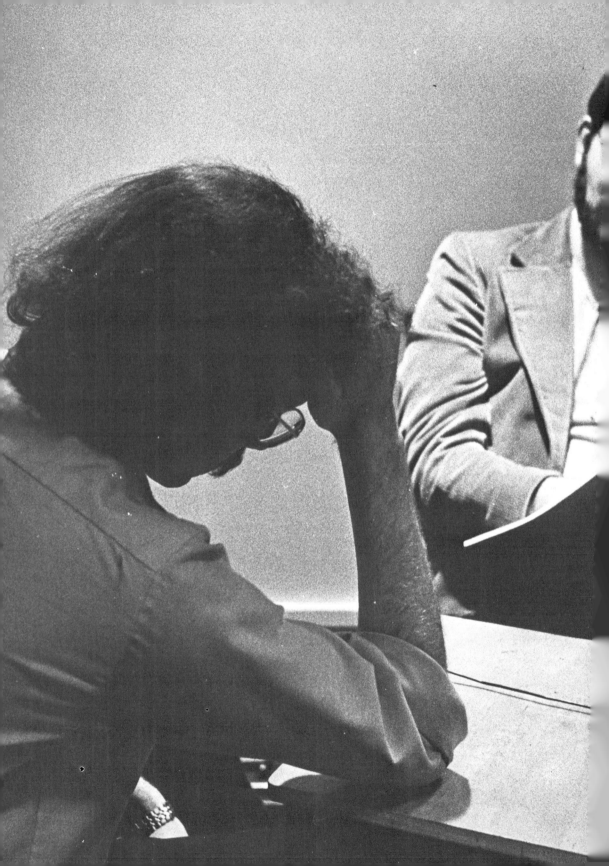

chapter **12**

Mental Health and Mental Illness

You would probably be surprised to learn that some psychologists think there is no such thing as mental illness. What we have, they say, are simply people with different problems in living. Certainly the majority of psychologists do not agree entirely with this point of view, but when it comes to defining the term "mental illness," there is no general agreement either.

You would probably also be surprised to know that you would not recognize the typical mentally ill person as being "sick." Furthermore, did you know that there are more seriously mentally ill people living outside mental hospitals than inside? Are you aware of the fact that only a very small percentage of these people are dangerous, either to themselves or others? Did you know that the number of patients in mental hospitals is steadily declining?

These are some of the things we will talk about in this chapter. First we will discuss some of the misconceptions most people have about mental illness. Then we will take a look at how we define the terms "normal" and "abnormal." After that we will examine some of the different kinds of mental illness. Finally, we will look at what is being done today to treat the mentally ill.

SOME MISCONCEPTIONS ABOUT MENTAL ILLNESS

Misconceptions about the mentally ill have existed throughout human history. Centuries ago it was believed that the devil or demons had taken possession of a person's soul. Sometimes the person was put to death, but at

Fig. 12–1   Years ago people thought the mentally ill were possessed by "demons" or "devils." They were thrown into jails or places such as Bedlam, shown here. On weekends the wealthy came to look at them for amusement.

other times and in other places the mentally ill were worshipped as having special powers.

More often than not mental illness evoked fear in other people, and often shame. Such people, it was believed, are dangerous and therefore should be locked away in some safe place. Particularly if the mentally ill person was a relative, great pains were taken to hide the fact of mental illness.

Today many of these misconceptions have disappeared. Others remain, however, and it will be worthwhile to take a look at them. Perhaps the most common of all misconceptions is that mentally ill people act crazy. For those who have never been inside a mental hospital, such a visit conjures up visions of raving maniacs, wild-eyed and dangerous. Nothing could be further from the truth. In fact, as we said earlier, you probably would not even recognize most mental illnesses as such.

If you were to visit a modern mental hospital what you would in all likelihood see is not a man pretending to be Napoleon or a woman who thinks she is Marie Antoinette, but rather a number of people who act much as you

Fig. 12–2   Unlike institutions for the mentally ill in past years, the modern mental hospital has no bars on the windows and few locked doors. Wards in such hospitals are largely indistinguishable from those in hospitals that treat physical illnesses.

and I do. This is not to say that there are no people who imagine themselves to be someone else; but such people are the exceptions rather than the rule.

In the typical mental hospital today you would find few locked doors or cells, but rather recreation rooms where patients watch television or play card games. Again, we do not suggest that such hospitals are holiday resorts or that everyone acts in a perfectly normal way. Instead, we are simply saying that most mental hospitals are quite different than imagined and that the mentally ill are, for the most part, not unlike you and me. It is misconception to think that there are normal people on the one hand and the insane on the other.

Another unfortunate notion about mental illness is that it is somehow shameful or a disgrace. Ideas in this respect have changed somewhat over the years, but not totally. It is, in fact, no more shameful for a person to be mentally ill than to have arthritis or a sinus infection. The unfortunate thing is that because mental illness is regarded as shameful by some, those who suffer these illnesses often either receive no treatment or are treated only after being ill for a long time.

Still another misconception is that close relatives of the mentally ill are very likely to have inherited such illnesses themselves. In this connection we should point out that there is very little evidence mental illness is inherited. Even in families where several members are affected, this may be because of close association with others in the same environment rather than heredity.

In addition to these misconceptions, many people worry unnecessarily about becoming mentally ill. "Sometimes I feel I am going out of my mind," one person says. Another person says, "I find myself thinking bad thoughts

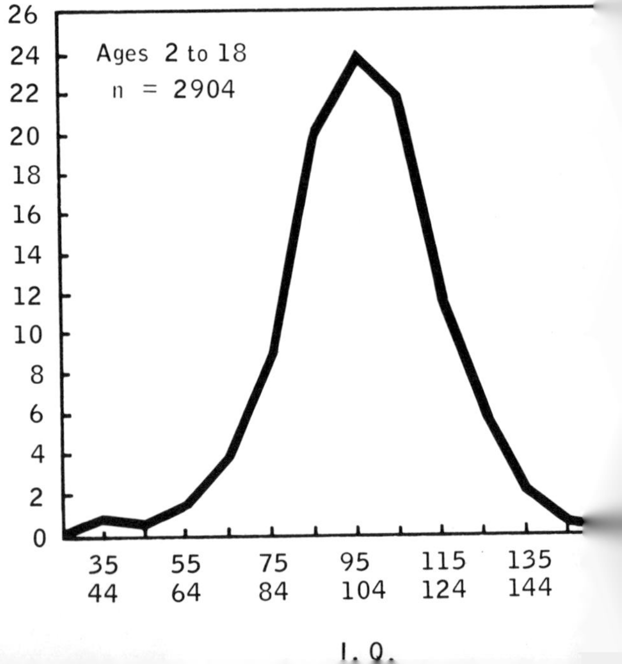

Fig. 12–3 Distribution Of Intelligence Quotients. The Revised Stanford-Binet Intelligence Test was given to 2904 people. Note that most of the I.Q.'s are around 100 with fewer at the extremes.

Ages 2 to 18
n = 2904

I. Q.

274

in church." Still another says, "I get very depressed and down in the dumps when things don't go right." Are these signs of developing mental illness? In most cases, certainly not. Such feelings are much more common in "normal" people than you would imagine.

Adolescents are more likely to worry about themselves and their behavior than older or younger persons in our society. Self-consciousness is particularly likely to be heightened at this time in one's life, and so are self-doubts. This in itself is "normal" behavior for this age. We said earlier, however, that it is not as easy to define such terms as "normal" and "abnormal" as you may think.

AM I NORMAL?

The first thing to understand about normality and abnormality is that the difference between the two is a matter of degree rather than one of kind. In other words, mental health and mental illness are like physical health and physical illness in one sense. No physician would tell you that there are only two kinds of people, the healthy and the sick. Some are healthier than others, or to put it the other way around, some are sicker than others. The same thing is true of mental health, as we can easily see when we try to describe the mentally healthy person. We will return to that in a moment, but before doing so we need to see how psychologists define the term *normal*.

Many psychologists define normality in statistical terms. If we measure the intelligence of a large number of people, for example, and plot their scores on a graph, we find a curve like that shown in Fig. 12–3. Most of the I.Q.s cluster around 100, with fewer scores below and above that figure. The score of 100, in other words, might be defined as "normal" or "average." An I.Q. of 20 or one of 200 then, would be defined as "abnormal."

You can probably already see some problems with this sort of definition. First of all, where does one draw the line between normal and abnormal? Second, does it make sense to call an I.Q. of 200 abnormal? The term "abnormal" in the minds of most people connotes something undesirable.

Other psychologists argue that normality can only be defined in terms of a particular society. Behavior that is considered normal in one society, may be considered abnormal in another. In our society, hearing voices or seeing visions is considered abnormal. In other societies, such behavior is perfectly normal.

If we talk in terms of a societal or cultural definition, we probably have to go even further and define behavior in terms of the individual's age as well

Fig. 12–4 Whether behavior is considered "normal" or "abnormal" depends in part on the culture in which it occurs. The behavior of these Zulu warriors is quite normal in their culture, but would it be in ours?

as the particular part of the society in which the individual grew up. Certain behavior may be considered normal at one age but not at other ages. By the same token, certain behavior may be considered normal in some parts of our society but not in others.

Some psychologists prefer not to talk in terms of normal and abnormal behavior at all, but rather in terms of *adjustment* and *maladjustment*. Adjustment or mental health can be discussed in terms of different characteristics that the well-adjusted person seems to possess in greater degrees than the maladjusted.

Some Characteristics of the Adjusted Person

There are several things we can say about the adjusted person in contrast to the maladjusted. First of all, adjusted people are productive and happy. This doesn't mean that such people never feel unhappy or that they never waste time. It simply means that, for the most part, such people are able to use their abilities effectively in work and in satisfying relationship with others. The maladjusted person, in contrast, often has little zest for living, sleeps poorly, and derives little pleasure out of his or her relationship with others.

An absence of tension and extreme sensitivity also characterize the adjusted person. Maladjusted people, on the other hand, frequently suffer anxiety and tension, and these are often reflected in a variety of symptoms. Such people often overreact to flattery as well as to minor frustrations. In fact, their overall tolerance for frustration is lower than in the adjusted person.

Still another characteristic of good adjustment is a healthy attitude toward bodily functions such as sex. Preoccupation with sex, as well as feelings of shame or guilt, are frequently seen in the maladjusted person. The adjusted person also feels he or she is an accepted part of society and, at the same time, can express anger or hostility when appropriate. They have reasonably strong feelings of security, in other words.

Finally, we can characterize adjustment in terms of self-esteem and insight. The well-adjusted person feels self-confident and sure of himself or herself. He or she does not feel inferior to most others, but rather feels equal to others in facing the situations that arise in day-to-day living. The maladjusted person often feels inferior to just about everyone else, and he or she may try to overcome such feelings by boasting or acting overconfident. Such people often have little insight or self-understanding. The adjusted person, in contrast, understands why he or she behaves in certain ways, or why he or she has particular feelings toward specific individuals or events.

The "Normal" Adolescent

In talking about the adolescent person in our culture, perhaps the first thing we should say is that it is normal for the adolescent to worry about being abnormal. In many respects our society does not spell out what is expected of the adolescent, and, furthermore, parents and other adults often react to adolescents in very inconsistent ways. Also, at this period in our lives, one faces new situations—particularly social ones—that he or she has not faced before.

The "normal" adolescent, then, may suffer from some feelings of inadequacy and lack of self-confidence. He or she may not always understand why certain feelings exist or why they behave in certain ways. Moods may fluctuate quite widely, from periods of great joy to periods of gloom and depression. Also, at least in later adolescence, preoccupation with the opposite sex is normal.

Recognizing that these are normal aspects of adolescent behavior is a valuable lesson to learn. On the other hand, it is just as important to know when to seek help. The adolescent who is depressed all the time, unable to do his or her work in school, with no interest in anything, needs help. In such cases, the school guidance counselor or psychologist should be contacted without hesitation.

What Can I Do to Maintain Mental Health?

There are a number of things one can do to maintain mental health. The first is to maintain good physical health. We all know that we are more irritable and easily upset when we are physically ill. It is important therefore to have periodic physical check-ups, to eat properly, and to get enough sleep. Adolescents in particular tend to ignore these things.

Psychologically, there are also a number of practices that enhance mental health. Accepting things that cannot be changed; making an effort to develop social skills such as dancing or conversation; accepting yourself and your feelings; and keeping busy with constructive activities are all important.

As we mentioned earlier in the book, it is also important to develop a sense of humor and a sense of perspective. It often helps dispel fear or apprehension if we can see the humor in a situation. It also helps to ask yourself, when things go wrong, "How important is this going to be to me ten years from now?"

Finally, it is important to know when to seek out help for emotional problems. Every human being from time to time faces situations that are difficult to handle. It is no disgrace to seek out a counselor or even a close friend to help one over the rough spots. Those who fail to do so sometimes develop a mental illness—an illness in many cases that could have been avoided. With these thoughts in mind we now turn our attention to some of the less severe mental illnesses—the psychoneuroses.

THE PSYCHONEUROSES

Psychoneuroses are less severe forms of mental illness that usually do not require hospitalization. No one knows exactly how many neurotics there are in the United States today, but conservative estimates put the number at around 8 million. Considering that the consumption of tranquilizers reached a staggering 300 tons in one recent year, this number is not surprising.

Neurotics are generally people who are unhappy, tense, and who manifest a variety of symptoms. Some of the symptoms may be physical in nature, and it is estimated that about half of all the patients seen by physi-

Fig. 12–5 *The patient with a psychoneurosis needs help. Feelings of fatigue, depression, and/or anxiety are common symptoms.*

cians have some emotional problem related to their physical complaints. Neurotics often sleep poorly, awaken tired and worn out, and have little energy or interest in work or anything else. Complaints of fatigue and nervousness are the most common symptoms.

What Causes a Psychoneurosis?

Often those suffering from a psychoneurosis complain that their nerves are bad or that they have suffered a nervous breakdown. These, however, are terms used by the layman and not by the professional psychologist or psychiatrist. While the nervous system is involved in neurotic behavior as well as in normal behavior, there is no evidence whatsoever that neuroses somehow involve something wrong with the nerves. In fact, no physical basis for psychoneurotic illnesses has ever been discovered, and it is likely that none exists. This, of course, does not mean that these conditions are imaginary or all in one's mind. There are causes, but the causes are psychological rather than physical. When a person says he has had a nervous breakdown, then, usually what this means is that the symptoms have become so severe he cannot any longer carry on normal life in even a very marginal way.

Here it should be emphasized that most neurotics do manage to function, in a less than satisfactory way, and often without professional help. In other words, the neurotic housewife manages to take care of the house, feed her family, and so on. She has little interest or energy for anything else, however. The neurotic businessman goes to work and does his job, but with substantially less efficiency than he could were he not suffering from a psychoneurosis. The neurotic, in other words, has a severe handicap which limits his or her effectiveness as a human being.

The causes of most psychoneuroses have their origin in childhood. Such disorders do not usually develop overnight, although symptoms may sometimes appear very suddenly. The specific causes of a neurosis in a particular individual are so numerous that we could not begin to describe them all. In very general terms, many professional psychologists believe that anxiety plays a central role in the development of neuroses. To understand how this may occur, we can examine a rather common type of psychoneurosis—obsessive-compulsive reactions.

What Are Obsessive-Compulsive Reactions?

Obsessive-compulsive reactions are neuroses in which the individual has disturbing thoughts which reoccur frequently and over which he or she has no control. In other cases, the most frequent symptoms are irresistible impulses to carry out certain acts of a repetitive nature.

All of us have experienced behavior somewhat similar to these symptoms. Sometimes we hum or whistle a tune over and over again—we cannot seem to get it out of our mind. Or we may develop a habit of smoothing down the back of our hair, or licking our lips. The difference between these behaviors and the symptoms of an obsessive-compulsive reaction is often a matter of degree. But there are frequently other differences as well.

Almost always in an obsessive-compulsive reaction, the obsessive thoughts are of a very disturbing nature to the person involved. Fears of uncontrollable impulses are quite common. A man may fear he will burn the house down. A woman may fear she will cut her children's throats while they sleep. Obsessive ideas like these are rarely carried out, but nevertheless they are highly disturbing to the patient and usually lead him or her to seek professional help.

Let us look at the case of a woman who comes to the psychologist because of fears she will kill her children. First of all, she finds it difficult to understand why she has such terrible thoughts. "I must be losing my mind," she says. "I love my children—I have given up everything for them. Why should I think such terrible thoughts?"

As the psychologist begins to treat this woman, he finds out what kind of person she is. She is, he notes, a perfectionist. She wants everything done on time—no exceptions. She keeps her house as neat as a pin; in fact, overly neat. She was raised in a strict family in which she was shown little affection by either parent. To be "loved" as a child, perfection was the key.

As she begins to find it easier to talk about her true feelings, it becomes apparent that she has ambivalent feelings toward her children. She both loves and hates them, in other words. Such feelings, incidentally, are not abnormal in most human relationships. Even those we love deeply irritate us at times. For most of us, however, when we get angry at someone we love, can accept this feeling.

In further discussions with this patient, the psychologist begins to discover the source of her resentment toward her children. He finds she had to give up a very attractive job when she became pregnant, and he also finds that she regards being a housewife as a life of drudgery and dullness.

Now we can begin to see the cause of this neurosis. The core of the problem really stems from the fact that our patient does not understand herself and her feelings. Her resentment toward the children causes her anxiety and guilt. Thus, these feelings have become unconscious. But even though unconscious, they pop up periodically into consciousness in the form of obsessive ideas of harming the children.

When through treatment she is able to recognize and accept her true feelings, her obsessive ideas disappear.

Not all neuroses are caused in this way but in a very general sense we can say that they stem from feelings that cause the individual anxiety. In many cases these feelings are unconscious. When the person learns to understand himself and his feelings, and to accept them, he is in a good position to recover from the neurosis.

Some Other Neurotic Reactions

Perhaps the most common of all neuroses is the *anxiety reaction.* In this neurosis the most common symptom is one of continual anxiety which does not appear to stem from any particular situation or person. Periodically, the person may suffer from severe anxiety "attacks" ranging from a few seconds to an hour or more. Heart palpitations, sweating, and other physical symptoms usually accompany such attacks. The causes of anxiety neuroses are numerous and such reactions may be treated through psychotherapy and other techniques which we will discuss later in this chapter.

Dissociative reactions often involve disturbances or peculiarities in memory. Amnesia, a condition in which the person forgets his name, where he lives, where he works, and so on, is one example. Contrary to the popular belief, amnesia is not usually caused by a blow on the head. Rather, the amnesia is typically a rather ineffective way of dealing with stressful situations which the person feels inadequate in handling. Fugue is another dissociative reaction, similar in some respects to amnesia. In fugue states, however, the person typically travels long distances from his home or place of work without remembering that he has done so. Multiple personality is still another type of dissociative reaction. If you remember the movie *The Three Faces of Eve,* or the book *Sybil* you know that in such cases there are two and sometimes three contrasting personalities in the same person. Typically, one personality is not aware of the others.

Phobic reactions are neuroses characterized by intense, unrealistic fears. They are fears of objects or situations which present no real danger. Thus, fear of house cats, birds, riding in elevators, and blood might be examples. Usually those suffering from phobias are not aware of the reasons for their fears but they react violently to the feared object and sometimes are unable to function because of them. Often phobias are developed through unfortunate childhood experiences which are traumatic. By *traumatic,* we mean they are intensely emotionally disturbing.

Other psychoneuroses include *hypochondriacal reactions*, *conversion reactions*, and *neurotic depressive reactions*. The first of these, as you might suspect, involves excessive concern over physical health. The second, conversion reactions, usually involves physical symptoms as well, but rather than vague aches and pains, often we see paralysis or loss of sensation in part of the body. Neurotic depressions tend to be over-reactions to stressful incidents in life. Life is a drag for such people, who find little happiness in anything. Rather, they tend to have lowered self-confidence, restricted interests, and a loss of initiative.

THE PSYCHOSES

Psychoses are much more severe than psychoneuroses. As we mentioned earlier, the psychoneurotic person is often able to carry on life in a more or less normal fashion. The psychotic, on the other hand, is usually incapacitated. He or she needs help badly, although some psychotics appear to recover without professional help.

The psychotic is generally disorganized to such an extent that he or she cannot socially function in a normal way. Frequently such patients must be hospitalized, although the length of stay in hospitals for the mentally ill has been drastically reduced.

Psychotics show a variety of symptoms which include loss of contact with reality, hallucinations, delusions, distorted emotions, and so on. As we discuss some of the different types of psychoses, we will explain the meaning of these terms.

It is estimated that there are about one million psychotics in the United States. Most of them, as we noted earlier in the chapter, are not in hospitals. Many of them are cared for at home or in a combination of home and community treatment center. Psychoses occur in all age groups, including young children, among all races, in all social classes, and in every country in the world.

Usually in discussing the psychoses, we differentiate between two types—functional and organic. *Functional psychoses* are those in which no physical basis for the disorder can be found, while *organic psychoses* have a clear-cut, though not necessarily curable, physical basis.

In this section we will discuss schizophrenia and manic-depressive reactions, two of the more common functional psychoses.

Schizophrenia

Schizophrenia is perhaps the most common of all the psychoses. It tends to develop slowly over a period of years and frequently is diagnosed

Fig. 12–6 Chronic Schizophrenia. Schizophrenia is one of the most common psychoses. Yet, despite years of research, we still do not know its exact cause or how to prevent it.

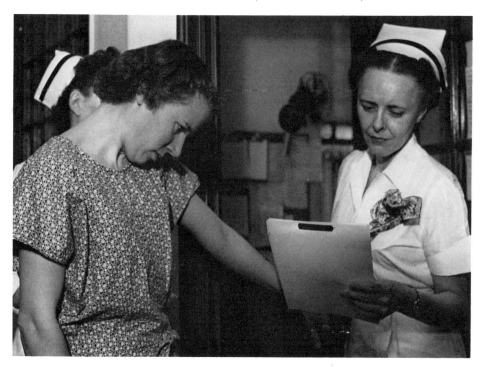

first in early adulthood, although it is not unknown in children.

Many different symptoms characterize the disorder, but the most common are apathy and withdrawal from others, a dulling of emotions, loss of contact with reality, and frequently delusions and hallucinations. At the beginning of this chapter we said that you probably would be unable to recognize a serious mental illness as such. The typical schizophrenic patient would probably strike you as a little odd, but not necessarily as a very sick person. We say this because many schizophrenics simply lose interest in life around them. They are content to sit quietly in the same chair hour after hour, and often day after day, doing nothing. They may smile to themselves occasionally, but otherwise take little or no interest in what is going on around them. Some of them have to be fed, in fact, or they would starve to death.

Frequently hallucinations occur in schizophrenia, as well as delusions. The patient may hear voices speaking to him—imaginary voices. These are *hallucinations*. Or he or she may imagine themselves to be someone else. These false ideas are called *delusions*. Sometimes the delusions involve persecution. Not uncommon are delusions that the FBI is following them or that the police have planted listening bugs in their room.

There are several different types of schizophrenia, and in fact, we may not be dealing with a single disorder at all. Some psychologists think that several different mental illnesses have been lumped under the heading "schizophrenia." Another problem is that we do not know the cause—or causes—of the disorder. There are many theories, but we need a great deal more research before we understand the nature of this illness.

Despite our ignorance about the causes of schizophrenia, we are able to effectively treat a great percentage of those who develop the disorder. Particularly if the disorder is diagnosed early, the prospects for successful treatment are good.

Manic-Depressive Reactions

Unlike schizophrenia, which tends to develop slowly and to become apparent first in younger people, manic-depressive reactions often have a sudden onset in middle age. These reactions are characterized by sudden changes in mood or emotion. The person may, over a period of a few hours, become suicidally depressed for no apparent reason. Or just as suddenly, they may become elated for no reason.

Some patients with manic-depressive reactions show only mood changes from normal to depressed and back. Others change from normal to elated and back to normal. Still others go through a cycle of normal-elated-depressed-normal.

As in schizophrenia, no one knows the cause—or causes—of manic-depressive reactions. Even without help, many people who have them recover, at least temporarily. But one thing we should point out here is that there is always a potential for suicide in any seriously depressed person. Thus such illnesses should always be treated.

Organic Psychoses

Unlike the functional disorders discussed above, we know the causes of most organic psychoses. Tumors of the brain, infections, circulatory disorders, and a number of other conditions, can cause an organic psychosis. Such disorders, however, cannot necessarily be cured even though we know the cause.

One of the most common of the organic psychoses, *senile brain disease*, occurs in elderly or aged people. Frequently, because of hardening of the arteries, the blood supply to parts of the brain is reduced. As a result we often see a general mental decline, with an impairment of memory and a lessening of efficiency. Other symptoms may include irritability, suspiciousness, and even delusions and hallucinations.

Fig. 12–7 Senile Brain Disease. As life expectancy increases, so does the number of people afflicted with organic psychoses, such as senile brain disease.

The sad thing about many of these people is that even though the disorder cannot be reversed, they are often locked away in mental hospitals and forgotten by those outside. This does not mean they do not receive adequate medical care or attention from personnel at the hospital. It simply means that occasional visitors from outside, even strangers, can do wonders to pick up the spirits and restore interest in life. Volunteer groups of young people can do great things in this regard.

How We Help The Mentally Ill

There are many different methods or techniques used in treating the mentally ill. Psychotherapy, for example, involves the treatment of such disorders by psychological means. Physical methods which utilize medication such as tranquilizers are also commonly used.

For the most part, psychoneurotics are treated by psychologists or psychiatrists in private practice. Mental health centers also treat a great many of these patients. Psychotics are more generally treated in mental hospitals. It is worth mentioning in this connection, however, that the length of hospitalization for psychotic patients has been steadily declining over the years. For the most part, a stay of four to six weeks in the hospital today is not uncommon. Some patients, of course, require much longer care. In addition, more and more general hospitals today have special wards for the care of the mentally ill.

What Is Psychotherapy?

As we mentioned above, the term *psychotherapy* refers to psychological methods of treating the mentally ill. While one goal of psychotherapy is to eliminate symptoms of the illness, others include the development in the patient of more effective methods of dealing with personal problems.

There are many different types of psychotherapy being used today. Here we will discuss only three of them briefly: psychoanalysis, short-term therapy, and group therapy. Of the three, psychoanalysis is less frequently employed, although some of the concepts in psychoanalysis may be incorporated into other therapies.

Psychoanalysis generally requires a minimum of six months and may last as long as two years, or even longer. It is a very intensive therapy which often delves deeply into the individual's early childhood. Earlier we discussed some of the methods used in Freudian psychoanalysis—the interpre-

Fig. 12–8   Play Therapy.

tation of dreams, free association, and so on. Modern psychoanalysts use some of these techniques, but others have been added as new theories of personality and mental illness have been developed.

Short-term psychotherapy may range in length from one session to treatment involving a year or more. For example, "crisis centers" have been set up in some cities to deal with problems such as threatened suicide. In some cases the patient requires only an hour or two of counseling in the center, and then he or she may be referred to a mental health clinic for further treatment.

High school or college counselors often use short-term therapy to help students over rough emotional spots. Several sessions in which the student talks out his or her problems with the counselor are frequently sufficient to alleviate the problem.

Group therapy involves several patients discussing their problems with one psychologist or counselor, and with each other. Often it is a help for the troubled person to know that others have similar problems. In *encounter groups*, the focus is on the feelings that emerge within the group and on the relationships among group members. The atmosphere in such groups encourages openness, emotional honesty, sensitivity, and expression of feelings, when the group is conducted by qualified professionals.

Fig. 12–9   In group therapy several patients discuss their problems with each other and with one counselor.

Behavior Therapy—A New Approach

In the chapter on emotions we discussed behavior therapy briefly. You will remember that it involves the application of operant conditioning techniques to behavior with a particular emphasis on changing the behavior in some way.

Unlike the methods of therapy discussed above, behavior therapy is frequently intended to simply eliminate the symptoms of a mental illness. Those who employ behavior therapy argue that the symptoms *are* the problem, rather than unconscious conflicts which must be resolved through psychotherapy. Psychotherapists often disagree with this position. Nevertheless we know that behavior therapy does seem to be effective in treating certain kinds of emotional problems.

In the chapter on emotion we talked about one form of behavior therapy—*desensitization*. This form of therapy is particularly useful in eliminating phobias. Fear of a particular stimulus is reduced by systematically reinforcing relaxation in the presence of the stimulus that causes fear or anxiety. In *aversive conditioning*, another form of behavior therapy, unpleasant stimuli are associated with certain behavior such as excessive drinking. Electric shocks or nausea-producing drugs are systematically associated with the undesirable behavior so that that behavior tends to be eliminated.

Other Methods

Tranquilizing drugs and other physical methods of treatment for the mentally ill are widely used today. Not everyone who takes tranquilizers can be considered mentally ill, of course. Such drugs are often used by well-adjusted individuals who need to relax during periods of stress. No psychologist believes that such drugs can cure mental illnesses, but they are often helpful in eliminating the disturbing anxiety that frequently is a part of mental illness.

Energizing drugs—those that perk up spirits and help eliminate severe depression—are also widely used today. Again, like the tranquilizers, such drugs do not cure mental illness. They only eliminate some of the symptoms and then only temporarily.

It is undoubtedly true that too many people overuse drugs in modern America. While there is nothing wrong with the occasional use of tranquilizers or energizers under a physician's supervision, continual reliance on such drugs is unwise. They do not, as we said, solve problems or cure mental illnesses. Those who feel a need to steadily use medication for emotional problems need the professional help of a psychologist or psychiatrist.

Other physical methods of treatment used with the mentally ill include electric shock treatments. These treatments involve passing an electric shock through the brain, causing unconsciousness. No one knows how or why they are helpful in some cases, but the fact is that they do have beneficial effects in the treatment of certain psychotic reactions. The use of shock treatments, however, is declining as new methods of treating the mentally ill are developed.

CHAPTER SUMMARY

1. Misconceptions about mental illness have existed throughout human history. More often than not, mental illness evoked fear in other people, and often shame. The fact is that the vast majority of mentally ill persons are a danger neither to themselves or others. It is no more shameful to be mentally ill than to have arthritis or some other physical illness.

2. Many psychologists define normality in statistical terms. The average or typical person is called "normal." Other psychologists argue that normality can only be defined in terms of a particular society. Behavior considered normal in one society may be considered abnormal in another. Still other psychologists prefer to discuss mental health in terms of "adjustment" or "maladjustment."

3. Adjustment can be discussed in terms of different characteristics that the well-adjusted person seems to possess in greater degrees than the maladjusted. The adjusted person feels self-confident in most situations. He or she understands his or her behavior. Adjusted people also are, for the most part, productive and happy. There is an absence of tension in such people and also healthy attitudes toward sex and other bodily functions. "Normal" adolescents in our culture sometimes suffer from feelings of inadequacy and lack of self-confidence. This does not mean that the adolescent is maladjusted. Rather, such feelings often stem from inexperience in meeting new situations, and particularly social situations.

4. There are several things that can be done to maintain good mental health. The first of these is to maintain good physical health. Accepting things that cannot be changed; making an effort to develop social skills; accepting yourself and your feelings; and keeping busy with constructive activities also are important.

5. Psychoneuroses are less severe forms of mental illness that usually do not require hospitalization. The causes of most neuroses have their origin in childhood. Such disorders do not usually develop overnight, although symptoms may appear very suddenly. There are many different causes of neuroses, but most psychologists believe that anxiety plays a central role in their development.

6. Obsessive-compulsive neuroses are characterized by symptoms which include recurring disturbing thoughts or irresistible impulses to carry out acts of a repetitive nature, or both. Anxiety reactions typically involve continual anxiety or tension with periodic attacks of anxiety which do not appear to stem from any particular situation or person. Dissociative reactions often involve disturbances or peculiarities in memory. Examples are amnesia, fugue, and multiple personality. Phobias are intense, unrealistic fears—that is, fears of objects or situations that present no real danger. Other neuroses include hypochondriacal reactions, conversion reactions, and neurotic depressive reactions.

7. Psychoses are more severe than psychoneuroses. Psychotics show a variety of symptoms which often include loss of contact with reality, hallucinations, delusions, distorted emotions, and so on. Schizophrenia is a rather common psychotic reaction. The most common symptoms of this disorder are apathy and withdrawal from others, a dulling of emotions, loss of contact with reality and frequently, delusions and hallucinations. Delusions are false ideas, while hallucinations involve false perception such as hearing voices or seeing visions.

8. Manic-depressive reactions tend to occur in middle-aged people more often than in the young adult. The symptoms usually involve sudden changes in mood from great elation to deep depression. Such changes in mood occur for no apparent reason and like schizophrenia, no one knows the cause of manic-depressive reactions. Organic psychoses, unlike schizophrenia and manic-depressive reactions, are caused by tumors, infections, circulatory disorders and a number of other conditions. One of the most common is senile brain disease, a psychosis often seen in the elderly.

9. There are many different methods or techniques used in treating the mentally ill. Psychotherapy involves the treatment of such disorders by psychological means. Physical methods of treatment include the use of drugs such as tranquilizers. Hospitalization is usually required only in the case of a psychosis and then typically for a period of between four and six weeks. Psychoneurotics are usually treated by private practitioners or in mental health clinics.

10. Different types of psychotherapy include psychoanalysis, short-term psychotherapy, and group therapy. Of the three, psychoanalysis is more intensive and requires more time. Behavior therapy involves the application of operant conditioning techniques to behavior with a particular emphasis on changing the behavior in some way. Two examples are desensitization and aversive conditioning.

Important Terms from This Chapter

adjustment	electric shock treatments	obsessive-compulsive reactions
anxiety reaction	energizing drugs	organic psychoses
aversive conditioning	maladjustment	phobic reactions
behavior therapy	manic depressive reactions	psychotherapy
desensitization	mental illness	schizophrenia
dissociative reaction	normal	tranquilizing drugs

Additional Readings to Help You Learn More

Grossberg, J. "Behavior Therapy: A Review." *Bobbs-Merrill Reprints*, P-465. Indianapolis: Bobbs-Merrill Company.

Lundin, R. *Personality: A Behavioral Analysis*, 2nd Edition. New York: Macmillan Publishing Company, 1974. Chapter 15, "Neurotic Behavior," and Chapter 16, "Psychotic Behavior," are two excellent up-to-date chapters on abnormal behavior that are highly relevant to the present chapter.

Munn, N., Fernald, L. and Fernald, P. *Introduction to Psychology,* 3rd Edition. Boston: Houghton-Mifflin Company, 1972. Chapter 19, "Therapy," elaborates on many of the different techniques of therapy used by psychologists.

Psychology Today: An Introduction, 2nd Edition. Del Mar, Calif.: CRM Books, 1972.

Chapter 30, "Adjustment and Disorder," deals with the concept of normality and adjustment as well as the classification of various mental disorders.

Ruch, F. and Zimbardo, P. *Psychology and Life,* 8th Edition. Glenview, Ill.: Scott, Foresman and Company, 1971. Appendix A, "A Case Study of a Psychotic Patient," is a good illustration of a case history of a psychotic.

Szasz, T. "The Myth of Mental Illness." *Bobbs-Merrill Reprints,* P-574. Indianapolis: Bobbs-Merrill Company. In this paper Dr. Szasz discusses some quite different ideas about the nature of mental illness.

Part VII.

THE OPPOSITE SEX

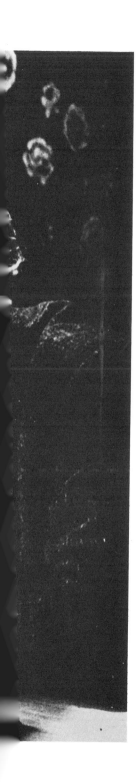

13

Two by Two: Dating

Aside from the time necessarily spent on studies, few topics are as compellingly fascinating to young men and women as the subject of dating. For those who are just beginning to date or who are very interested but have yet to start, questions such as, "How do I get a date?" "Why does everybody seem to be more popular than I am?" and "How can I make sure I won't do or say something stupid on a date?" often come up. Many who already have had some dating experiences have wondered whether or not they should go steady, or how to tactfully break off a relationship, and especially how far to go.

In this chapter we will try to shed a little light on these questions and the relationship dating has to other aspects of adolescent life. Perhaps we can best begin by finding out how dating practices have changed over the years and whether dating is just frivolous fun or if it serves a real purpose in becoming a mature person.

HOW HAS DATING CHANGED?

You have undoubtedly noticed that any reference on your part to who dates and when, where they go, and what they do often causes comment on the part of your parents. They may have told you how they went to the movies, dances, parties, proms, and athletic events when they were in high school. Sound familiar? It should, for these are undoubtedly still very com-

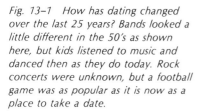

Fig. 13–1 How has dating changed over the last 25 years? Bands looked a little different in the 50's as shown here, but kids listened to music and danced then as they do today. Rock concerts were unknown, but a football game was as popular as it is now as a place to take a date.

mon dating situations. Accessibility of automobiles was just as important to dating in the 1950s as today. Popular music, current slang, and favorite hangouts were all part of the whole picture in the fifties. The initial impression, then, is that perhaps dating has not changed very much in the past 20 or 25 years. This is far from the truth. There are obviously situational similarities, but young people today have far more to contend with, and they also have opportunities to develop much more insight into their own behavior and that of others than their parents ever did.

We all realize that accurate information is a good basis for making sound decisions. Some of these decisions concerning dating will be your own answers to questions such as, "What shall I do if the people I'm with start drinking?" "How do I handle a party situation where kids are smoking and maybe passing around some pills?" "Does kissing mean the same thing to both boys and girls, and how do you stop without hurting feelings?" Your parents, if they were fortunate, received accurate information from their parents. But more likely, they learned to handle various aspects of dating through trial and error, and with little information from their parents or anyone else.

Some situations which you may face were largely unknown to your parents as teen-agers. The growing problem of drug use and pot-smoking on dates and at parties was simply not a factor in the 1940s and 1950s. Schools have become increasingly aware of the need to present adolescents with as much sound information as possible about alcohol, its ill effects on the body and judgment, drugs, marijuana, and smoking. The course in psychology that you are now taking is recognition that if you understand your behavior and that of others, you will have a better basis on which to make decisions in situations which are as emotionally charged as dating is.

The Real Meaning of Dating

On Wednesday, as you plow through the week with homework up to your ears, get ready for another test in English, and finally get a report together for that one picky teacher, you find yourself really looking forward to Friday night. You are going to the game; you like the person you are going with; everybody is going to the same place to eat, and you can hardly wait. The primary function then seems to be to have a good time away from the grind of obligations. It is true that dating serves a very valuable purpose in your life strictly from a recreational viewpoint. We need the good times; we need to pursue some activities simply for the enjoyment and relaxation they bring us. Changes of pace and of scene, and the realization that we are giving ourselves a break are universally recognized by psychologists as being very important to maintaining mental health. Naturally, this is not uppermost in anyone's mind on a date—that is, what a good thing we are doing for ourselves. In fact, it may be just a little hard to believe, considering that most activities which we have come to label as "fun" somehow are really divorced in our minds from "work" or "serious" pursuits. We have our particular culture to thank for this. It is common for the average child to be taught that business comes before pleasure, and we know we should keep our noses to the grindstone. In other words, we tend to grow up feeling just a little guilty about having a great time.

The main thing to remember is that it is important to balance work and play. We are made continually aware of how valuable school work, good grades, and doing a good job of whatever we undertake is to our future. We need to be equally aware that having some recreational outlets which in-clude dating are also very important to becoming a mature person.

Aside from the recreational aspect of dating, psychologists have found that dating serves a number of other needs which may not be so obvious to you. One social scientist says that sociologists and psychologists feel that dating is also a part of the socialization process, that self-esteem needs are served, that needs to maintain and raise our status in the eyes of others can be met, and finally, dating leads to the selection of the person we marry. Let's take a little closer look at each of these functions and begin with dating as a part of being socialized.

Dating as Socialization

If you will recall the discussion of socialization in Chapter 3, we said that becoming "human" involves learning what we may or may not do in various situations, which personality qualities are approved of and thus desirable to cultivate. In other words, we learn to behave in ways that are approved and accepted by those who are important to us.

Your dating experiences can most certainly be seen in this light. However tentatively you may start out, dating affords you the opportunity to learn a great deal about the opposite sex. Young men come to understand what girls are like, how they think, what their values are, and to view them

Fig. 13-2   Ask this boy what he thinks of girls. Do you really need to ask?

in terms of their common bonds rather than as beings apart. It is a rediscovery period in many respects. To illustrate this, all one need do is ask a ten-year-old boy what he thinks of girls. His likely reply at this age will be "Girls? Yuk!" His culture has taught him that at this stage in his life they are contemptuous creatures who are totally undesirable. This rediscovery idea holds true for girls also. At the pre-high school level, boys are generally regarded as somewhat interesting, but they are usually stereotyped as "loud, aggressive mannerless creeps." Only through interacting with one another are these ideas gradually replaced by those deemed more appropriate to the adolescent.

Boys and girls begin to try on their adult roles when they date. Despite the development of women's liberation, boys still do most of the asking out, and girls the accepting. These are part of our culture's traditional definition of how young men and women "ought" to go about initiating dates. Many high schools have turn-about events, usually dances, where girls must ask the boys to go with them. There has been some additional reversal in the usual way dates are obtained in the past couple of years with more girls asking boys of their choice to go out with them. But it is still far from being the rule. One way girls get around appearing to be the aggressor is to initiate what could be called the "almost date." She may suggest that a boy come over to her house to watch T.V., or "study," or "talk" thereby enabling the two to get

Fig. 13–3   Watching TV is less formal than a date, as well as being less expensive.

together but not obligating him to take her out. Little by little, both sexes learn which roles feel the most comfortable and meets with the most approval by their peers and parents.

Self-Esteem from Dating

All of us like and need to be important to those who are important to us. Any dating experience which leaves us with the feeling that we are of real worth in the eyes of another person adds to our feelings of self-esteem. This is true for people of all ages, but it is particularly important to the adolescent who is steering into adulthood. We all like to have our ideas listened to, to have the feeling that we have been understood. There are, of course, some dating experiences that do not turn out as we had hoped and which, without insight, could serve to lower our opinions about ourselves. For example, suppose your date rejects some of your ideas in an untactful way. You could, after thinking about it, decide that you really did not have such good ideas and that they would only be shot down if you did express them. This would reflect lowered self-esteem. On the other hand, after consideration, if you decided that the ideas were O.K., but you could have presented them in a more favorable light, and that your date was immature for being untactful, you have maintained your self-esteem despite the experience.

Dating and Status

You will recall from the discussion in Chapter 11 that even though nothing specific is said or written down, we all have a pretty good idea of how we rate with others and how we rank in comparison with others in the informal friendship groups to which we either aspire or belong. It should come as no surprise then, that if we date and whom we date can add to or subtract from our status. Suppose, for example, that dating is very much the thing to do among members of your friendship group. If one of your friends is not dating yet, he or she is very likely to be thought of as having lower status than those members who are going out. If all members of a particular bunch are already dating, statuses may be raised or lowered in others' views depending on how "desirable" their dating partners are in the eyes of the group. There are many factors which go into making up an adolescent's opinion of a good date. Among them are good looks, athletic ability, manners, morals, grades, family status, and personality characteristics. What are some other factors that help you determine how datable someone is?

Gradually, as dating experiences continue and adulthood looms ahead, young men and women come to form ideas about what qualities they will seek in a marriage partner. As one psychologist said, "One dating situation eventually leads to a marriage partner choice." In the next chapter we will discuss some ways in which adolescents make mistakes in choosing their spouses. We will also look at the changing patterns of marriage in America. The point to remember here is that many of the qualities which at first seem so important to making casual dating fun, such as good looks or nice clothes, are very unimportant when it comes to choosing a helpmate for the long haul.

Becoming Datable

The age at which boys and girls begin to date has lowered considerably over the past few years. Surprising as it may seem, some youngsters begin the social whirl in fifth and sixth grades. More are dating in junior high school, and the percentage of those who have never dated is very small by the time senior high school is completed. There are different norms or accepted ages for beginning dating depending on the area of the country, the attitudes held by parents of the particular youngsters involved, and the sanctions spoken or unspoken by the schools among other factors.

How Does It All Begin?

Since dating is part of the American scene, and widely recognized to serve desirable functions in adolescents' lives, our institutions often give first impetus to boy-girl get-togethers. A junior high school may sponsor an after-school dance, for example, or a church may have a social for its young members. Events of this kind get boys and girls together under adult supervision and from the participants' viewpoint can run the gamut from being seen.

Fig. 13–4 Churches often have social events for teenagers. At this one, even the Bishop gets into the swing.

Fig. 13–5 Early marriage (before 20) is frowned upon in Japan as well as China. This Japanese couple is considered to be just about the right age to "tie the knot."

as a "great time" to "pretty good" to "a flop." At any rate, adolescents often begin their boy-girl experiences in this manner in our culture. Let's take a look for a minute at what other youngsters experience around the world at your age.

Dating in Other Cultures

Dating as we know it simply does not exist in many areas of the world. From the few glimpses we have been allowed to date of Mao's China, young people are very much discouraged by the government from becoming too interested in each other too early. From the Chinese government's point of view, this is an immensely practical matter. If young people can be kept from keeping company until their late teens or early twenties, then they will marry later and produce fewer children. Feeding her people has always been a vast problem for China, and early dating and early marriage, if permitted, could keep China's food problem at crisis levels far into her future.

In Latin America, dating patterns have been changing in recent years, but in general boys and girls do not date or keep company until much later than American youngsters. Argentine girls, for example, could scarcely believe the statistics which this author relayed to them regarding teen-age marriages in America. Middle and upper-middle class girls' activities are

Fig. 13–6   Some arranged marriages still take place in India. This young lady may never see her prospective husband until their wedding day.

rather strictly supervised and even today are chaperoned in many Latin countries. However, once they are allowed to begin going out, they are fairly free to choose whom they like.

In India, some young people never date. Marriages are simply arranged for them by their families when they reach "marriageable" age. In most European countries on the other hand, dating practices are similar to those in this country, although the average age at which dating begins is somewhat later than the United States.

Getting Dates

For some students, the big worry is finding someone who will ask them to go out or getting someone to go out with them. For others, the problem is fitting studies and other responsibilities into their heavy social schedules. Both sides of the dating coin can give adolescents problems, and often teens have questions which they will not ask of their friends for fear of appearing stupid, nor of their parents for other reasons.

Let's consider first the concerns of those who are not yet dating. Girls may wonder, "Why hasn't anyone ever asked me for a date?" They may try very hard to act as if such a state of affairs is of little importance, but in fact not being asked out may become an over-riding concern. Classroom performance may deteriorate, relationships at home may become tense, and friendships with peers may become more distant unless a girl can view the situation in perspective. There may be reasons for the no-date situation which have nothing to do with the particular girl at all, although she may be slow to see them. The boys in whom she is interested may not be ready to date yet, or they may feel that they do not have enough money to take a girl out. They may well be avoiding dating for fear of rejection by the girl of their choice and subsequent loss of face if this is found out by their friends. Boys commonly feel very unsure of their own social skills at this age, and girls should realize that is the case.

On the hand, girls might want to take stock of their own behavior and whether or not they may be unwittingly behaving in ways which signal go away to boys. If you are a girl, are you friendly? Do you at least smile and speak to people on your bus, in the halls, in class? That small gesture can become, first of all, a very good habit; and secondly, it can encourage boys to think that if they do speak to you, you will not act as if they are some slimy specimen beneath your notice.

How do you look? Does your appearance signal, "I consider myself important enough to look as well as I can? "Not enough money" is sometimes used as a catchall excuse for poor appearance. Don't kid yourself. Clean hair and clean skin not only look good, they also help keep skin blemishes down. What about clothes? Unless the girls in your school wear cashmere sweaters, suede pants, and fur jackets, you should be able to be fashionable with a little effort, a little ingenuity, and a little advice from someone who sews.

What about outside-the-classroom social contacts? Do you hole up with a book? Have you joined any of the clubs at your school? church? community? You may not be giving boys a chance to meet you.

What about the girl who says, "But I'm too fat," or "I'm just plain ugly"? If being overweight is the problem, take action! If you feel you cannot go to your parents or friends about the problem, ask your school counselor to help you get an appointment with a physician. Psychologists and counselors know that being overweight and the emotional difficulties that go with it are not insurmountable. There are very effective ways of helping the overweight girl or boy bring their weight down and also bring eating habits to within healthy limits. The important point to remember is that you may be fat now, but you do not have to stay fat.

It is also no wonder that many adolescent girls consider themselves homely in this society. The media bombard young girls with impossible examples. Magazines aimed at this age group typically portray teen-age girls who have perfect skin, hair, eyes, and figures, surrounded in their ads by boys who look like young Greek gods. T.V. commercials are even worse. The fact is that 95 per cent of us have some flaw in our physical appearance; or we think we do. Again, it is not impossible to disguise or play down such real or perceived defects. Exercises can slim a chunky waistline, makeup can compensate for smallish eyes. Medical care can help keep skin problems under control. Most important is for the teen-age girl to evaluate herself and her appearance realistically, to allow herself pluses as well as minuses in her evaluation, and to keep in mind that she will be an adult a lot longer than she will be a teen-ager. As an adult she will consider the kind of person she is becoming to be far more important than whether or not she is "beautiful" compared to some T.V. or magazine standard.

Boys Have Troubles, Too

Sometimes from a girl's standpoint it looks as if boys have it made. All they have to do is call up anybody they want and presto! They have a date. Right? Wrong! Psychologists have found that more often than not boys have felt that it was very hard for them to ask a girl out for the first time. They worry that they will be turned down, that they won't know what to talk about, that they will somehow embarrass themselves. They, too, are concerned about their appearance, but in different ways than girls are. Boys in high school are subjected to the same kind of media bombardment as girls. From their viewpoint, most of the boys portrayed in commercials or ads are virile, look self-assured, and are athletic geniuses. Boys need to remember that these supposed paragons of male perfection are actors in well staged mini-productions.

One point which is often overlooked is the fact that dating is competitive. Boys face this everytime they ask a girl out and must contend with possible rejection. What really makes the picture even more clouded is that sometimes a boy cannot be certain of the reason he was given by a girl for not going out with him. He may wonder is she really does have to babysit or go with her parents, or if she is just waiting for something better to come along.

Some of the factors mentioned in the discussion of girls obtaining dates certainly apply to boys. If a boy is having trouble, he can ask himself the same questions we posed for girls. Is he friendly? Is he active in school and community affairs? Does he maintain his appearance? Are his manners up-to-snuff? Does he know how to dance?

High school students who feel that their social life is less satisfactory than it should be can and should take measures to expand their interpersonal contacts.

Managing Everything

We mentioned earlier that some students try to wedge their studies, job and home responsibilities into a jam-packed social schedule. Since there are literally only so many hours in a day, some other areas in a socially whirling teen's life will suffer. Usually that means deteriorating grades, increased tensions at home between the adolescent and parents, and the possibility of illness due to lack of proper rest and diet.

Why do some adolescents press and insist on going out almost every night? Among other reasons we know that some will try this to escape unpleasant situations at home or to show how grown-up they are. Others simply have a hard time saying no or are afraid that they will miss out on something. Allocating time for each activity one wishes to pursue is not always an easy task. As we mentioned in an earlier chapter, if you feel you are swamped, try to evaluate how important each activity is going to be to you in the long run, whether it be school work or social commitment. You may then be able to see how you can manage to sustain your responsibilities without really causing your social life to suffer.

POPULARITY AND UNPOPULARITY

Everyone wants to be "popular," yet there are difficulties in pinning down just what adolescents mean by their use of the term. It includes, psychologists have found, being liked by many individuals, being in demand socially, and having a pleasing personality. Girls who are popular with other girls usually are characterized as being attractive, having a good sense of humor, having the right clothes; they are not necessarily top students. Girls who are popular with boys are usually physically attractive, spend less time talking to girls, and are available for dates. Boys who are popular with other boys are generally admired for their athletic capabilities. Boys who are popular with girls are liked for their manners, looks, and pleasing personalities.

There are few adolescents who feel that they are popular enough. It is perfectly understandable to wish that we were held in just a little higher esteem by those who are important to us than we perceive ourselves to be. There are qualities which are consistent with becoming a mature young man or woman that can certainly lead to anyone's becoming more popular. These qualities can be learned. You might want to strive for some of them if you feel they would help you feel more comfortable in social situations.

Fig. 13–7 It does take an effort to make others feel comfortable in your company, especially when you're the size of this fellow. Seriously though, indicating interest in others by listening to their problems helps you win friends.

1. Cultivate good manners. Rather than say the "wrong" thing, adolescents often clam up. The result is that they may be looked upon as loners, shy, rude, or indifferent. It does take effort to make others comfortable in your company, but it is well worth it. Such simple questions as "How did it go today?" or "What have you been up to?" indicate interest in others. Answering adults' or peers' inquiries in some detail also makes social contacts more smooth. The little courtesies of "please" and "thank you" are absolute musts.

2. Look at yourself positively. None of us are perfect physical specimens. We all have pluses and minuses. Teen-agers sometimes tend to dwell on one or two minor features they consider disappointing and blow them up all out of proportion to their real importance. The point is to give yourself credit! Certainly in any realistic appraisal you may find some need for improvement, but be honest enough to admit your good qualities to yourself! Your attitude about yourself comes over loud and clear to your peers and adults. If you present a very negative picture by having dirty hair, unkempt clothes and monosyllabic responses, fewer people will seek out your company.

3. Take part in activities. If you are involved in a few extracurricular activities, you're going to find several things happening. You will have more to talk about; you will widen your social contacts; and you just might do some good!

Besides the clubs that your school inevitably has, and the athletics programs, your community could certainly use an hour or two a week from you. There are "candy-striper" programs in your local hospitals.* There are children with cerebral palsy who would love to go swimming or just to a park. There are old folks who have no one to visit them. As hoky as it may seem, the fact is that when you do a little something for someone else, you benefit too!

4. Attempt to reduce friction points. Suppose you have just received a miserable grade on a test, or on your report card. You are unhappy with yourself, your parents are undoubtedly less than pleased, and the teacher may be disappointed. Talk to the teacher—talk to your parents. An honest effort on your part to straighten things out will make everyone happier.

*"Candy-striper" programs are volunteer programs in which teen-agers distribute books and magazines, read to patients, and generally help to cheer people up.

Fig. 13-8 *Just as these boys discuss mistakes in football with their coach, so should you discuss a poor grade with your teacher. The teacher, after all, is your academic coach.*

Real friction can develop between parent and teen-ager. The subjects of debate are usually choice of friends, hours to be kept, number of times allowed out in the week, grades, help around the house, cars, dress, music, smoking, drinking, and drugs.

However grown-up you may feel, the fact is that you are a dependent minor. The rules you may consider unreasonable are almost always laid down with protecting you in mind. Try to understand that letting go is sometimes very difficult for parents. They remember when you were totally dependent on them as infants. Sometimes their picture of you is not as grown-up as you feel it should be. Usually, however, you and your parents can work things out. The more responsibly you behave, the better the chances to be accorded more responsibility. For example, if you are keeping up your end of things by pitching in around home without being nagged, by keeping your grades up relative to your ability—then you are in a much better position to ask for some new privilege. If the rules seem hopelessly stringent, enlist your counselor or pastor and try to work things out.

In addition to the sore points just mentioned, another frequent source of worry to parents is the American custom of going steady. Does it mean the same thing in all areas of the country? Is going steady really a boon? What happens when you break up? We will take a look at these and other questions in the following sections.

GOING STEADY

In your school going steady may indicate a very serious commitment between two people, a sort of engaged-to-be-engaged arrangement. In others, it is simply fashionable to declare that you are going steady, but the level of involvement of the two people is much less. Whatever the emotional commitment, the arrangement usually means that one person is dated to the exclusion of all others. Rings or pins or bracelets are often exchanged as tokens of going steady. In the following discussion we will look at the pros and cons of this type of dating, the age-old problem of love versus sex, the problems of breaking up and what going steady now can mean to you in terms of the long view.

One big plus in the minds of adolescents is that going steady offers date security. Boys do not have to compete for a girl's attention, and girls don't have to wonder whether they will have someone to go out with each weekend. A sense of belonging makes going steady very attractive to teens. Prestige or status often enter the picture. A girl who is the steady date of a boy who is highly regarded finds her own status raised. The same holds true for a boy who can command the sole attention of a highly regarded girl. People who go steady may enjoy more status than those who do not simply because such arrangements are viewed as the thing to do in a particular school. Date security and looking good in the eyes of one's peers are very big pluses to adolescents. An additional plus is that the couple also come to know each other's hopes, plans, likes, dislikes, religious views, and so on. They may regard part of the steady arrangement to include privileged communication, in that they feel that they can divulge their feelings freely to at least this one person.

Love or Sex?

Those who are going steady usually say they are in love with each other. What do they really mean? Does being in love mean the same thing to a girl as it does to a boy? Philosophers, poets, the clergy have all attempted down through the ages to define love between men and women. There has been a considerable amount of disagreement and still is. Being in love has come to mean a general enchantment with the object of one's affections, wanting to be with that person as much as possible, being miserable at separation, strong physical attraction and a willingness to deny seeing any faults in the loved person. Girls tend to see the relationship very much this way. Boys find being in love rather less romantic and put more emphasis on sexual attraction.

Some boys will develop very convincing arguments designed to lead their steady into consenting to have intercourse. The argument is usually, "If you love me and I love you, then it's O.K." Girls who do consent face several unpleasant possibilities. They may become pregnant, or they may find the boy's attachment to them cooled considerably. Guilt feelings may be unbearable, and there is always the possibility that the word will get out and parents may find out.

Sexual urges reach a peak in adolescence among males, and the wish to experiment may be hard to control. Boys and girls should be fully aware of the attitudes each brings to a going steady arrangement. They need to be aware that sexual exploitation on the part of either person certainly does not mean love. Getting carried away is a result of frequent long opportunities for private love-making on the part of steadies. Interviews include statements such as "We didn't plan to. . . ." One psychologist suggests that in developing into a mature person it would be much better for the boy and girl if their behavior in regard to sex desires were regulated by an understanding of what was good for themselves and their companion, accompanied by the ability to govern their behavior.

In general, adolescents today are only a little more well informed about sexual development than were their parents, despite sex education programs in the schools. It is just as important to understand the opposite sex in terms of their attitudes, feelings, fears, and so on as it is to know how specific organs function. If your school has no sex education program and you do not feel free to take your questions to your school counselor or parents, by all means consult the library! Do not rely on information from friends. More likely than not it will be at best incomplete; and even more likely, wrong.

Going steady, then, does have considerable attraction for adolescents and seems to offer many advantages. Some disadvantages of going steady are recognized by teenagers; however, they sometimes fail to include that a steady arrangement usually leads to progressively physical intimacies and that as one level of necking or petting becomes old hat, it is much easier to rationalize moving just a little farther. In the next chapter, we will discuss some of the tragic results of early steady relationships—teen-age mothers raising babies alone, seeking abortions, then forced into marriage by irate families, and divorce in such marriages. The intention here is not to paint a completely dark picture of going steady, but to give the student an idea of both sides of the picture.

The Long View Again

As you date and begin thinking about those qualities you wish to find in a husband or wife, keep your long-range goals in mind. Do you plan on going to college? Will you be going into one of the services upon graduation? Will you be seeking employment outside your immediate area when you finish school? You may find yourself viewing your dating relationships very differently in the light of these questions. Breaking up with your steady may enter the picture. As some of you may already be aware, at best it is not a pleasant process. Rarely do steadies part without some hurt feelings to one of the parties. A parting, of course, is rarely anticipated at the beginning of the steady relationship. Boys and girls have reported that they have felt the least hurt when the breakup was mutually agreed upon, or when one partner couched the end of going steady in terms of not being really ready for this type of involvement.

In summary, then, dating provides a culturally acceptable way for boys and girls to enjoy each other's company and to accumulate and weigh those personal qualities which they seek in a life partner. Going steady offers both advantages and pitfalls to the maturing individual. And finally, we do know that the experience of some dating in an adolescent's life in general leads to better marriage partner choices and to longer lasting, more satisfying marriages.

CHAPTER SUMMARY

1. Many dating situations revolve around some of the same activities that were prevalent in dating twenty years ago. Teens still flock to athletic events, parties, dances, and the movies. Cars and popular music are central to dating as they were in the past.

2. Although the events to which adolescents go have changed only a little, other elements have been added. Alcohol, pot, "soft" and "hard" drugs often pop up in group situations. Many teens have difficulty handling these aspects of dating.

3. The primary functions which dating serves in our culture are: (1) Recreation—we go out to have a good time; (2) Socialization—we learn about the opposite sex and come to know them as human beings. We learn to try on our adult roles as men and women; (3) Self-esteem—we form new opinions of ourselves as we see ourselves interacting with others; (4) Status—whether a boy or girl is dating or not and whom he or she dates is important in determining how peers rate a person and how the person rates himself or herself; (5) Marriage partner selection —with a moderate amount of dating, we become able to more clearly define what sort of person we would like to have as a husband or wife. One dating relationship eventually leads to marriage.

4. Dating may begin in groups at the junior high level. It is also not uncommon to see pairing off begin at school and church sponsored events.

5. Dating in other cultures is different from the average American teen's experiences. In China, young people are not encouraged to think about seeking a partner until their late twenties. Latin Americans still keep a wary eye on boy-girl relationships, and in some cultures dating is virtually nonexistent.

6. Dates are very hard to find for some and crowd out all other activities for others. Becoming datable involves one's personal habits, dress, accessibility, and friendliness.

7. Some time honored tips on popularity include suggestions to (1) cultivate good manners, (2) give yourself credit (3) take part in extracurricular activities, and (4) reduce friction points between yourself and others.

8. Going steady offers date security and increased status, which are viewed as big pluses by teens. Steady dating also increases the likelihood of more and more intimate sexual behavior, with the danger of an unwanted pregnancy. Breaking up a steady relationship is often very painful.

9. A moderate amount of dating as a teen does appear to enable individuals to make better and longer lasting choices in marriage partners.

Important Terms
from This Chapter

recreation	status	competitive dating
socialization	arranged marriage	popularity
self-esteem		date security

Additional Readings
to Help You Learn More

Haas, K. *Understanding Adjustment and Behavior,* 2nd Edition. Englewood Cliffs, N.J.: Prentice-Hall, Inc., 1965. Chapter 4, "Adolescence and Adulthood," discusses such things as dating and mate selection, marriage counseling, as well as education and work life.

Longstreth, L. *Psychological Development of the Child,* 2nd Edition. New York: The Ronald Press Company, 1974. Chapter 14, "Moral Development and its Determinants," goes into morality, environmental determinants of moral behavior, and child rearing and moral behavior.

Malm, M. and Jamison, O. *Adolescence.* New York: McGraw Hill Book Company, 1952. Chapter 6, "Heterosexual Adjustment," discusses problems in dealing with the opposite sex in a straightforward and objective manner.

Readings in Psychology Today, 2nd Edition. Del Mar, Calif.: CRM Books, 1972. "Who Likes Whom and Why?" Students will find this particular paper most helpful.

Wertheimer, M. *Confrontation: Psychology and the Problems of Today.* Glenview, Ill.: Scott, Foresman and Company, 1970. Today's teen-agers will find the various papers in Section 1, "Identity and the Identity Crisis," very helpful in terms of understanding their own problems.

chapter

14

Marriage and the Family

In the previous chapter, we indicated that at some point in a person's dating experiences one relationship may deepen and lead to marriage while others do not. Popular romantic myth in this culture tells teens that they will know when the "right" person comes along. How you are expected to know is left to the imagination. Prospective husbands and wives do not drop in front of us from the blue, so where do they come from? How do people really choose their partners? What if they make a mistake? The selection of a marriage partner is one of the most important decisions you will make as a young adult. In the following sections we will discuss some of the most important factors that should go into such choices, the changing patterns of marriage in our culture, teen marriages, emerging sex roles, the implications for raising a family, and some projections for the future.

CHOOSING A PARTNER

Most of you taking this course have not even met the person whom you will ultimately marry, but you have probably given some thought to the qualities you hope to find in your prospective mate. You may also have the feeling that the number of prospective mates is almost limitless—that you have the whole world to choose from. In the following section we will take a look at the qualities which may make a person a good date but a poor partner. We shall also see if we really have the whole world to choose from.

Fig. 14–1. Major choices that high school students face as they approach graduation: 1. Should I go to college? 2. Should I go to technical school? 3. Should I go take some time off and travel? 4. Should I get married?

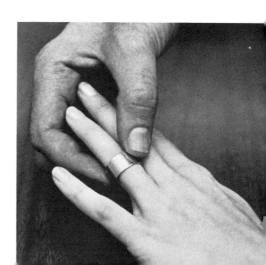

Adolescents frequently emphasize how much fun someone is to be with or how good-looking and what a great dancer or athlete a date is. These qualities undoubtedly contribute to having a good time, but what are their implications for being a good marriage partner? Psychologists and other social scientists know that physical attractiveness, an up-to-the minute grasp of the latest hair styles, clothing trends, slang, and the ability to dance will say nothing about what kind of marriage partner a person will be. It is possible to possess all of these qualities and be a very poor husband or wife. What, then, should one look for in a prospective mate? Certainly we do not want to go through life never having any fun, but we do not want to choose so poorly or on such an inadequate basis that divorce is the only answer.

Major Questions in Mate Selection

The casual dating you engage in now will help you to clarify both the assets and liabilities you will bring to marriage as well as defining what you seek in a partner. The main questions teens need to ask if they find themselves becoming serious about someone include: "Are we really ready to marry? Will marrying now prevent us from reaching other goals in our futures? Does the welfare of the person we love equal our concern for self? Do we see each other as we really are? Do we have major differences on matters vital to the success of our marriage?" The following areas have proven to be those in which major differences often spell a poor future for marital satisfaction. They are also areas that many young persons do not discuss with their prospective partners out of a mistaken belief that "if we love each other, everything else will be okay."

1. *Maturity:* Couples need to assess their prospective partners as to emotional maturity. Is he or she jealous of activities and friendships outside their relationship? Does he or she have a quick temper? Does either demand having their own way? How would each be likely to behave in a crisis? Are either of the pair overly dependent or obstinate or sulky? Do they seem to view marriage as an escape from parental authority? Do each have healthy attitudes towards sex? Is each aware that the other has emotional needs, and is each willing to meet the needs of his or her partner?

2. *Religion:* Young couples frequently give very little attention to or tend to downgrade the importance of differences in religious beliefs. This is one area that should be thoroughly explored together. Vast differences in belief and practice will strain even the most loving couples. Marriages in which the couples' religious backgrounds are similar are known to have a better chance for success. Mixed marriages—that is, marriages between Prot-

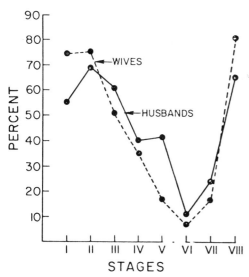

Fig. 14–2. Percent of individuals reporting that their present stage of the family life cycle is very satisfying. Dispelling the myth about family life, that marriage is least satisfying at the beginning, this chart shows the variety of fluctuations that occur at different stages. The stages shown are I. Beginning marriage (before children), II. Oldest child an infant, III. Oldest child a preschooler, IV. Oldest child an elementary school child, V. Oldest child a teenager, VI. Oldest child living away from home, other children at home, VII. All children living away from home and VIII. Husband retired.

estant and Catholic, Catholic and Jew, Moslem and Christian, etc., can work out very well, but the partners must make varying accommodations in terms of family practices on holy days, religious education of their children, and so on.

3. *Education:* The number of college and university students who marry before completing their education is growing, as is the number of couples who marry soon after high school graduation. The potential for strain on a student marriage is often very great. Before blithely assuring themselves that they can take care of each other, some very practical questions such as, "Will we be able to maintain our studies if we have other responsibilities?" and "Will we have enough money, or will a restricted budget be a big sore point?" should be asked. Another area concerns couples whose individual educational levels are very different. If one of the pair has a great deal more education than the other, this can serve to pull the couple apart.

4. *Money:* What contribution will each make to the family income? How are major financial decisions to be made? More arguments occur in this area than in almost any other in a marriage. Does the couple understand how to budget? Which partner is the better manager? Will they have enough to live on or must they seek parental support? Should both work?

5. *Children:* Most couples do want children, but do not realize what a vast change it is from two-ness to three-ness. What is the couple's attitude towards children? Do they agree on when to begin their family? How many children do they feel are ideal? How would they deal with a surprise preg-

TABLE 14-1: MEDIAN AGE AT FIRST MARRIAGE, BY SEX: 1890 TO 1971

Year	Male	Female
1890	26.1	22.0
1900	25.9	21.9
1910	25.1	21.6
1920	24.6	21.2
1930	24.3	21.3
1940	24.3	21.5
1950	22.8	20.3
1960	22.8	20.3
1971	23.1	20.9

Although you will note that the marriage age has declined over the years, note also that most people marry partners in their own age range and that the girl is almost always slightly younger than the boy.

nancy? Do they share similar beliefs about family planning? Do they have very clear ideas about what each feels a mother and father should be? What about adoption? What about discipline? Do they agree? There should ideally be plenty of time before marriage to talk freely and thoroughly about these questions. It can be startling and disruptive at the very least to find that your partner does not agree with what you consider to be very reasonable feelings about these matters.

6. *Relatives:* Each member of a pair brings relatives to their marriage in greater or lesser degrees. What if you really cannot stand his father? Perhaps her brother lives nearby and is a complete slob, but she cannot see why you dislike him. What will situations like this do to the couple's feelings about each other? Interfering relatives on either side have torn many marriages apart.

7. *Recreation and companionship:* During courtship it is quite normal to simply be content to be with the one you love, doing nothing special. But for the long haul, just sitting around together becomes intolerably boring. If one of the couple enjoys relaxing by going to concerts, curling up with a good book, or playing cards, and the other much prefers participating in a rigorous tennis game or shooting 18 holes of golf, the couple may find themselves growing apart.

8. *Personal habits:* We tend to excuse and magnanimously overlook little faults when we feel we are in love. These little faults can be major sources of irritation in marriage. Small things like leaving socks on the floor

or not capping the toothpaste can cause blow-ups unless the couple is aware before they marry of the impact and cumulative irritation such habits can produce.

9. *Sex:* Many young people come to marriage woefully ignorant about many aspects of their sexual relationship despite sex education in school and the numerous books on the market. Couples should talk freely together about their attitudes and preferences. A good sexual relationship depends heavily on the willingness to discuss this aspect of marriage before marriage. Proper techniques are simply not enough. Keeping any disappointment quiet and not talking about it can be disastrous. A joyful loving sexual relationship must be based on good information, great mutual consideration, and open communication.

Obviously the preceding points are not meant to be exhaustive. They are raised here to point out that the better a couple knows one another and the more fully they have explored the various aspects of their future life together, the better prepared they will be for it. If something bothers you about your prospective spouse before you marry, you can be certain that it will cause trouble after you are married.

Outside Influences: Peers and Family

Often teens are not fully aware of the pressures that their friends and families bring to bear on their choice of mates. Parents want their children to be happy but often have very different ideas than their children about what will make them so. Usually, the harder parents try to push, the more adolescents will back off from the direction their parents desire them to take. What teens need to understand is that many parents are afraid that their children will either marry too early or choose unwisely, and their pushiness is designed, from their point of view, to protect their children.

Peers can cause adolescents to be swept in certain directions. Suppose that most of the girls in a particular group are going steady, talking about getting married, getting jobs, and getting away from home. If only one or two are planning to further their education and not get serious until later, they can be most uncomfortable. The point to remember is that the end of high school is a major choice point in life. Neither peers nor parents can map the future to perfection. Although it may be very difficult to step to your own drummer, particularly in the face of pressures from friends, their plans and enthusiasms may not be as well thought out as yours.

Limits on Choice of Partners

It may seem, as mentioned previously, that you have the whole world from which to choose your mate. Our culture, however, subtly in some cases, baldly in others, prescribes rather narrowly the general limits within which our choices should take place. Since most marriages take place when people are in their early twenties, this is generally agreed upon as the "right" time of life to marry. Women who delay marriage until their late twenties or early thirties are still stigmatized as old maids. Men may begin to be stigmatized as odd if they are not married by their middle thirties. Our culture, in other words, considers being married as the normal state. Some girls, despite the advent of women's lib, begin to feel somewhat desperate if they have not managed to land a husband by the time they are 21 or 22. The nagging feeling that "if I don't marry this one, I might never get married" has driven more than one girl into an unhappy alliance.

There are also norms for acceptable ages of prospective spouses. The unwritten ideal is that the man be two to four years older than his wife. "May–December" marriages, in which the age difference is fifteen to twenty years, are uncommon and are frowned upon, especially if the woman is much older than her husband.

Inter-racial marriages are still comparatively rare in the United States. Despite the apparently genuine efforts on the part of many in our culture to encourage people to look beyond differing skin colors, the differences remain as effective limits on partner choices.

The old saw that "it's as easy to marry rich as marry poor" is very far from the truth. Those in upper socio-economic circumstances try to control the field of choice for their children by seeing to it that they attend very expensive private schools where, with few exceptions, children from families equally well off will be found. The middle class discriminates in its own way by trying to steer their children away from lower-class matches. Social scientists have found that when class lines are crossed, more frequently the man will choose a girl from a lower class than the other way around.

Religion forms yet another restriction on possible choices. Most people choose partners of their own faith and meet with some resistance if they do not. Members of the Jewish faith are most likely to choose partners of their own religion; next are Catholics; and it is only somewhat less likely that Protestants will not choose a fellow Protestant.

Another very important factor in mate selection is the community in which you live at the time you are beginning to think seriously of marriage. For those of you who remain in your home town or city after high school, chances are that your choice of a partner will also be living there. For those of you who go away to a college or university, your prospective partner will most likely be found there. These points should serve to demonstrate that in effect we really do not have the whole world from which to choose. Multiple influences have subtly shaped a limited field from which we may make a "suitable" and comfortable selection.

Most of you will not marry while you are still in high school, but some teens do marry; and the rate of divorce in such marriages is so high that we need to take a look at the problems of teen marriages.

READY OR NOT: TEEN MARRIAGES

It is quite likely that you know several people in your class or neighborhood who are engaged or "pre-engaged." Perhaps you are one of them. Many of these young people have very little idea of just what it is that is propelling them towards marriage while still in their teens. Many sail blithely into partnerships that will falter within a year. Most of these couples profess to be very much in love with each other, to know "everything" about each other, and to know their own minds. Few are truly prepared.

Pressures to Marry Early

One of the more subtle influences on adolescents which may propel them into early marriages is the cultural confusion in our society about who is and who is not an adult. There are cultures in which passage from childhood to adult status occurs at a specified time with specified ceremonies. Thereafter the person is expected to assume adult responsibilities and has been so prepared. There is no sharp delineation of adulthood for us to latch onto in our society. Many of the marks of adult status occur at varying times during a teen's development.

Sexual maturity occurs in girls and boys at an age when most are defined legally and culturally as children in this country. The privilege of driving a car comes at age 16 for the majority of American youth, and though certainly it is an adult thing to do, it does not of itself mark the 16-year-old as grown-up. Boys and girls may join the military forces at age 18 and may vote, but they may not enter into binding legal agreements in some states until they are 21 years old. The age at which drinking is permitted varies from state to state, as does the legal age to marry without parental consent. Adolescence, then, tends to be a drawn-out affair in our culture, with the main legal status of an adult becoming available finally at age 21. Even at age 21, there are exceptions. One may not become a United States Senator until one is 30 years old, nor run for the United States House until age 25. Political maturity, then, is deferred even longer.

Getting married, however, tends to confer immediate "adult" status on the married couple. They are expected to establish their own place of residence, provide for their own needs, be responsible to their partners rather than their parents, and in general wend their own way. These factors alone may have enormous appeal to the teen who feels his or her life is too restricted by parental demands. Marriage is thought of as a way, at last, to be one's own boss.

Escape: The Frying Pan and the Fire

Something new and different like being married may seem far more desirable than a given teen's present circumstances. If there are fights at home, or indifference to their children on the part of "too busy" parents, or a shortsighted wish to be done with school and books, marriage can seem like a great escape route. The idea seems to be that if the couple just gets away, everything will fall their way. For life to actually work out in this Cinderella fashion for married teens is rather rare.

Most teens find that when they escape from home into an early marriage things are not quite what they thought they would be. The couple may be shocked at all the expenses that the money they have available each week must cover. The cute little apartment may begin to seem dinky, dumpy, and dull after a few months. Each may try to keep up their friendships with those still in high school only to find their marital status a barrier.

Lack of money for recreation may come as a stunning revelation to the young couple. When their main concerns at home were spending money on dates, clothes, and paying for a car or bike, there seemed to be sufficient money. Paying for food, clothing, shelter, heat, lights, and so forth tends to leave a teen couple with very little money for any extras such as a movie or dinner at a nice restaurant.

Sometimes the very things that made a young couple flee their homes come cropping up in the new marriage. The couple may find their time together even more restricted than when they were dating if both are working full time.

Just as perceived impossible situations at home can thrust a couple into marriage, so can an unexpected development in their physical relationship precipitate marrying. Even in this age of the pill, many high school girls find that they have somehow become pregnant. There are few choices once a pregnancy is established. The girl may seek an abortion legally or illegally. This option can be an awful experience, depending on the girl's religious beliefs and the kind of care she receives. Abortion is very controversial in our culture. Attitudes toward it as well as the legal status of such operations range from "murder of the unborn" to "removal of tissue." The girl can reject abortion and marriage and have the baby out-of-wedlock. The big questions of what will happen to the child and to the girl after the baby's birth can have a devastating impact on a girl's life as well as on the life of the young father.

The slightly more common choice is for the couple to marry. In addition to everything else, they must immediately prepare for the next generation. Rarely is either partner delighted at the prospect. Should any arguments occur, there is always the possibility of one partner throwing it up to the other that they had to marry; they did not choose to do so.

WHY TEEN MARRIAGES FAIL

We have already noted in previous sections some of the pressures on teens which may precipitate their marrying while still in high school or shortly thereafter. Do these marriages really fail to last and if so, why?

It is not just scare tactics on the part of parents seeking to keep their children from getting too serious about their dates that makes them say that teen marriages often do not work out. From census statistics, we know that whether you are male or female, if you are in your teens and marry, your chances of that marriage ending in permanent separation or divorce are quintuple that of the rest of the population. It is even worse if you live in the Western United States or if you are a member of a minority group. Statistics do not measure human suffering, however. A broken marriage means more than two broken lives. However estranged a young couple might be from

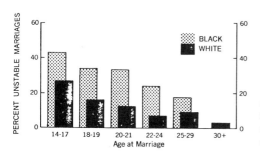

Fig. 14–3. Statistics show that youthful marriages are unstable. This is, they end in divorce or separation in a large number of cases.

their families, their families will still be affected by the dissolution of their marriage. If the young couple happen to have children when they part, the divorce will almost undoubtedly scar them too. What are the major reasons for the high rate of teen marriage failure?

Immaturity: On Both Sides

As we indicated earlier in the chapter, emotional immaturity has a great deal to do with the shattering of many teen marriages. Both boy and girl may have unrealistic expectations of their partners. Interviews with teens whose marriages have failed include such complaints as: "He thought I was going to mother him and bow down to every whim," "She just sat around all day and watched T.V.—didn't even clean up the place," "He was always feeling sorry for himself because he couldn't hang around with his friends the way he used to," "I got sick of hearing her whine to her mother on the phone every day," and "We fought all the time about everything." Comments such as these indicate that each person came into the marriage with very little insight or understanding of how their behavior and feelings would affect their partner. We can see, too, that some girls have rushed into the partnership with the notion that they will be taken care of and that they need do little or nothing to make a go of things. Some young husbands find that the sexual freedom that they expected once they were married is viewed as exploitation by their wives. The girl may have had the idea that all the romantic cuddling and caressing would increase with marriage, only to find that her partner no longer sees a need for it.

The main point to remember here is that success in marriage demands that each come into the partnership with as full an understanding as possible of their own and their partner's motives, behavior, expectations, and short-comings. They must also bring a deep concern for each other's feelings and be able to compromise. This does not mean that there will be no bumps in the road. But it will certainly help to keep the bumps from becoming insur-mountable barriers.

Inadequate Preparation for Responsibility

In high school, you may feel that you are a responsible person if you are making adequate grades and not getting into trouble with your teachers. Some teens fail to realize that there is more to responsibility than this—particularly in marriage. When teens whose marriages have fallen apart say they "just weren't ready," they most often are alluding to the fact that they were not prepared for the total responsibility of managing their own lives down to the last detail. In many cases this is not the fault of the young people involved. They have not been prepared by their culture to do so. As we mentioned earlier, adolescence is a prolonged affair in our society, and certain kinds of responsibility are not allowed until one reaches a certain age. On the other hand, parents are expected to clothe, feed and provide lodging and laundry service for their children. While teens may have certain chores to do around the house, very few have been trained to manage a household completely on their own, from bed-making to cooking to taxes. Young couples often find themselves overwhelmed with duties that they had previously taken for granted when they lived at home.

Money Problems

Probably the heaviest burden that teen marrieds must bear is the struggle to live on their income. If the couple has married just out of high school, it is almost inevitable that both must work to make ends meet. In addition, high school graduates rarely make as much as those who further their education in some way. Even if the couple is not particularly materialistic, lack of what each perceives to be an adequate income causes more grief in teen-age marriages than almost any other factor. Recriminations crop up. The young husband may feel that his wife is wasting money on clothes and cosmetics. His wife may resent the money he spends on bowling and beer with the boys. Thousands of young couples slide deeply into debt, and nasty letters from creditors add more tension and strain to their lives.

Unless the couple is really fortunate, the specter of unemployment usually looms over them. Young men with little experience or seniority are the first to be laid off if the firm they work for has to retrench for some reason. Millions of Americans each year go through the hard times of being out of a job and trying to find another. Even a very good marriage of long standing is severely tested in such times. It can be particularly hard for a young husband to be out of work himself and be dependent on his wife's job to see them through. Deep divisions that may be difficult to mend can occur in financially tight circumstances.

Money management requires knowledge of planning, budgeting, and good buying practices that few teens have had the chance to experience if they marry immediately out of high school. It may look very easy when a boy or girl is living at home in comfortable middle-class circumstances. The average teen's money managing experience comes from handling his or her allowance or income from a part-time job. While this is certainly good experience, it falls short of the knowledge teen couples need when they are thrown on their own. Families and schools alike need to prepare teens much more thoroughly in the various aspects of management of personal and family finances.

Instant Families

No one would disagree with the statement that the birth of a child should be a wanted and welcome event. But, as mentioned previously, it is a vast change from two-ness to three-ness, and many couples do not realize what it will mean to have a tiny human being totally dependent upon them. Pregnancy is not always welcomed by teen couples, nor is the expense involved reckoned with. Teen-age mothers frequently resent being tied down to the demands a baby makes on their time, and teen-age fathers are sometimes unwilling to share their wife's attention with the newcomer.

If the couple begins their marriage with a baby on the way, they have only a very short time to get used to each other before the new roles of

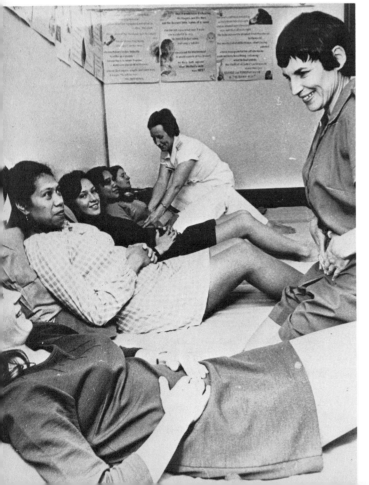

Fig. 14–4. These expectant mothers are attending a Prenatal clinic. Good prenatal care is essential for both mother and child.

Fig. 14–5. This little fellow has unwittingly thrust additional responsibilities onto the shoulders of his young father.

mother and father are upon them. If both prospective parents are working before their baby comes, they will also become aware that good prenatal care is not cheap. Many prospective teen mothers forego adequate care during pregnancy, and it is partially this factor that keeps the infant as well as the maternal mortality rates much higher than they should be. Income also tends to drop for the teen couple just when they need it most. Even if the young wife has managed to retain her job right up until her baby comes, she must still take time off to have the baby. Most firms and businesses do not have generous maternity leave and benefits available, and in many cases the job may not be held open for the mother.

Infant day-care has become more widely available at reasonable cost in urban areas in recent years, and young couples need these services. Grand-mothers and aunts are not likely to be as readily handy as baby-sitters as they were when three generations lived in the same house or at least in the same town. As we will see in the next section, it is sometimes better for young couples not to have their relatives right at their elbows.

Problems with Relatives

Comedians have long made mother-in-law jokes a standard part of their routines, but to anyone who has an in-law problem, the joke is difficult to see. Actually, the emphasis on mothers-in-law is quite unfair, as problems with relatives can just as easily develop from some other relationship. There is also the possibility that the attitudes of the young couple may lead them to look for in-law trouble. The young wife may feel that her mother-in-law disapproves of her housekeeping or cooking. The husband may perceive that his wife's family does not think he will ever amount to much. If either set of parents or relatives disapproved of the match in the first place, the chances that they will keep their feelings to themselves are fairly slim. Sometimes the pressures are great enough to break up the marriage.

Many parents, of course, are warmly supportive of the young couples in their families. They help out financially or with services and encouragement and do not interfere or criticize. In-law problems are not inevitable for teen marrieds any more than they are for those who marry later. When such difficulties do crop up, however, their potential for causing strain on a young marriage is severe.

HELP FOR MARRIED TEENS

There are sources of help for couples who find themselves in difficulty of one sort or another in almost every community. Licensed competent marriage counselors can often help a young couple work through emotional, sexual, or family problems. The clergy of all denominations have always been generous and ready to help young marrieds with their problems. Legal aid is frequently available at low cost. State-sponsored family service agencies can help with advice and assistance in terms of employment and child welfare.

The best possible favor that a couple can do for themselves and their respective families is to plan ahead. Premarital counseling sessions are often useful, for they serve to make the couple aware of the many facets of married life to which they might not have given much consideration. Such courses are usually provided by churches in the community, and frequently are included in high school curricula.

But the best efforts of family and community are sometimes not sufficient to keep a couple together, and one or the other seeks a divorce or separation. As we pointed out earlier, this is five times as likely to lie in store for those who marry in their teens as for those who defer marriage until their early twenties.

DIVORCE AND CONSEQUENCES

Some of you have already seen firsthand what divorce is like and what it can do emotionally to a couple, their children, and families. There are few friendly divorces. Despite the fact that no-fault divorce laws are apparently the coming thing, it is necessary now for blame to be established in many states. One partner must charge the other with mental cruelty or with desertion or infidelity in order to satisfy legal grounds for dissolution of the marriage. The families of each partner frequently harbor and express very negative feelings about the member of the pair whom they consider to be the villain.

Divorce is still viewed by many in our population as a stigmatizing admission of failure. Few religious bodies condone divorce, and many actively oppose it. The general population since World War II has become somewhat more acceptant of divorce, if for no other reason than that it has become such an increasingly common occurrence. Attitudes toward divorced persons still carry some unfavorable overtones. The divorced woman is generally regarded to be more free with her sexual favors and is sometimes pictured as a poor mother, whether she is or not. The divorced man is regarded traditionally as the cause of many divorces. The mantle of failure and guilt after a divorce is hard for many to discard.

Children frequently become emotional pawns in divorce proceedings. They are usually "awarded" to one parent or the other, and are frequently lost to the grandparents on one side of the split family. One parent is reduced to the status of a visitor in the life of his or her children. The children not infrequently develop the idea that they are somehow at fault in causing the split. In any event, when children are involved in divorce serious emotional problems can and often do result.

What of a young couple who part before they have started a family? A high proportion remarry within one to five years, and while many second marriages are successful, many of these subsequent partnerships also dissolve. The human cost in time, energy, and pain in the dissolution of a marriage and restructuring of lives is almost impossible to measure. It would seem that our society is trying to help those couples who for one reason or another find themselves on the verge of breaking up. State and local governments have vastly increased their family service programs over the last few years in an attempt to help iron out behavioral, emotional, occupational, and financial difficulties and thus aid families to stay together.

CHANGING SEX ROLES IN MARRIAGE

The traditional roles of men as the breadwinner and head of the house and women as head of the home have come under attack in recent years. Hundreds of thousands of women entered the labor force in the United States during World War II, and the percentage of married women who seek employment outside the home has been steadily rising ever since. What happens to families in which both husband and wife are employed?

Whether the family is in an apartment or single family home, there is still housework to be done. When the husband alone is employed, the division of labor between men and women is still rather sharp. The man earns the family's living, takes care of the car or cars, the yard, and the outside of the house. If the woman remains at home, she usually performs most other tasks from laundry to cooking to cleaning and shopping. She chauffeurs the children to lessons, doctors' appointments, and for the most part manages the family's social life. Her husband expects to help her with the heavy work, such as moving furniture and carrying heavy loads. He is also typically expected to have some skill at fixing things around the house. When both work, the division of labor is less clear and often worked out in very individualized ways depending on what suits the couple.

Contributing significantly to the family income usually raises the wife in status in the family. Even though the income may be very welcome, some men's egos are wounded by this lack of dependence on them and resent their wives' outside employment. When this happens, the larger portion of the housework may still be done by the wife despite the fact that she usually puts in the same number of hours away from the home as her husband does. The increasing independence of married women has in fact brought about a restructuring of families in our society. Men have begun to feel that shared responsibility for household tasks does not impair their masculinity. Women are gaining in terms of equality in family decision-making without being branded as pushy or henpecking. Both increasingly see the benefits of sharing the traditionally feminine tasks involved with child rearing. The attitude that "work is work," without the traditional male-female divisions seems to be seen as only sensible among young couples today.

Men's Liberation

There are a few couples experimenting with complete role reversal. The men in these cases have either quit their jobs or work at home while the wife is employed outside the home. They have become "house husbands," and have taken on all traditional housewife tasks. Whether or not their numbers will increase remains to be seen; right now they are a very small percentage of the 200,000 men (widowed, divorced, and single) whom the United States Department of Labor lists as male homemakers.

Women's Liberation

During the late 1960s and early 1970s, there has been a great deal of discussion of the position which women occupy in the total society as well as their position within the family. Militant feminists have been very vocal and effective in changing attitudes toward and laws concerning women in recent years. Whether one agrees with all of their arguments or not, there is considerable merit in much of what the leaders of the movement say. Although they represent a little more than half the population, women are vastly under-represented in all professional fields except for teaching and nursing. Equal pay for equal work may be the law, but women's salaries still lag behind their male counterparts who hold identical jobs. The proportion of women who seek Ph.D.s and M.D.s has not risen significantly, and women are largely absent from upper managerial positions across the board of United States economic life.

Ardent feminists claim that men conspire to keep things this way. What is little realized is that women do also. There is considerable ambivalence on the part of many talented women, and some difficulty in seeing themselves as equal competitors in a "man's world." Many secretly fear that they will not be considered as marriage material if they are too bright or too successful, and few openly opt for a single life.

The effects of the women's lib movement on the present and future generations may be the most telling in how families organize themselves and rear their children. If the common humanity aspect of women's lib is generally accepted, we should see far less sexual differentiation in early childhood. Boys may be able to express fear and cry more readily without parental disapproval. Girls may be encouraged very early to think of themselves as potential engineers or auto mechanics. We may see more paper girls and boy baby-sitters. There may, however, turn out to be more smoke than fire in terms of the overall ways in which men and women see themselves and each other's roles in our society. The trend, at present, does appear to be toward more sharing and cooperative efforts in male-female relationships. Further research and demographic data from the next census year (1980) will help to clarify whether or not the changes we seem to see now are reflected statistically.

What Future for the Family?

There are some psychologists and sociologists who point to the high rate of divorce, desertion, and juvenile crime as evidence of the decline of the family as a successful institution in America. Most social and behavioral scientists are not that pessimistic. They see that the functions and structure of the average American family have certainly changed under the impact of industrialization, inventions, and increased population in urban areas, but deny that the family is on the decline. Let us turn our attention for a moment to what has happened to the structure and functions of the family since the turn of the century.

Changes in Family Structure and Function

In the early 1900s, the unquestioned head of the family was the father. His wife and children were subject to his authority. Laws governing property, inheritance, and political life all reflected this. Kinship ties were relatively stronger than today, due to the fact that most new families remained fairly close to the area in which they had been born and raised. It was also fairly common for at least one member of an older generation to be present in the home. One sociologist explains that under such authoritarian leadership, whether benevolent or not, the family in 1900 was still a fairly self-sufficient economic unit. Much that the family consumed was produced at home, including food and clothing. Religious and secular instruction was begun at home and supervised there. Protection of the family fell to the father, and recreation was largely a family affair. The status of each member of the family was clearly defined, and a primary function of the family was the procreation and rearing of children.

The structure of the average American family today is somewhat different, and many of its previous functions have been assumed by other institutions in our society. The leadership of the family is much more of a joint or shared leadership than previously. The children often have a great deal of weight in major family decisions. Industrialization and the automobile have moved most families far from their origins, and it is now rather rare to have an extended family (grandmother, aunts, or uncles) under one roof. As an economic unit, what the family consumes in goods and services comes primarily from outside sources, although there has been an increasing trend in recent years to do it yourself. Recreation, as one sociologist notes, is now a vast multimillion dollar business, and each member of the family is likely to participate in something different. Protection of the family is now shared with the state. Laws protect children and women. As women come to share more equally all the formerly male prerogatives, some status relationships within the family have tended to become obscured. With the discovery of effective contraceptives, families are having and planning fewer children. This has all led to bring one particular function of the family into high relief. Companionship and affection have come to be more and more important as the glue which holds a family together. One psychologist notes that families are successful today because they want to be, rather than because they have to be.

An Optimistic Projection

Despite the stresses placed on the family as an institution by the enormous demands placed on it, the vast majority of families show them-

Fig. 14–6. Despite the complexities and pace of a highly industrialized, mobile society, the family as an institution is still strong.

selves to be resilient and adaptable. Young men and women are preparing themselves for a long life together and increasingly speak of the necessity for commitment to each other. They seem to be much more aware of how strongly a family can influence its children in terms of value systems and attitudes. Social scientists have taken note that there is now more emphasis on interpersonal communication, affection, and cooperation among newly forming families. The pressures of living in a fast, industrialized, urban-exploding society will continue to tax families and split many. The overall prediction, however, is not for the decline of the family but for its increasing importance and strength.

CHAPTER SUMMARY

1. Choosing a marriage partner is one of the most important decisions young men and women make. The emphasis in our culture on having a good time with someone who is attractive often leads couples to gloss over discussing and exploring many questions on which the success and longevity of the marriage may depend.

2. The primary areas which couples should explore together in premarital counseling or in courses designed to prepare them for marriage are (1) each other's emotional maturity, (2) their overall health, (3) religious beliefs, (4) education, (5) financial matters, (6) children, (7) their respective family relationships, (8) recreation and companionship, (9) personal habits, and (10) sexual attitudes. If you find some area that bothers you before marriage, it will certainly bother you within that marriage.

3. Our culture limits the range of choice of acceptable partners. The "ideal" mate is neither a great deal older nor younger than his or her partner and has a similar background. Peers and parents can bring considerable pressures to bear..

4. Those who marry in their teens often have little awareness of the pressures which have led them into early marriages, nor are they prepared for life in tandem. Some of the pressures come from teen culture in that the excitement of being together and being in love are embedded in music as well as attitudes. Added to this is the unclear status of teens in this country. In some matters they are viewed as adults, in others as children. Marriage tends to confer adult status and is looked upon by some as a happy escape from school and parental control. An unplanned pregnancy often precedes and precipitates marriage. In addition, it may appear much more exciting to be planning a wedding than planning to work one's way through further schooling. Parents may unwittingly push their teens into early marriages by opposing the alliance so strongly that their child rebels and asserts his or her independence by marrying.

5. Teen marriages are five times as likely to fail as those which are begun when the partners are in their twenties. Among the multitude of causes for teen

marital failure are immaturity, inadequate preparation for responsibility, financial difficulties, lack of education, difficulty adjusting to becoming parents, and problems with relatives.

6. Many families and public and private agencies are available to help young people over the rough spots. Often, despite such help, divorce is the end result with the consequent emotional turmoil for all concerned.

7. Sex roles are changing as increased numbers of married women work. For those who remain at home, the traditional roles of the husband as the breadwinner and head of the family and the wife as head of the home are more usual. Children have an increasing voice in today's family, and the structure is far less authoritarian than before.

8. The family as an institution has shown how flexible and adaptive it is even in the face of the fantastic pace of our society. The projection is that the increasing emphasis on greater interpersonal communication, affection, companionship, and commitment will lead to stronger family ties in the future.

Important Terms
from This Chapter

maturity	peer pressure	immaturity
budgets	choice limitation	women's liberation
companionship		sex roles

Additional Readings
to Help You Learn More

Coser, R. *The Family: Its Structure and Functions.* New York: St. Martin's Press, 1964. Part 2, "Limitations on Marital Selection," deals with the selection of marriage partners in various cultures as well as the nature of love and its relationships to physical attraction.

Doby, J., Boskoff, A. and Pendleton, W. *Sociology: The Study of Man in Adaptation.* Lexington, Mass.: D. C. Heath Company, 1973. Chapter 7, "The Family As an Agency of Adaptation," discusses various kinds of families, the life cycle of the family, and new family forms.

Kephart, W. *The Family, Society, and the Individual,* 3rd Edition. Boston: Houghton-Mifflin Company, 1972. Part 2, "American Family Patterns," has five chapters which deal with the heritage of American families, experimental family organizations, and minority family types. Part 3, "Premarital Behavior Patterns," deals with mate selection, romantic love, and premarital sex codes. Part 5, "Family Disorganization and Reorganization," has three chapters which deal with divorce and the preservation of family values.

Part VIII.

EVERYDAY PROBLEMS OF
LIFE IN AMERICA

chapter 5

Psychology and Social Problems

chapter **15**

No one who reads a newspaper or watches television, even occasionally, can fail to be aware of the immensely complex social problems facing our own country and the world at large. The economic gap between the nations of the world is widening, not narrowing. Population is increasing so rapidly that we can expect to see over 7 billion people in the world by the end of this century—a figure double the current population. Crime in the United States has reached the point where millions of people live in almost constant fear. In addition, prejudice and racism prevent millions of people from reaching their full potential.

If we turn our attention to the quality of life, we can see that for many there has been a steady erosion amidst increasing material affluence. Most of our cities have virtually become places unfit for human habitation. Health care, despite medical breakthroughs undreamed of in past years, is distributed poorly and available mainly to those who can afford to pay. And, finally, in the background is the continuing threat of thermonuclear war.

As we said at the beginning of this book, these problems exist not because we need a greater understanding of the physical world around us, nor because of a lack of men and women of goodwill. We understand enough about the physical world now to be able to solve most of these problems. Furthermore, there are men and women of goodwill in our own country and in other countries as well. But as we have seen, technology is not enough, nor is goodwill enough to solve these problems. We do not need further scientific discoveries nor larger numbers of men and women of goodwill—we need a better understanding of human behavior.

No psychologist would pretend that psychology alone can come up with the solutions to most human social problems. But together with economists, political scientists, sociologists, anthropologists, and others concerned with human behavior, we should be able to make a start down the road to finding solutions.

In this chapter we will look at our current state of knowledge concerning the major social problems facing men and women of the modern world. We will examine some of the efforts being made to tackle these problems and, at the same time, some of the obstacles to their solution. Finally, we will talk about what you can do to help.

POPULATION PROBLEMS

It is probably more correct to speak about the problems—plural—of population, rather than to suggest that there is one single problem. In the countries of the West, the biggest problem is not so much one of overpopulation as it is of a maldistribution of population. We have, in other words, too many people concentrated in too small an area. In many other countries of the world, the main problem, in contrast, is one of too many people, given the resources of these countries.

Most experts agree that even with current farming practices we could feed all of the world's population for an indefinite period—providing that population did not increase. But as we shall see in the following section, it is quite apparent that population will increase, unless human behavior in many parts of the world can be altered.

The major problem facing the world today then, is not so much one of overpopulation in general, but rather a poor distribution of the resources of the planet. In the future, unless things change, the problem will be mainly one of too many people.

Some Facts and Figures

At present the population of the world is roughly 4 billion people. Given the present rate of population increase, we can expect to see over 7 billion within 25 years. Despite the development of new seeds and fertilizers —the so-called green revolution—there is little hope that chronically hungry nations such as India will ever become self-sufficient in food. Furthermore, we know that today about half of the world's population, mainly in Asia, Africa, and Latin America, live in perpetual hunger.

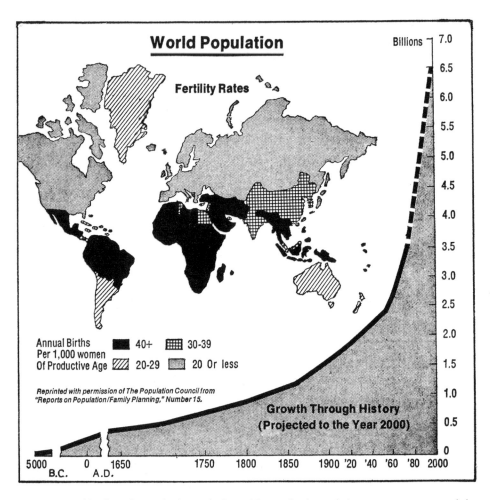

Fig. 15–1. This chart shows the increasingly rapid growth of population as we move toward the year 2000. Unless certain countries can control these birth rates, disaster looms for many of the world's people.

The fact is that food production is not growing fast enough to meet increasing needs. Some estimate that to meet these needs, the world's food crops would have to double in the next 18 years. If we could bring more land under cultivation, and if we could raise the output of areas already being farmed, we could feed the world's population for perhaps two decades. But after that, most experts agree, there would be disastrous starvation in many of the world's developing countries.

Population and the Revolution in Medicine

At the time the first settlers arrived in America in the early 1600s, there were about one-half billion people on the earth. Since that time, population has grown at ever increasing rates, but unevenly around the world. The population explosion really began in the mid-1600s, and mainly in Europe. Why? What variations have there been around the world and what accounts for them?

Any increase in population is due either to an increase in the birth rate, or a decrease in the death rate, or a combination of both. In the countries of the West, long before the medical revolution, food production was increasing and the death rate due to starvation and inadequate diet was decreasing. Population began to increase rapidly. Furthermore, it increased most rapidly in those countries involved in the industrial revolution. Europe's population increased from 17 to 23 per cent of the world's population, while the population of both Asia and Africa declined in terms of percentages.

The reduction of death rates in the late 1800s in the West was brought about by medical discoveries which eliminated diseases most common in infants and children. With the reduction in death rates along with high birth rates, population began to skyrocket. Between 1871 and 1941, the rate of population increase in America was five times that of India! This was despite the fact that the American birth rate was only about half that of India.

The results of the revolution in medicine did not reach most of the developing countries until the end of World War II. Through the United Nations World Health Organization, diseases like cholera, malaria, typhus, and typhoid were largely eliminated. The death rate dropped, while the birth rate remained largely the same. The result was a population explosion unprecedented in the history of the world.

In Western countries, population today has largely stabilized. The death rate has continued to drop, but the birth rate has also dropped significantly. Thus even though people are living longer, fewer are born, and the population remains about the same. The reason for this is that means have been adopted to control population, that is, the birth rate.

Population Control: The Issues

Religious opposition to population control has been one (and only one) of the reasons that the world's population has increased rapidly. In the twentieth century, however, such opposition has significantly diminished. The

Catholic Church still opposes artificial means of birth control, but it does not oppose the idea of population control in general. Abstinence from sexual relations is the means of birth control acceptable to the Catholic Church today.

But it is not only religious obstacles to birth control that has resulted in a worldwide population increase. Even if the Catholic Church dropped its opposition to artificial methods of birth control today, there would be only the slightest effect on population figures. One reason is that Christianity is not the largest of the world's religions. More people are Hindu, Moslem, and Buddhist than Christian. Another reason is that most of the people in the world are farmers or peasants. Large families are as beneficial in many parts of the world today as they were in the United States earlier in our history. More children mean more hands to work the land.

In many countries such as India there is considerable fatalism about life in general. Millions believe that little can be done to change things and that somehow provision can be made, however meager, for large numbers of children. In other countries there are beliefs that a large number of children reflects favorably on a man's masculinity.

These are some of the reasons why the world's population is increasing at an unprecedented rate. To put it simply, there is little motivation to limit family size in many parts of the world. There is thus no simple answer to the question of how population can be controlled.

In general, it seems apparent that people must be convinced that it is possible to control family size. They must also be made aware that limited family size does not necessarily lead to undesirable consequences. Finally, they must be convinced that limited family size has certain desirable consequences. Certainly no single program will accomplish these objectives. Many programs will undoubtedly be needed, because attitudes toward family size vary from one culture to another and from one individual to another. Furthermore, before we can even begin to think in terms of large-scale programs, we need much more understanding of the attitudes toward family size that will have to be changed.

CRIME AND DELINQUENCY

It is clear that various social problems are inter-related to some extent. Of course it would be ridiculous to argue that large families are the cause of crime. But larger numbers of children are more frequently associated with poverty, and we know that poverty is related to crime in more than an

Fig. 15–2. Prisons have changed little in the last 100 years. Today however, people are beginning to realize that prisons should do more than simply serve as places of punishment.

incidental way. We might call this a kind of chicken-and-egg dilemma. Which comes first? Does poverty cause large families, or are large families the cause of poverty? Both are true in some instances and false in other instances. The point here is that it is not always so easy to pinpoint the cause (or causes) of social problems. Typically, social problems such as crime have many causes, and because of this there are no easy solutions to such problems.

In this section we will look at some of the causes of crime and at what is being done today to deal more effectively with the problem. Before doing that, however, we need to know something about the nature and extent of crime in the United States.

Some Facts and Figures

Recorded crimes have been increasing rapidly in recent years. Major crimes nearly doubled between 1940 and 1960, for example, while the population increased only by about one-third in this period. To some extent, however, such figures are misleading, because we know that there has been an increase in the number of reported crimes. Has there really been an increase in the number of crimes, or are more simply being reported? Both questions can be answered in the affirmative. More crimes are being committed today than in the past, and more are being reported to the police.

The same thing is true of delinquency, defined as acts committed by juveniles that would be considered crimes if committed by adults. Before the Second World War, only about 1 per cent of children between ten and seventeen were delinquent. But the figure had doubled by the early 1950s. In addition, as with adult crime, there is evidence that more acts of delinquency are being reported today than in the past.

Crime, then, is a major social problem in the United States. It is a problem not only in terms of the effects on the direct victims of crime, but also in terms of the effects produced by the fear that crime generates. To the extent that crime has produced fear, we all may be said to be victims of crime.

Types of Crime

Most of us tend to think of crime in terms of violent incidents we see on television or in the movies. Violence, however, is only one type of crime, for obviously criminal offenses are not always those that are injurious to others. Crime ranges from casual offenses such as speeding or double-parking through white-collar offenses such as embezzlement to organized criminal gangs that commit robbery, hijackings, and murder. Delinquency is no different, except in the fact that the offense is committed by one not considered to be an adult. Delinquent acts include theft, vandalism, murder, sex offenses, and so on, just as in adult crimes.

Who is most likely to be the direct victim of crime? The answer is that, to a certain extent, it depends on where you live. Most crime occurs in cities rather than in rural areas. Furthermore, urban crime is much more common in poor inner-city slum areas than in the suburbs. Both the criminal and his victim are likely to be residents of the same area and members of the same social class.

Crimes of violence, including murder, are more frequent in urban areas that are in transition from residential to business and industrial. Murder, it should be added, almost always involves people who know one another. Yet, despite the fact that very few of us are likely to be the victims of violent crimes because of where we live, the fear of becoming a victim has permeated suburban life as much as in the inner city. The effects of crime have to be evaluated not only in terms of the effects on the direct victim, but also in terms of the effects on the quality of life for all of us.

What Causes Crime?

Spokesmen against the registration and licensing of hand guns like to say, "Guns don't commit crimes, people do." On the face of it, certainly, it does not look as if one could argue against this statement. But we know that in those countries that restrict the sale of hand guns, the incidence of violent crimes is much lower than in our own country. As is well known, for example, policemen in England do not carry guns. Fewer of these policemen are murdered by criminals, and fewer crimes are committed in that country with lethal weapons such as hand guns. Restricting the availability of such weapons, then, and particularly the cheap so-called "Saturday-night specials," would undoubtedly reduce the incidence of violent crime in the United States.

Restriction of the sale of hand guns would not entirely eliminate crime, since there are many causes. Poverty certainly is one cause. Emotional disturbances are also the causes of crime. It has been estimated that as many as one-fifth of all criminals are people who are mentally ill. In addition, there are professional criminal cultures, in which one learns specialized techniques that can be used in a full-time criminal career. Delinquency, in contrast to adult crime, tends to occur almost always in gang settings. Delinquents tend to have friends who are also delinquent much more often than they have friends who are nondelinquent. Feelings of frustration, rejection of the values of adults, and negativism often result from the adolescent's feeling of powerlessness in society. In the company of others with similar feelings, adolescents may turn to criminal activities for sources of income, or vandalism and violence, or drugs.

Changing Views in Corrections

Since about 1800, when modern prisons were first introduced, confinement of criminal offenders was believed to serve three purposes: protection of society, deterrence, and rehabilitation. Unfortunately, even today the emphasis tends to be on the first two of these purposes. It is true that while the convicted criminal is in custody, he or she cannot commit additional crimes. Thus society, at least in the short run, is protected. But what most people fail to grasp is that close to 95 per cent of those now in prison will eventually be released. Without rehabilitation, society gains little in the way of long-term protection.

Prisons have been traditionally been places of punishment. The term "penitentiary," in fact, means a place where one does penance. Justice is done, many people believe, when the offender has "paid his debt to society." The idea behind punishment is that the offender will change his behavior, and that the threat of punishment will make others think twice before committing crimes. But does this really happen? The answer seems to be largely no.

We know that about 75 per cent of those released from prison commit additional crimes. Punishment does not appear to act as a deterrent, and in fact there is good reason to consider prisons as little more than schools of crime. Prisoners typically learn to be more proficient criminals while confined behind bars.

Perhaps, you may think, the problem is that we are too lenient with law breakers. Tougher law enforcement and longer sentences will do the job. But will they? Suppose we consider the ultimate sentence for a moment— the death sentence. Does the threat of death deter the criminal from committing murder or other crimes that may lead to the death penalty? Those who have worked closely with convicted offenders, including those condemned to death, tell us that it does not.

Warden Duffey of San Quentin prison in California talked with many men before they were executed in the gas chamber. He asked these men if, at the time they were committing the crime, they considered that they might be executed. Not one of them, according to the warden, considered this possibility. Was this because they thought they could escape detection? In most cases probably not. Some made no effort to escape, while others made only half-hearted attempts. Murder, as we pointed out earlier, usually involves people who know each other well. Often victim and killer are members of the same family. Furthermore, such crimes are typically not premeditated. They occur in the heat of an argument, or when both parties are highly emotional. In addition, drunkenness often is involved in murder and other capital crimes. Under such circumstances it is easy to see that consideration of the consequences of his act is highly unlikely by the person committing a crime punishable by death.

The death sentence has now been abolished, at least temporarily, by the Supreme Court. Murders have not increased since the suspension of capital punishment, nor are they lower in countries where such punishment still exists. The important point here is that if the ultimate sentence of death does not deter crime, why should longer sentences or tougher law enforcement be expected to do so?

Most of those who work with convicted offenders today believe that much more emphasis should be placed on the rehabilitation aspect of prisons than has been the case in the past. The purpose of confinement should be not so much to punish the person for his offenses as to change his behavior. The mentally ill prisoner needs to be treated. The unskilled and semiliterate offender needs to be taught skills he can use to lead a productive life. These should be the real purposes of confinement.

In line with these views, we are slowly seeing changes in the correctional system in the United States. Probation is more widely used today than in the past. Also, a number of states have established community treatment programs in which offenders are rehabilitated in their own communities rather than being confined in institutions. These changes certainly make a great deal of sense. In terms of the tremendous cost to society, it makes no sense at all to continue handling criminals as we have in the past.

POVERTY

The term "poverty" is a relative one. No one can draw an arbitrary line and say that people below that income line are poor while those above it are well-off, if not rich. Those we consider to be the poor in the United

Fig. 15–3. For intellectual growth, home stimulation is as important as good food. Even in poor conditions, a stimulating home environment can help to repair damage caused by malnutrition in infancy.

353

States would be considered quite well-off in countries like India or Zaire. Obviously, though, it is not only pointless but heartless as well to tell the poor in America that they are better off than the Indian poor or the poor of Zaire. As one author has said, "I should put it another way. I want to tell every well-fed and optimistic American that it is intolerable that so many millions should be maimed in body and spirit when it is not necessary that they should be. My standard of comparison is not how much worse things used to be. It is how much better they could be if only we were stirred."*

Being Poor amid Plenty

In the late nineteenth century, poverty was often attributed to biological or genetic inferiority. Those in the upper class, in contrast, were believed to be biologically superior. In line with these views, little could be done to alleviate poverty. It might be added that there are still some who cling to these views today.

Still others believe that the poor are basically lazy people who prefer to accept handouts rather than work. In addition, some believe that being poor builds character and that a poor childhood is necessary for achievement later in life.

We reject these views as being unsubstantiated by any scientific evidence, as we reject any view that blames the poor for their plight rather than the economic system in which these people live. Circumstances beyond one's control tend to cause poverty rather than some shortcoming on the part of the individual such as lack of effort. It should be noted that "circumstances" tend generally to be the explanation given by poor people to account for their situation. Wealthy people, on the other hand, tend to attribute poverty to some personal shortcoming of the poor. This is particularly true of one who rose to affluence from a poor background. "I made it," such people often say, "and they could, too, if they wanted to work."

What are the "circumstances" that tend to create poverty? To discover the answer, let us take a closer look at poor people.

Who Are the Poor and What Are They Like?

Poverty is a distinctive way of life that is often transmitted from one generation to the next. As one sociologist has noted, "The poverty stricken

*M. Harrington, *The Other America.* New York: The Macmillan Co., 1962.

share common experiences: unsteady work, crowded housing, educational handicaps, inadequate diet, frequent illness, and inadequate medical and dental care, and uneconomic buying."* In addition, poor people often believe that there is little they can do to change things. Schools are not considered to be of any great importance, nor is work considered to be a way of getting ahead. More often than not, work is simply a way of surviving.

Close to 75 per cent of the poor in America are white, but nonwhites are disproportionately represented. There is, in other words, a larger percentage of nonwhite poor than their numbers in the population. In fact while about 10 per cent of the population is nonwhite, about 20 per cent of the poor are nonwhite. By region of the country, the South and Appalachia are disproportionately represented. And in addition, poverty is more likely among certain groups such as the elderly, farm workers, and families with no father in the home.

Programs to Eliminate Poverty

In the 1960s a "war on poverty" was launched by the federal government. Programs were provided for youth through the job corps and work training agreements with state and local governments. Community action programs were set up to aid local antipoverty programs and to institute adult education, particularly in teaching reading and writing. Other programs were aimed at the rural poor through improving the conditions of migrant workers and through small loans for farm and nonfarm enterprises or businesses. Small business loans were made more accessible to nonwhite applicants. In addition, programs such as Head Start were inaugurated in an effort to improve the academic performance of four- and five- year-old children from impoverished backgrounds.

How have these programs worked out? Certainly it is obvious that the problem of poverty has not been solved. But it is equally obvious that many people are better off today than they were before these programs began. We have in fact, made a beginning—a commitment to end poverty. No one in his right mind believed that the "war on poverty" could be won in a year or even a decade. It will take a long time, and there will be failures in many of the specific programs. But we can learn from those failures and implement better programs if we understand the causes of poverty, and if we have the determination to eliminate these causes.

*J. Davis, *Social Problems*, Glencoe, Illinois: The Free Press, 1970.

RACISM AND PREJUDICE

One of the causes of both poverty and crime is racism or prejudice. *Prejudice* may be defined as a negative attitude which leads to discrimination against members of a particular group. Prejudice is an attitude, while *discrimination* refers to behavior. When a particular prejudicial attitude is directed toward members of a specific race, this is called *racism.*

How extensive is racism and prejudice? Is prejudice reciprocal? That is, do people against whom others are prejudiced feel prejudice in return? Is it possible for different racial groups to live together without prejudice? These are all questions that have been studied by psychologists.

In one recent study of attitudes of whites towards blacks, it was discovered that about 95 per cent of the whites favor equal employment opportunities. Only about half favored open housing legislation, however. In terms of age, younger people tended to be less prejudiced than older people, and the same was true of better educated people. However, most whites in the study tended to blame blacks for their inferior housing, employment, and education. Few thought that these things resulted from discrimination.

Among blacks, most believed that racism causes a large number of them to miss out on good jobs and housing. Only about 25 per cent thought that discrimination was not a serious problem. One-third of those interviewed thought whites were hostile and repressive. Another third thought that whites were indifferent, while the remaining third believed most whites had good intentions. Some 80 per cent of the blacks believed it possible to get-ahead despite racism, but a significant minority thought that no matter

Fig. 15–4. Prejudice is not inevitable among different racial groups. Lasting friendships can and do develop between those of different races, providing the causes of racism are removed.

how hard a black works, he cannot succeed in the United States. Less than 20 per cent believed in the separation of the races, while about 40 per cent believed blacks should develop a positive cultural identity.

Many studies over the years have shown that prejudice occurs in all parts of the United States and that differences from area to area are slight. Furthermore, we know that prejudice does tend to be reciprocal. Finally, it is apparent that prejudice is not inevitable when different racial groups live in the same society. One good example of this is Hawaii, in which many racial groups have lived together in harmony for years.

How Much Does Prejudice Cost?

Prejudice is immensely expensive not only in terms of those who are subjected to discrimination but also to society as a whole. In Chicago, less than ten years ago, it was found that black college graduates earn less than white high school dropouts. Two-earner black families earned less than one-earner white families. Comparing whites and blacks in that city, it was reported that the black person is less well schooled by one year, four times as likely to be unemployed, one-half as likely to have a skilled craft, one-third as likely to be a sales person or manager, three times as likely to be a laborer, and eight times as likely to be a domestic.

Among other minority groups the situation is similar. American Indians, for example, have a life expectancy of only 44 years in contrast to 71 years for white Americans. The Indian, in fact, is worse off than any other minority group in the country. His economic, educational, social and physical situation is at the very bottom in American society.

Fig. 15–5. In 1965, this was an American Indian house in Muskogee, Oklahoma. It was typical of the substandard conditions now being eliminated by the Bureau of Indian Affairs housing programs.

Prejudice and discrimination are directed not only against racial and ethnic groups but against women and the elderly as well. Women have a much harder time in gaining admission to medical schools, for example, than men. Fewer women are in professional careers, and those that do manage to secure the necessary qualifications are almost always paid less than men.

Older people, regardless of sex, have a much more difficult time in securing employment than do younger people. In fact, if an average man over 40 loses his job, the results may be almost disastrous in terms of finding another. Why is this? What causes prejudice? We turn our attention now to this important question.

What Causes Prejudice?

There are both individual and social causes of prejudice. Historians point out, for example, that racism directed against blacks has its roots in slavery and the economic exploitation of members of that race. Even today it may be said that such prejudice has an economic basis, at least in part. But prejudice against blacks in particular cannot be fully explained on an economic basis. Other groups which came to America as migrants (Irish, Italians, and Germans) were subjected to economic exploitation, but they never suffered the results of the prejudice directed against blacks and Jews. Furthermore, such explanations do not help us understand why some individuals are prejudiced while others are not.

One psychologist has said that there are several ways in which individuals learn prejudice. One is that a person may have had so much contact with members of another group in certain inferior roles that they cannot accept them as social equals. Another is that dramatic or fearful firsthand experiences may create negative attitudes. Thus the white person mugged by black juveniles may develop an intense prejudice against all blacks. Finally, attitudes may be adopted ready-made. In other words, the individual develops attitudes through contact with others holding the same attitude.

Most psychologists are convinced that prejudice and racism are acquired or learned through contact with others holding the same attitudes. In particular, children learn such attitudes from their parents in the same way they learn other attitudes such as patriotism, and even food preferences. Frequently such attitudes are reinforced in social groups with which the individual is affiliated later in life. Few people are prejudiced because they have had any bad firsthand experiences with members of a particular group.

Can such attitudes be changed? The answer is yes. Studies of attitude change have shown that two ways are most effective. One way involves changing the prevailing social norms within a group—the norms from which attitudes are derived. The other involves changing group affiliations. In other words, when a prejudiced person becomes a member of a group whose members are not prejudiced, his or her attitudes change.

Discrimination, of course, can be eliminated in part by passing laws which make discrimination illegal. We have seen that the civil rights laws, for example, have done a great deal to eliminate the more blatant forms of discrimination. Subtle forms of discrimination, on the other hand, are more difficult to eliminate through legal means.

ENVIRONMENT AND URBAN LIFE

It is apparent to behavioral scientists that behavior both affects and is affected by the environment. We have heard more and more in recent years about the necessity of controlling pollution—cleaning the air we breathe and the streams, rivers, and lakes of the country. We have also become aware of the fact that the density of population affects human behavior as well as conditions such as temperature, humidity, and noise. In this short section we will examine some of what we know about the inter-relationships between behavior and the environment.

Hot and Crowded

Psychologists have only recently begun to look at such things as the effects of population density and climatic conditions on human behavior. But with the urban riots of the mid-1960s, the role of environmental conditions with respect to social behavior has become of crucial importance.

Few scientific studies have been conducted to determine how such things as weather affect behavior. From observations we know that aggression seems to be related to temperature and humidity. Arguments, agitation, fist-fighting, and even knifings appear more prevalent in midsummer than in winter. The United States Commission on Riots in the 1960s reported that in nine of eighteen disorders, the temperature reached 90 degrees or more during the day.

Overcrowding or high population density has also been found to be associated with aggression. The Riot Commission, for example, said that crowded ghetto living conditions, worsened by summer heat, was a basic factor in civil disorders. Furthermore, from studies of overcrowding among animals, we know that behavior such as courting, nest-building, social organization, and even physiological functions are adversely affected. But exactly what are the relationships between aggressive behavior and environmental conditions? Is there a temperature beyond which aggression is more prevalent? Is there a density level beyond which aggressive behavior is more likely?

One recent study compared two temperature conditions (hot and normal) and two density conditions (high and low) in terms of their effects on mood, attitudes toward others, and performance on a task. As one might expect, high temperatures and crowded conditions made people irritable, aggressive, and likely to accomplish less work. One of the problems with this study, however, is that we still cannot define "overcrowding" accurately nor can we say that a particular density level coupled with a certain temperature will produce aggressiveness. About all that can be said for sure is that conditions as they exist in American urban ghettos are subjectively evaluated as overcrowded and unpleasant. In part, it may be this subjective evaluation that leads to resentment, hostility, and aggressiveness.

The Quality of Life

Even though we know riots tend to be associated with overcrowding and high temperatures, we cannot say that these factors alone are responsible. Many other cities in the world are as crowded as Chicago or New York and as hot in the summer, but violence and crime are much lower than in most American cities. Thus it is apparent that other factors must also be involved. Nevertheless, regardless of what those factors may be, it is becoming increasingly apparent that the quality of life in the United States is gradually eroding. *Quality* can perhaps be best defined in terms of subjective feelings of satisfaction and well-being.

For a long time, quantity and quality were not differentiated. If one had material possessions—and the more the better—that constituted the desirable goal in life. In recent years, however, an uneasy feeling has begun to develop that how much one has is not necessarily related to how satisfied one feels. Put another way, one might say that bigger is not better, or that other things are more important than growth.

In the United States we are beginning to give more thought to the quality of life than ever before. How big should cities be? Should we sacrifice more of the environment in order to secure even greater material comfort? What restrictions, if any, should we place on growth? How should we plan for the future? These are questions that will occupy the time of increasing numbers of people as we move closer to the twenty-first century.

HEALTH CARE

Despite the massive breakthroughs in medicine, inadequate health care is still a major social problem in the United States as well as in most countries of the world. The problem is not so much that we need new medical discoveries, but rather that we make the benefits of existing knowledge widely available.

In the United States there is a clear relationship between economic status, illness, and the availability of health care. Part of the problem is that we are training too few physicians, and another part of the problem is that physicians tend to avoid rural areas. Let us take a look at some of the facts concerning health care in America.

Some Facts and Figures

Families with low incomes are more frequently ill, lose more days of work, have less health insurance, and receive less medical care than families with high incomes. Poverty, then, undoubtedly contributes to illness despite claims by some that free medical care is available to all those who cannot afford to pay.

Infant mortality rates (death rates) are twice as high for nonwhites in the United States as they are for whites. Overall, the country ranks ninth in the world in terms of infant mortality. In other words, eight other countries have better records for low death rates among infants than we do. In terms of maternal mortality (death of the mother during birth) nonwhites have a rate four times as high as whites. Furthermore, life expectancy for whites is higher than for all other racial groups.

Even among the affluent portion of our population, there is little or no protection against catastrophic illnesses such as kidney failure or hemophilia. Even families with health insurance, in other words, can be easily wiped out financially by such illnesses.

Those who say that the United States has the best medical care in the world simply do not know what they're talking about. For some people, the medical care they receive may be unsurpassed. But for the country as a whole, we are not in first place or even second place compared with countries like Sweden, Norway, or New Zealand. But it could be argued that these are small countries while the United States is very large. Size alone, however, does not necessarily determine the quality of health care for a country's citizens. Other factors, such as organized health plans, are probably of greater importance.

Recent Public Health Measures

It is apparent that a completely unrestrained free enterprise system with regard to health care will not work. Government must intervene to help people in those instances where they cannot help themselves. For example, until recently older people were those most likely to be affected by illness and, at the same time, those least likely to be in a position to pay. The provision of health care for such people through Medicare and Medicaid— programs passed by Congress—has done much to eliminate the suffering and economic destitution formerly associated with illness among the aged.

Some countries, such as those mentioned earlier, have socialized health care plans. In New Zealand, for example, all hospitalization is free, as are all prescription drugs. Free dental care is also provided for all children up to the age of 14. Office visits to a physician are nominally charged. Tax rates are higher in New Zealand than in the United States, but the added cost means generally overall better health care for New Zealand citizens.

Socialization is not necessarily the answer to the health care problems of Americans. In fact it seems unlikely that we shall see such a plan in this country. Compulsory health insurance, however, is another matter, and we are almost certain to see such a plan in the very near future. Protection against catastrophic illnesses will almost certainly be included in such a plan.

Fig. 15–6. Medicare and Medicade have significantly improved health care for our older citizens, many of whom formerly could not secure adequate health care.

Compulsory insurance will not solve all health problems. Even when such a plan comes into existence we will still be faced with the problem of too few physicians and a poor distribution of physicians in the country as a whole. Additional government and private action will be required to solve these deficiencies.

WAR AND VIOLENCE

War, and particularly nuclear war, is undoubtedly the greatest social problem of them all. If we cannot prevent such a war, there will be little need for concern over the social problems we have discussed in this chapter. Yet even small wars diminish men, and violence in general diminishes the quality of life. How much do we know about the causes of violence? Can wars be prevented? These are perhaps the most important questions that psychologists should try to answer.

What Causes Violence?

For centuries wars were regarded as stemming inevitably from human nature. But as we learned earlier in this book, there are some cultures in which warfare is unknown. Have the inborn aggressive urges of some people somehow been repressed, or have they found other outlets for their aggression? People like Konrad Lorenz, who have studied animal behavior extensively, suggest that aggression is instinctive. The answer to man's aggressive impulses, they say, is to find acceptable outlets for aggression. But others argue that angry people may feel better when they can attack some scapegoat, although this does not necessarily mean their aggressive tendencies have been lessened.

Most psychologists reject the idea that aggressive behavior is instinctive. Some argue that aggression results mainly from feelings of frustration. Eliminate frustration, they say, and you will eliminate aggression. Others argue that aggression and violence have no simple, single causes. Social and economic frustrations may contribute to violence. Overcrowding and heat may trigger riots. Political extremists may incite people to attack others. But in most cases there are many causes of aggressive behavior all operating together. There are thus no easy solutions to the violence we see and read about. Only through careful systematic research will we understand the multiple causes of aggression. And only when we fully understand the causes will we be able to prevent wars.

Can Wars Be Prevented?

As suggested above, the prevention of war really requires that we understand the causes of human aggression much better than we do today. But it is not only understanding of the causes that will prevent wars. We will also need a much better understanding of such things as negotiation than we have today. How is interpersonal bargaining affected by the need to save face? What incentives can be found to induce nations to negotiate rather than fight? Can we find a way to set up a system of compulsory international arbitration? These questions go beyond a search for the causes of aggression.

Just as there are probably no simple, single causes of aggression or violence, there are no such answers to the question of how wars can be prevented. When we ask the question, "Can wars be prevented?" however, the answer does seem to be a simple yes. "Yes, but," it might be added. But only if we commit ourselves to the idea that they can be prevented, and if we are determined to find the means for their prevention.

WHAT YOU CAN DO TO HELP

Often the average person feels powerless in the face of such social problems as those we have discussed in this chapter. What can I do to help prevent war, to change prison conditions, to improve the quality of life, or to help secure better health care for all Americans? You have already taken the first small step, and that is to be informed. Every citizen, regardless of age, has a responsibility to learn as much as he or she possibly can about the social problems facing our own country and the rest of the world. Too often people feel that these problems do not affect them directly. But as we pointed out in this chapter, these problems affect us all in one way or another. No man is an island, one author wrote, and to that we might add that no country is completely independent of the problems of other nations.

A second step you should take is to become active in the political process of the United States. Even if you still cannot vote in elections, you can take part by working for candidates whose views reflect your own. Too often Americans think that they have discharged their responsibility by simply voting in elections. But the system cannot function as our forefathers intended if the vast majority of Americans do nothing more than vote. It should be added here that almost half never even bother to vote.

In connection with some of the specific problems we discussed, there are a number of other things you can do. Relative to crime, for example, do not let yourself become a victim. Make sure if you drive that you never leave the keys in the ignition. Take precautions around the house so that your family is not victimized by burglary. Listen to your own conscience. Do not let yourself be drawn into activities that you know are against the law. In adolescence especially, it takes considerable courage to fly in the face of peer pressures and hold to your own sense of right and wrong.

Individuals can certainly do a great deal to fight racism and prejudice. Examine your own attitudes and those of your friends. Do not fail to object to remarks that are obviously racist in nature, and do not tolerate jokes that demean members of another race or religion. Resolve to raise your own children to be free of prejudice.

In connection with the environment, there are many things you can do. Avoid pollution, for one thing. Do not litter roadsides with empty containers. Take part in clean-up campaigns, and encourage others to do so. Your high school and its organizations can be very active in campaigns like these.

Something else you might consider is entering one of the professions or occupations that deal directly with these problems—psychology, medicine, social work, economics, planning, government service, and so on. In the next chapter we will take a closer look at some of these fields.

CHAPTER SUMMARY

1. There is no single population problem, but several. In the West, the problem is mainly a poor distribution of population. In the developing countries, the problem is mainly overpopulation. World population is expected to almost double by the end of this century. One of the obstacles to population control has been religious opposition to birth control. But in many world areas there is little motivation to regulate family size anyway.

2. Various social problems tend to be interrelated. Thus overpopulation is to some extent, related to poverty, while poverty is related to crime. Social problems such as crime, however, have many causes in addition to poverty. Emotional disturbances are apparent in about 20 per cent of all criminals. While guns do not cause crime, there is a clear relationship between crime and the availability of guns.

3. Confinement of criminals in prisons has traditionally been for the purposes of protecting society, deterrence, and rehabilitation. The emphasis, however, has tended to be on the first two of these purposes. We know today that prisons do little to deter crime. More emphasis is clearly needed on programs to rehabilitate offenders.

4. The term *poverty* is a relative one. Those considered poor in one country would be considered average or even well-off in another. Poor people are largely victims of circumstances beyond their control. In the United States, the federal government launched a "war on poverty" in the 1960s. Many different specific programs were included in this "war." While poverty has not been eliminated, at least we have made a commitment to end it, and a significant beginning has been initiated.

5. Prejudice is a negative attitude that leads to discrimination against members of a particular group. When a particular prejudicial attitude is directed toward members of a specific race, we call this *racism.* Prejudice occurs in all parts of the United States. Furthermore, prejudice tends to be reciprocal. Finally, prejudice and racism are not inevitable; in some societies different racial groups live together in harmony.

6. There are both individual and social causes of prejudice. Racism against blacks, for example, has its roots in slavery and the economic exploitation that this involved. There are several ways in which individuals learn prejudice. In most cases such attitudes are adopted ready-made from family members or from other groups with which we affiliate.

7. Human behavior both affects and is affected by the environment. Psychologists have only recently studied the effects of such things as population density and temperature on behavior. We know that both overcrowding and high temperatures tend to be associated with aggressiveness, at least in the United States. However, we still cannot define "overcrowding" exactly, nor can we specify the exact relationships between density and certain kinds of behavior.

8. Inadequate health care is another major social problem in the United States. Some people receive excellent health care, but the poor person, the rural dweller, or the minority group member generally is unable to obtain high quality health care. In some countries medical practice has been socialized. While we probably will not see this in America, in all likelihood we will see a national compulsory health insurance plan.

9. The greatest social problem of all is war and violence. In the past war was regarded as reflecting human nature. We no longer accept war as inevitable, however, or aggression as an instinctive aspect of human behavior. Violence, aggression, and war have no simple, single causes, and there are no simple, easy solutions to the problems of violence and aggression. We do need a greater understanding of the causes of war and also more understanding of such things as negotiation and arbitration.

10. There are a number of things you can do to help solve social problems. *First,* be informed. Learn as much as you can about their causes and possible solutions. *Second,* take an active part in the American political process. Vote when you are eligible, and work for candidates whose views you support. *Third,* learn what you can do to help solve specific problems such as crime or racism. *Finally,* consider entering one of those professions that deal directly with social problems.

Important Terms
from This Chapter

overpopulation

delinquency

corrections

deterrence

poverty

war on poverty

racism

prejudice

discrimination

overcrowding

infant mortality

socialized medicine

Medicare

Additional Readings
to Help You Learn More

Brickman, P. *Social Conflict: Readings in Rule Structures and Conflict Relationships.* Lexington, Mass.: D. C. Heath Company, 1974. Chapter 6, "Problems of Communication in Conflict Situations," includes three papers that give the student some insight into how misperceptions can be a basis for conflicts between groups.

Davison, G. and Neale, J. *Abnormal Psychology.* New York: John Wiley and Sons, 1974. Chapter 9, "Sociopathy and Legal Responsibility," deals with antisocial personalities and gives a number of cases as illustrations.

Doby, J., Boskoff, A. and Pendleton, W. *Sociology: The Study of Man in Adaptation.* Lexington, Mass.: D. C. Heath Company, 1973. Chapter 11, "Major Consequences of Population Changes," enlarges upon some very important points made in the present chapter.

Griffitt, W. and Veitch, R. "Hot and Crowded: Influences of Population Density and Temperature on Interpersonal Affective Behavior." *Bobbs-Merrill Reprints,* P-751. Indianapolis: Bobbs-Merrill Company. This paper elaborates on some of the discussion in the present chapter.

Johnson, R. *Aggression in Man and Animals.* Philadelphia: W. B. Saunders Company, 1972. Chapter 6, "Violence and Society," discusses violent crime in the United States, guns and violence, prisons, drugs and violence, and interracial violence.

Pettigrew, T. "Complexity and Change in American Racial Patterns: A Social Psychological View." *Bobbs-Merrill Reprints,* S-613. Indianapolis: Bobbs-Merrill Company.

Quinney, R. *Criminal Justice in America: A Critical Understanding.* Boston: Little,

Brown and Company, 1974. Chapter 6, "Custody and Corrections," deals with the nature of prisons and their functioning in the United States.

Raab, F. and Selznick, J. *Major Social Problems,* 2nd Edition. New York: Harper and Row, 1964. This is an excellent book that discusses a variety of social problems such as juvenile delinquency, crime, the family, religious conflict and world-wide problems. Several chapters in the book, such as 1, 2, 4, 7 and 11, would be especially helpful in enlarging on the present chapter.

Wertheimer, M. *Confrontation: Psychology and the Problems of Today.* Glenview, Ill.: Scott, Foresman and Company, 1970. Section 3, "Racism and Race Relations," is an extremely good discussion of the nature of prejudice and new views on race relations.

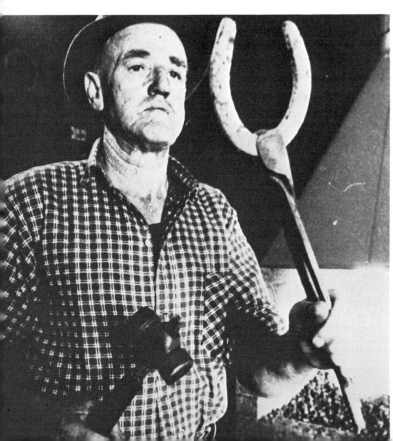

Work, Work, Work

chapter **16**

Fig. 16–1. Boys tend to have less realistic occupational aspirations than girls when very young. Almost every boy, for example, would like to become an astronaut. Girls of the same age however, more frequently tend to think of becoming teachers or nurses.

"What are you going to be when you grow up?" A few years ago I had some of my students ask this question of boys and girls in the first through the fourth grade. To our surprise we found that by the fourth grade all children were making quite realistic predictions about their probable occupations as adults. We were further surprised by the fact that girls make rather realistic predictions much earlier than boys, and also that the social class backgrounds of children affect their choices as early as the fourth grade.

In this study all boys, regardless of background, made the expected choices in the first grade—fireman, policeman, astronaut, athlete, and so on. Girls, on the other hand, spoke of becoming nurses, teachers, or housewives. They not only thought in terms of fewer occupations than boys, their expectations were more in line with occupations traditionally associated with women. Social class did not seem to affect the girls' choices. Boys, however, not only seemed to think in terms of a greater number of occupations, but by fourth grade their social class clearly affected their choices. Boys from poor backgrounds spoke of becoming factory workers, truck drivers, or delivery men, while those from wealthier families talked of becoming doctors, accountants, or lawyers. Boys from minority groups more often spoke of becoming musicians or athletes than did other boys.

What does all this mean? To some extent it means that what we become (or expect to become) is determined by what others expect of us. It also means that by nine or ten years of age we have a pretty good idea, if only in general terms, of the kind of job we will hold as adults. In addition, it

suggests that girls have fewer choices than boys—or think they do—and that members of racial minorities think in terms of limited choices.

In this chapter we will talk about the factors that influence one's choice of vocation, whether or not one goes to college, and what you should know to make the right decision. We will look at the options open to young people, how discrimination affects occupational choice, and how psychology can help you in choosing. We will begin by looking at some of the mistakes young people make in one of the most important decisions of life—selecting a vocation.

Mistakes People Make in Choosing a Vocation

Probably the biggest mistake most people make in choosing a vocation is making that choice on the basis of information that is too limited. There are over 40,000 different kinds of jobs in the United States today. Yet most young people think in terms of perhaps two dozen at most. Women and members of minority groups, as we mentioned earlier, tend to think in terms of still smaller numbers.

Not only are most young people unaware of the thousands of possible jobs, they often have inadequate or incorrect information about the jobs they do consider. One fellow thinks of becoming an engineer, for example, but does not know that engineering requires extensive training in mathematics

Fig. 16–2. Of the 40,000 different kinds of jobs available in the U.S., the average high school senior knows something about perhaps fifteen or twenty. Who has ever considered becoming a winetaster as shown here? Seriously though, there are many uncommon jobs that you should consider along with the ones everybody knows about.

—a subject he hates. Another one considers becoming a surgeon but has no idea of the years of study required. A girl wants to become a teacher but has no idea of the job prospects for teachers over the next thirty years. Another girl thinks it probably makes little difference anyway since she will get married after high school and raise a family.

Vocational choices are sometimes made on the basis of economic considerations alone—another mistake. "I want to be a lawyer," one boy says, "because they make a lot of money." Another one says, "I'm going to be an airline pilot—commercial pilots can earn as much as $60,000 a year." Money, as we will learn later in this chapter, is a poor substitute for satisfaction in one's work. There are more important things to consider when selecting an occupation.

Still another mistake made by many young people is in letting others decide what they will become. Parents can sometimes be very pushy when it comes to making decisions for their children. "You should go to college," one father says, "because that's the only way to get ahead." Another one says "Very few millionaires ever went to college—some of them didn't even finish high school."

Parents not only can influence vocational choice (sometimes for the worse) but friends often influence choices as well. High school students sometimes decide to go to college because all of their friends are going. And the reverse of this is true—some decide to go to work after high school because most of their friends are going to do that. Friends as well as parents can help you make an intelligent decision. But in the final analysis you are the only one in a position to make the decision that is best for you.

Friends not only influence the nature of decisions about occupations but sometimes when these decisions are made as well. Often it appears to adolescents that everyone else knows exactly what they are going to do—therefore, "I should too." Thus there are frequently social pressures to decide before enough information is known and before the individual is ready to make an intelligent decision. In this connection it should be noted that many young people change their minds about what occupations they should enter as they gain more information. Furthermore, we know that changes of occupation, sometimes several times, are not uncommon among adults.

What should you remember from this? *First,* find out as much as you can about as many occupations as you can. The kinds of information you need will be discussed later in this chapter. *Second,* listen to what parents and friends have to say, but remember that you will have to live with whatever choice you make. *Third,* do not let your decision be determined by only one factor such as the salary or income of a particular occupation. *Finally,* do not

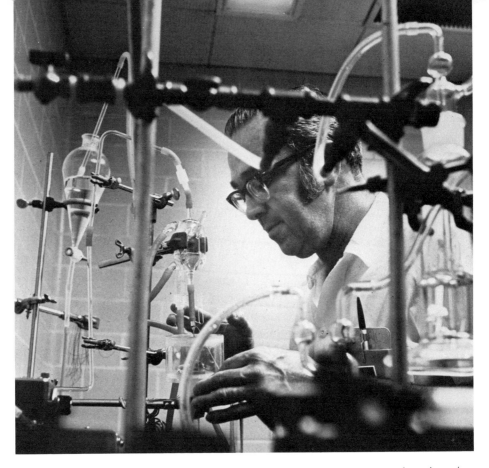

Fig. 16–3. *Work in a research laboratory is not for everyone. But for some people such work insures maximum job satisfaction.*

worry if you are not sure of what you want to be. Remember, it is better to worry a little about not knowing than it is to make the wrong choice.

What Is Job Satisfaction?

Several years ago one of my professors (a biologist) told me that he felt he had the ideal job. "If I weren't a professor," he said, "I'd be doing my research at home in my spare time. This way I'm doing what I enjoy, and I'm getting paid for it." For this man, research work in biology was the ideal job, and he experienced a great deal of job satisfaction.

Not everyone, of course, would be happy as a research biologist, but the point is that for each of us there is at least one occupation in which we can experience considerable job satisfaction. From the above example we can see that job satisfaction must at least in part stem from the nature of the work itself. But psychologists know that there is more to it than this. Opportunities for achievement, the degree of recognition possible, the degree of responsibility in the job, and opportunities for advancement all are relevant in the worker's evaluation of his job.

Job dissatisfaction, in contrast, stems from the lack of these things as well as undesirable company policies and administration, lack of supervision or poor supervision, poor salary, bad interpersonal relationships, and bad working conditions. It is, of course, often difficult to know in advance such things as company policies, type of supervision, or the nature of interpersonal relationships in any work situation. But for particular types of work it is possible to determine opportunities for achievement, advancement, recognition, and salary—all important in job satisfaction. It is also possible to determine what interests you and what you might be good at. Here it should be noted that generally we enjoy doing things that we find interesting and for which we have some aptitude. The main goal of vocational choice, then, should be to find a vocation in line with our interests and aptitudes, and one which offers the other opportunities mentioned above.

The ideal job for anyone is one in which he or she can become self-actualized. The term *self-actualization* refers to the need for self-fulfillment and the realization of potentialities; in other words, to become what one is capable of becoming. For some, self-actualization involves becoming a baker, carpenter, or nurse. For others, it involves becoming a professional musician, attorney, or sociologist. In some cases, then, further education beyond high school is necessary if one is to become self-actualized. For some people this means attending a college or university, while for others it means attending a business school, junior college, or trade school. Whether you decide to continue your education after completing high school should be determined not by what others do or by supposed status or prestige in more education, but by whether you need that education to become self-actualized.

COLLEGE OR WORK?

Some students know long before they near the end of high school that they will need further education if they are to qualify for a vocation they have chosen. Others know that a high school diploma is sufficient to qualify them for their chosen vocation. Still others, however, often approach the end of high school undecided about further education. Is it absolutely essential that one decides before high school graduation about going to college or business school? The answer is no. In many cases a decision to work for a year before going on is a wise one.

Fig. 16–4. This girl may not want to do this kind of factory work the rest of her life. But often a job like this after high school helps one decide what they want to do for a life's work.

Taking a Year Off

Too often high school seniors feel they must continue on to a college or university immediately after they graduate. Frequently parents have pressured them to follow this course, and often they feel compelled to do so because friends are doing so. In many cases these students thrash about for a year or two in college and either flunk out or drop out. In fact we know that about 50 per cent of entering college freshmen will never graduate.

Many college students who fail to graduate should never have chosen to come to college in the first place. They could have found a satisfying vocation, in many cases, with nothing more than their high school diplomas. Others should have pursued training in business or vocational colleges which could have qualified them for a vocation in which they could become self-actualized. Still others were not ready to begin college or university work immediately after high school. In these cases, a year of work before beginning college could have salvaged the situation.

With a year of experience in work after completing high school, some students have a better understanding of themselves and what they want to achieve. Frequently when such students do begin college or university work, they are more highly motivated and mature. They often can see the relevance of college work to some ultimate vocational goal. In these cases, a year off was a good idea.

Choosing the Right School

For those students who know they need more specialized training after high school, the most important choice is that of selecting the right school. By "right," we mean that school which will provide the student with the skills needed to qualify him or her for a particular vocation. In some cases this will be a business college or commercial school where one learns bookkeeping or secretarial skills. In other cases it means a school of hair fashion or laboratory technology. In still other cases it may be a junior college or computer institute. Finally, for some, it means a four-year college or university.

What kinds of information does the student need in order to make an intelligent choice? He or she needs to know first, what kinds of training are available. With regard to particular schools, what are the course offerings, entrance requirements, costs, accreditation, size of student body, and location? Is the school co-educational? What kind of student social life is there at the institution? What placement services are available? How successful have graduates of the institution been? Are financial aids available? Where can the answers to these questions be obtained? The best source is your school guidance counselor or psychologist. They not only have books and catalogs you can read, but they usually have firsthand knowledge of the institutions as well.

Most students who go on to post-secondary education attend one of three main types of institutions: junior colleges, vocational schools or colleges, and four-year colleges and universities. It will be worth our while here to take a brief look at each of these.

Junior Colleges

The number of two-year junior colleges (sometimes called "community colleges") has increased dramatically in the United States over the past twenty years. These colleges typically offer two-year training programs of a preprofessional, liberal arts, or terminal nature. Terminal programs are frequently vocational in nature, and emphasize development of skills in hair styling, auto mechanics, computer technology, and others. Preprofessional and liberal arts programs are often designed to prepare the student for entering into the last two years of a four-year college or university.

Junior colleges have several advantages. Often they are publicly controlled and operated. Tuition costs, therefore, are frequently much lower than in private institutions. In addition, they are generally smaller than four-year colleges and universities and thus can offer more individualized help than larger schools. A disadvantage frequently is that they cannot offer the wide range of subjects and activities available in larger institutions.

Vocational Colleges

Technical schools may be either public or private. As mentioned above, the courses offered in such schools may also be available in junior or community colleges. The yellow pages of your telephone book generally list the schools in your town or city which offer vocational training. You can obtain facts about such schools from special brochures or catalogs available from the school. In addition, you should ask your guidance counselor for information he or she may have concerning such schools.

Many vocational or technical schools offer work-study programs. Such programs usually combine classroom work with practical on-the-job experience for which the student is paid. The advantages of such programs lie in the practical experience one obtains plus the opportunity to offset tuition or enrollment costs.

Four-Year Colleges and Universities

Liberal arts colleges offer four-year programs that are generally not specifically vocationally oriented. Within such colleges, however, preprofessional courses such as pre-med or pre-law are designed to prepare the individual for specialized postgraduate professional training.

Because liberal arts colleges do not specifically try to train people for jobs, this does not mean that one's course work has no relevance to later employment. In fact we know that many companies hire graduates of such colleges for lower level sales, management, and administrative positions, in addition to other kinds of positions. Students in these colleges typically major or specialize in a certain subject, such as mathematics or English. At the same time they take these courses, however, they also take other courses designed to turn out a broadly educated person.

Fig. 16–5. One advantage of the larger universities is that they frequently have distinguished faculties, however, for many students, there are disadvantages too.

Universities are collections of colleges under a single administration. The typical university includes a college of liberal arts, college of business, college of agriculture, college of engineering, and so on. In addition, universities often include professional schools in law and medicine as well as graduate schools for specialized, high-level study in particular subjects.

Universities often can employ distinguished faculties because of the size of the institution. In addition there is usually a wider range of courses available than in a college, and usually more student activities are available as well. A disadvantage for some students is the size of the larger universities. Younger students often feel insecure and uncomfortable on a campus of 25,000 students, but it should be pointed out that many universities are much smaller than this.

Four-year colleges and universities can be public or private. One disadvantage of private schools is that they are always more expensive than public ones. However, scholarships and other financial aids are available in all institutions. Private schools, it should be pointed out, are not necessarily better than public ones because of their greater cost. Some of the finest academic institutions in the country are public or state supported.

Adjusting to College

Many students who fail to graduate from four-year colleges simply never make the adjustment that is required by the differences between high school and college. This is especially likely to be true in cases where the student is away from home and on his or her own for the first time. The individual, rather than parents or teachers, is responsible for making virtually all decisions—when to eat, when to sleep, when to study, whether or not to attend class, how many dates to have, and so on.

Differences between College and High School

For many students, the freshman year in college is the most difficult. Not only is the individual faced with almost total responsibility for budgeting his or her time, one also is often faced with some of the most difficult courses in college. Regardless of what the student wants to major in, first-year students generally take very similar courses—English, history, physical science, and mathematics. These courses are often required for graduation. Specialized study in one area generally does not come until the last two or three years of college.

In the freshman year, many of the courses are called survey courses; they give an overview of an entire field. Outside reading in such courses is generally very heavy, and it is difficult to obtain a passing grade without doing the reading. For many students who have never done much work outside the classroom, the reading load is "impossible." Often accustomed to cramming for tests, they try to read the entire assigned material the night before an examination—with disastrous results.

In some cases, college professors have few, or even only one examination, in a course. Passing or failing hinges on putting all one's eggs in one basket. Particularly if the student is unfamiliar with the type of test given—multiple choice or essay—examinations in the freshman year are likely to be unpleasant.

Still another problem that many freshmen face, believe it or not, is homesickness. In the first few weeks of college life, students often feel overwhelmed by the size and unfamiliarity of the college or university campus. Particularly if one left behind at home a steady date and has had little or no luck in obtaining dates in the college community, homesickness is likely to be a problem.

What can be done to make the transition from dependence to independence, high school to college, easier? *First,* you can reread Chapter 6 in this book. Adopting good study habits is one of the most important keys to success in college. *Second*, before signing up for classes try to ask some of the sophomores on campus about classes they took in their freshman year. When you meet your faculty adviser, he or she will generally go along with your ideas about the classes you want to take. If you were not a particularly strong student in high school, you may want to ease into the college routine by taking a lighter load than normal. This you can suggest to your advisor as well. *Finally*, every college and university has a counseling center set up specifically to help students with problems, personal as well as academic. Often it helps to talk over such problems with a friendly listener.

Financing Further Education

For many students the most difficult problem faced concerning education beyond high school is how to pay the bills. Junior or community colleges are often the answer to many students' financial problems, because tuition is generally low and one can live at home. Vocational colleges, as we mentioned earlier, frequently have work-study programs in which the student can earn enough to pay tuition and living costs. But what of the four-year college or university? Public institutions, as we pointed out, are less expensive than private ones. However, every college and university has some scholarship or other assistance plan which can help students in need of financial aid. There is usually a financial aids officer on campus to whom you can talk.

Many students believe that to secure financial assistance one has to have a top scholastic record in high school. But this is not the case at all. There are many forms of financial assistance available to almost any student who qualifies for admission to a four-year institution. These may involve partial remission of tuition fees, outright grants, or even loans.

Often students (and their parents) are reluctant to take out loans to pay the cost of education beyond high school. In most cases, however, this is shortsighted, particularly since many loans are interest free and need not be repaid until the student has graduated. For a qualified student, if the difference between going to college or not going is a loan—take the loan. In most cases the additional income one can earn by completing a college education more than offsets the entire loan.

It should also be mentioned that the majority of college students work in order to pay at least part of their expenses. Some work at full-time jobs in the summer, and others supplement this income with part-time work during the school year. Most colleges and universities have officials, usually in the dean of students' office, who help students to find part-time jobs.

DISCRIMINATION: RACE, SEX, AND AGE

Racial discrimination in employment was not uncommon before passage of the Civil Rights Act which made such discrimination illegal. But racial discrimination was not the only kind of discrimination in the United States. In particular, women and older people of both sexes found many doors closed to them.

Discrimination, in one sense, has tended to be a two-way street. Educational opportunities and jobs were often denied to people because of their race, sex, or age. But at the same time, those discriminated against, often took themselves out of the running. To some extent this is still true today. Blacks, Mexican-Americans, Indians, women, and older people often tend to lower their sights because they feel they will be denied opportunity anyway. As we learned at the beginning of this chapter, both white girls, and boys and girls from racial minorities tend to think in terms of fewer vocational choices than do white boys.

One interesting example of a subtle form of discrimination is revealed in a study of the effects of listing job openings by sex in the newspaper. A large eastern newspaper listed employment opportunities under "Jobs-Male Interest" and "Jobs-Female Interest." Two psychologists conducted a study to see if listing jobs in this way discouraged female job seekers from applying for jobs listed in the "Male" column.

They prepared two sets of booklets listing a number of jobs that had appeared in the newspaper. One set listed the jobs under "Male" and "Female" columns, while the other listed the identical jobs with no sex labeling. Two groups of women were then given the booklets and asked to indicate if they would be willing or unwilling to apply for each of the jobs. They were told to assume they had the necessary skills for each of the jobs.

When the jobs were listed by sex, only 46 per cent of the women were as likely to apply for the "Male Interest" jobs as for "Female Interest." When the jobs were listed without the sex designation, however, 81 per cent of the women preferred the "Male Interest" jobs to those listed under "Female Interest."

Times have changed. Although there is still undoubtedly subtle discrimination against various groups, such discrimination is less than was true in the past, and furthermore it is illegal. Thus every young person should think in terms of whatever vocation will enable that person to become self-actualized.

Much has been written about the problem of racial discrimination, and to the high school student the problem of discrimination against older people is often not as relevant as sex discrimination. Therefore we will turn our attention to the specific problem of discrimination against women.

Women and the World of Work

Sex has been more important than social class as a determining factor in women's choice of vocation. As we learned earlier, girls tend to think in terms of fewer vocational choices than boys, and they are apparently aware of vocations considered appropriate for women at an earlier age. Apparently our society very clearly teaches little girls that they are expected to become housewives, teachers, nurses, or secretaries before boys learn that they should become engineers, doctors, or lawyers. Boys learn that there are

Fig. 16–6. Women today are found in machine shops, flying commercial airplanes, riding race horses, and doing innumerable jobs formerly done only by men. How many jobs can you think of that require skills or abilities possessed only by one sex or the other? Not many!

greater numbers of vocations to choose from, and the possible choices include those that require a high degree of professional training and skill.

Two mistakes are commonly made by younger girls in thinking about vocations. One is to believe that this is relatively unimportant anyway, since they plan to marry and raise a family. If anything, in many cases they believe that training for a vocation is little more than "insurance"—insurance against the possibility that one might not marry or that one might have to support a family through death or disability of the husband. The second mistake is to think only in terms of those vocations traditionally considered to be woman's work in our society.

It is true that the majority of girls will marry and raise families. And it is equally true that many women become self-actualized in the role of housewife and mother. What many girls fail to realize, however, is that there will be about 25 years after the children have grown and left home in which to pursue a vocation. The point is that many women are not self-actualized solely in becoming a housewife and mother. For these women, training for a specific vocation is extremely important.

Many women could become successful doctors, engineers, architects, or truck drivers. Why don't they? In the past certainly these occupations were not considered very ladylike. Today, however, we never hear this phrase even though the vast majority of girls do not choose to train for or enter such vocations. In many cases, family and friends exert subtle pressures on girls to enter vocations considered feminine or appropriate for girls. The tragedy is that many girls can never achieve any sense of job satisfaction or self-fulfillment in such vocations. What can be done?

Probably the best advice to offer a high school student thinking about a career is, "Don't sell yourself short, don't underestimate yourself, and do your own thing." If you think you might be interested and fulfilled in a particular vocation, give serious thought to training for entry into that vocation, whether it be medicine, engineering, pharmacy, or whatever. You will find that it is much easier for girls to be accepted today into courses of study formerly considered to be the domain of men. You need, then, basically the same kinds of information about occupations that boys need—information we consider in the following section.

WHAT YOU NEED TO KNOW ABOUT OCCUPATIONS

Occupations may be classified by the kinds of activities in each, and by the degrees of responsibility and skill each requires. In terms of the kind of activities, there are several categories: service, business contact, organization, technology, outdoor, science, general cultural, and arts and entertainment.

Service occupations are mainly concerned with the needs and welfare of others. Guidance, social work, and police work are examples. *Business contact* involves sales of investments, real estate, and other products. *Organization* refers to managerial and white-collar jobs. *Technology* includes such occupations as engineering and machine trades, as well as transportation. *Outdoor* includes farming, forestry, and so on, while *Science* involves occupations concerned with scientific theory other than those under technology. *General cultural* includes such jobs as journalism, teaching, and the ministry. *Arts and entertainment* includes both performers and creators, that is, composers and playwrights.

Classifying occupations by the degree of skill and responsibility they require yields the following categories: professional and managerial, levels one and two; semiprofessional and small business, skilled, semiskilled, and unskilled. The top level under management refers to jobs in which the individual has independent responsibility for policy making. Less significant responsibilities are involved in level two. Semiprofessional and small business involve the application of policy or determination of activities in a small business. Skilled occupations require special training and experience, while semiskilled require less of this. Unskilled jobs, of course, require no special training.

Where education is relevant to jobs in these categories, level one management requires the Ph.D. or equivalent. Level two requires completion of college. Semiprofessional and small business require high school completion or technical school study. Skilled occupations require completion of apprenticeship training, while semiskilled usually involve somewhat less of this practical on-the-job experience.

In order to make an intelligent career plan, you need to know the answers to a number of questions concerning the widest possible number of occupations. *First,* what are the duties involved; what is the nature of the work? *Second,* what are the qualifications needed for entry into the job? Are there special physical, mental, social, or personal qualifications? *Third,* what are the educational requirements? What general education is required? What subjects or skills must be mastered? Where can training be obtained? How much will it cost, and how long is it? *Fourth,* what is the employment outlook? Are workers in demand in this occupation? What are the prospects for the future? *Finally,* are there related occupations one might enter in the event of changes in the economy?

In addition to answers to these questions, you also need to know about the working conditions for different occupations. Also you need to know the salary associated with each occupation—the beginning wage range, average salary, and maximum that one can expect. As we mentioned earlier, many students tend to think that salary is the most important factor to consider. However, this is not the case; it is only one of several factors associated with job satisfaction. Within certain limits, it is possible to earn a living wage in almost any occupation. Other factors tend to be of greater importance in career planning.

Just as salary is only one of many factors a person should consider in career planning, the status and prestige of jobs is also only one of a number of factors to consider. Too often students reject out of hand certain jobs because they do not seem important enough. The main thing to remember, however, is that it is not how important the job appears to others that counts, but whether the individual in that job feels self-actualized.

Where to Get Information

Many high schools have information on various careers in the library, and usually the guidance counselor has additional information. Some schools maintain files on job opportunities in the local community as well. In addition, many schools offer courses in occupations, orientation psychology, and group guidance.

In addition to these sources, high schools often hold special conferences or career days in which speakers are invited in to make presentations on their specialties. Also, field trips frequently present the student with an opportunity to learn firsthand information about different kinds of jobs.

To plan intelligently for a career, however, you not only need information about jobs, you need information about yourself as well. What are your interests and abilities? Do you have the personality characteristics required in a particular job? To answer these questions, psychology can often be of help.

HOW PSYCHOLOGY CAN HELP

Many high school students have a good idea of their interests and abilities, as well as their personality characteristics. Given information about various occupations, these students have little difficulty in selecting the kind of job in which they might become self-actualized. For many students, how-ever, this is a problem "I don't know what interests me," one student says. Another reports, "I seem to be interested in just about everything." Still another says, "I'm interested in engineering, but I don't know if I have the mathematical ability it requires."

Psychological Tests

For students such as these, psychological tests are often of help. Basi-cally four kinds of tests are helpful in vocational guidance: (1) general intelli-gence tests; (2) aptitude tests; (3) interest tests; and (4) personality tests. General intelligence tests (I.Q.) can often provide an indication of whether or not a student has the intelligence required for entry into a specific class of occupations. Aptitude tests, on the other hand, are designed to predict the extent to which a given individual may profit from a specific kind of training. Thus, for example, the medical aptitude tests predict probable success or failure in medical school.

Interest tests tell the extent to which the student's interests coincide with those of successful people in a variety of occupations. In these tests it is assumed that if your interests are similar to those of teachers, for example, or geologists, you would find such work personally interesting. Finally, per-sonality tests can be used to determine if you have the kind of personality required in a specific class of occupations.

There are two things to remember about such tests. One is that no test will predict success in a specific job. Psychological tests are generally most useful in predicting success for a class or category of occupations. Within that category, you have to decide on specific jobs. Second, no psychological test is infallible. They all make mistakes, in other words, by predicting success when failure is inevitable or by predicting failure when success is probable.

Of what use are tests, then? For many people they are of help in clarifying ideas and in making up one's own mind. Even though no test will pick out the job for you, they will help you to focus on a class of occupations in which you would probably be satisfied. Furthermore, even though no test is perfect, test results are often the best evidence to use in planning for a career. Tests, in fact, were developed to improve on older and less satisfac-tory methods.

When psychological tests are interpreted by a trained guidance coun-selor or psychologist, they can be of great help to the individual in making up his or her mind. Here the importance of the guidance counselor or psychologist needs to be stressed.

The Guidance Counselor

Almost all high schools have trained guidance counselors to help students with personal problems as well as career planning. In fact, your teacher in this course may be such a counselor. While no counselor is infallible, they have a range of experience with young people and a knowledge of their problems that can be invaluable. As you come closer to graduation you should take the opportunity to talk over your career plans with your counselor. He or she may do no more than agree with your choice. On the other hand, if you are undecided, they may be able to give you special assistance through testing and counseling.

In the final analysis there is only one person that can make the right decision for you, and that is you yourself. No counselor will tell you what to do. They will simply lay out what seem to be the reasonable options you have. You then have the choice to make, based on what you know about yourself and about the thousands of jobs open to young people today.

CHAPTER SUMMARY

1. The biggest mistake most people make in choosing a vocation is making that choice on the basis of information that is too limited. Young people overlook thousands of possible jobs, and they often have inadequate or incorrect information about those they do consider. Another mistake often made is to consider only one factor, such as salary. Also, in many cases other people such as parents or friends exert too much influence over choices.

2. To make an intelligent career plan, you should learn as much as possible about as many occupations as you can. Secondly, listen to what parents and friends have to say, but do not let them decide for you.

3. The most important thing to consider in choosing an occupation is job satisfaction. The job you choose should offer opportunities for achievement, advancement, and recognition, if at all possible. In addition, you should pick an occupation that you will find interesting and for which you have some aptitude.

4. The ideal job for anyone is one in which he or she can become *self-actualized*. This term refers to the need we all have for self-fulfillment and the realization of potentialities. In other words, we should seek to become what we are capable of becoming. Whether or not you decide to seek more education after high school should be determined by whether you need that education to become self-actualized.

5. Some students often approach the end of high school undecided about further education. In many cases taking a year off from school is a good idea. Frequently, when such students continue, they are more highly motivated, mature, and sure of what they want to do.

6. Not every student should go to college. Some can find a satisfying vocation with nothing more than their high school education. Others should pursue further training in business or vocational colleges. For those who know they need more training after high school, the main problem is often in choosing the "right" school. By "right," we mean that school which will provide the student with the skills needed to qualify him or her for a particular vocation. In some cases this means a business or commercial college. In other cases, a junior college; for still others, a four-year college or university.

7. Many students who decide to attend four-year colleges or universities do not graduate. Some should not have come at all. Others cannot make the adjustment necessary for success. Often these students fail to realize the differences between high school and college. They cannot handle the responsibility for budgeting their time; they have inadequate study habits; and in some cases they are homesick. College counseling services can often help such students.

8. Discrimination in employment of members of minority groups and women is less of a problem today than in the past. But the problem has not completely disappeared, even though there are laws against discrimination. Nevertheless, times have changed and every young person should think in terms of whatever vocation will enable that person to become self-actualized.

9. Girls often make two mistakes in thinking about vocations. One is to think it is relatively unimportant anyway, since they will be married after high school. Another is to think only in terms of those occupations traditionally considered to be "woman's work" in our society. Some women, of course, are self-actualized as housewives and mothers. But others should remember they will live a long time after raising families. They should consider the same range of potential occupations considered by boys.

10. Occupations are classified both by the kinds of activities they involve and the degrees of responsibility each require. In order to plan for a career, you need to know the answers to many questions concerning the largest possible numbers of occupations. The questions include details related to: duties, qualifications, employment outlook, working conditions, and salary.

11. Occupational information can be obtained in your school library, from your guidance counselor or school psychologist, and in special programs such as career days. You also need a clear picture of your overall intellectual ability, aptitudes, interests, and personality. Again, your guidance counselor can be of great help in clarifying these important factors in choosing a vocation.

Important Terms
from This Chapter

job satisfaction	community college	university
self-actualization	four-year college	vocational college

work-study programs

survey course

interest tests

liberal arts college

aptitude tests

I.Q.

Additional Readings
to Help You Learn More

Adams, J. *Understanding Adolescence: Current Developments in Adolescent Psychology,* 2nd Edition. Boston: Allyn and Bacon, Inc., 1973. Chapter 17, "Career Development in Adolescents," deals with theories of vocational choice and career development and occupational trends. Chapter 18, "Vocational Counseling with Adolescents," discusses exactly what the guidance counselor tries to do in talking with teen-agers about the problems they face in vocational choice, as well as the use of tests and a number of other subjects.

Herzberg, F. *Work and the Nature of Man.* Cleveland: The World Publishing Company, 1966. Chapter 3, "Industry's Concepts of Man," is interesting in that it looks at assumptions managers and other employers have about human motivation in work situations.

Malm, M. and Jamison, O. *Adolescence.* New York: McGraw Hill Book Company, 1952. Chapter 10, "Vocational Adjustment," is an excellent discussion of many of the problems teen-agers face in terms of vocational adjustment.

Resnick, W. and Sachs, H. *Dynamic General Psychology: An Introduction.* Boston: Holbrook Press, 1971. Chapter 16, "Psychology and the Student," discusses among other things high school problems and college problems and the challenge the student faces in playing the role of the student.

Wertheimer, M. *Confrontation: Psychology and the Problems of Today.* Glenview, Ill.: Scott, Foresman and Company, 1970. Section 7, "Man and Technology," discusses such things as "the good life," "men and machines," and "the human engineer."

Glossary

Active learning. Involves more than simply reading material through. An active learner makes an effort to remember what he reads or hears.

Adjustment. A term used to refer to the extent to which a person is able to accept himself as he is and to deal effectively and realistically with his environment.

Adolescence. Refers to the physical and sexual maturity of an individual. Also used in a social sense to refer to that period between childhood and adulthood.

Adrenal gland. A gland located above the kidney which has several functions in terms of use of various chemical substances by the body.

Affect. A term used by psychologists to refer to emotion. (See also effect.)

Affiliation. The motive to be with other people.

Aggression. An attack on others, either in physical or verbal form.

Alpha rhythm. An electrical pulsation which emanates from the brain at the rate of 10 per second.

Ambivalence. Antagonistic feelings. As, for example, simultaneous feelings of love and hate on the part of a child for his or her parents.

Ambiverts. A psychological term used to describe people who at times enjoy being with others, and at other times enjoy being by themselves. Most people fall into this category.

Anal stage. A stage in personality development, according to Freud, which lasts between one and three years of age and during which the child goes through toilet training.

Anthropology. One of the behavioral sciences. Concerned primarily with the behavior of individuals in primitive societies.

Anxiety. A state of tension which is frequently highly motivating. Worry or apprehension.

Anxiety reaction. A neurosis in which the most common symptom is one of intense anxiety.

Approach-Approach conflict. A type of conflict that occurs when the individual is faced with two mutually exclusive attractive goals.

Approach-Avoidance conflict. A conflict situation that occurs when the individual is faced with a goal he or she finds both attractive and unattractive at the same time.

Aptitude test. Psychological tests designed to measure one's ability to profit from future training. Examples would be the medical aptitude test and tests that are given to potential pilots for the U.S. Air Force.

Arranged marriage. A marriage performed in certain cultures in which the couple frequently never see one another before the actual ceremony.

Association. A learning theory which holds that ideas become linked together simply through their close occurrence in time or space.

Attention. The focus of perception. Attention may be either voluntary or involuntary.

Attention-Rejection. A characteristic of emotional states.

Autonomic nervous system. The part of the nervous system that controls the involuntary functions of the body such as heartbeat and respiration.

Aversive conditioning. A form of behavior therapy particularly useful in treating such conditions as excessive drinking.

Avoidance-Avoidance conflict. A conflict situation which occurs when the individual is faced with choosing between two unattractive goals.

Basilar membrane. A structure found in the cochlea which contains the neurons essential to hearing. (See also cochlea.)

Behavior. Any observable movement of an animal, including speech or verbal behavior by human beings as well.

Behavioral geneticist. A psychologist who studies the role of genetics in certain behavior.

Behavioral sciences. Psychology, sociology, and anthropology are the three behavioral sciences, in that they are all concerned with the behavior of human beings and other animals.

Behaviorist. A psychologist who believes that psychology should study only behavior.

Behavior therapy. The application of principles of operant conditioning techniques to changing abnormal behavior.

Biological motive. A motive which has its origin in the biological functioning of the body. Such motives are unlearned and include, for example, hunger and thirst. (See also motive.)

Brightness. The degree of lightness or darkness of a color.

Budget. A plan for utilizing income in the most intelligent way.

Cardinal traits. Traits that are seen only rarely but are nonetheless very dominant and obvious.

Central traits. Those personality traits that might be mentioned, for example, in a letter of recommendation.

Cerebral cortex. The part of the brain in which higher thought processes occur.

Chemical senses. The sense organs of the body that govern taste and smell. They are called chemical senses because chemical reactions seem to be involved in some way in their functioning.

Choice limitation. Refers to the fact that each of us is limited in terms of members of the opposite sex from which we choose potential marriage partners.

Chromosome. A structure found in the nucleus of all living cells, along which the genes are distributed.

Classical conditioning. A very simple form of learning in which a stimulus and response become connected through close association.

Clinical methods. Research methods involving the use of psychological tests or psychotherapy for purposes of systematic study of behavior.

Clinical psychology. Involves the application of psychological principles in the treatment of the mentally ill as well as in adjustment problems of the normal individual.

Clique. Another term for an informal group. Usually used to refer to a small group of close friends.

Cochlea. That portion of the inner ear which is responsible for our hearing sound.

Color blindness. The inability of the individual to perceive color. Most color-blind people fail to see red and green, but see other colors.

Community college. A two year junior college which provides both vocational and academic courses.

Companionship. A relationship providing a sense of security.

Compensation. Overcoming feelings of inferiority by excelling in some activity other than the one in which the individual feels inferior. A defense mechanism.

Competitive dating. A situation characteristic of dating in the Western world in which members of both sexes must actively compete with one another for the attention and affection of members of the opposite sex.

Conditioned response. The response made to a conditioned stimulus. (See also conditioned stimulus.)

Conditioned stimulus. The stimulus that causes a response it did not originally cause. Stimuli become conditioned through close association with unconditioned stimuli. (See also unconditioned stimulus.)

Cones. Found in the retina of the eye, these are light-sensitive cells which are responsible for color vision.

Conflict. In psychology the term is used to refer to the presence of two or more motives at the same time that cannot both be satisfied.

Conformity. Behaving in accordance with the social norms of a particular group to which a particular individual relates psychologically.

Contiguity. One of the so-called laws of association which says that ideas become associated when they occur close together. "Table-chair" would be an example.

Contrast. One of the laws of association which states that ideas become associated because of their differences. "Black-white," and "up-down" would be examples.

Control group. The group of subjects in an experiment which are matched with subjects in the experimental group. Such subjects provide a baseline for evaluating the effects of an independent variable upon members of an experimental group.

Cornea. The outer portion of the eye, through which light rays pass.

Corpus callosum. The part that connects the two cerebral hemispheres of the brain.

Corrections. A term used to refer to the attempt to rehabilitate and change the behavior of criminal offenders.

Counter-culture. The "drop-out" scene. A subculture which rejects the traditional values of our culture as a whole.

Culture. A term which refers to the products of a human society. Such products include both material objects and nonmaterial things such as language or social norms.

Date security. One of the motives for going steady.

Delinquency. Under the law, delinquency refers to acts that would be considered crimes had they been committed by adults.

Dependent variable. The factor in a psychological experiment which the psychologist is interested in studying.

Desensitization. A form of behavior therapy particularly useful in eliminating phobias.

Deterrence. The act of inhibiting or preventing; one of the objectives of imposing prison terms and heavy fines on criminal offenders.

Differentiate. To tell the difference. To make clear the differences between things.

Discrimination. A reaction stemming from prejudice which categorizes people in certain ways depending upon their sex, race or religious beliefs.

Dissociative reaction. A neurosis which involves disturbances or peculiarities in memory. Amnesia in some cases is an example.

Distributed learning. Learning distributed over a period of time—in contrast to massed learning or "cramming."

DNA A substance found in chromosomes that is believed to be the carrier of genetic information.

Dominant gene. A gene which when present determines the nature of a particular physical characteristic.

Dynamic theory. A theory of memory which accounts for change in *how* we recall something, rather than just in *how much* of it we recall.

Ebbinghaus, H. One of the early psychologists who studied learning and memory.

EEG. The electroencephalogram, a device which measures the electrical activity in the brain.

Effect. A result. Something that occurs as the result of something else.

Ego. That part of personality according to Freud which works out compromises between the id, the superego and reality. (See also id and superego.)

Electra complex. According to Freud, a stage of personality in which girls learn to identify sexually with the mother.

Electric shock treatments. Treatments that involve passing an electric shock through the brain causing unconsciousness. This form of treatment is sometimes used with psychotic patients.

Emotion. A stirred-up state which may lead either to activity and goal-directed behavior, or to inactivity.

Endocrine glands. Ductless glands that secrete hormones directly into the blood.

Energizing drugs. Drugs that perk up the spirits of the depressed person.

Environment. Any and all influences affecting animal or human behavior from the moment of conception.

Ethnocentrism. The term means literally the state of being centered on one's own culture, i.e., the belief that one's own culture represents the normal way in which human beings behave.

Experimental group. The group of subjects in an experiment that are treated differently from members of the control group: a group in which there is manipulation of some independent variable.

Experimental method. The method preferred by most psychologists for research purposes because the investigator has greater control over the variables involved.

Experimental psychology. That part of psychology concerned with research and the development of research techniques.

Extinction. The elimination of a conditioned response through withdrawal of reinforcement.

Extrinsic incentives. Incentives to learn that are external to the individual involved. When an individual learns something solely because of the grade he will receive in school, for example, the grade is an extrinsic incentive.

Extraverts. A term used to describe people who are outgoing and who enjoy being around other people

Formal group. A group which is formally constituted. That is, where officers are elected and rules are written down.

Four-year college. A college which offers academic and preprofessional programs leading to a bachelors degree.

Free association. A technique devised by Freud for use in psychoanalysis in which the patient says whatever comes to mind while relaxing on a couch

Freud, S. The physician who developed psychoanalysis for the treatment of the mentally ill.

Frustration. The interference with the satisfaction of a motive. May be used to refer either to the events involved or to the feeling the individual has.

Frustration tolerance. The degree to which an individual is able to withstand the effects of frustration.

Genes. Located along chromosomes, these chemical substances determine certain inherited physical characteristics.

Genetics. A science concerned with the study of heredity. (See also heredity.)

Gestalt theory. A theory of memory accounting in particular for how we remember shapes and sizes.

Gonads. Another term for the sex organs: testes in the male and ovaries in the female.

Group. Two or more individuals who share certain social norms in common and who also have common motivation. Such groups also affect the behavior of individual members in particular ways.

Halo effect. An impression which is carried over to some other situation. A student who does particularly well on a project, for example, may be perceived by the teacher as a very good student in other areas as well, even though this is not necessarily the case.

Heredity. Refers to inherited characteristics passed from parents to offspring via the genes.

Hierarchy. An order or arrangement of things. An example would be the hierarchy of motives as discussed by Maslow.

Hormones. Chemical substances secreted by the endocrine glands.

Hue. The aspect of color that defines it as red, green, yellow, or blue.

Human nature. An unscientific term often used to account for behavior that appears to be instinctive. (See also instinctive.)

Hypnosis. A mental state in which the subject is highly suggestible.

Id. According to Freud, that part of personality consisting of the instinctual urges with which the individual is born.

Identical twins. Twins that are born from the same fertilized egg. Such twins have inherited exactly the same genetic makeup from the parents.

Illusions. False perceptions of stimuli.

Immaturity. Refers to both physical and sexual development as well as to an emotional state in which the individual is not totally capable of managing his own affairs without guidance.

Independent variable. The factor in a psychological experiment which the psychologist is interested in studying.

Industrial psychology. The application of psychological principles in industrial or work settings.

Infant mortality. The death rate among newborn infants.

Inferiority. A feeling that one is not as good as other people in certain activities or characteristics.

Informal group. A group which is not formally constituted. There are no specifically designated status and role relationships, although these exist nonetheless.

Instinctive. A term used to refer to behavior that is inborn and that is not affected by learning. Such behavior occurs in every single member of a particular species.

Intelligence. The ability to act with purpose, to think logically and to deal effectively with one's environment.

Intelligence quotient (I.Q.). An index of the relationship between physical age and mental age. For example, one may be 15 years of age but have a mental age of 17 years. Such a person would have an I.Q. above 100.

Interdisciplinary. Refers to a scientific approach emphasizing the interdependence of the behavioral sciences in answering questions about human behavior.

Interest tests. Tests which determine the extent to which an individual's interests coincide with the known interests of members of various professional and occupational groups.

Interference theory. According to this theory of forgetting, we forget because we learn other material which interferes with our recall of the material we originally learned.

Intrinsic incentives. Reasons for learning that lie within the individual himself. For example, an interest in something often causes the individual to learn about that particular thing.

Introverts. A psychological term used to describe people who are rather solitary and who do not necessarily enjoy being with other people.

Involuntary. Something over which we have no control, as, for example, heart-rate.

Iris. The opening in the front of the eyeball through which light passes.

Job satisfaction. The satisfaction that derives from one's employment aside from the salary one receives.

Jung, C. The psychoanalyst who coined the terms introversion and extraversion in developing a theory of psychological types.

Learning. The modification of behavior that occurs as a result of experience.

Level of aspiration. The goal an individual sets for himself and that he strives to achieve.

Liberal arts college. A college which offers a four-year academic program leading to the development of a broad and well-rounded person.

Maladjustment. The opposite of adjustment. (See adjustment.)

Manic depressive reactions. A psychosis in which there are sudden changes in feeling or emotion with no apparent reason.

Maslow, A. The psychologist who developed a theory of motivation which stresses that biological motives are more fundamental than social motives. Motives in his view may be thought of as a pyramid with biological motives at the bottom and social motives, including self-actualization, at the top.

Massed learning. Learning which is crammed into a short space of time. Often referred to as "cramming."

Maturation. A term that refers to the development of certain behavior as the result of physical growth rather than learning.

Maturity. Refers to physical and sexual maturity as well as emotional maturity necessary to establish the sound relationship necessary or prerequisite to marriage.

Medicare. A program of health care for the elderly in the United States.

Mental illness. A condition in which the person is perceived by others to be abnormal or maladjusted in some way.

Method of approximations. A technique of animal training which involves the gradual shaping of behavior through the use of reinforcement.

Mnemonic devices. Gimmicks or devices used to improve one's memory.

Motivation. An internal condition of the animal which causes it to become active and to seek some means of satisfying a motive.

Motor area. That part of the brain concerned with the movement of voluntary muscles in the body.

Motor neuron. A nerve cell which carries nerve impulses from the brain toward the muscles and glands.

"Natural" experiment. An experiment conducted in a real-life setting in which the participants are unaware that an experiment is in progress.

Nerve impulse. The electro-chemical charge which moves through the nervous system.

Nerves. The basic building blocks of the nervous system. (See also neurons.)

Nervous system. The network of nerve cells or neurons that help maintain human life and that allow us to do virtually everything we do. The brain is part of the nervous system.

Neurons. The individual cells that make up the nervous system.

Nonconformity. A term used to refer to behavior which deviates from commonly accepted social norms. The nonconformist is one who does not behave in normally accepted ways.

Normal. A term used in one of two ways. In connection with mental illness, it is often used in a statistical sense. Typical or normal behavior, for example, in one culture, may be atypical or abnormal in another. In another sense, the term is sometimes used to refer to variation from some "ideal" behavior. By this definition entire cultures can be considered abnormal or normal.

Obsessive-compulsive reactions. Neuroses in which the individual has disturbing thoughts which reoccur frequently and over which he or she has no control. In other cases the individual feels irresistable impulses to carry out certain acts.

Oedipus complex. A concept developed by Freud to account for sexual identification in boys.

Operant behavior. Behavior that produces some effect on the environment in which the animal finds itself. For example, when the rat presses the lever in a Skinner box, food is presented.

Operant conditioning. A type of conditioning that involves waiting for a particular response to occur and then reinforcing the occurrence of that response.

Oral stage. The stage in personality development occurring from birth until about one year of age during which the infant derives pleasure from the mouth.

Organic psychoses. Psychoses that are caused by some conditions such as tumors, infections, circulatory disorders and other conditions.

Otolith organs. Those sense organs responsible for our being able to maintain balance. (See also semicircular canals.)

Overcompensation. Overcoming feelings of inferiority by excelling in the activity in which the individual feels inferior. A defense mechanism.

Overcrowding. A term referring to the density of population in a given area.

Overlearning. Learning beyond the point of mere mastery. When we can repeat something correctly once, for example, we have learned it. Additional study beyond this point is called overlearning.

Overpopulation. A situation in which there are too many people in relationship to the products necessary to sustain life.

Pancreas. A gland located above the liver which controls the amount of sugar in the blood.

Parasympathetic division. That part of the autonomic nervous system which slows down various organs of the body when we relax after being emotionally aroused.

Parathyroid gland. A gland located close to the thyroid gland which regulates the use of calcium by the body.

Passive learning. In passive learning the learner does little more than simply listen or read through the material.

Pavlov, Ivan P. A Russian psychologist who discovered classical conditioning.

Peer pressure. Pressure exerted from friends to behave in certain ways. Often peer pressure brings about early marriages, for example.

Perception. A process that intervenes between the activities of the senses and behavior. Perception is initiated by information from the sense organs but not completely determined by it.

Personality inventories. Psychological tests designed to measure the inner characteristics of personality.

Personal motive. A particular motive which is unique or nearly unique to a particular individual.

"Phantom" pain. A feeling of pain a person with an amputated limb often seems to feel in the missing limb.

Phobic reactions. Neuroses characterized by intense unrealistic fears.

Physiological changes. Changes which occur within the various internal organs of the body.

Pituitary. The so-called master gland which secretes a number of hormones affecting other endocrine glands.

Planaria. Often used in scientific experimentation, these flat worms have been used to study memory.

Pleasantness-unpleasantness. Characteristics of emotional states.

Polygraph. Another term for the lie detector.

Popularity. Being liked by many individuals, being in demand socially, and having a pleasing personality.

Poverty. A relative term referring to lack of money or certain material possessions.

Prejudice. An attitude or predisposition to react in a negative way to certain individuals.

Primary reinforcement. A stimulus which directly reduces an animal's motive.

Primary sex characteristics. Refers to the male and female sex organs *per se*.

Projection. A defense mechanism in which we attribute our own shortcomings to others.

Projective tests. Tests used to measure personality which generally involve the interpretation of ambiguous or unclear material such as inkblots.

Psychiatry. A specialized branch of medicine concerned with the treatment of the mentally ill.

Psychoanalysis. A method of treatment developed by Freud for use with the mentally ill.

Psychological types. Refers to personality theories that are based on types of personalities rather than traits.

Psychology. The study of the behavior of human beings and other animals.

Psychoneurotic. Describes a person suffering from a less severe form of mental illness.

Psychosomatic reactions. Illnesses that are physical in nature but caused by psychological disturbances.

Psychotherapy. A psychological method of treating the mentally ill.

Psychotic. Describes a person suffering from a type of mental illness that is usually quite severe.

Puberty. The time at which an individual becomes sexually mature.

Racism. A form of prejudice directed at a particular racial group.

Rating scales. Scales that are used to assess personality.

Rationalization. Finding logical but false reasons for past, present or future behavior. A defense mechanism.

Reaction formation. A defense mechanism in which the person gives strong expression to the opposite feeling from that he actually has.

Recessive gene. A gene which affects a particular physical characteristic only when another recessive gene is present at the same locus on the opposite chromosome.

Reconditioning. Learning again to make a conditioned response once extinction has occurred.

Recreation. Various forms of activities important in maintaining good mental health.

Reference group. A group to which the individual relates in a psychological sense whether or not he is a member. In other words, the social norms that exist in that group serve to influence or affect the individual's behavior.

Reinforcement. Any stimulus which causes a response to occur again and again. Food, for example, is a reinforcement for a hungry person.

Reliability. Refers to how consistent or reliable test results are, or how consistent or reliable the results of experiments are.

Repression. According to Freud, a defense mechanism by which certain feelings or ideas become unconscious.

Response. Something an animal does when presented with a stimulus. (See also stimulus.)

Retina. The light-sensitive layer of the eye. Contains the rods and cones.

Retroactive inhibition. This occurs when learning one thing has a negative effect on our memory of something else we learned previously.

RNA. The substance found in chromosomes which is believed to be modified in some way when an animal learns. Thus, it apparently has some very close connection with memory.

Rods. Located in the retina of the eye, these are light-sensitive cells which respond to light and dark.

Role. Refers to the particular kind of behavior manifested by an individual in a group situation. One role in a group, for example, is that of the leader.

Rorschach, H. The Swiss psychiatrist who developed the inkblot test for investigating and measuring personality.

Saturation. The purity or richness of a color.

Schizophrenia. A psychosis characterized by apathy and withdrawal from others, a dulling of emotions, and loss of contact with reality.

School psychology. The application of psychological principles in school settings. Involves counseling and/or the use of psychological tests.

Science. The systematic study of events using a particular method known as scientific method. Scientific method consists essentially of making objective observations under controlled conditions.

Secondary reinforcement. A stimulus that acquires reinforcing properties through its association with a primary reinforcement. For example, a buzzer that always sounds when food is presented to a hungry animal will become a secondary reinforcement.

Secondary sex characteristics. Refers to sex characteristics which develop at the time of puberty such as the breasts in women and the beard in men.

Secondary traits. Less conspicuous personality traits that are less frequently seen in a person's behavior than central or cardinal traits. (See also central traits and cardinal traits.)

Self. Sometimes defined as the feelings, attitudes, and evaluations that the person holds about himself or herself as an object.

Self-actualization. The need to utilize one's capabilities to the fullest extent.

Self-esteem. The good feelings that we have about ourselves often stemming from various accomplishments.

Semicircular canals. Those sense organs responsible for our being able to maintain balance. (See also otolith organs.)

Sensory area. That part of the brain that receives nerve impulses from the various sense organs of the body.

Sensory neuron. A neuron that carries nerve impulses in the direction of the brain.

Serial position effect. Refers to the ease or difficulty of learning something as a function of where it appears in a list.

Sex roles. The behavior that each of us learns to manifest as a function of whether we are male or female.

Sibling rivalry. The rivalry between two children in the same family for the attention and affection of the parents.

Similarity. One of the laws of association which states that ideas become associated because of their similarity.

Skinner, B. F. The psychologist who discovered operant conditioning.

Skinner box. An apparatus used in the study of operant conditioning, typically with white rats.

Socialization. The process of learning to behave in accordance with the social norms of the group into which one is born.

Socialized medicine. A health plan utilized in some European countries in which health care is free to the individual, but is paid for out of taxes.

Social motive. A motive which has its origin in the social life of the individual. Such motives are learned and include, for example, acquisition and achievement.

Social norms. Standards existing in all human groups which regulate or determine the behavior of members of those groups.

Society. The largest social unit in which an animal, including human beings, lives.

Sociology. One of the behavioral sciences. Concerned primarily with the behavior of human beings in groups.

Sperry, R. The psychologist who discovered that information is transferred from one half of the brain to the other through the corpus callosum.

Status. Refers to the particular position of an individual within a group in terms of his influence on the group.

Stimulus. Any physical energy such as a light or sound that brings forth a response on the part of an animal. The term "stimuli" refers to more than one stimulus.

Superego. That part of personality according to Freud which consists of the conscience.

Survey course. A college course usually given in the freshman year covering an entire field such as General Psychology or Introduction to Biology.

Symbol. Something that stands for something else. In language, for example, particular sounds have particular meanings. The sounds are symbols.

Sympathetic division. That part of the autonomic nervous system which is activated when we become emotional.

Synapse. The gap between two nerve cells or neurons across which the nerve impulse must travel.

Systematic observation. Observation made of behavior in natural settings in which the investigator does not attempt to control or manipulate variables, but simply observes things as they occur.

Temporary social situations. Social situations in which the participants have no established social ties. Examples would be crowds at a football game or a railroad station.

Tension-relaxation. A characteristic of emotional states.

Theory of disuse. A theory of forgetting which says that we forget when we do not have to remember particular material for a long period of time.

Thorndike, E. L. One of the early psychologists who studied learning and who formulated a number of "laws" of learning.

Thyroid gland. A gland located in the throat area which regulates the metabolism of the body.

Trait theories. Theories of personality that utilize a limited number of dimensions for descriptive purposes. Such dimensions are masculinity, femininity, introversion-extraversion, etc.

Tranquilizing drugs. Drugs that cause the tense person to become more relaxed. These are nonaddictive drugs.

Unconditioned response. An unlearned response which exists prior to the beginning of the classical conditioning procedure.

Unconditioned stimulus. The stimulus that normally causes an unconditioned response. For example, electric shock is an unconditioned stimulus that causes an animal to withdraw its leg from the source of the shock.

Unconscious. Something of which we are unaware. A mental state or part of the mind that may affect our behavior without our realizing it.

University. A collection of four-year colleges offering a variety of degrees.

Variable. One of the factors affecting behavior in some way.

Vocational college. A college specializing in preparation for various vocations such as auto mechanics, carpentry, and plumbing.

War on Poverty. A program initiated during the Johnson administration designed to improve the standard of living of the poor in the United States.

Women's liberation. A social movement advocating greater freedom and equality for women.

Work-study programs. Programs in colleges which allow the student to study at the same time he or she holds down a part-time job.

Acknowledgments
and Copyrights

Figures

Author page—Fred Prouser; Opening page, Chapter 1, New Zealand Herald.

1–1	Syndication international
1–2	New Zealand Herald
1–3	Garvin McCain
1–4	Dr. Jose Delgado
1–5	Jerry Richardson
1–6	National Aeronautics and Space Administration
1–7	Mirror Pic

Chapter 2, Opening page—H. F. Harlow, University of Wisconsin, Primate Laboratory.

2–1a	H. F. Harlow, University of Wisconsin, Primate Laboratory
2–1b	H. F. Harlow, University of Wisconsin, Primate Laboratory
2–1c	H. F. Harlow, University of Wisconsin, Primate Laboratory
2–1d	H. F. Harlow, University of Wisconsin, Primate Laboratory
2–2a	H. F. Harlow, University of Wisconsin, Primate Laboratory
2–2b	H. F. Harlow, University of Wisconsin, Primate Laboratory
2–2c	H. F. Harlow, University of Wisconsin, Primate Laboratory
2–2d	II. F. Harlow, University of Wisconsin, Primate Laboratory
2–3	From *Principles of Human Genetics,* 3rd ed., by Curt Stern. W. H. Freeman and Co., Copyright 1973.
2–4	U.S. Navy Medical Research Laboratory, Groten, Conn.
2–5	The Psychological Corporation
2–6	National Association for Mental Health

Chapter 3, Opening page—Auckland Star.

3–1	New Zealand Herald
3–2	From *Introduction to Psychology,* 3rd ed., by Ernest R. Hilgard, Copyright 1962 by Harcourt, Brace, Jovanovich, Inc., and reproduced with their permission.
3–3	M. F. Soper
3–4	Shirley, M. M. The First Two Years: A Study of 25 Babies. Child Welfare Series No. 7, 1933. The University of Minnesota Press, Minneapolis. Copyright 1933 by the University of Minnesota.
3–5	Wayne Dennis
3–6	Shuttleworth, F. K. 1939. The Physical and Mental Growth of Girls and Boys age 6 to 19 in Relation to Age at Maximum Growth. Monogr. Soc. Res. Child Development 46, No. 210.
3–7	ANTA

3–8   New Zealand Herald

Chapter 4, Opening page—Auckland Star

4–1   Australian Associated Press Limited
4–2   G. Suttles. Social Order of the Slum. 1968. Copyright University of Chicago Press.
4–3   New Zealand Herald
4–4   Australian Associated Press Limited
4–5   Ash, S. Opinions and Social Pressure. 1955. Scientific American. Courtesy of William Vandivert.
4–6   Ash, S. Opinions and Social Pressure. 1955. Scientific American.

Chapter 5, Opening photograph—Animal Behavior Enterprises

5–1   Thorndike, E. *Animal Intelligence*. 1911. New York: Macmillan.
5–2   Whittaker, J. *Introduction to Psychology*, 2nd ed. 1970. Philadelphia, Pa.: W. B. Saunders Co.
5–3   Yerkes, R. and Morgulis, S. 1909. The Method of Pavlov in Animal Psychology. Psychological Bulletin 6: 257–273.
5–4   Sears Roebuck and Co.
5–5   Auckland Star
5–6   Charles Pfizer, Inc.
5–7   B. F. Skinner, *Cumulative Record*. 1959. Reprinted by permission of Prentice-Hall, Inc., Englewood Cliffs, N.J.
5–8   John Fairfax and Sons Limited
5–9   Pierrel, R. and Sherman, J. 1963. Barnabus, The Rat with College Training. Brown Alumni Monthly.
5–10   Auckland Star
5–11   Pan Asia

Chapter 6, Opening photograph—Roger Cornell

6–1   Fred Prouser
6–2   New Zealand Herald
6–3   Lafayette Instrument Co., Lafayette, Indiana.
6–4   Ebbinghaus, 1885 from Woodworth, R. *Experimental Psychology*. New York: Henry Holt, 1938.
6–5   Luh, C. 1922. The Conditions of Retention. Psychological Monographs 31: 142.
6–6   Krueger, 1929
6–7   Carmichael, L., Hogan, H., and Walter, A. 1932. An Experimental Study of the Effect of Language on the Reproduction of Visually Perceived Form. Journal of Experimental Psychology 15: 73–86.

Chapter 7, Opening photograph— Magnum

7–1   Haas, K. 1965. *Understanding Adjustment and Bheavior,* 2nd ed. Englewood Cliffs, N.J.: Prentice-Hall, Inc.

410

7–2	Mirror Pic
7–3	Butler, R. 1954. Curiosity in Monkeys. Scientific American 18: 70–75.
7–4	Berlyne, D. 1966. Curiosity and Exploration. Science 153: 25–33.
7–5	The Central Press Photos Limited
7–6	New Zealand Heraold
7–7a	Embassy of India
7–7b	Boys Clubs of America
7–8	National Association for Mental Health
7–9	Saturday Evening Post, 1949, Curtis Publishing Co.

Chapter 8, Opening Paragraph—New Zealand Herald

8–1	New Zealand Herald
8–2	Pennsylvania State Police
8–3	Syndication International
8–4	Bridges, K. 1932. Emotional Development in Early Infancy. Child Development 3: 324–341.
8–5	New Zealand Herald
8–6	Medical Audiovisual Dept. Walter Reed Army Inst. of Research
8–7	Coleman, J. 1956. *Abnormal Psychology in Modern Life*, 2nd ed. Chicago, Ill.: Scott, Foresman and Co.
8–8	Mary Lynn Ranalli

Chapter 9, Opening photograph—Dr. Theodore Rasmussen, Montreal Neurological Institute.

9–1	Thompson, R. 1967. *Foundations of Physiological Psychology.* New York: Harper and Row.
9–2	Munn, N. 1956. *Introduction to Psychology.* Boston: Houghton Mifflin Co.
9–3	Modified from Pennfield and Rasmussen, 1950 in Ranson S. and Clark, S. *The Anatomy of the Nervous System.* Philadelphia, Pa.: W. B. Saunders Co., 1959.
9–4	New Zealand Herald
9–5	Smith, D. W. and Wilson, A. 1973. *The Child With Down's Syndrome.* Philadelphia, Pa. W. B. Saunders Co.
9–6	Maier, N. and Schnierla, T. 1935. *Principles of Animal Psychology.* New York: McGraw Hill.
9–7	Roger Sperry
9–8	New Zealand Herald
9–9	Institute of Living, Hartford, Conn.
9–10	Webb, W. 1968. *Sleep: An Experimental Approach.* New York: Macmillan.
9–11	Dr. Wilse B. Webb
9–12	Reprinted from *The Tides of Life* by R. G. Hoskins, Ph.D., M.D., by permission of W. W. Norton and Co., Inc. Copyright 1933 by W. W. Norton and Co., Inc. Copyright renewed 1960 by R. G. Hoskins.

Chapter 10, Opening photograph— Lynn J. Hollyn

10–1	After Polyak, F. 1941. The Retina. Chicago: University of Chicago Press.

10–2	Whittaker, J. 1970. *Introduction to Psychology,* 2nd ed. Philadelphia, Pa.: W. B. Saunders Co.
10–3	Whittaker, J. 1970. *Introduction to Psychology,* 2nd ed. Philadelphia, Pa.: W. B. Saunders Co.
10–4	Ittelson, W. and Kilpatrick, F. 1951. Experiments in Perception. Scientific American 185: 50–55.
10–5	Davis, H. and Silverman, W. 1970. *Hearing and Deafness,* 3rd ed. New York: Holt, Rinehart and Winston, Inc.
10–6	Whittaker, J. 1970. *Introduction to Psychology,* 2nd ed. Philadelphia, Pa.: W. B. Saunders Co.
10–7	New York Office of Midtown Planning and Development.

Chapter 11, Opening photograph—New Zealand Herald

11–1	U.S. Information Agency
11–2	Culver Pictures Inc.
11–3	Baughman, E. and Welsh, G. 1962. *Personality: A Behavioral Science.* Englewood Cliffs, N.J.: Prentice-Hall, Inc.
11–4	New Zealand Herald
11–5	New Zealand Herald
11–6	New Zealand Herald
11–7	Gough, H. and Weider, A. (ed.) 1953. *Contributions toward Medical Psychology.* New York: Ronald Press.

Chapter 12, Opening photograph—National Institute of Mental Health, U.S.P.H.S.

12–1	Sir John Soane's Museum, London
12–2	National Institute of Mental Health
12–3	Terman, L. and Merrill, M. 1937. *Measuring Intelligence.* Boston: Houghton Mifflin.
12–4	Durban Publicity Association
12–5	National Institute of Mental Health
12–6	National Institute of Mental Health
12–7	National Institute of Mental Health
12–8	National Institute of Mental Health
12–9	National Institute of Mental Health

Chapter 13, Opening photograph—New Zealand Herald

13–1a	New Zealand Herald
13–1b	Australian Associated Press Limited
13–1c	Boys Clubs of America
13–2	New Zealand Herald
13–3	Dale I. Leiseste
13–4	Syndication International
13–5	New Zealand Herald
13–6	Embassy of India

13–7	Department of HEW, Office of Youth Development
13–8	Department of HEW, Office of Youth Development

Chapter 14, Opening photograph—New Zealand Herald

14–1a	Pennsylvania State University
14–1b	Charles Pfizer, Inc.
14–1c	New Zealand Travel Association
14–1d	Fred Prouser
14–2	Rollins, B. and Feldman, H. 1970. Marital Satisfaction over the Family Life Cycle. Journal of Marriage and the Family, 20–28.
14–3	Sweet & Burmpass 1973
14–4	New Zealand Herald
14–5	Camera Press
14–6	Auckland Star

Chapter 15, Opening photograph—U.S. Department of Defense, New Zealand Herald, and Agency for International Development

15–1	The Population Council
15–2	New Zealand Herald
15–3	World Health Organization: National Nutrition Institute, Mexico.
15–4	Boys Clubs of America
15–5	Bureau of Indian Affairs
15–6	New Zealand Herald

Chapter 16, Opening photograph—Delta Airlines, New Zealand Herald, New Zealand Herald, Fred Prouser.

16–1	National Aeronautics and Space Administration
16–2	New Zealand Herald
16–3	Charles Pfizer, Inc.
16–4	New Zealand Herald
16–5	Harrisburg Area Community College
16–6	New Zealand Herald

Tables and Boxes

Box 4–1	Remers, R. and Radler, R. 1957. *The American Teenager.* Indianapolis, Ind.: The Bobbs Merrill Co.
Box 4–2	Reprinted by permission of G. P. Putnam's Sons from *Son of the Great Society* by Art Buchwald, Copyright 1965, 1966 by Art Buchwald.
Box 5–2	Excerpted with permission from the National Observer, Copyright Dow Jones and Co., Inc., 1973.

Box 5–3   Boulder Daily Camera, July 22, 1970. Copyright ms says © Knight news-
                papers & written by Michael T. Mulloy, Los Angeles Times and reprinted
                by permission of L.A. Times/Washington Post News Service
Box 11–1   Robert Tyson
Table 14–1   U.S. Current Population Reports
(Box 1–2   Five Things that Worry 10th Grade Students) A. Frazier and L. Lisonbee,
                "Adolescent Concerns with Physique," *School Review*, 58, 1959: 397–
                405.

SUBJECT INDEX

NAME INDEX